Linguistics in Context: Connecting Observation and Understanding

Lectures from the 1985 LSA/TESOL and NEH Institutes

edited by

Deborah Tannen

Georgetown University

Volume XXIX in the Series
ADVANCES IN DISCOURSE PROCESSES
Roy O. Freedle, Editor

ABLEX PUBLISHING CORPORATION
NORWOOD, NEW JERSEY

Printed in the United States of America

Library of Congress Cataloging-in-Publication Data

Linguistics in context: connecting observation and understanding / edited by
  Deborah Tannen.
    p.   cm.—(Advances in discourse processes; v. 29)
  Selected lectures and an introduction from the 1985 LSA/TESOL and NEH
Institutes, held at Georgetown University, June 24-Aug. 2, 1985.
  Bibliography: p.
  Includes index.
  ISBN 0-89391-454-1. ISBN 0-89391-455-X (pbk.)
  1. Linguistic analysis (Linguistics)—Congresses. 2. Language and languages—
Study and teaching—Congresses. 3. Poetry—Study and teaching—Congresses.
I. Tannen, Deborah. II. LSA/TESOL Institute (1985: Georgetown University)
III. Series.
P126.L54 1987
410—dc19   87-19704
                                                                      CIP

Ablex Publishing Corporation
355 Chestnut Street
Norwood, New Jersey 07648

To Michael

Contents

Preface to the Series

Roy O. Freedle
Series Editor

This series of volumes provides a forum for the cross-fertilization of ideas from a diverse number of disciplines, all of which share a common interest in discourse—be it prose comprehension and recall, dialogue analysis, text grammar construction, computer simulation of natural language, cross-cultural comparisons of communicative competence, or other related topics. The problems posed by multisentence contexts and the methods required to investigate them, while not always unique to discourse, are still sufficiently distinct as to benefit from the organized mode of scientific interaction made possible by this series.

Scholars working in the discourse area from the perspective of sociolinguistics, psycholinguistics, ethnomethodology and the sociology of language, educational psychology (e.g., teacher-student interaction), the philosophy of language, computational linguistics, and related subareas are invited to submit manuscripts of monograph or book length to the series editor. Edited collections of original papers resulting from conferences will also be considered.

Volumes in the Series

Contributors

A. L. BECKER is Professor Emeritus of Linguistics and Anthropology at the University of Michigan, currently affiliated with the Malay National University. He received his B.A. and M.A. in English literature and his Ph.D. in linguistics at the University of Michigan. He has had field experience in Burma and Indonesia and has written extensively on Southeast Asian languages and arts. At present he is concentrating on the theory, history, and practice of translation. He can be reached through the Center for South and Southeast Asian Studies, University of Michigan.

PAUL FRIEDRICH is Professor of Anthropology and Linguistics at the University of Chicago. He grew up in Massachusetts and Vermont, was trained at Harvard and Yale (his MA is in Slavic languages and literature), and has done over five years of anthropological and linguistic fieldwork among Russian dissidents, the Nayars of the Malabar Coast, and the Tarascan Indians of southwestern Mexico. He has taught and published widely in ethnographic semantics, historical linguistics, political anthropology, mythology, language and culture, and poetry and poetics. His many books include *Language, Context, and the Imagination; The Princes of Naranja; The Meaning of Aphrodite;* and *The Language Parallax.* He has been teaching at the University of Chicago since 1962, and has been a Guggenheim Fellow.

PAUL HOPPER is Professor of Linguistics and Anthropology at the State University of New York at Binghamton. He has studied in Europe, the USA, and Southeast Asia (he received his Ph.D. in linguistics at the University of Texas, Austin), and has held fellowships from the Guggenheim Foundation, the Fulbright Program, and the American Council of Learned Societies. He has taught at several Linguistic Institutes; he was Collitz Professor of Comparative Philology at the 1983 Institute at UCLA. He has taught at several universities in the US, including Washington University and the University of Hawaii. He is the author and editor of books and articles on Indo-European, Germanic, and Austronesian linguistics, and on linguistic typology and pragmatics.

ix

STEPHEN D. KRASHEN is Professor of Linguistics at the University of Southern California. He received his Ph.D. in linguistics at the University of California, Los Angeles. He is the author of over 100 articles and books in the fields of neurolinguistics and language acquistion. He was the winner of the 1982 Mildenberger Award, given by the Modern Language Association, for his book *Second Language Acquisition and Second Language Learning,* the Ludwig Distinguished National Leadership Award, given by the New York Foreign Language Teachers Association in 1986, and was co-winner of the Pimsleur Award, given by the American Council of Foreign Language Teachers, in 1986. His most recent books are *Inquiries and Insights* and *The Input Hypothesis: Issues and Implications.*

WILLIAM LABOV is Professor of Linguistics at the University of Pennsylvania. He received his B.A. from Harvard in 1948, and worked as an industrial chemist in northern New Jersey until 1961. He began the study of linguistics at Columbia University in 1961, received his Ph.D. in 1964, and taught at Columbia until 1970. His dissertation, *The Social Stratification of English in New York City,* was published in 1966. Further results of work on sociolinguistics are reported in *Sociolinguistic Patterns.* From 1966–1968, he carried out research on the Black English Vernacular in South Harlem, with results published in *Language in the Inner City.* From 1968 on, he has engaged in the study of ongoing linguistic change, as reported in *A Quantitative Study of Sound Change in Progress,* with M. Yaeger and R. Steiner. In 1971, he moved to the University of Pennsylvania, and carried out research on sound change in Philadelphia. In the years 1981–1984, he examined the transmission of language features across the black/white/Puerto Rican boundary in Philadelphia. He is the director of the Linguistics Laboratory at the University of Pennsylvania, and is currently engaged in research on cross-dialectal comprehension.

R. P. McDERMOTT is a Professor in the Department of Family and Community Studies, Teachers College, Columbia University. He received his B.A. in philosophy and Asian Studies from Queens College, CUNY, and his Ph.D. in anthropology from Stanford University. He has done field work in the urban United States and Japan. His research interests include language in classrooms and other institutional settings, Japanese, nonverbal communication, literacy, and the Irish Literary Renaissance.

KENNETH L. PIKE is Professor Emeritus of Linguistics at the University of Michigan and President Emeritus of the Summer Institute of Linguistics. He received his Bachelor of Theology from the Gordon

College of Theology and Missions and his Ph.D. in linguistics from the University of Michigan. He is the author of numerous books and articles. (For a full bibliography see Eunice V. Pike, *Ken Pike: Scholar and Christian* and Ruth M. Brend, *Kenneth Lee Pike: Bibliography*.) He was President of the Linguistic Society of America 1961–70. He can be reached at Summer Institute of Linguistics, Inc., 7500 W. Camp Wisdom Road, Dallas, TX 75236.

HAROLD ROSEN is Professor Emeritus at the University of London Institute of Education where he was Head of the Department of English and Media Studies and the first holder of the Chair of Education with special reference to English in Education. He is currently a Visiting Professor at the Open University. He taught for many years in secondary schools, mostly in inner-London, and for four years in a College of Education before taking up teaching and research at the Institute of Education. He has directed research projects concerned with linguistic diversity in schools and the relationship between language and learning. His most recent publications are *Stories and Meanings* and contributions to a guide for the study of language and literacy (Open University, 1987). He is at present working on a book, *The Theory and Practice of Narrative in Education.*

MURIEL SAVILLE-TROIKE is Professor of Educational Psychology and Linguistics and Chair of the Department of Educational Psychology at the University of Illinois, Urbana-Champaign. She received her Ph.D. from the University of Texas at Austin and was on the faculty of the Linguistics Department, Georgetown University, 1974–81. Her research interests are primarily in Navajo and related Athabaskan languages, first and second language acquisition, and the ethnography and sociolinguistics of communication. She has published extensively in all these areas, including *The Ethnography of Communication: An Introduction,* and has edited *Linguistics and Anthropology* (Georgetown University Round Table on Languages and Linguistics 1977) and, with Deborah Tannen, *Perspectives on Silence.* She is continuing her research on the processes of communication, first and second language development, and language loss among speakers of Chinese, Japanese, Korean, Arabic, and Spanish, and is editing the works of Edward Sapir on Navajo for publication.

EMANUEL A. SCHEGLOFF is Professor of Sociology at the University of California, Los Angeles. He received his Ph.D. from the University of California, Berkeley. A pioneer in the area of conversation analysis, he has published numerous articles, including the classic "A Simplest Systematics for the Organization of Turn-taking for Conversation" (with Harvey Sacks and Gail Jefferson). He has been on the faculty of several Linguistic Institutes.

PETER STREVENS' academic career began in West Africa before he moved into phonetics and applied linguistics at Edinburgh University. In 1961 he moved to Leeds University as Professor of Contemporary English Language, then to Essex as Professor of Applied Linguistics. Currently he is a Fellow of Wolfson College, Cambridge and Director-General of the Bell Educational Trust. He was Chairman of the International Association of Teachers of English as a Foreign Language 1984–7. He has published widely in the fields of applied linguistics, English as a foreign language and teacher training. His books include *British and American English* and *Teaching English as an International Language.*

DEBORAH TANNEN is Associate Professor of Linguistics at Georgetown University. Her B.A. and M.A. are in English literature. Before receiving her Ph.D. in linguistics at the University of California, Berkeley, she taught remedial writing, freshman literature and composition, and English as Second or Foreign Language in Greece, Detroit, California, and Lehman College, CUNY. She was a Danforth Fellow and a Rockefeller Humanities Fellow. Her publications have been in discourse analysis, including conversation, spoken and written discourse, frames theory, doctor-patient communication, cross-cultural communication, and modern Greek conversation and literature. She is currently investigating the relationship between ordinary conversation and literary discourse with support from the National Endowment for the Humanities. Her books include *That's Not What I Meant!: How Conversational Style Makes or Breaks Relationships* and *Conversational Style: Analyzing Talk Among Friends.*

H. G. WIDDOWSON is a Professor in the Department of English as a Second Language, University of London Institute of Education. He received his Ph.D. from the University of Edinburgh. He was a founder and editor of the journal *Applied Linguistics* and former editor of the English in Focus series. His books include *Stylistics and the Teaching of Literature, Teaching Language as Communication, Explorations in Applied Linguistics I and II,* and *Learning Purpose and Language Use.*

Preface

From June 24 to August 2, 1985, Georgetown University was host to the 1985 LSA/TESOL Institute, combining the 52nd Linguistic Institute of the Linguistic Society of America and the 7th Summer Institute of Teachers of English to Speakers of Other Languages. It was my privilege to organize and direct this joint six-week Institute, "Linguistics and Language in Context: The Interdependence of Theory, Data, and Application," as well as a concurrent four-week Institute nestled within the larger one, supported by a grant from the National Endowment for the Humanities. The NEH Institute, "Humanistic Approaches to Linguistic Analysis," highlighted the humanistic focus of the LSA/TESOL Institute and brought to it three additional faculty members; I was the fourth NEH faculty member. Each of us taught one week of the NEH Institute. Participants in the NEH Institute were twenty-five college and university faculty who teach introductory and intermediate level linguistics and language-related courses; many are accomplished researchers as well.

In addition to regularly scheduled courses and ancillary meetings and workshops, the 1985 LSA/TESOL Institute included nightly lectures. Each week a different scholar-in-residence delivered a series of lectures and seminars, beginning with a lecture on Monday night. On Tuesday nights the traditional Forum Lectures were delivered by scholars who came just for this purpose. Each Wednesday night, that week's NEH Institute faculty member delivered a public lecture. This volume includes most of those lectures, as well as a keynote address delivered by an Institute faculty member, Henry Widdowson, during the TESOL Summer Meeting held at the Institute.

This volume, then, reflects many of the themes, issues, and approaches that characterized the tripartite Institute. It is a companion to the 1985 Georgetown University Round Table on Languages and Linguistics (GURT) which was held at the end of the first week of the Institute and in which all visiting faculty then in residence were invited to participate. Those lectures appear in the GURT volume and are listed as an Appendix to the Introduction.

The remainder of this Preface, based on my remarks at the Institute's opening ceremony, places the Institute in personal and historical context and acknowledges the many people who contributed to it.

The 1985 LSA/TESOL Institute

In 1973, I was a teacher of remedial writing, freshman composition, and English as a Second Language at Herbert H. Lehman College of the City University of New York. That summer I went to the Linguistic Institute at the University of Michigan. I attended classes all day, and I went to lectures in the evenings. It was at, and because of, that Institute, "Language in Context," that I decided to become a linguist. So I have a personal debt to Linguistic Institutes. My way of repaying that debt was organizing and directing the 1985 LSA/TESOL Institute: the first one since 1973 to focus on language in context, or, broadly speaking, sociolinguistic/discourse approaches to language.

The History of Linguistic Institutes

Nineteen eighty-five was the second year the LSA and TESOL Institutes were jointly held, and the third time Georgetown University hosted a Linguistic Institute. The first and second times were 1954 and 1955. (It was then standard for a university to host the Institute two years in a row.) The 1985 Institute took its place in a long tradition. (The following information comes from "The History of Linguistic Institutes" by Archibald Hill and from earlier Institute brochures, all of which were provided by the Linguistic Society of America.)

The first two Linguistic Institutes were held in 1928 and 1929 at Yale University. The next two, in 1930 and 1931, were held at the College of the City of New York. All four of these Institutes were directed by Edgar Sturtevant. Hill reports, "Preliminary costs . . . were guaranteed by a group of thirty-two of the most distinguished members of the Society" including Boas, Bloomfield, and Sapir. Because of economic conditions, Institutes were then discontinued until 1936 when they began again and were held five years in succession at the University of Michigan, directed by Charles Fries. At these Institutes, the connection between linguistics and the teaching of languages was central.

The 1936 Linguistic Institute included "luncheon conferences." The brochure explains, "These luncheon conferences will be held in one of the private dining rooms of the Michigan Union and will cost each member attending fifty-cents for his luncheon." (It most likely was "his" luncheon. The list of 16 faculty members includes not a single woman.) The maximum fee for tuition was $39; a single room cost $3–5 per week; board was $4–7 per week. The railroads offered a special

1 + ⅓ fare for Institute participants. Visiting scholars were admitted free.

The University of Michigan again hosted the Linguistic Institute from 1945 to 1950. About the 1945 Institute, Hill writes, "In addition, the lectures contained the first appearance of what has come to be the most theatrically and linguistically effective performance of many Institutes, Professor Pike's "Demonstration of an Introductory Analysis of a Language Unknown to the Linguist." Exactly 40 years later, Professor Pike performed a similar demonstration at the 1985 Institute.

Participants

I was particularly pleased to have on the faculty of the 1985 Institute someone who had also been on the faculty of the 1955 Institute at Georgetown: Charles Ferguson. Indeed, the 1985 Institute had a large and stellar faculty, including seven scholars from abroad (Michael Canale, Robert Cooper, Florian Coulmas, Beatriz Lavandera, Andrew Pawley, Suzanne Romaine, Henry Widdowson); five from the Washington, DC area (Jo Ann Crandall, Robert Johnson, Scott Liddell, Richard Tucker, Walt Wolfram); and fifteen from Georgetown University, including members of the French (Simon Battestini), English (Daniel Moshenberg), and Philosophy (Steven Kuhn) Departments as well as Linguistics (Walter Cook, S.J., Francis Dinneen, S.J., Ralph Fasold, Charles Kreidler, Robert Lado, Peter Lowenberg, Solomon Sara, S.J., Deborah Schiffrin, Shaligram Shukla, Roger Shuy, John Staczek, Michael Zarechnak). The twenty-three visiting faculty members from other states were Kathleen Bailey, Russell Campbell, Wallace Chafe, Mark Clarke, Jenny Cook-Gumperz, Frederick Erickson, John Fanselow, Lily Wong Fillmore, John Gumperz, Evelyn Hatch, Shirley Brice Heath, Robin Lakoff, Diane Larsen-Freeman, Michael Long, James McCawley, Marianne Mithun, Joan Morley, William Moulton, Susan Philips, Haj Ross, Leonard Talmy, Rita Wong, and Vivian Zamel. One-week scholars-in-residence were Emanuel Schegloff (week one); Elinor Ochs and Bambi Schieffelin (week two); Charles Fillmore (week three); and Paul Hopper (week four). Forum lecturers were Kenneth Pike, Paul Friedrich, Stephen Krashen, Peter Strevens, Muriel Saville-Troike, and William Labov. The NEH faculty were A. L. Becker, Ray McDermott, Harold Rosen, and I. John Gumperz held the Linguistic Society of America Chair. William Moulton held the Herman Collitz Chair.

There were also numerous lectures, meetings, workshops, and conferences which contributed to the richness and excitement of the Institutes. These events and their organizers were: Jens Allwood and Per

Linell ("Reconsidering structuralist linguistics"); Paul Chapin ("Everything you ought to know about how to apply for an NSF grant"); Florian Coulmas ("The national language question"); Hans Dechert ("Current trends in European second language acquisition research"); Richard Frankel ("Exploring the medical encounter through microinteractional analysis"); Roy Freedle ("Cognitive and linguistic aspects of language test performance"); Donald Freeman ("Experiential language teacher education: A workshop in issues, practices, and techniques"); David Hiple and Judith Liskin-Gasparro ("Four-day oral proficiency workshop"); Joyce Hutchings (TESOL Summer Meeting); Leah Kedar ("Language and power"); Joan Morley and Sandra Silberstein ("The art and science of materials development"); Livia Polanyi ("Syntactic and semantic aspects of discourse structure"); Deborah Schiffrin (Linguistic Institute summer meeting); John Staczek ("Colloquium on Spanish, Portuguese, and Catalan linguistics"); Len Talmy and Deborah Tannen ("Analyzing videotaped interaction: Loud family tapes"); Jackie Tanner ("Media software development for ESL teachers"); and Anne Walker and Judith Levi ("Language and the judicial process"). I organized a concluding NEH Conference 'Interpretation in Linguistic Analysis,' as well as a public presentation entitled 'Women and Men Talking,' which featured Robin Lakoff, Susan Philips, Frederick Erickson, John Gumperz, and actors from Horizons Theater.

These faculty members, lecturers, and organizers; those who participated in these events; and the students and visiting scholars, constituted the Institute. The nearly 550 students and visiting scholars also came from all over the world. Some (by no means all) of the countries they came from are Argentina, Australia, Bangladesh, Belgium, Brazil, Canada, China, El Salvador, Costa Rica, Dominican Republic, Holland, Honduras, Egypt, Finland, Gabon, Germany, Greece, Guatemala, Hong Kong, India, Iran, Israel, Jamaica, Japan, Korea, Kuwait, Malaysia, Nigeria, Norway, Peru, Philippines, Saudi Arabia, Singapore, South Africa, Sweden, Switzerland, Syria, Taiwan, Tobago, Togo, Trinidad, Turkey, and Venezuela.

Acknowledgements

The last part of my opening remarks were devoted to thanking the many people who helped make the 1985 LSA/TESOL and NEH Institutes happen. Such thanking behavior is a ritual within the ritual which is the opening ceremony. The fact that it is a ritual does not mean that it is not sincere. Quite the contrary, the thanking is ritualized because it is so universally true that such events do not materialize without the efforts of a great many people.

First, my earnest thanks go to the Institute staff. Associate Directors Diane Larsen-Freeman and Wallace Chafe helped define the themes, design the curriculum, and select faculty for the TESOL and LSA components, respectively. Assistant Director Heidi Byrnes helped with administrative tasks, especially those associated with the 1985 GURT. Maya Mozoomdar was an exemplary special assistant before the Institute began; Fiona Burnett was our incomparable secretary during the period of the Institute.

I was helped by a great many student volunteers, including Larry Bell, Gayle Berens, Susan French, Susan Hoyle, Carolyn Kinney, Katherine Langan, Clare O'Leary, Cindy Roy, Stuart Showalter, Fran Smith, Edwin Solis, Belle Tyndall, Lucy Vanderwende, and Monique Wong. Venetta Acson was a special consultant. The LSA staff offered continual and varied support, especially John Hammer, Margaret Reynolds, and Bernarda Erwin; likewise, the TESOL staff, especially Carol LeClaire and Susan Bayley. The LSA Committee on Institutes and Fellowships and the TESOL Committee to Select the Ruth Crymes Fellow deserve thanks too.

It was James Alatis, Dean of the School of Languages and Linguistics and Executive Secretary of TESOL who initiated the idea for a joint LSA/TESOL Institute at Georgetown. His support was crucial throughout, and others in his office provided invaluable help: Richard Cronin, Jose Hernandez, John Staczek, and Josette Selim. The Linguistics Department secretary Carolyn Leilich cheerfully absorbed many pressures exerted by the presence of the Institute.

The Institutes were under the direct jurisdiction of the School for Summer and Continuing Education, of which I thank Dean Michael Collins and Esther Rider, Director of Summer Sessions. Outstanding for their patience and organization were the Registrar, John Peirce, and Associate Registrar Jan Doehlert.

I also thank those who provided funding for aspects of the program: the National Endowment for Humanities, and staff members David Wise and Jack Meyers, for support of the NEH Institute, "Humanistic Approaches to Linguistic Analysis"; the National Science Foundation for support of the conference "Language and the Judicial Process"; and the DC Community Humanities Council, the British Council, the Adrian Akmajian Memorial Fund of the Linguistic Society of America, and WAMU radio host Diane Rehm, for making possible the special public presentation, "Women and Men Talking: A Cultural Approach to Understanding Male/female Communication."

There are two people I haven't mentioned because mention alone is inadequate to the task of acknowledging their contributions. Every person I have named enabled some aspect of the Institutes, but there are two people who enabled every aspect. They are Carol Kaplan, my assistant, and Gerald Sullivan, Associate Dean of the School for Summer and Continuing Education.

I dubbed Carol Kaplan Ms. A&B because she cheerfully, tirelessly, and ably handled the masses of details and people that besieged her, always working Above and Beyond what might reasonably be expected.

Gerald Sullivan was the Institute's Guardian Angel from the time I first wrote the proposal, three years before the Institutes took place. He continued to be a stalwart, untiring, and unflappable support at every stage. He was the key person in making all arrangements from budget and fellowships to parking and field house membership. His unwavering faith in the Institutes' success became a self-fulfilling prophecy.

Time and place to prepare this volume were provided by a sabbatical leave from Georgetown University and affiliation with the Joint Program in Applied Anthropology of Teachers College, Columbia University for which I am grateful to Lambros Comitas. Ray McDermott provided invaluable dialogue on the issues discussed in the Introduction, and he as well as Jo Anne Kleifgen, Clifford Hill, and Michael Macovski gave helpful comments on an earlier draft. I thank, finally and especially, the contributors who helped make the 1985 LSA/TESOL and NEH Institutes a success, and, through their extra efforts, made this volume.

Deborah Tannen

New York, NY

Introduction

It is an exciting time in linguistics. With the burgeoning of research in discourse, our field has seen a broadening of scope and diversifying of methods of inquiry. This window-opening has ushered in invigorating debate about the nature of language and of linguistics: the relationship between the individual and the social, the fixed and the novel, the theoretical and the empirical, the humanistic and the scientific. As Clifford Geertz (1983:8) demonstrates in his essay "Blurred Genres" (an essay which uses as one of three examples the work of a scholar included here: A. L. Becker), current scholarship is experiencing "significant realignments in scholarly affinities," so that "a growing number of people trying to understand [human behavior] have turned to linguistics, aesthetics, cultural history, law, or literary criticism for illumination rather than, as they used to do, to mechanics or physiology."

Paul Hopper concludes in his lecture included in this volume that our field reflects "two competing ideologies, corresponding broadly to the two major intellectual trends of our day: structuralism, with its belief in and attention to a priori structures of consciousness and behavior, and hermeneutics, with its equally firm conviction that temporality and context are continually re-shaping the elusive present." The 1985 LSA/TESOL Institute brought together scholars who represent the latter trend or are actively struggling with the challenges it poses. Institute participants who attended the daily classes and listened to the nightly lectures took part in their interchanges. This volume, which includes all but a few of the lectures delivered at the Institute, invites a wider audience of readers to participate as well.

Part of the excitement of this new dialogue comes from its interdisciplinary roots. To better understand the nature of language, linguists are working alongside colleagues from anthropology, sociology, psychology, literature, and education. All these fields are represented in this volume (and in its companion volume of lectures from the 1985 Georgetown University Round Table on Languages and Linguistics, composed of papers by Institute faculty members listed in an Appendix).

In its very title, reflecting its joint nature, the 1985 LSA/TESOL Institute was about connecting the field of linguistics with related

1

disciplines, in particular the teaching of English to speakers of other languages. The subtitle of the Institute was "Linguistics and Language in Context: The Interdependence of Theory, Data, and Application." "Theory," "data," and "application" were intended as constitutive, not additive. The conviction underlying this choice of subtitle is that linguistic research should entail all three at once. It needs a simultaneous commitment to close observation of real language in context, a broad and inclusive theoretical perspective, and attention to the uses of our research. The Institutes grew out of a wish to bring together researchers who were working in this spirit, to communicate with each other and to display a panorama of the work they are doing. In a sense, the need to link scholars who ordinarily work in relative isolation is a human counterpart to the need to link microanalysis with wider perspectives of theory and application.

The title of the NEH Institute, whose faculty members gave lectures to the larger Institute which are included here, was "Humanistic Approaches to Linguistic Analysis." The focus of this Institute was the relationship between the language of everyday conversation and the language of literature, including poetry. This theme runs through a number of the lectures included in this volume, not only those of the NEH faculty.

The Institutes thus represented a range of research—a range, moreover, that in itself contributes to an understanding of the relationship among theory, data, and application. The volume as a whole, reflecting the crystalline microcosm of individual lectures, is about connecting observation and understanding, and putting them to use.

SECTION ONE: HUMANISTIC APPROACHES TO LINGUISTIC ANALYSIS.

The four lectures in Section One are by the faculty who taught for one week each in the NEH Institute. A. L. Becker begins "Language in Particular: A Lecture" by asking, "If there is a linguistics in the humanities, . . . what might it be and how might we do it and why would we want to do it . . . ?" For him, the road to such a linguistics has been "the particular." Noting some philosophical strands of humanistic linguistic analysis, Becker suggests that we need humanistic linguistics, not to replace the scientific kind, but to do work that cannot be done within it.

Sounding a theme that is also discussed by Friedrich, Pike, and others in succeeding lectures, Becker notes that humanistic linguistics puts the observer back into our work. Demonstrating with sentences produced on the spot by audience members, Becker proposes an understanding of grammar similar to what Hopper, in a later lecture, calls the "emergent grammar hypothesis": that language is modeled on prior text, "drawn from lingual memory and reshaped to present circumstances." He explains, "Our discipline and our rigor in humanistic linguistics comes . . . from the particularity of the text-in-context, not from the rigor of the rules." Put another way, the discipline "comes not from theory but from a language."

To answer the last of his initial questions, why would we want to do this kind of linguistics, Becker, following Geertz, reminds us that our goal is "to learn to converse with those we have difficulty conversing with," "our own neighbors and family or people halfway round the world," and, Becker concludes, to learn to respect others "as the practical first step in having my own differences respected." Thus, Becker's lecture provides a foundation for the collection by expressing the Institute's theme: our understanding of language (i.e. theory) and observations of particular bits of language (what might be called data) are inseparable from each other and from the practical use of language in everyday life (application).

Becker cites Ortega y Gasset's observation that "speech consists above all in silences. A being who could not renounce saying many things would be incapable of speaking." This could be a lead-in to the second NEH lecture. Ray McDermott shows that "Inarticulateness" can be "organized": "occasions on which people are left without words are systematic outcomes of a set of relations among a group of persons bound in a social structure." McDermott illustrates "two ends of a continuum of mastery and disappointment . . ." At the apparently articulate end he considers the writers of the Irish Literary Renaissance, showing the inarticulate in even their work and the "institutionalized use of their texts—riot, exile, and condemnation." At the "mutterance" end, he introduces Horace, who fails at school, and White-Thunder, a Menomeni Indian described by Bloomfield and discussed by Hymes, who lacked facility in both Menomeni and English.

McDermott is interested in "institutional arrangements." For both the apparently articulate and the apparently inarticulate he asks, "First, what was their situation and what language resources did they have available for explicating and transforming their situation? Second, what effects did their talk have on the conditions that so limited them?" McDermott invites us to "move slowly away from a linguistics of speakers towards a linguistics of participation . . ."

McDermott offers a supremely social view of language. He also claims that an amoral linguistics is not worth having: Insight must become a means to "organize a better world." Like Becker, he is concerned with understanding not only speakers of different languages and cultures but "your spouse or your neighbors." Moreover, insight into what makes some (others) inarticulate is inseparable from insight into what makes others (us) articulate. Self-knowledge is a goal of analyzing others.

Harold Rosen's NEH lecture is, like Becker's and McDermott's, an essay. Including his own creative writing as material (as Friedrich and Pike also do), Rosen argues for the centrality, force, and pervasiveness of "The Autobiographical Impulse." He asks, Why is narrative so universal? And why is it "so constantly thwarted, put down, and often explicitly outlawed in our educational system and in 'high' discourse"? In counterpoint to McDermott, Rosen cites de Certeau to the effect that "memory emerging as narrative is one means available to us for asserting our authority against institutionalized power . . ."

Rosen shows that narrative, like dialogue, is a way of thinking and learning. Narrative is a social activity, a means of presentation of self. Furthermore, telling the past negotiates it: "The existence of a genre, learnt in thousands of tellings, offers us a framework which promises order and control." He concludes with a practical recommendation: that narrative be recognized and incorporated in educational and other institutional discourse.

Rosen argues, "Autobiographical stories often lie completely concealed beneath the genres which come to be defined precisely by their omission of personal stories." He cites Gilbert and Mulkay's observation of the excitement that emerges when scientists tell about their discoveries, contrasted with the burial of that excitement in their scholarly writing. This discussion prefigures a theme of the next and last NEH lecture, my own, "Hearing Voices in Conversation, Fiction, and Mixed Genres." I discuss a passage from a book by Mary Catherine Bateson who, because of her conviction that suppressing emotion in scholarly discourse obscures meaning, used fictional techniques in writing the proceedings of a scholarly conference. This example highlights the emotional basis of understanding in language which is the key to my idea of "involvement."

My lecture begins with discussion of the centrality of dialogue in storytelling, and the role of storytelling in creating involvement. Then, to support the claim that dialogue in conversational storytelling is constructed, not reported, I examine the dialogue in a story told in conversation. I then demonstrate that constructing dialogue is part of a pattern of vivid storytelling by reference to a pilot study by Mary Ott comparing how Brazilian and American speakers told Little Red Riding Hood. Next, I present dialogue from an American novel which was introduced by graphic verbs. I turn then to three spoken and written genres produced by junior high school students: a school writing assignment evidencing stilted dialogue; a sharply contrasting conversational story; and a kind of written conversation: notes passed to friends which are strikingly similar in idiom to the conversational story. In conclusion, I cite the dialogue of a Hasidic Jew as rendered by a journalist, to emphasize the impossibility of deriving meaning from text without interprepretation by individuals in interaction.

All the NEH lectures provide examples of "humanistic approaches to linguistic analysis," where "humanistic" is language-focused, context-sensitive, and concerned always with the effects of language use on people.

SECTION TWO: THE NATURE AND USE OF LANGUAGE AND LINGUISTIC THEORY.

In "Emergent Grammar and the A Priori Grammar Hypothesis," Paul Hopper identifies two approaches to grammar "whose polar extremes are dominated by radically different understandings of the nature of human language." The "a priori grammar attitude" (APG) sees grammar as "a discrete set of rules which are logically and mentally presupposed by discourse," so that "grammar is logically detachable from discourse and precedes discourse." In contrast, the "emergence of grammar attitude" (EOG) sees "grammar as the name for a vaguely defined set of sedimented (i.e. grammaticized) recurrent partials whose status is constantly being negotiated in speech . . ." The two approaches to grammar are "competing ideologies, corresponding broadly to the two major intellectual trends of our day: structuralism, with its belief in and attention to prior structures of consciousness and behavior, and hermeneutics, with its equally firm conviction that temporality and context are continually re-shaping the elusive present."

Like Widdowson, Hopper notes that divergent paradigms entail different ideas of data (intuition and made-up sentences vs. real language) and different attitudes toward temporality (grammar as static, an object existing in speakers' minds vs. grammar as a real-time activity, not homogeneous). Whereas APG is "indifferent to prior texts," not distinguishing between repetitive utterances (such as idioms and proverbs) and "bizarre fictional sentences," EOG is concerned with "strategies for building texts."

Supporting the EOG, Hopper demonstrates the efficacy of "a textually-based argument concerning some aspects of emergent clause structure" in a nineteenth century Malay written narrative. Adopting Becker's term "text-building strategies," he argues, "It is from such natural ways of constructing discourse . . . that the phenomena we think of as 'grammar,' such as the classification of verbs into transitive and intransitive, perfective and imperfective, and so on, develop and become sedimented."

Finally, Hopper takes up the "debate over functionalism." He questions the simplistic correspondence of sentence grammar and discourse grammar and observes, "The assumed priority and autonomy of the Sentence are at the head of a line of implications which lead to the 'modularity' of syntax, semantics, and pragmatics—the separation of structure from meaning, and meaning from use." Thus, like many of the authors in this volume, Hopper argues against atomism in favor of a holistic view of language.

In the next lecture, Emanuel Schegloff demonstrates the pioneering and still most influential paradigm for analyzing conversation. Like McDermott, Schegloff is interested in "the organization of social action." Conversation becomes the focus of analysis because it is "the primordial site of sociality and social life." Essential to Schegloff's approach is continual return to the data. For him, the observation of a phenomenon in a videotape of interaction is not the end of observation, but its beginning: occasion for rerunning the bit of tape innumerable times to refine and check analysis.

In "Discourse as an Interactional Achievement II: An Exercise in Conversation Analysis," Schegloff examines two short segments from a casual conversation videotaped by Marjorie and Charles Goodwin. To give a sense of his analysis, I will summarize a small part.

In one segment in the videotape, a speaker, Mike, produced two head shakes, one horizontal and one vertical, both accompanying similar verbal utterances. Thus the negativity or positivity of the head shakes reflects not grammatical negativity or positivity but agreement or disagreement, that is, a feature of the relationship of the utterance to a preceding utterance. The lateral shake is also used as an intensifier. Furthermore, head gestures are unusual gestures in that they can be produced by hearers rather than speakers. In another segment, Mike, this time apparently a listener, also shakes his head, beginning just after Curt utters a word with a pitch peak and raised amplitude. Since a pitch peak can be a way of marking that a turn is about to end, Mike's head gesture may be that of an incipient speaker, about to disagree with what Curt has just said. Schegloff argues that the continuation of Curt's utterance must be seen as a response to this incipient disagreement, and therefore as an interactional product and achievement.

Schegloff goes on to show that the whole sequence is topic-proffering, characterized by several tries. He accounts for two cut-offs of the first component of Curt's turn. The first is a repair probably occasioned by an overlap. The second takes into account a remark made by another speaker, Phyllis, which otherwise seemed to have been ignored. Schegloff proposes, finally, that the placement of the second repair is responsive to the impending possible completion point of the utterance.

Based on analysis of such details, Schegloff addresses the theoretical problem, "How is it that with the use of abstract formal resources interactional participants create idiosyncratic, particularized . . . interactions?" In conclusion, referring to the incorporation in his analysis of such traditionally nonlinguistic concerns as gesture and interactional contingencies, Schegloff reminds us that "the fabric of the social world does not seem to be woven with seams at the disciplinary boundaries." As a result, we need "a stance toward the organization of inquiry concerning social life which interweaves linguistics, together with other traditional and not-so-traditional disciplines, as parts in a larger social science, one which is both humanistic *and* scientific."

The last chapter in this section, William Labov's "The Judicial Testing of Linguistic Theory," looks at the nature of theory through the lens of its use. Labov reports on his participation in three legal cases. Consideration of the reception of his and his colleagues' linguistic evidence by the courts casts light on "the familiar problems of the relations between theory and practice, theory and data, theory and facts."

In the first case, linguists were asked to testify as to whether the wording of a letter was biased. The letter, to be sent to black steel workers in Pittsburgh along with a check in settlement of a national class action suit, explained that accepting the check entailed relinquishing claim to a potentially much larger settlement in a pending local class action suit. The lawyers representing the steel workers in the local suit felt that the letter's explanation of the recipients' options was biased in favor of accepting the check and waiving rights to the pending claim. Labov and his colleagues agreed. Their analysis indicated that the letter was comprehensible and objective, "but where the document was comprehensible, it was not objective; and where it was objective, it was not comprehensible."

The judge was sympathetic to the perspective of the expert witnesses but allowed the letter to go out with only minor changes. In the second case, however, involving letters notifying welfare recipients that their benefits would be curtailed, the judge ordered that a new letter be sent, one which made clearer the possibility of appeal. The result was that far more recipients appealed the curtailment of their benefits.

The third and last case involved the incarceration of a man accused of having made threatening telephone calls. Comparing tapes of the actual telephone threats to tapes of the defendant uttering the same words, Labov determined that the caller spoke in Eastern New England dialect whereas the defendant spoke in New York City dialect, and phonetic differences between the two exist at levels beyond conscious control. Using a variety of types of linguistic analysis, Labov convinced the judge that his findings were fact, not opinion. The defendant was freed.

Labov notes that many academic linguists see theories as their end product, so that "facts are valued to the extent that they serve a theory . . ." He suggests, instead, that theories be created to resolve questions about the real world; that they be based on observation and experiment; and that it is "the application of the theory that determines its value." Labov's own paper offers a model of the use of linguistic theory in the pursuit of social justice.

SECTION THREE: POETRY: LINGUISTIC ANALYSIS AND LANGUAGE TEACHING.

All three chapters in the third section deal with analysis of poetry. Two are also concerned with language teaching, as are two of the chapters in the final section.

Widdowson begins his lecture, "Poetry and Pedagogy," by observing that poetry is normally placed outside the scope of applied linguistics and language teaching. (One might also observe that it has been infrequently included within the scope of linguistics.) Citing a literary scholar who believed poetic language is unique in requiring the reader to fill in meaning, Widdowson notes that all language requires this. In poetry, however, meaning is more often by association, or correspondence. (It is just this observation that leads Paul Friedrich, in the book from which the subsequent lecture is taken, to argue that all language is more or less poetic.) In language teaching, as in linguistics, there is a continuum between two poles (Hopper's two poles of grammatical theory are recalled by association): on the one hand, the study of language as science, associated with rules and assumptions of objectivity; on the other hand, the study of language as art, associated with focus on the particularity of the data.

Widdowson joins others in this volume in opposing "the needless opposition between form and meaning." Studying poetry along with other forms of discourse calls attention to the language as well as its meaning. Literature, by representing life rather than commenting on it, can be "a means of engaging the previous experience of learners as mediated through their mother tongue and bringing it to bear on the learning of the new language," fulfilling a goal of pedagogy to observe the formal properties of language by using language in context.

Paul Friedrich, in "The Unheralded Revolution in the Sonnet: Toward a Generative Model," also posits a continuum, "from a routine conversation to stylized and deeply conventional poetic forms." The sonnet "illustrates one extreme case of 'poetic language,' with acutely constraining rules, patterns, and conventions of all sorts for all levels of sound and meaning."

The language of the sonnet illustrates "the fissures and even the breakdown of order and convention in several ways." After outlining the history of the sonnet, its varying forms, its determining structures, and its rules and how they are broken, Friedrich examines the place of the sonnet in contemporary poetry. Asking why the form has endured, he considers the richness of prior text: echoes of all the sonnets that came before.

Friedrich applies to language the principle of indeterminacy in physics ("the observer is an integral part of the universe of observation"). He includes in his exploration his own experience of writing sonnets. In this argument and this practice, his lecture prefigures the next one, Kenneth Pike's "Bridging Language Learning, Language Analysis, and Poetry, via Experimental Syntax."

Like Friedrich, Pike reflects a theme of the NEH Institute: the relationship between poetry and conversational language. He further relates both to second language pedagogy. He uses his own creative writing as objects of analysis and introspection, seeing the two as inextricable (echoing Friedrich and also McDermott). The rejection of autonomy is central to Pike's view of language and linguistics. Like many others in this volume, he discusses the concept of context.

Pike suggests that an understanding of language and poetry, and the process of language learning, can be enhanced by experimenting with syntax: "the deliberate, systematic, patterned changing of a text in order to force the student to use different grammatical forms to paraphrase the same referential material." Whereas Widdowson discusses the benefits to language learners of reading poetry, Pike suggests that students write poems, and poems paraphrasing poems, to get a kaleidoscopic view of the poem's linguistic parts.

In keeping with the spirit of the Institute, Pike states at the outset that he wants to build bridges between theory and application, science and philosophy, form and meaning, the intellectual and the personal: "I wanted a theory that would allow one to live outside the office with the same philosophy one uses inside it. This required the development of a view which allowed one to integrate research with belief, thing with person, fact with aesthetics, knowledge with application of knowledge." He notes that "pure formalism as such, without attention to referential social axioms, is powerless to capture the relevance of many discourse grammatical functions."

SECTION FOUR: LANGUAGE LEARNING AND TEACHING.

Muriel Saville-Troike ("From Context to Communication: Paths to Second Language Acquisition") reports on research conducted over the previous four years on the acquisition of English by children of varied language backgrounds. She joins the chorus of Institute voices when she notes, "collecting data only to confirm or disprove a priori hypotheses is likely to exclude crucial evidence for phenomena which occur in the process of language acquisition . . ."

Saville-Troike's study suggests stages of development in language learners within which she finds two types of learners: Type A ("other-directed") and Type B ("inner-directed"). Within each stage, learners of each type exhibit different communicative tactics. For example, at Stage II, when English first appears, she finds "two basic developmental strategies": "holistic" or "message-oriented" and "analytic" or "code-oriented."

Saville-Troike discusses implications of her study for second language acquisition theory as well as for teaching. For example, "the process of natural language learning is not unitary, and may take different paths." Whereas "meaningful context is critical for language learning," "over-emphasis on providing contextual meaning for students may actually inhibit their development of context-reduced/academic competence." She ends with a note of concern for the young subjects of her study: The acquisition of English by very young children "is quite likely to be at the expense of their native language development."

Stephen Krashen's "Do We Learn to Read by Reading?: The Relationship Between Free Reading and Reading Ability" represents an entirely different disciplinary and methodological mode of argumentation: quantitative analysis. Yet his approach to the teaching of reading is similar in spirit to the approach to language found in the other chapters in this volume. He argues for an integrated, holistic rather than atomistic view of language ability: Reading is not a bundle of autonomous, independently functioning skills, but an organic, context-bound, humanly motivated activity.

Krashen reviews the results of quantitative studies aimed at determining whether children who do more pleasure reading are better readers, as measured by tests of reading comprehension. He is concerned with reading programs implemented in schools, students' reports of free reading outside of school, and the availability of books and other forms of print. He concludes that "free reading consistently relates to success in reading comprehension." If children spend a portion of their class time simply reading books—or comics!—of their own choosing, while their teacher silently reads for pleasure, their reading ability improves as much as or more than it does if their time is spent entirely on "skills" lessons.

In the final chapter of this section and this volume, "Language Learning and Language Teaching: Towards an Integrated Model," Peter Strevens notes that an "intellectual base" for the "massive array of published materials, of teaching techniques, and of professional support for the teacher and the learner . . . is supplied principally through applied linguistics . . ." He identifies four paradigms presently in use. The one he feels embraces the others and is seriously conducive to language learning is the teaching/learning paradigm. He discusses the components of language learning and how language teaching can successfully respond to an understanding of these components.

REINTEGRATING LINGUISTICS.

An intriguing analogue to the mission of this volume in linguistics is provided by neurologist and essayist Oliver Sacks' (1986, 1987) account of neuroanatomy. Sacks (1987:41) notes that advances in modern medicine resulted in "a real gain of knowledge but a real loss of understanding" because of compartmentalization into motor, intellectual, and affective domains and excessive abstraction associated with "narrow formulations or theories" (40) which he contrasts, citing William James, with " 'the light of the world's concrete fullness . . .'(41)." To regain understanding, he recommends that his colleagues "listen minutely" to patients and "observe them, everything about them, with a comprehensive eye" (40). Sacks calls for "a neurology of living experience."

The lectures in this volume represent a reach for a "linguistics of living language," indeed of "living experience." The scholars whose voices are heard here are striving for a linguistics rich in the details of description, not blindered by "narrow formulations and theories," not blinded to the "concrete fullness" of language by excessive abstraction, not blocked from understanding by compartmentalization into autonomous parts. Like Sacks' (1986:3) call for a "personalistic" science of neurology, is the call for a linguistics grounded in human experience, perhaps a "personalistic" linguistics.

A NOTE ON THE DIVERSITY OF EXPOSITORY VOICES.

All volumes of collected papers are characterized by a diversity of voices. Since this volume seeks to give a sense of the LSA/TESOL and NEH Institutes as an event, I see that diversity as a strength. The expository voices of the authors differ, even as individual voices and lecturing styles differ.

In addition to personal stylistic variation, perhaps a reflection of it, there is variation in the degree and type of correspondence between what is printed here and what was heard by those present at the lecture. This range in what is represented by a written "paper" is a corollary in writing to a phenomenon I have discussed elsewhere (Tannen 1988): the diverse nature of the activity commonly referred to as "giving a paper" at a scholarly conference—an activity that takes a myriad forms, resulting from a variety of intertwined uses of speaking and writing and linguistic patterns associated with each. In a lecture series, no one tries to make individual speakers speak in the same way. Similarly, I did not try to make the Institute lecturers transform their lectures into writing in the same way.

Moreover, the diversity of expository voices reflects the disciplinary diversity of our field. The study of language is interdisciplinary by nature, so any volume seeking to include a range of linguistic approaches is, in effect, cross-disciplinary, representing a variety of theoretical and methodological paradigms.

The risks of interdisciplinary efforts are described by Henry Widdowson (Chapter Seven):

> The conventions of the paradigm not only determine which topics are relevant. They determine too the approved manner of dealing with them: what counts as data, evidence, and the inference of fact; what can be allowed as axiomatic, what needs to be substantiated by argument or empirical proof. The paradigm, therefore, is a sort of cultural construct . . . So the way language is conceived by another discipline, informed by another set of beliefs and values (the culture of a different tribe of scholars) tends to be seen as irrelevant, inadmissible, or misconceived. . . . This means that those who try to promote cross-cultural relations by being interdisciplinary are likely to be ostracized by both sides and to be stigmatized twice over as amateur or mountebank. The role is even less enviable for those who would seek to mediate not only across disciplinary boundaries laterally at one level of abstraction but also across different levels of abstraction by referring academic enquiry to the realities of practical applicability. This is what applied linguists try to do.

This is also what the 1985 LSA/TESOL and NEH Institutes tried to do, and what the present volume tries to do in representing the Institutes. I hope that readers who affirm the need for interdisciplinary and applied cum theoretical studies, will attune their eyes to the varying voices much as we attune our ears to the cadences of different languages or varying accents in our own languages.

As lectures delivered at the LSA/TESOL Institute, the chapters in this volume represent a range of research in linguistics. The authors do not agree on all issues, methods, and approaches. Yet, diverse as they are, they share a commitment to gaining understanding through close observation of language in use, and to exploring ways that our discipline can be of use to people in their lives. They share a commitment to rigorous inquiry of theoretical and practical import.

Deborah Tannen

New York, NY

REFERENCES

Geertz, Clifford. 1983. Local knowledge: Further essays in interpretive anthropology. New York: Basic Books.
Tannen, Deborah. 1988. The commingling of orality and literacy in giving a paper at a scholarly conference. American Speech 63:1.
Sacks, Oliver. 1986. The man who mistook his wife for a hat and other clinical tales. New York: Simon & Schuster.
Sacks, Oliver. 1987. Tics. New York Review of Books, January 29, 1987, 37–41.

APPENDIX

Papers by LSA/TESOL Institute faculty included in *Georgetown University Round Table on Languages and Linguistics 1985. Languages and Linguistics: The Interdependence of Theory, Data, and Application*, edited by Deborah Tannen and James E. Alatis. Washington, DC: Georgetown University Press, 1986.

William B. Moulton (Emeritus, Princeton University). An unexplored semantic relation between verb and complement: Reciprocal

Walt Wolfram (University of the District of Columbia and Center for Applied Linguistics) (with Deborah Hatfield). Interlanguage fads and linguistic reality: The case of tense marking

Suzanne Romaine (Oxford University). The syntax and semantics of the code-mixed compound verb in Panjabi/English bilingual discourse

Marianne Mithun (SUNY Albany). Disagreement: The case of pronominal affixes and nouns

Leonard Talmy (University of California, Berkeley). Force dynamics as a generalization over 'causative'

Scott K. Liddell and Robert E. Johnson (Gallaudet College). American Sign Language compounds: Implications for the structure of the lexicon

Andrew Pawley (University of Auckland). Lexicalization

Beatriz R. Lavandera (University of Buenos Aires). Intertextual relationships: 'Missing people' in Argentina

Florian Coulmas (Universität Düsseldorf). Nobody dies in Shangri-La: Direct and indirect speech across languages

Susan U. Philips (University of Arizona). Reported speech as evidence in an American trial

Robin Tolmach Lakoff (University of California, Berkeley). My life in court

Haj Ross (Massachusetts Institute of Technology). Languages as poems

Charles A. Ferguson (Stanford University). The study of religious discourse

Wallace Chafe (University of California, Berkeley). How we know things about language: A plea for catholicism

Rita Wong (San Francisco State University). Does pronunciation teaching have a place in the communicative classroom?

John F. Fanselow (Teachers College Columbia University). You call yourself a teacher? An alternative model for discussing lessons

Michael Canale (Ontario Institute for Studies in Education). Language assessment: The method is the message

G. Richard Tucker (Center for Applied Linguistics). Developing a language-competent American society

Robert L. Cooper (The Hebrew University of Jerusalem). Selling language reform

Shirley Brice Heath (Stanford University). Literacy and language change

Frederick Erickson (Michigan State University). Listening and speaking

Mark A. Clarke (University of Colorado at Denver). Conversational narratives as altered states of consciousness

Jenny Cook-Gumperz (University of California, Berkeley). Keeping it together: Text and context in children's language socialization

NEH LECTURES: HUMANISTIC APPROACHES TO LINGUISTIC ANALYSIS

CHAPTER ONE

Language in Particular: A Lecture*

A. L. Becker

Universiti Kebangsaan Malaysia

The point of this talk might also be stated as, "If there is a linguistics in the humanities, if there is a humanities, what might it be and how might we do it and why would we want to do it in the first place?" In the title as it is given, the notion of the "particular" has been my road to a kind of linguistics in the humanities. It is a road that was first laid out by a very great teacher whom you heard last week, Kenneth L. Pike. It was Pike who said to me when he left Michigan, "What you should really work on is particularity. What is linguistics when it focuses on particularity?" It was a nice challenge, although I really had no idea what he meant. It was one of many challenges Pike gave me as a teacher. One thing we all do as linguists—or nearly all of us—is teach at one time or another. It is an important part of our activity as linguists and Pike has been one of the very best.

But there are many paths to the kind of linguistics that we might locate in the humanities, and many of you will already be further along, on other paths than mine. There will be some paths that you have already rejected. There are paths from Heidegger (1971) which carry one through such great rhetoricians as Ernesto Grassi (1980) from Italy or José Ortega y Gasset (1957, 1959) from Spain, both students of Heidegger. They had to leave Germany in 1931, disturbed by the "basic 'Germanic' characteristic of Heidegger," as Grassi writes in his book, *Rhetoric as Philosophy: The Humanist Tradition.* But they carried the lessons back and applied them in very interesting ways in their own cultures, as do, in our time, people like Hans-Georg Gadamer (1976)

---

* This text was transcribed and edited from a tape recording. I would like to thank Deborah Tannen, Haj Ross, Andrew Pawley, John Lawler, and J.O. Becker for useful comments, and Carolyn Leilich for making the transcription.

and Paul Ricoeur (1981) and, closer yet to us, Clifford Geertz (1983). I think there is a Heideggerian tradition of thought about language that these names represent.

There is another path. It's a path from Wittgenstein (1958) which brings us closest to home with people like Erving Goffman (1981), who took the notion of language games and turned it into those beautiful investigations and explorations that he spent his too short life describing, showing us the variety and particularity of the games that we play with language. Many of Erving's students are here tonight.

There is also, I believe, a tradition which is less well known, an American tradition which, on the eve of the Fourth of July, seems appropriate to talk about, a little academic patriotism. This tradition starts for me with Ralph Waldo Emerson (1836) and his essays on language which, I think, still have a lot to teach us if we can relearn how to read them. For one thing, it takes a lot of slowing down to read someone like Emerson, who wrote with pen and ink, not with a word processor; the kinds of things he wrote then took longer to write and hence to read than the kinds of things we write and read now. So when I recommend Emerson to my linguist friends, they often have difficulty, mainly because they try to read too fast. But you can go along and join this tradition wherever it gets easy, with any of the people who developed it, people like William James and Charles Peirce, and closer to our times, John Dewey, who as a language philosopher has been neglected. He sat in Peirce's classes at Johns Hopkins and tried to figure out the obscurity of that strange man, Peirce. At the celebration of his ninety-second birthday in New York, someone asked Dewey if he could sum up what he'd learned of importance in all those years, and he said something Emerson could have said, "Democracy begins in conversation." (Lamont 1959:58)

And there is one student of William James who is not usually recognized as a student of William James, though she is recognized as one of the most subtle explorers of everyday conversation. I'm talking about Gertrude Stein. I would like to play for you, in her own voice, an excerpt from *The Making of Americans*. It's a voice from the past, and so this is a little bit of what the Javanese call jarwa dhosok, taking old language, old voices, and trying to make them speak to us in the present. This is the traditional task of the philologist: trying to make old or distant language speak to us in the present. Jarwa dhosok in Javanese means, literally, taking old language (jarwa) and forcing it, pushing it (dhosok) right into the present. It takes several kinds of effort. But I think Gertrude Stein's voice is part of the Emersonian tradition I am talking about (see for example, Stein 1974). (Pike's is, too.) She had one of the great lingual imaginations. She was one of those who can look at a particular bit of language and just play with it and see things in it of great richness. If you read any of her works, again slowly like Emerson's, you will know what I am talking about. So I'd like to make her, with your permission, Patron Saint of Humanistic Linguistics, and I'd like to play a bit of her voice reading from *The Making of Americans,* talking about repeating ("repeating then is in every one"), and ending with the statement, "That was all there was then of discussing."

[A tape recording of Gertrude Stein reading the following passages]

Repeating then is in every one, in every one their being and their feeling and their way of realising everything and every one comes out of them in repeating. More and more then every one comes to be clear to some one.

Slowly every one in continuous repeating, to their minutest variation, comes to be clearer to some one. Every one who ever was or is or will be living sometimes will be clearly realized by some one. Sometime there will be an ordered history of every one. Slowly every kind of one comes into ordered recognition. More and more then it is wonderful in living the subtle variations coming clear into ordered recognition, coming to make every one a part of some kind of them, some kind of men and women. Repeating then is in every one, every one then comes sometime to be clearer to some one, sometime there will be then an orderly history of every one who ever was or is or will be living.

. . .

It happens very often that a man has it in him, that a man does something, that he does it very often that he does many things, when he is a young man when he is an old man, when he is an older man. . . . One of such of these kind of them had a little boy and this one, the little son wanted to make a collection of butterflies and beetles and it was all exciting to him and it was all arranged then and then the father said to the son you are certain this is not a cruel thing that you are wanting to be doing, killing things to make collections of them, and the son was very disturbed then and they talked about it together the two of them and more and more they talked about it then and then at last the boy was convinced it was a cruel thing and he said he would not do it and his father said the little boy was a noble boy to give up pleasure when it was a cruel one. The boy went to bed then and then the father when he got up in the early morning saw a wonderfully beautiful moth in the room and he caught him and he killed him and he pinned him and he woke up his son then and showed it to him and he said to him 'see what a good father I am to have caught and killed this one,' the boy was all mixed up inside him and then he said he would go on with his collecting and that was all there was then of discussing and this is a little description of something that happened once and it is very interesting. (Stein 1966:284, 489–90)

So if you had any doubts about Gertrude Stein as an ancestor, I hope that this passage has erased them, because there is such a great deal in these words about the kinds of things we are trying to study and understand today. What makes there be an end of discussing? Or, as William Labov (1982) asked here a few years ago, what makes fights in bars? Or on the Mediterranean?

That's all fine and interesting, you may say, but why a linguistics in the humanities? What's wrong with the linguistics we have now? The answer is, probably nothing. It's just that there is a lot of other work to be doing which involves a close look at languaging, and other ways to be doing it, and I would like to present some thoughts on this linguistics in the humanities that these ancestors have opened up for us. I speak not in opposition to another kind of linguistics, but rather to identify a kind of work which needs doing. I don't want to replace scientific linguistics with anything else. I want to look at something which I think is important to do but which can't be handled within scientific linguistics.

Others will object and say, "Didn't it take years for every linguistics department to drive out the humanists, often called philologists? What possible reason could there be for asking them back?" Let me say right away that the reason is not to restore some genteel and elitist kind of great thoughts or great books program in linguistics, a kind of old philology or new humanism. It's not a matter of old books and old manners and things like that, but of something quite different and new. I think the job to do is simply the one Paul Friedrich asked of us last night, to put the observer into our work. Put the observer back into our knowledge. Put the knower back into the known. In simplest words, I think, that is what linguistics in the humanities is all about. Years ago Kenneth Pike (1978) called it emic analysis. It took a long time to understand what he was talking about and what it meant. Questions come up about what things are in our analysis because of the observer. What parts of our analyses are observer parts? Can we separate these things out? Can we say, this is language and that is the observation of language? I think not.

In our seminar here this week we did an experiment which demonstrates these things more clearly than talking about them will. It's one of the quickest ways to demonstrate what I would like to talk about. By doing a short experiment I can evoke an experience which we all share and which will save many words—something worth doing in the beautiful Georgetown twilight. (In Burmese this time of day is called 'ugly-things become beautiful-time'.) I'm going to ask you to write a sentence for me. I'm going to ask you to write a sentence which can be as long as you like—as many clauses, compoundings, and embeddings as you feel inclined to, in which you describe the simple action that I'm going to do. The only constraint is that it be a single sentence. Then I'm going to look at some of these sentences and use that personal experience of writing that you will have had as the particularity we will focus on. In a linguistics of particularity, you have to have a particularity to start with (that's where the discipline or rigor comes from!) and the particularity is what you are making right now. So I'll say "start" and then I'll say "stop" and that episode between those words is what I want you to describe.

Start . . . [the speaker performs a simple act, walking up the steps to the podium] . . . Stop.

[There is a long pause while the audience writes.]

There are slow writers and fast writers. Just like there are slow speakers and fast speakers, and slow readers and fast readers. Some of you will have already written the first page of your novels.

What I'd like to do now is hear some of these sentences. If we did this in a smaller group we would stop with each one and we would talk about it and parse it and describe it and then compare it with the previous ones and think about what was different about them. What are the dimensions of the differences? What are the kinds of differences appearing between these sentences? At this point the experiment gets a little unwieldy because of your numbers, so, in the interest of saving time, I would like for you to read what you wrote in a loud clear voice and we won't make much comment on each one but rather hear a bunch of them and then come back and try to summarize the dimensions of difference. I'll work a little less inductively because of the size of the crowd and the time constraint, but even in a seminar it can take weeks.

Fred Erickson, would you start?

"He walked up the steps across the stage to the podium, and slapped the book down on it as he arrived there."

Thanks. Ray McDermott?

"Repeating himself, he walked up a well travelled path in this shrine of knowledge and took a place at the podium, where, repeating himself . . . [laughter]"

Wow! I said we weren't going to comment but you can see why this takes a long time when you are doing it in a seminar, because of the differences you see in each one. But let's go on. Deborah?

"You stepped onto the stage holding a book, walked to the podium, and put the book on the podium."

Rosalia?

"He walked slowly toward the podium, placed the book he was carrying on it, and looked at us."

Haj?

"Pete walked up the three steps to the stage carefully, continued carefully, watching his feet, stepping over the tangle of wires, came up to the podium, raised his arms opening them wide to grasp both sides for it was wide, slowly raised his head and eyes to look at us gravely."

Wow! Gertrude Stein took, I see.

Let's continue. Would you read yours?

"He was walking up the steps to the podium being careful not to trip."

The next one?

"The man with the small paperback book in his hand who was standing at the edge of the stage began to walk up the steps onto the stage and then crossed the small semicircular platform to the podium where he put the book down onto the surface of the podium."

Very careful! Next one, please?

"Under the curious watchful eye of the assembled group, A.L. Becker engaged in a simple act in hopes to illustrate particularity."

That's what happens when someone does it twice in one week. She's in the seminar. Let's go on.

"He climbed the stage with a book in his hand and was approaching the podium where he put the book in front of the microphone."

Good. He got there, I think. Do you have one?

"The man walked to the place where he said 'start' and then to the place where he said 'stop.' "

No nonsense about that. How long is it going to take us to get to the back of the room? We'll probably never get to the back of the room but we have to do a few more.

"Calmly and deliberately, he climbed the stairs, watching the podium, set his book on the podium and looked at his audience."

"The linguist, though he had removed his spectacles, walked up the stairs without tripping."

The major accomplishment of the evening. Anyone else? Yes, please?

"The knower being entirely the known walked across the stage to the lectern."

Emersonian! Yes, Andy Pawley.

"A vertical figure moved across a [noise] field, then it ceased to move, its lower part obscured by a square object."

There's a Martian in every audience, isn't there?

That was the voice from the etic side!

You see how this thing sets you up and you know you could go on for a whole week, and there's nothing else you'd have to do except this. The thing we haven't done is talk about the ways these sentences differ. But I would like first to make a general comment about them. The one thing that you have noticed from the start was that there were no two alike. And if we went through the whole hall, even if there were five hundred people, there would be no two alike. If there were two alike, we would be surprised, and suspicious. It hasn't yet happened to me in the twelve or so years I've been doing this experiment that there were ever two alike. What does that mean? What does that say about what is happening here, about what languaging does, about how languaging works?

On the other hand, I could have set up the experiment so that there would have been more than two alike. There is a very easy way to do it, and I have tried it that way. That would be to ask you not to write your sentences down but to just speak out your sentences from aural memory. As you might guess, after about five or six, people start saying, "Well I said just what he said." The inventiveness of new versions, of new "takes" on this situation seems to dry up under the pressure of the oral situation. This is fascinating, and it means that one of the things important in shaping these sentences you wrote is the fact that I asked you to write them and the writing itself, the medium itself, is part of what shapes them. It is a basic part, which we don't have a real contrast for here because all of you read them. [Points to someone.] Except you, and yours was very short. It says interesting things about living within societies in which writing is common and those where it isn't and how deeply different these can be. One of those "inevitabilities" that everyone believes in right now is the notion that going from orality, to writing, to printing, to post-printing is a natural law of human cultures. And that we are getting a better and better noetic sphere to live in—that we are getting better at shaping and remembering and communicating knowledge. It is something that large parts of the human population are not quite sure about yet. It has to do with the pollution of the noosphere, if you want a nice political name for it.[1]

Well, we could make a list of the differences between your sentences.

---

[1] The term "noosphere" is from Pierre Teilhard de Chardin. Walter Ong talks of the "noetic sphere" with, I think, the same sense. Inscribed over the door to the hall where this lecture was held, there were these apt words of Teilhard's: "The age of nations is past. It remains for us now if we don't wish to perish, to set aside the ancient prejudices and build the earth." That a major part of these ancient prejudices are right down there in our language is also something common to the thinkers invoked at the beginning of the lecture. In Wittgenstein's (1958:114) clear phrasing: "One thinks that one is tracing the outline of the thing's nature over and over again, and one is merely tracing round the frame through which we look at it."

We could see that interaction between you [points to one] and me was different from that between you [points to another] and me. You used my name, you said "he," and you used "the man." These are a set of variants and they specify a dimension of variation, the interpersonal dimension.

Some of your sentences sounded like the beginning of poems, or novels, or short aphorisms, or metacomments, or newspaper stories, or police reports. We had many different language games going on here. Each of you reached back in memory to prior texts and made this one, the one you wrote, a variant of those prior texts. We recognized them as we went along, as they evoked memories of sentences we had heard before. Each of those sentences has a past, a history. I do not believe that they were generated by rules but rather they were drawn from lingual memory and reshaped to present circumstances. We are thrown into language, says Heidegger, we don't create it. Jarwa dhosok, say the Javanese.

And of course the structure was different in your sentences, the grammar was different. The way the clauses were put together was different. Here linguists have a fine and subtle language, describing the hierarchy of part-whole relations we call structure.

In order to use language, it must have transparency, so that if I say, "Look at Haj over there," I want you to look at Haj, not my words. In order to use language, we all have to believe in a world beyond language, although the world beyond one language is not the same as the world beyond another. The things you observed in the world here, the things that were seen happening up here were different. Some of them weren't mentioned, some of them were not even seen by everyone. If I were to ask you now a question like, "What really happened?" or "Who among you was right?" or "Which one of these sentences was most correct, which of them gave the truest explanation of what happened?"—are these possible questions anymore? Can we still say that truth value is correspondence of language with an event? What event? Was there an event apart from all of these "takes"? Is there a true event that makes the other "takes" fictional? In this sense, as many have said, language does not represent the world, or reflect it. Describing it creates it. Our language pushes us into those very biased ways of saying things. Ours is a world experienced in the act of interacting with it lingually, in the act of languaging it. As Gadamer (1976) wrote, "Being that can be understood is language."[2]

All of you had not to say many things in order to be able to say

---

[2] This phrase appears often in Gadamer's writings. See the essay "Aesthetics and Hermeneutics" in *Philosophical Hermeneutics*.

some things. What was unsaid is one of the major differences between your sentences. It is a minor difference here compared to what happens with other languages. Ortega (1957) has a nice comment about that, in his essay on the difficulty of translation:

> The stupendous reality that is language cannot be understood unless we begin by observing that speech consists above all in silences. A being who could not renounce saying many things would be incapable of speaking. And each language represents a different equation between manifestations and silences. Each people leaves some things unsaid in order to be able to say others. Because everything would be unsayable. Hence the immense difficulty of translation: translation is a matter of saying in a language precisely what that language tends to pass over in silence.[3]

So there is a dimension of the said and the unsaid in your sentences. Each one of those dimensions I have sketched is a dimension of difference:

1. negotiating interpersonal relationships
2. shaping the medium
3. making a grammatical sentence
4. looking through language to a believed world
5. evoking prior language
6. leaving many things unsaid, some of them unsayable

All of those things come together to shape the events that were happening when each of you was languaging about what I did. You will notice that I shift from the word "language" to the word "languaging." That is one of the easiest ways I know to make the shift from an idea of language as something accomplished, apart from this activity we have shared, to the idea of languaging as an ongoing process. That, too, is something that those thinkers I mentioned earlier were all pressing: a movement away from language as something accomplished, as something apart from time and history, to language as something that is being done and reshaped constantly. That is why we can never run out of new sentences for that little episode that just happened here. We can never run out because old language (prior text) is always being reshaped to present needs. It's always being created.

---

[3] The quotation is from the chapter, "What People Say: Language. Toward a New Linguistics" in *Man and People*. This chapter is also the source of my use of the term "philology." What is translated into English as "a new linguistics" is in Spanish "una nueva filología."

So how do our various "fictions," as Wittgenstein called them, our various "takes" on that episode differ? In all the ways that language can mean, they differ. The check list I just gave you of six dimensions of difference is only a personal one. And the question of what "really" happened? Well, we could negotiate a joint statement. But in negotiating that statement, which we all might vote on, then, as being the most accurate negotiated description for some purpose, the negotiated statement itself would be subject to all the particular constraints that I just mentioned above and would not be a way of escaping them. So the observer is part of the observed. The observer is more than part of the observed. The observer is shaping the observed just as the observed is shaping the observer. They are interlocked.

The movement across languages, philology, is one of going to a place like Burma or Java or Bali and spending one's lifetime trying to converse with the people there in ways that make sense and ways which also allow them to preserve their worlds, allow them their descriptions of what is happening. I've done that little experiment in several of those countries when I was teaching there. It's amazing the things they say and do not say. In Java they would very often say things like, "The teacher seems very annoyed with us today." With a Japanese audience I recall almost everyone in the audience referred to the size of the steps, with medium-sized steps or small steps or long steps—they didn't agree, except that steps were important.

What we are doing here is all in English. When we get to those other languages the differences are in the same dimensions I listed above—the interpersonal relationships, the prior texts, the reference to a world believed beyond language, and all the others—making sentences, breaking silence, shaping a medium. All of these things we did together are also the dimensions that can be different from one language to another. None of them is unchanged from language to language. Every one of those dimensions changes as we go into another language and we can often not predict how they will change: in the dimension of structure, the coherence of things, the ways things are put together. In the dimension of prior texts. The hardest thing to do in Burma or Java or any place foreign is to know when something somebody has told you is original with that person or has a past in that culture which everyone there would recognize. Prior text is the real a priori of language, not some logical deep structure or anything like that. Prior text is the real source, the real a priori of speaking, in the view that I'm trying to develop here.

And that great difference between languages, between ways of languaging, that profound difference is also one of the themes that those ancestors I claimed earlier share.

But the recognition of this variety and diversity in different languages leaves us with several demons. There are fears about where this kind of thinking can lead us, and those demons are very real ones and they are very scary ones. Learning to cope with demons is a lot of what living in certain parts of Southeast Asia is about. In many places, perhaps all places, the world beyond the world that language shapes is full of demons. And so I'm going to tell a demon story mainly because I want to refer to it again in a minute, and now I've just mentioned demons, so it's relevant and timely. If I tell a story, you will recognize that I'm doing what humans do in human linguistics, as Haj calls it. One of Gregory Bateson's favorite stories was about the guy who asked the computer, in his best computerese, "Will you ever think like a human?" They put that into the computer, and it whirred and clicked for a while and out came a slip of paper that said, "That reminds me of a story."

Mentioning demons reminds me of a story, but that's not quite honest either. It says right here in my notes, "Tell the demon story." Erving Goffman (1981) was on to tricks like this, and he taught us to be sure that all of these little stories and asides we happen to remember are the most planned and rehearsed parts of any lecture.

In Bali they give shadow plays and readings of old texts and things when there are a lot of demons around, when someone dies or someone is suffering or something chaotic is happening. A puppeteer or a reading club comes to the place of difficulty and begins to perform nonstop until the corpse is cremated or some other imbalance has been brought back to balance. I watched the shadow plays and fell asleep many nights to the voices reading and translating Old Javanese texts and finally asked a Balinese friend:

"How does it work? You know how DDT kills bugs and then the malaria doesn't come. How does a story work? What goes on? How does a story get rid of a demon?"

And he said, "It's like doors."

"Like doors?"

"Yes." He acted as if I should be satisfied with that, or maybe it was just that in Bali you have to prod a story along more than we are used to prodding, so I said,

"Like doors? Okay. What do you mean like doors?"

"You know how our doors are, around our homes and our temples. You have a wall. You have a gap in the wall and behind the gap you have a slab of wall a little wider than the gap. To enter, you have to go right or left around the slab. That's the first door. Then there is another wall with a gap backed by a slab, and this second door is not right across from the first door but offset a little. Do you understand how these doors work?"

"I never thought about it," I said. "I thought they were there so you could get privacy in your house so no one could see you . . . You could sit in there relaxed."

And he didn't know what I was talking about, I suspect, for he said, "Why would anyone want to do that?"

He returned to the topic, "It's to keep out demons."

"How does it work?"

He said, "Demons can only move in straight lines. It's people move in curves, they move around like this." And he demonstrated the way a lot of Balinese move on the street, around in curves all the time, nothing in straight lines. "Demons can't get in the doors because they bounce off the slabs. Humans just move around them. If a demon by luck gets through the first door, it just bounces off the next wall. So if you build a series of concentric walls with offset doors, you're safe from demons."

That made real sense. "But what about stories?"

"Demons think in straight lines, too. Our stories, you know how they are all so tangled and thick, one story inside another . . . or our music with many things happening at once in different rhythms."

"Yes," I said, prodding.

"Humans love that. Demons can't stand it."

And thus I was taught one of the big lessons, that tangles should be welcomed as good news—they keep out demons.

There are demons in the air with this talk about observers and fictions and some of the other things we have been talking about this evening, this collection of experiences. The recognition of the immense variety of language games leaves one at the end of a Goffman essay with an almost oceanic feeling. It's the same at the end of reading Wittgenstein's later works. The variety of kinds of things that we can do with language defeats cataloguing, except at the most general levels. And at those general levels, the particularities that we're concerned with here, the things that make you different from you and you different from you, these particularities wash out. If we are interested in those differences, if we're interested in getting across those differences to talk to another person, then those things which wash out at higher levels of generality are just the things we need and just the things we can't afford to wash out. And that's why Wittgenstein talks about particularity. The things that make your sentences different, or that make English different from Balinese.

This kind of thought often is called subjectivism. There seem to be no constraints on one's fantasy in interpreting what other people say. One demon is fantasy.

Another demon of particularity is that it seems to shut out generalization. If we are not generalizing, if we are not capturing generalities, then what are we doing? It's what we get rewarded for, seizing on generalizations. If we turn toward particularity, one of the demons says, then that's all over. That's no longer something we do. Isn't that too much to give up?

Clifford Geertz (1983) has some interesting things to say about this matter of particularity and its demons as it applies to the social sciences. I think what he says applies to linguistics as well. He distinguishes two ways of approaching the work of the social sciences. One he calls "rules and instances" and the other "cases and interpretations." In the rules and instances approach, the rigor comes with the setting up of a body of rules which instances illustrate. Instances come and go. If, when you are setting up a rule, your example doesn't fit, get a better example. It would be silly to use a bad example. The rules are the main source of discipline and examples come and go. In the "cases and interpretations" approach, the examples sit there. They don't go away. You spend twenty years trying to figure out a Burmese sentence. (See, for example, Becker 1984.) You go over a text the way Manny Schegloff did so beautifully on Monday night, over and over and over one passage for six months, eight months, a year, and then you begin to see the particularity of it. Particularity is not something we begin with; particularity is something we arrive at, by repeating. Particularity is something we learn. We don't distinguish birds until we learn their names and hear their songs. Up to that point we hear "bird" around us and then we begin to pick up their particularity along with the language. Particularity is something we achieve.

Our discipline and our rigor in humanistic linguistics comes right there, from the particularity of the text-in-context, not from the rigor of the rules. By context I mean the six sources of constraints I laid out a few minutes ago. For one working on interpreting a text-in-context, you pick up all the new theories that come along in linguistics, all the thirty million theories of grammar that Jim McCawley (1982) writes so well about—they come along and you take them and apply them to your text-in-context and they each show you something you didn't notice before, often something beautiful. But then you cast them aside because there's another one coming along that is going to show you something else. The discipline of the philologist comes not from theory but from a language—the texts and conversations he or she is trying to understand.

So you can see that there is a kind of reverse behavior for these two approaches Geertz identifies. The one working with a particular text grabs the theories as they come by and celebrates them by applying them and learning their lessons. But the discipline is not in the theories. The discipline is in the particularity of the text-in-context. One is grateful to the theories. Again, I'm not trying to replace anything in linguistics, but to describe a kind of linguistics I call philology, the historic matrix from which linguistics was abstracted.

I want to say one more thing about particularity. Notice that all of the constraints that I talked about earlier—structural, interpersonal, generic, referential, medial, and silential—the sources of constraints on the unique sentences you wrote earlier about my walking up on the stage: all of those different constraints which were working on each of you in different ways can only be seen and can only come together in particularity. They don't come together at more general levels. They come together in the particularity of the sentences you wrote. Holding on to the experiences that we just shared is our discipline. That's what is going to keep us talking about the same thing, not necessarily the logic or lack of it in the superstructure.

There is one more demon. Relativism. This all sounds like relativism, and the conversation goes off into aspects of morality. Aren't we just loosening up morals? Are there no standards anymore? Is this the 1960s all over again? (No, I assure you it's the 1940s talking, the decade of Einstein and Gertrude Stein.) Relativism is one of the demons some people conjure up, but I think that they get it wrong. A relativist like me doesn't think anything goes. A relativist does think, however, that many things go, and that many different languages and their cultures around the world have learned, over thousands and thousands of years, to attune themselves to their worlds in much better ways than other people tell them they must or should. Relativism doesn't mean anything goes but it means that the world the Balinese live in and that they shape into understanding with their language is a valid, real, true, good world to be in and doesn't have to be destroyed and replaced. So relativism does not seem to be a real demon for us either, unless we insist on thinking in straight lines.

If the demons of relativity and particularity are at least at bay, there remains subjectivism. There was something we might call "the personal" in the sentences you wrote tonight, something very close to particularity: your own voices sounding out of your own memory, shaping old texts coherently to new situations. This personal part is not best described, as it often is, as characteristic choices among varying possibilities, but something much less intentional. You must examine yourselves in this. I am not planning the sentences I speak to you or choosing from a grammatical/lexical menu. I am not reading, but as we all do as teachers, just speaking from notes, old language shaped to the present situation—jarwa dhosok. I can look back at what I said and parse it or explain it in different ways, but one thing I cannot do, and I assume you can't either, is parse and speak a new sentence at the same time. I can do a lot of other things simultaneously to speaking—like wave to a passing friend or wonder if my shirt is hanging out in back—but I can't parse as I speak. This, too, is something Wittgenstein and Goffman liked to talk about, the deep difference between speaking and an analysis of speaking.

There is a huge personal dimension in languaging that makes each of your sentences different, and that's just what I want to get at. Most of the languaging we do most of the time is not conversation, but rather that inner newsreel which goes on all the time, replaying today's events and trying to make ourselves come out more heroically by adjusting all sorts of things and getting our replay fictions right, or rehearsing an upcoming task. Buddhist teachers sometimes call it gossip. That continual personal play of language within us is probably where we spend most of our time. I'd bet a goodly number of you are there right now. This is not to say that conversation is not essential in order to learn languaging. I'm aware of Wittgenstein's arguments against the possibility of a private language, but the language which we are thrown into becomes a part of our consciousness—how great a part we are only now beginning to realize. This is hard to discuss, the huge personal dimension of language, this thing we are thrown into and which we experience at such a personal level.

The problem many of us have with science is that it does not touch the personal and particular. Doing science means making sentences which meet certain criteria, one of which is that the sentences be impersonal. The criteria for scientific statements include explanatory hypotheses which will give mechanisms for generating whatever you are observing and which will then lead to deductions and predictions about other things and include actual tests that you can carry out to demonstrate what you are talking about. Can we do that? In the world that I am talking about, is it possible? If we study the particular, the differences between each one of your "takes," can we meet all of the criteria for scientific statements? I think the answer is no.

I do not think we should worry that the answer is no. There are other ways of making true and useful statements; there are other disciplines, just as rigorous, just as important, and just as necessary as scientific statements are—if our study is of particularity. By adopting scientific constraints on the statements we make, we move away from the very thing we want to study. This seems to me to be one of the major points of Wittgenstein's (1958) *Philosophical Investigations*. The nonuniversality of scientific statements, their cultural embeddedness, is clear to many anthropologists—one thinks immediately of the work of Gregory Bateson (1972) and Clifford Geertz (1983) and Stephen Tyler (1978)—and to many philosophers, from John Dewey (1934) to Richard Rorty (1986).

What then must we do? What do we do that is different than what we did before? Our goal, following Wittgenstein, is description, as careful and self-conscious as we can make it. And why describe languages—that is, languaging in different societies? I think the answer, as Geertz often puts it, is to learn to converse with those we have difficulty conversing with. Whether they are our own neighbors and family or people halfway around the world, the same kinds of differences are involved, I think, and learning about one teaches about the other. Recognizing the dramatic differences I confront in speaking to a Balinese prepares me to recognize the more subtle differences I confront in speaking to my wife or my children, and it teaches me to respect them, not out of some abstract moral principle, but as the practical first step in having my own differences respected. I know as a lifelong language teacher that this is very difficult to do, particularly with people who believe in the myths about universality of logic and emotion.

All of this is clearly reflected in the ways we write. What we do as scholars is determined mostly by the final product we anticipate, the kind of statements we will be making and the criteria with which it seems proper to evaluate them. There are many things humanist linguists do. Sometimes we describe words. (People like Raymond Williams [1977] and Gaston Bachelard [1969] and others have done brilliantly with that.) We describe language games and how they work, different plots and rhetorical figures in different languages, all with the goal of helping us to better converse with those we have difficulty conversing with.

One of the main things we do, one of the central activities of the modern philologist, is translating. We often make translating the focus of our work, the way parsing is the center for a linguist. I am often asked, by deans and such, what it is every linguist must know, humanistic linguist or scientific linguist or linguist of any kind, and I think that the answer is clearly "parsing"—detailed, rich, and subtle parsing. But for the philologist, parsing is subordinate to the greater discipline of translating. Parsing is still essential, but it is not the goal. Translating is. I mean here the process of translating as a method of analysis and exploration, going back and forth and forth and back from source text to translation and translation to source.

In that process, back and forth, what we are doing, in the words of Ortega (1959), is learning what our exuberancies and deficiencies of interpretation are. What is happening in this process of translating is that the observer is changing. We put before us a line of Javanese and then we put beside it an English translation, any English translation, from a linguist's glosses to a poet's well-wrought figure; it doesn't matter which. And then we look at all the things in the English that are not in the Javanese: the exuberancies. We find almost always that exuberancies account for more than half of the stuff in the English translation. (Given our experiment tonight, I'm sure you can believe that.) Then we look at the Javanese and we see all the things in the Javanese that didn't get across into the English because there is nothing in English that can be a counterpart of those things. These are the deficiencies, and they almost always account for more than half of the stuff in the Javanese text we are translating from. The exuberancies are those things in your translation which are there only because your language demands them, and the deficiencies are the things in the original language which don't get across.

In too many articles by linguists, what is being parsed is the exuberant and deficient translation, often in the form of a set of glosses which evoke English prior texts. And that is why parsing, I think, must be subordinate to translating.

I think the point about exuberancies and deficiencies is clear without an example. I invite you to try it on your own turf. At all linguistic levels there are these exuberancies and deficiencies, from the tiniest grammatical "facts" to the largest rhetorical ones.

The products of this exploration are not scientific articles, not statements that meet the criteria of science I mentioned earlier, but essays. Essays are disciplined by particularity. They are exercises in correcting the exuberancies and deficiencies of an observer—with the goal of helping us to converse with those people we have difficulty conversing with. Attuning ourselves to another language, another person's languaging and keeping his or her philology, his or her world, intact (or nearly so) in doing it. It's a necessary kind of work, I think. It's an important kind of work, if Dewey was right—and I think he was—that democracy begins in conversation.

It is also very tough, because particular texts are unmerciful disciplinarians. Like doors. And like clocks. So, I'll stop.

REFERENCES

Bachelard, Gaston. 1969. The poetics of space. Boston: Beacon Press. (See especially the introduction, in which he discusses the differences between the philosophy of science and that of the humanities.)

Bateson, Gregory. 1972. Steps to an ecology of mind. New York: Ballantine. (See especially the essay: Style, grace, and information in primitive art.)

Becker, A.L. 1984. Biography of a sentence: A Burmese proverb. Text, play, and story: The construction and reconstruction of self and society, ed. by Edward Bruner, 135–55. Washington: American Ethnological Society.

Dewey, John. 1934. Art as experience. New York: Putnam.

Emerson, Ralph Waldo. 1836. Nature. Boston: Munroe. (See especially Chapter IV: Language.)

Gadamer, Hans-Georg. 1976. Philosophical hermeneutics. Berkeley: University of California Press. (See especially Chapter 4: Man and language.)

Geertz, Clifford. 1983. Local knowledge. New York: Basic Books. (See especially Chapter 1: Blurred Genres; and Chapter 7: The way we think now: Toward an ethnography of modern thought.)

Goffman, Erving. 1981. Forms of talk. Philadelphia: University of Pennsylvania Press.

Grassi, Ernesto. 1980. Rhetoric as philosophy: The humanist tradition. University Park: The Pennsylvania State University Press.

Heidegger, Martin. 1971. On the way to language. New York: Harper & Row.

Labov, William. 1982. Speech actions and reactions in personal narrative. Analyzing discourse: Text and talk. Georgetown University Round Table on Languages and Linguistics 1981, ed. by Deborah Tannen, 219–47. Washington, D.C.: Georgetown University Press.

Lamont, Corliss (ed.). 1959. Dialogue on John Dewey. New York: Horizon.

McCawley, James. 1982. Thirty million theories of grammar. Chicago: University Press.

Ortega y Gasset, José. 1957. Man and people. New York: Norton. (See especially Chapter 11: What people say: Language. Toward a new linguistics.)

Ortega y Gasset, José. 1959. The difficulty of reading. Diogenes 28.1–17.

Pike, Kenneth L. 1978. Here we stand—Creative observers of language. Approches du langage: Actes du colloque interdisciplinaire tenu a Paris. Sorbonne, Serie 'Etudes' 16.

Ricoeur, Paul. 1981. Hermeneutics and the human sciences. Cambridge: Cambridge University Press.

Rorty, Richard. 1986. Method and morality. Values and the social sciences, ed. by Robert Bellah & Paul Rabinow. (See also, more recently, "The Contingency of Language" in London Review of Books, 17 April 1986.)

Ross, Haj. 1982. Human linguistics. Contemporary perceptions of language: Interdisciplinary dimensions. Georgetown University Round Table on Languages and Linguistics 1982, ed. by Heidi Byrnes, 1–30. Washington, D.C.: Georgetown University Press.

Ross Haj. 1986. Languages as poems. Languages and linguistics: The interdependence of theory, data, and application. Georgetown University Round Table on Languages and Linguistics 1985, ed. by Deborah Tannen & James E. Alatis, 180–204. Washington, D.C.: Georgetown University Press.

Stein, Gertrude. 1966. The making of Americans. New York: Something Else Press.

Stein, Gertrude. 1974. How writing is written. Los Angeles: Black Sparrow Press.

Tyler, Stephen. 1978. The said and the unsaid: Mind, meaning, and culture. New York: Academic Press.

Williams, Raymond. 1977. Marxism and literature. Oxford: University Press.

Wittgenstein, Ludwig. 1958. Philosophical investigations. New York: Macmillan. (See especially paragraphs 109, 114, and 115.)

CHAPTER TWO

Inarticulateness*

R. P. McDermott

Teachers College, Columbia University

> Scientifically speaking, the basis of life—the energy of life, as Aristotle would call it—is simply the desire for expression.
>
> Oscar Wilde ([1889] 1956)

> One has only learnt to get the better of words for the thing one no longer has to say.
>
> T.S. Eliot (1943)

There are times in everyday life that are well organized for us to have a say. On such occasions, the words seem to come easily. A simple greeting exchange is a clear enough example. One "Hello!" demands another; it is hard not to follow up. Other times are well organized to not encourage our talk; getting a word in edgewise during a church service or court appearance can be most difficult, even if we know exactly what we would want to say if asked. This paper is about a third occasion—one in which, although one is invited to say something, the words are not available. On such an occasion we can be struck

---

* The most immediate inspiration for this essay comes from John Montague's "A Flowering Absence," happily reprinted here as an Appendix. My understanding of the Irish materials relies heavily on the work of Declan Kiberd. I talked the paper through in lectures at the University of Pennsylvania, the University of Virginia, the Graduate Center of the City University of New York, and the Socialist Scholars Conference in New York City. At Georgetown, participants at the LSA/TESOL/NEH Institutes were subjected to a week of various versions of the paper. There, Deborah Tannen organized about the most invigorating environment imaginable—a linguist's Camelot. My deepest appreciation to Deborah and the many gentle, careful, and amazingly intelligent friends she gathered for a few wonderful weeks of breakthroughs to articulateness. Keith Basso, Dell Hymes, and Deborah Tannen offered helpful comments on an earlier draft.

dumb. The cat can run off with our tongue. We can experience inarticulateness.

Situations that can organize inarticulateness are legion, and it is easy to name the most obvious occasions. Funerals, police inquiries, job interviews, exams, class and race border encounters, tax interrogations, sex talk with children, group therapy, television interviews, and first dates—all are potential tongue stoppers. A folk account would have it that whenever our words can be immediately consequential and long remembered, the pressure can get to us, and new heights of eloquence or new lows of inarticulateness are frequent. The folk account, I want to suggest, hides a much deeper malaise.

There are two reasons for writing this paper and for becoming more articulate about our inarticulateness. One is to defend the inarticulate by putting up for notice that occasions in which people are left without words are systematic outcomes of a set of relations among a group of persons bound in a social structure. The claim is that inarticulateness is not well understood as an individual disability, but better understood as a well orchestrated moment in which inarticulateness is invited, encouraged, duly noted and remembered, no matter how much lamented. As we have seen in the careful and gentle papers of A.L. Becker (1982, 1984), any text can be understood from the point of view of both its deficiencies and its exuberances. In defending the inarticulate, we can focus on the exuberances and find great powers of expression in the most diminished text. Every utterance has its biography and cuts its own figure, and, if we are careful enough to describe its points of contact with ongoing events, we can learn a great deal about the powers of the talk that constructs, maintains, and resists the order of those events.

The second reason for the paper is to display how much inarticulateness is a problem in all our lives, far beyond what even the most articulate of us allow ourselves to consider. Near the end of a lifetime of describing the communicative worlds of birds, octopi, Iatmul transvestites, Balinese trance dancers, porpoises, and schizophrenics, Gregory Bateson was asked what one question he might ask any organism if he could for a moment share its code. He answered that he would ask that organism under what conditions it would be possible for it to tell the truth.[1] This is not so much a case of Bateson being interested in the "truth," as much as Bateson being interested in the limits of what we can articulate about our situation. What would we have to know about our surroundings, and our ongoing, reflexive contribution to our surroundings in order to answer Bateson's question? We would have

---

[1] The story is told in Birdwhistell (1977). Equivalent formulations can be found throughout Bateson's (1972) essays.

to specify unfortunately what we cannot, and every attempt to articulate our conditions necessarily falls short. The only hope is that some of our efforts come closer than others, in the sense that they fit our experience and do not guide us to what William James called "false connexions."[2] What is on the surface articulate may hide more limits on the truth than any of us anticipate. In addition to celebrating the powers of the inarticulate, we may have to mistrust the confidence of those who seem to know what they are saying. Bateson (1977:146) warns us directly: "God, language is a lousy invention, isn't it".[3]

If the inarticulate may have the most to say and the articulate only

---

[2] The significant lines are: "Woe to him whose beliefs play fast and loose with the order which realities follow in his experience; they will lead him nowhere or else make false connexions" (James 1907:205). For essays on the importance of this advice for philosophy and for practical affairs, see John J. McDermott (1976, 1986).

[3] If our everyday life language is systematically inadequate to the description of the order in our experience, imagine the insanity of relying on it for the categories we need to work in the human sciences. We were warned long ago. In his work on botany, Goethe railed against received categories for classification:

I must confess that after Shakespeare and Spinoza, Linnaeus had the greatest influence on me—and just through the reaction he provoked in me. That I may be clear about those circumstances, think of me as a born poet, seeking to mold his words and his expressions immediately on the objects before him at any time, in order to do them some measure of justice. Such a poet was now to learn by heart a ready-made terminology, to have a certain number of words and epithets ready, so that when he encountered any form, making an apt selection he should know how to apply and order them into an appropriate description. Such a treatment always seemed to me like a mosaic, in which you put one finished piece next to another, in order finally to produce out of a thousand individual pieces the semblance of a picture: and so in this sense I always found the demand to some extent repugnant (quoted in Cassirer, 1945).

Marx was no less elegant in his brevity: "Science would be superfluous if the outward appearance and the essence of things directly coincided." This sentiment is crucial throughout Marx. This particular version, from the third volume of *Capital,* comes to us from quotation and translation by Eric Wolf (1982:44).

In a line displaying both Goethe and Marx, Bakhtin claims that the comprehensiveness of our words is resisted not only by the complexity of the phenomena they purport to describe, but by the role of our words in the organization of our lives:

Indeed, any concrete discourse (utterance) finds the object at which it was directed already as it were overlain with qualifications, open to dispute, charged with value, already enveloped in an obscuring mist—or, on the contrary, by the "light" of alien words that have already been spoken about it. It is entangled, shot through with shared thoughts, points of view, alien value judgements and accents. The word, directed toward its object, enters a dialogically agitated and tension-filled environment of alien words, value judgements and accents, weaves in and out of complex relationships, merges with some, recoils from others, intersects with yet a third group: and all this may crucially shape discourse, may leave a trace in all its semantic layers, may complicate its expression and influence its entire stylistic profile (1934/35:276).

In such a world, what could articulateness be?

the most predigested and most mystified reality to put before us, what then might a paper on inarticulateness be about? Just what is the phenomenon being put before the readers for consideration and analysis? I suggest a three-tier answer. For a starting place, there is a surface level phenomenon: We can all recognize a speech performance that flops as different from one that wins admiration. This is an important experience, and we do not want to give it away too easily. At the same time, we do not want to mistake a surface level account of our experience for a richer account that might reveal to us a configuration of conditions that organize our behavior and limit our access to what might be in the way of telling the truth. To this end, we can first consider a surface version of what articulateness is. For an intermediate step, we can erase that record with contrasting cases, suggesting that a surface level inarticulateness might just carry the day on occasion and that apparent articulateness can hide more than it reveals. At the third level, the phenomenon is recovered in a new set of theoretical clothes. By this third answer, the surface level of inarticulateness represents not a disability, but an invitation to listen in a new way. If you cannot understand your spouse or your neighbors, consider yourself duped and work hard to alter the conditions that keep you unable to discover what you need to be talking about, with whom, and to what end.

If this procedure of finding a phenomenon and recasting it in new terms helps to make things a little clearer, we can call it science; if it helps to make our lives better by having us appreciate people where previously we could only find disability, we can call it a blessing and a call to organize a better world.

For a surface version of inarticulateness, we can turn to Fillmore's (1979:93) account of its opposite: fluency. A fluent speaker can be appreciated for:

1. "the ability to talk at length with few pauses, the ability to fill time with talk."
2. "the ability to talk in coherent, reasoned, and 'semantically dense' sentences."
3. "the ability to have appropriate things to say in a wide range of contexts."
4. "the ability some people have to be creative and imaginative in their language use, to express their ideas in novel ways, to make up jokes, to attend to the sound independently of the sense, to vary styles, to create and build on metaphors, and so on".

There is a commonsense framework in which all this makes great sense, and there is a sociocultural framework in which it makes very bad sense. Certainly, the term "ability" is loaded; it stops inquiry where it should begin. The issue is not so much who can do what, but what is there that can be done and under what conditions. From the commonsense point of view, the list offers an accurate account of what we mean by fluency and articulateness in our culture. From the sociocultural point of view, it is exactly this easy acceptability of the list that is our topic. From the commonsense point of view, we can separate the articulate from the inarticulate and wonder why respectively they are the way they are. From the sociocultural point of view, we can only wonder how full members of the culture can come together and arrange for each other to look differentially able. It is not speaker abilities that we need to understand. For a sociocultural account, we must describe (a) the situations that bring speakers and hearers together, (b) the particular relational jobs available for them to work on together, and (c) the language resources, exuberant and deficient, the people have available for talking about what they are doing together.

The commonsense framework allows us to set up our problem as a contrast between the inarticulate and the articulate performances. If we put aside questions of individual abilities and instead address sociocultural questions to the performances, we can develop new sensitivities to the efficacy of different kinds of talk. In the long run, we shall see that it is neither the length of the utterance nor its finesse that organizes the relevance of an utterance. The force of an utterance is rarely dependent simply on matters of form; it is not the utterance alone that makes a difference, as much as the conditions for its being delivered, heard, acted on, remembered, and quoted. The same utterance in different settings can do a quite different job. A single utterance can be simultaneously an example of inarticulateness and articulateness, depending upon how it is made sequentially relevant over time.[4]

---

[4] The term "sequential relevance" has been given a substantial empirical base by the work of Sacks, Schegloff and their now many followers (Atkinson & Heritage, 1984; Goodwin, 1982; Schegloff, 1979, 1980). It is their stand that utterances can only be analyzed with a detailed attention to their most local circumstances on a case-by-case basis. This is a radical starting place for any description, for it reduces most of our received units of analysis—word meanings and the "things" named by the words—to arbitrary conventions, into categories that should be the topics of analysis rather than tools for carrying out an analysis. This paper takes a less radical cut to the extent that I address a social issue, inarticulateness, as it is framed by commonsense categories. For the conversational analyst, inarticulateness is a folk category for speech performances that likely bears little resemblance to any of the behavioral facts of conversation. I proceed less deliberately, similarly claim that inarticulateness is not the problem it appears to be, but hold out for the possibility that the term glosses an important phenomenon at some level at which we do not yet know how to look. I can be less deliberate only to the extent that I control my conclusions in a way consistent with my methods; I assume that it is a foolish error to proceed without using conversational analysis (for

Nota bene. Introductions should formulate what is to come next and what is not. This paper is not about the explanation of individual inarticulateness. It does not offer a social as different from an individual explanation of inarticulateness. The social-individual contrast set is never applicable in analytic talk, for it mediates between two ends of a continuum that analytically does not exist: no individual, no social; no social, no individual. The argument of this paper is not that society determines inarticulateness in individuals, for such an argument would harbor four analytic errors in one line: society, individual, causal connections, and inarticulateness. It would be too exhausting to argue against all these distinctions in one paper, and only inarticulateness is reframed as part of the relations among people rather than as a thing to be explained. The notion of inarticulateness is socially organized. However it is used by members to label individuals, it takes a culture to make it a designation available for use. Given its origin in the collective lives of many speakers across generations, we can suspect that the notion of inarticulateness is likely not well designed for describing specific speech performances or individual persons; as a cultural resource available to all speakers, it would seem to be better designed to guide members to look for, recognize, record, remediate, avoid, condemn, and explain individual speech performances as instances of inarticulateness. Any use of the notion of inarticulateness is likely organized according to constraints in place long before any specific speaker has a say.

FROM MUTTERANCE TO BREAKTHROUGH

This paper is organized around the illustration of two ends of a continuum of mastery and disappointment onto which all our talk falls. At the level of mutterances, a speaker can be reduced to grunts, groans, quips, expletives and a wide range of nonsense in the service of apparently unformulated ends. Fluency is missing. At the level of breakthrough, words flow, new things are said, and the world is tem-

---

its use of a principled starting place and its detailed analyses of conversations) as a corrective to any conclusion we might reach about human talk. There is no reason to assume that our own metalinguistic awareness will give us a trustworthy foundation for inquiry (Silverstein, 1981).

Details on the sequential relevance of any behavior should be crucial to any analysis invoking a notion of context. Unfortunately, context is called on often and described rarely. Of the many ways to refer to context in Japanese, one term, zengo (前後), makes the importance of sequential relevance directly available; it is made up of the words for before (前) and after (後). In theoretical verve, this greatly outstrips the spatial imagery demanded of our own inside/outside sense of con-text.

porarily altered. Between the two ends of the continuum, there is the level of mundane talk, at which a person can fill up time with words, but only in service of a status quo. In most situations, people can talk with each other a great deal, but the conditions that bring them together for the most part erase their words in the long run and render them effectively dumb, as if they had not spoken at all. This situation is farily endemic to life in any society; it is the human situation under stable conditions. The two ends of our continuum simply extend this middle to more volatile conditions.

Examples of the two end points of the continuum are taken from quite different kinds of work. Among the mutterers, it is easy to count the kinds of people who most often run into situations without words for ready use: the autistic, the schizophrenic, the shy, the stupid, those without grace, and those with a foot in their mouth. In this paper, I rely on the mutterances of children in trouble in school to present the case. They offer us the opportunity of saying what they cannot say, namely, how they managed to get into such trouble. Once the particulars of their troubles are established, their mutterances can make great sense. At first we can feel sorry for them, for only we seem to have the capacity to state their case. The empathy can give way to guilt when we realize that the conditions that foster their inarticulateness are the same ones that have rendered us articulate. Upon further listening, they appear to have known this all along; only we did not know how to listen.

Among those who breakthrough into performance, to use Dell Hymes's helpful phrase,[5] I turn to persons whose names and words we are all

---

[5] Hymes (1975) uses the "breakthrough into performance" phrasing to capture the transition point between knowing about a tradition and reporting on it, on the one hand, and knowing how a tradition works and doing it, on the other. It is a slippery notion that takes on some stability in Hymes's comparison of various ways of telling stories. One could write a paper, as Hymes has done, distinguishing the reported tellings from the live performances, or one could write a paper, as Hymes would have to appreciate, collapsing the tellings and performances as different versions of a single kind of speech effort within the polyphony allowed by a community. I use the breakthrough to articulation notion both ways: I distinguish persons who have access to diminished as different from enhanced language resources for having a say; no sooner than I force the distinction, I erase it and then try to recover it in new terms.

A more profound similarity between this paper and Hymes's "breakthrough" effort is that they share a view of language, well stated by Hymes (1973:73): "Every language is an instrument shaped by its history and patterns of use, such that for a given speaker and setting it can do some things well, some clumsily, and others not intelligibly at all. The cost, as between expressing things easily and concisely, and expressing them with difficulty and at great length, is a real cost, commonly operative, and a constraint on the theoretical potentiality of language in daily life." This is a reason to investigate, see expected to know, namely, the writers of the Irish literary renaissance of the first decades of this century. Finding the inarticulate in their work moves us obviously from their texts, which seem to say well mostly everything that has to be said, to the institutionalized use of their texts—riot, exile, and condemnation—as a unit of analysis. This is the same move to be made in the interpretation of the mutterances of failing school children. In the language of this paper, it makes no more sense to celebrate Yeats's lone genius than to isolate the mutterances of failing children as the products of simple minds. In anthropological theorizing, apparent geniuses have always been trimmed to an account of how much their cultures have equipped them with both the problems they solved and the tools with which they constructed their solutions; similarly, the supposedly stupid have been generally enlarged by an account of their accomplishments under degrading circumstances (Kroeber, 1944; White, 1949). In seeing how even the most magnificent, ingenious words can be subverted, we come full circle to asking questions about our own situation and our relation to saying what we might have to say to make the world, for one precious moment, the world we would like to have created.

As we will end with Yeats, so might we begin. In his poem, "Among School Children" (1983 [1928]:217), he asks:

O chestnut tree, great rooted blossomer,
Are you the leaf, the blossom, or the bole?
O body swayed to music, O brightening glance,
How can we know the dancer from the dance?

In the same vein, we should ask how anyone could possibly tell the inarticulate from the situations in which their inarticulateness is organized, or the articulate from the situations in which they are allowed to have their words emerge and listened to and even remembered. We need to move beyond the simple prejudice that some dancers, and some talkers, are simply better than others, without looking to see what kind of dance, and what kind of conversation, they are asked to put into action. Inarticulateness is a dance in which we all engage, either by suffering it ourselves or by arranging for others to carry the burden. If Wilde is right in claiming that the stuff of life "is simply the desire for expression," then our death is in the concerted suppression of the resources we need to talk to each other.

Before we take up the two ends of the fluency continuum, there are orienting stories to be told about how inarticulateness has been con-

---

through, and reorganize constraints, not a reason to condemn those who are having trouble talking in ways we know how to hear.

ceived in the literature. They can offer some theoretical preliminaries and bring Yeats's question into full relief.

INARTICULATENESS AS PERSONAL TRAIT, POLITICAL RESIDUE, AND CREATIVE RESISTANCE TO THE COLLECTIVE SETTING

> All actors have some degree of discursive penetration of the social systems to whose constitution they contribute.
>
> Anthony Giddens (1979)

In 1927, Leonard Bloomfield performed a great service in writing his small paper on "Literate and Illiterate Uses of Speech." It was popular then, perhaps more than now, to understand a person's articulatory powers as a function of their reading habits. The more read, the more to be said, and in just the right way, ad captandum vulgus, perhaps even in Latin, diem ex die. Bloomfield's service was to point out that among the Menomeni Indians with whom he was working, there was a considerable range of individual differences in speaking skill that was in no way tied to erudition. Our way of handing out high scores for talk was simply our way and accordingly arbitrary. He concluded with a conceptual disservice. The real source of the differences was personality; some can, some can't, it depends on the person.[6]

Forty years later, Dell Hymes (1967) highlighted Bloomfield's accomplishment by taking up the case of White-Thunder, a man Bloomfield described as massively inarticulate, unable to perform in either Menomeni or in English. Hymes moved us from personality to politics as the key category for understanding inarticulateness. How sad, he wrote, that White-Thunder could have been caught between languages; he gave up Menomeni, the language of the home, for English, the language of the marketplace and the forces of the occupying white man. Outside the participation net of both languages, he fell, in effect, into a silence. He may have talked a great deal, but without access to the words he needed to say what had to be said, to say what others might have had to hear.

---

[6] The crucial passage reads as follows:

The nearest approach to an explanation of 'good' and 'bad' language seems to be this, then, that by a culmination of obvious superiorities, both of character and standing, as well as of language, some persons are felt to be better models of conduct and speech than others. Therefore, even in matters where the preference is not obvious, the forms which these same persons use are felt to have the better flavor. This may be a generally human state of affairs, true in every group and applicable in all languages, and the factor of Standard and Literary Language versus dialect may be a superadded secondary one (Bloomfield, 1927:396).

When I first read Hymes's account in 1975, I was moved to defend White-Thunder's powers of communication. I wrote to Hymes and complained that he left out a consideration of how much power the man might gain from his silence. Given the situation of the Menomeni, those "dreamers without power" (Spindler & Spindler 1973), what better way to handle those above him? Inarticulateness seemed a quite potent weapon, and we should not forget for a second that White-Thunder was likely an adaptive, sense-making, and demanding person as much as the rest of us. We did not yet have in hand Basso's (1979) account of the Apache understanding of silence as a counter to the White Man, nor was Bauman's (1983) volume on the potency of silence among the Quakers available. But we did have Labov's (1972) de-mythologization of the "nonverbal" Black child and the appreciations by Basso (1971), Dumont (1972) and Philips (1972) of the "silent" Native American. And I had my father, who controlled his large and complex flock with a quiet insistence that we figure out what he would say would be the right thing to do if in fact he would ever say it. There was power in silence, sometimes as much as there can be in Latin, dum tacent clamant, and it was unfair to White-Thunder to forget it. If we cannot tell the dancer from the dance, it is certainly unfair to complain about the dancer if there is no music.

Hymes wrote back an important letter. Certainly it would be wrong to forget the powers inarticulateness might bring to White-Thunder in his most local circumstances. But Hymes was making a different point. How sad it is that the only articulatory powers available to White-Thunder were in his display of apparent disability. How sad that he never wrote a poem, or an account of his troubles. How sad that he never was able to transform his situation. How sad that only we could tell the story of how powerful he might be, we who were so much a product of the forces that contributed to his own distress.

This account of White-Thunder has moved us quite far in an understanding of inarticulateness. His inarticulateness was not simply an absence of skill due to his lack of education or his own personal makeup. Nor was it simply an absence organized and maintained by a difficult political situation. It was rather a creative and powerful step along a road built by us all. There was something wrong with the road. White-Thunder was the most obvious deposit point or symptom of the wider system as that system was played out in the daily lives of the Menomeni, but his inarticulateness belongs to us all. How can we know the dancer or the dance from us?

If White-Thunder had written an account of his life, he might have started with the question of how inarticulateness is possible. How can people learn how not to talk? All members of the species can acquire a language, even many of them. But is their language always ready to acquire them? This turn of phrase, given us by Sankoff and Laberge (1973), is crucial. We need a Saussurian challenge to our psycholinguistic bias. Languages seem to come to us "stacked," not in the sense that differential amounts of them enter our heads for possible use, but in the sense that they are brought to life in conversations to which we as speakers have differential access. Competence is a bad lead term for our approach to the language people use in their lives together. Language, Saussure's (1915) *la langue,* is only incidentally in the head. It is much more crucially, much more sensually, much more materially, in the conversations we make available to each other for participation. Language is an institution, and language performances, be they fluent or inarticulate, upper class or lower, male or female, smart or dumb, can well be studied as situated, concerted activities carefully constructed from and reflective of the tensions and constraints that organize all the institutions of the society. As Hymes (1973:60) has said well, "in actuality, language is in large part what users have made of it."[7]

White-Thunder had a limited conversation available to his life. Does this really make him very different from the rest of us? His situation seems quintessentially human. Only the particulars differentiate him from us. The particulars are all important, of course, and most of us would prefer the limits of our own situation to the limits of White-Thunder's situation. To the extent that our conditions are preferable (because we sometimes organize to confront or at least to write papers about our predicament), there is no reason to add to White-Thunder's troubles by not noticing the power in his performance. Nor is it fair to point to his apparent disability when it is the product of the conditions that render English and our use of it powerful. If White-Thunder were to write his poem, it would likely condemn us. In working for conditions that organize our own articulateness, we cannot afford to make others systematically inarticulate.

The next two sections lay out the continuum from utterance to breakthrough. In a concluding section, we return to an understanding of how articulateness and inarticulateness are different versions of the same effort. It is a distinction we must move beyond.

---

[7] In a letter critiquing the exuberances of this paper, Dell Hymes has urged that in defending the inarticulate, we cannot assume that even in the best of all possible worlds everyone would have equal access to the powers of talk. Of course he is right. There is never reason to not appreciate the varying insights and sensitivities different individuals bring to a conversation. Indeed, one reason to focus, as I have done, on social constraints on what can be said and by whom is to allow us to focus on the powers of the individual given the situation in which he or she must operate.

MUTTERANCES

Well, uh, I would like to start this section, ok, with the claim that, you know, much of our talk can't be found in a heh dictionary. It's like, we make a lot of noise while talking, that, you know, to be honest with you, doesn't seem to carry much, how should I say, referential meaning. One rich supporting example comes from Gail Jefferson's (1978) account of *nyem,* a neat combination of mostly No and a little Yes, with the sequential relevance of making the hearer responsible for deciding what is being said. Thanks to conversational analysis we are gaining a sense of how incredibly precise talk can be. Every sound seems to do an important job in constructing the relations between conversational partners. One of the jobs to which all the precision can be directed is obfuscation. Human conversations appear well designed for making delicacy, avoidance, mitigation, and duplicity generally possible. Jefferson's account of *nyem* details one device by which a person who is asked a question can arrange to not give the answer while simultaneously not demonstrating "a recognizable refusal to give it" (p. 139). Techniques for the avoidance of "troubles talk" seem almost endless (Jefferson, 1984, 1985). Mutterances are not only ubiquitous, they seem to be extremely well organized. They seem often to be required.

As much as mutterances are sometimes required, they are also a bar to fluency; too many of them, or their appearance at the wrong time, can invite the characterization of a speaker as inarticulate or dumb. For many years I have been examining videotapes of children and adults in school settings, primarily in classrooms; in an afternoon cooking club; and in some kitchens for homework scenes. What has fascinated me has been the occurrence of apparently disruptive, disorganized, or otherwise nonsensical moves on the parts of the children often precisely at the moments when it is their turn to perform some task: moves such as a whine, a curse, a scream, a burp, a gaze away, a silence, something in the eye, a wisecrack, a complaint; tasks such as answering, getting a turn, taking a turn, reading, or simply showing attention. In trying to understand the organizational import of each of the moves, my job was to locate what came before and after in order to situate them as moves of a particular kind (McDermott, Gospodinoff and Aron 1978; Dore and McDermott 1982). What first appeared to be a simple scratch often turned out to be a way of changing the focus of the group; what first appeared to be a disruption often turned out to be a call to order; and what first appeared to be a call for a turn came up as an effort to not have a turn. Timing was of the essence. Members could not easily explain what was going on, and it took me years to locate the range of institutional relevancies served by the fast-paced moves I was examining.

Through all that work, I found myself increasingly able to speak for the children who were having the hardest time in school. Their well-timed moves, when situated in the conversational fabric, showed them to be saying all that could be said given the constraints of the relations between the participants. In the well-placed tear or the apparently misplaced call for a turn we could find children showing a profound understanding of their circumstances, and even a resistance to the established order that had them in exactly these conversations built around the differential display of school learning and school failure. A formulation of the American classroom as the place in which we ask our children not just to learn to read and write, but to display at appointed times reading and writing better than each other, was available in the most inarticulate mutterances of all the children.

Detailed descriptive work was necessary in order to gather categories appropriate to the study of the lives of children at school. When I went to describe the behavior of the apparently stupid, disorderly, or inarticulate children, I found myself to be similarly caught short. The culture had not equipped us with an adequate language for the interpretation of our own children. Labels were readily available, of course, but they did not seem to mean much. Before I could study our not-so-fluent children, I had to confront our all-too-fluent, well-institutionalized, but diagnostically baseless labels that were used to describe our children without much careful attention to the complexities of their behavior. The categories derived from careful description stand in considerable opposition to the commonsense categories that guide our more institutionalized interpretations of our children. Whereas our commonsensically-derived categories are well-tuned with educational psychology and the competitive sorting machinery of the schools, the new categories are finely tuned to behavioral realities and better aligned with political critiques of schooling in America (Goldman & McDermott 1987, Wexler 1982). With the detailed context analyses in hand, it is possible to defend the failing children, deemed unable, slow, inarticulate, disturbed, and even minimally brain damaged by official school lore, as instead bright, articulate, and appropriately resistant to the community-wide tensions over access to resources that get played out in their conversations at school.

A full illustration of the articulatory power of a not-so-fluent utterance requires a most detailed analysis. Fortunately, many are now on record.[8]

---

[8] Schegloff's accounts of "uh" (1979) and "uh huh" (1982) are seminal. Accounts from school settings are in Dore and McDermott (1982), McDermott and Tylbor (1986) and

Although the more detailed analyses stand behind what follows, for our purposes I am simply going to tell a story from my first days as a teacher of children in New York City.

It was my first day in front of a classroom. It was a bottom class, everyone's idea of what a sixth grade classroom should not be. We made it to two o'clock on the strength of my frenzied rush through anything that would be interesting to burned-out twelve-year-olds. I had prepared for weeks, but was already running out of materials. I was exhausted. Horace seized the moment. From his seat in the back right part of the room he marched to the front left—across the tops of the desks. "Horace, sit down," said I. "Fuck you," said he. And so started a difficult year.

Across the months at PS 118, I gradually learned how to handle such moments. A full range of teacher cant, can't, and insult got us all through the days with more pain and less dignity than we deserved, but we emerged full-blooded members of the culture with a normal range of success and failure for that kind of class—most of them failed miserably and I went on to teach in another school.

Horace's words had a context. He did not do it alone. Horace had me to say it to, and a classroom of variously appreciative children to look on. Nor was his classroom an unimportant place. Aside from the thousands of dollars the city was paying out annually for every child in the room, there was also the picket line of teachers around the building. It was 1968, and the community control of schools by minority people was becoming an institutional possibility. The teachers' union went on strike to check the rise of parental power, and, with generations of Irish union blood coursing through my veins, I walked through a picket line in the name of civil rights. All I wanted to do was to teach some kids how to read, and the whole world showed up to comment and complain. In Joyce's words, "Here comes everybody." In Horace's words, "Fuck you."

I have often had to worry about Horace's words. While I arranged during the course of the year to hear less of his "request for action" and to defuse any situation where it might show up, the experiences behind his words seemed not to go away. They were also terribly

---

the bibliographies cited in those papers. Although they deal less obviously with mutterances, linguistic anthropologists often offer accounts of verbal ingenuity from people rendered voiceless in the earth's market of words. Examples are too numerous to list, although mention must be made of Conklin (1959) and Rosaldo's (1984) accounts of word play routines from the mountains of the Philippines, of Becker's (1979, 1984) appreciation of the poetics of texts from Southeast Asia, and of W.P. Murphy's (1981, 1986) description of political intrigue in West African talk. Ross's (1982) call for a human linguistics puts the appreciation of speaker ingenuity at the forefront of linguistic studies.

difficult to describe. Surely a literal interpretation would not get me far. What would I have to do to explain all that he might have been saying and all that I sometimes thought I heard? Horace did not talk at length, nor in coherent, dense terms; he was thoroughly inappropriate and not very creative. Despite his lack of fluency, he might have been saying a great deal about the conditions that were organizing our collective access to the telling of the truth. Three years either side of Horace's "Fuck you," the same words were used to instigate the Berkeley Free Speech movement and to cap off the final line in one of anthropology's finest theoretical treatises (Murphy 1971). Horace might have been driving a far sturdier vehicle of articulation than was immediately obvious.

Keys to understanding Horace's talk came slowly. One key developed a few months later when an assistant principal at the school came to my room to show me how to give an approved Board of Education lesson. I happened to be working on longitude and latitude with the class, and he stayed with the topic when he took over the chalk. As even assistant principals can make mistakes, after a few minutes, he asked Horace, "What's latitude?" Horace answered, "Latitude an attitude." The answer made no sense to the man, and he said so. There was some artfulness to the rhyme scheme, of course, but it could be dismissed as a weak joke. The rest of Horace's fluency was well below the surface, where the school official did not have to look. An attitude had a special place in the black community at the time, and, indeed, years later, has become a catch phrase for difficult children in informal teacher talk (Gilmore 1985). One did not just have an attitude, or even take one on. Rather, one could "cop" an attitude and be assured a response. To cop an attitude was to take a strong stand in opposition to whatever was going on, which of course Horace was doing at just that moment. The move was lost on the assistant principal, but a quick look at the faces around the room showed that Horace was once again not alone. For only a second, Horace had said what the rest of us would not. The school strike was now over, but the inequality and racism that occasioned its rhetoric were still in the classroom. Few people were showing up to hear Horace's every word, and the television news no longer carried daily accounts of life in the classrooms. I am probably the only person to remember Horace's effort to cop an attitude. As social structure marched on, Horace and his words were erased. As articulate as his words were upon analysis, Horace was rendered inarticulate.

One untried way to appreciate Horace's talk is with the question of its erasure. The assistant principal brushed the words aside to get on with the lesson, and the rest of the world has moved on without knowing all that they could mean. Horace's words were made inconsequential, as indeed was Horace throughout his life in school. His records listed him as a terrible behavior problem and a bad student. There seemed to be so much institutional firepower available for documenting Horace's problems, and so little for hearing his words. In Bakhtin's ([1934–1935] 1981, [1940] 1984) terms, the tension between the verbal-ideological core and the small revolutions that inhabit our every utterance had been adjudicated against Horace in favor of the more institutionalized meanings. Horace's words had been absorbed by the core, the chafe removed, and turned to grist for the record keeping of the school system; by way of his records, his march to a safe periphery had been waylaid, and efforts to reach a new ground, to say what he had to say, would become less and less sensible to any who happened to hear. To whom did the inarticulateness belong? Horace or the institution? The dancer or the dance?

Given the power potential in Horace's words, we should ask about the institutional arrangements that are so easily available for erasing his words. Questions about Horace's talk are first and foremost questions about his institutional possibilities. In the bottom sixth grade of a terrible school and in his third foster family, Horace's possibilities were restricted in the extreme. There were few hospitable institutions poised for acquiring him. Nor was he to be acquired by mainstream American English. Without it, he would often be inarticulate. After an examination of the contacts made with the world by his talk, we can know better, as the beaming children in the class may have known better. Horace was copping an attitude against the conditions that were inhibiting his expression. But such insight is a small force against the institutional arrangements poised to erase him. Horace may have said much more than could be heard institutionally. He may have said much more than we can ourselves say. We may not find out until it is too late for Horace and too late for us. God, fluency is a lousy invention, isn't it?

BREAKTHROUGH TO ARTICULATENESS

Your training has been Catholic, Irish and insurrectionary; mine, as it was, was scientific, constructive and, I suppose, English. The frame of my mind is a world wherein a big unifying and concentrating process is possible (increase of power and range by economy and concentration of effort), a progress not inevitable but interesting and possible. That game attracted and holds me. For it, I want language and statement clear as possible . . . It seems a fine thing for you to defy and break up. To me not in the least.

(H.G. Wells, in a letter to James Joyce,
23 November 1928. In Ellmann 1982:608).

It is possible to say that writers of the Irish Literary Renaissance were among the most articulate persons of our century. William Butler Yeats (1865–1939) leads the way. His poems have reached every part of the globe (as his face, carried on some Irish currency, reaches daily into millions of pockets). Irish drama still plays at his Abbey Theatre, and Yeats's claim that the Irish literary revival was part of the "great stir of thought which prepared for the Anglo-Irish war" seems reasonable when placed alongside his own service in the first Senate of the Irish Free State. Perhaps most crucially, Yeats's version of Ireland and its tradition is still accepted as a reality rather than the farfetched invention it most certainly was. His cold eye and silver tongue continue to move us all.

Yeats was much less alone than White-Thunder or Horace. His efforts to say what had to be said were supported by a strong cast of collaborators: most immediately, Lady Gregory (1852–1932), George Russel (or AE) (1867–1935), John Millington Synge (1871–1909), and George Moore (1852–1933). Within two decades of their rise to prominence, they were joined by James Joyce (1882–1941) and Sean O'Casey (1880–1964) in what has been recognized as an all important revolution in articulateness. On what grounds can they share the focus in this paper with the likes of White-Thunder or Horace? Such a comparison leaves our mutterers looking quite short, but only if we limit ourselves to a content record of their words. One of the attractions of the Irish writers is that they seem to say so well precisely what the others would say if they had a little more support. They put into words, onto transcripts and drama sets, what White-Thunder and Horace could not. Neither White-Thunder nor Horace had ever quite reached the difficult times of Synge's Playboy or O'Casey's Paycock; nor can we imagine them suffering the internal intellectual torments of Joyce's Stephen Daedalus or Leopold Bloom. But the heroes in the fiction were allowed to speak, sometimes against great odds; through the pens of their authors, their voices echoed across the land, and each said what other Irish in their situation, or White-Thunder or Horace in their situation, or likely we in our situation, could not say. They spoke, and in some ways, they were heard.

Although we can celebrate the Irish writers for what they could say, we must not rest on their laurels. We can balance our appreciation by attending to what they did not accomplish with their words. The intention of this move is not to demean them, but to put up for notice that they were special precisely in ways that made a difference for that time and place complete with limits on what could be accomplished. In our lives in contemporary America, we are faced with the same situation. We do not know how to describe the limits of what we can accomplish with our words. In Bateson's terms, we do not know how to specify the conditions under which we would be able to tell the truth.[9]

In approaching the Irish writers, we have the same questions that emerged from trying to understand the articulatory powers of White-Thunder and Horace. First, what was their situation and what language resources did they have available for explicating and transforming their situation? Second, what effects did their talk have on the conditions that so limited them?

Their Situation

The English language with which the Irish writers worked did not come to any of them as a neutral medium for expressing their thoughts. The history of English in Ireland is the history of oppression, exploitation, starvation, and bloodshed (Bliss, 1979). No word was free of this history. No word was neutral. Every word and every act stood poised in allegiance between Empire and Ireland, between city and country, between tradition and modernity, between Catholicism and the Church of Ireland. Every Irish author mentioned cursed the words available for making great art or taking a strong stand. Although they all wrote in English, each played with different dialects, registers, and languages as they honed their own skills. Every word, says Bakhtin ([1934/35] 1981:294), is "populated—overpopulated—with the intentions of others. Expropriating it, forcing it to submit to one's own intentions and accents, is a difficult and complicated process." What was easy to notice in Bakhtin's postrevolutionary Russia was apparently easy to experience in prerevolutionary Ireland.

For the writers in search of a language, the alternative to English was the Irish language. By 1850, Irish was marching out of the country with famine and migration (O Cuiv 1950). Ireland opened the nineteenth

---

[9] There is no intention here to imply that the Irish writers are in any way unique in their search for a language of expression. On the contrary, we all have this struggle all the time. This is why Horace, for certain analytic and political purposes, can be said to stand even with Yeats. The Irish writers, however, are a particularly rich case through which to examine the problem, because (a) the conditions working against their artic- ulateness were so very harsh and, in retrospect anyway, easy to discern, and (b) they were so very successful at challenging those conditions in the sense that they said so much so well and in the sense that they supplied an "imagination" to a revolution (Thompson, 1967).

Other cases could prove equally useful. Virginia Woolf has noted that when women turned to writing novels, worse than "discouragement and criticism," they faced an absence of language: "when they came to set their thoughts on paper . . . they had no tradition." This line, from *A Room of One's Own,* is discussed in relation to Chinese developments in Feuerwerker (1975).

century with eight million people and the twentieth century with half that number. Most of the casualties were Irish speakers. Because the tongue generally follows the demands of the market place, English was taking over even where Irish speakers were still vibrant. In many homes, Irish-speaking parents without any English in their heads forced their children to speak only English. It is as if White-Thunder were making language policy for the peasants of Ireland. From his perspective of a few generations later, in his poem on "The Severed Head," John Montague (1979:39) paints a vivid portrait of the language situation in Ireland over the last century.

(Dumb,
bloodied, the severed
head now chokes to
speak another tongue:—

As in
a long suppressed dream,
some stuttering garb-
led ordeal of my own)

An Irish
child weeps at school
repeating its English.
After each mistake

The master
gouges another mark
on the tally stick
hung about its neck

Like a bell
on a cow, a hobble
on a straying goat.
To slur and stumble

In shame
the altered syllables
of your own name;

and find
the turf cured width
of your parent's hearth
growing slowly alien:

In cabin
and field, they still
speak the old tongue
You may greet no one.

To grow
a second tongue, as
harsh a humiliation
as twice to be torn.

Decades later
that child's grandchild's
speech stumbles over lost
syllables of an old order.

By the turn of the century, Irish writers were already lamenting the role of English in their life. Trying to put the severed head back on its body became a driving preoccupation. A major development was the Gaelic League, an urban, middle-class organization for reinstituting the treasures of Irish language and culture. In his founding statement, Douglas Hyde (1892:313), 46 years later the first President of the Republic of Ireland, sounded the revival theme that shows up in most of the language complaints of many authors of that time:

What the sword of the Dane, the sword of the Norman, the wile of the Saxon were unable to perform, we have accomplished ourselves. We have at last broken the continuity of Irish life, and just at the moment when the Celtic race is presumably about to largely recover possession of its own country, it finds itself deprived and stripped of its Celtic characteristics, cut off from the past, yet scarcely in touch with the present.

It was to the sound of such a call that George Moore, already a successful and mature writer in England, returned to his native Dublin and announced that he was there "to give Ireland back to her language." Without a word of Irish to his name, he insisted on laundering his prose of English impurities: he would write first in English, have it translated into Irish, and then back again into English. Critics wondered if Ireland would ever give its language back to him (Kiberd 1982).

At the same time, Synge, Lady Gregory, and Yeats were experimenting with various country dialects of Hiberno English in their plays. Synge went the furthest (Kiberd 1979). He walked the roads with the tinkers and the dispossessed and lived with the fishing folk of Aran. Across the six plays he gave the world before his early death, he made increasing use of Irish words and syntax (Bliss 1972a,b). In his preface to *The Playboy of the Western World,* Synge (1982 IV:53) stated his aim forcefully:

In writing *The Playboy of the Western World,* as in my other plays, I have used one or two words only, that I have not heard among the country people of Ireland, or spoken in my own nursery before I could read the newspapers.

George Russel (AE) took a different path away from the English language and back into the wonders of the past. Dreams and spirits were the stuff of his insights, and painting and poetry the media for expressing the transcendent. English, he complained, could not lead Irish writers to what they had to say; the spirit of the past was not available in the harsh tongue of modern commerce.

The handicaps facing the Irish writers of the time are nowhere better stated than by Stephen Daedalus in his conversation with an English priest in Joyce's *A Portrait of the Artist as a Young Man* (1916:189):

The language in which we are speaking is his before it is mine. How different are the words *home, Christ, ale, master,* on his lips and mine! I cannot speak or write these words without unrest of spirit. His language, so familiar and so foreign, will always be for me an acquired speech. I have not made or accepted its words. My voice holds them at bay. My soul frets in the shadow of his language.

English, of course, was the native language of both Stephen Daedalus and James Joyce. Why would perfectly sensible English words give him "unrest of spirit"? Critic Hugh Kenner (1983:71) offers the following guess at the specifics:

> *Home.* An Englishman's was his castle, an Irishman's a shelter from which he might momentarily be evicted.
> *Christ.* When he cuts his thumb on a bottle, an Irishman does not cry 'Chroist!' but 'Jaysus!'
> *Ale.* Metonymy for wholesome English custom, scattered throughout the language as in *bridal* (bride-ale); but in Ireland they prefer a porter allegedly discovered in the eighteenth century by a man named Guinness who had burned the hops by mistake.
> *Master.* In England your teacher, your Saviour, or one before whom you are pleased to place your forelock; in Ireland the owner of a pack of hounds or the racker of a pack of tenants.

No wonder the Irish writers of the time had to seek an alternative language. English could not bend to their demands. In using the language of the Empire they could erase their efforts to say what had to be said by their very efforts to say it. Some of the Irish chose Horace's road and their invectives were incorporated into the political upheavals of the day. Some we will never know about went the way of White-Thunder. The great bulk of the people, fluent to the core, talked without saying anything that made a difference, nothing to which many people had to attend. Still others pushed for a breakthrough.

The most ambiguous breakthrough in articulation came from Yeats. Although he publicly regretted that he could not speak Irish, his own articulation crisis seems to have been better served by English than were the crises of Synge and AE or later Joyce and O'Casey. Early in his career, Yeats (1901:15–16) was responsible for surprisingly trenchant statements:

> All Irish writers have to choose whether they will write as the upper classes have done, not to express but to exploit this country; or join the intellectual movement which has raised the cry that was heard in Russia in the ˙seventies, the cry 'to the people.'
>   Moses was little good to his people until he had killed an Egyptian; and for the most part a writer or public man of the upper classes is useless to this country till he has done something that separates him from his class. We wish to grow peaceful crops, but we must dig our furrows with the sword.

Some would say that Yeats spent the rest of his life being an Egyptian.

He bought the King's English, as different from the peasant English of Synge, the laundered English of Moore, the tenement English of O'Casey, or the polyphonous cacophony of Joyce. In Ireland at that time, English could only speak to the intentions of the institutional fabric of which it was a part, and even Yeats could be absorbed. In his defense, we must remember that Yeats pressed the English language with an eloquence that no king nor any mortal soul had ever brought to the task. According to Kenner (1983:83), Yeats often took possession of English and expropriated it to his own accents. Small, solid, and dependable Anglo-Saxon words—cast, cold and eye, for example—take on a new life in his writing; "these are no longer 'English' words but *his* words, almost accidentally coincident with English ones . . . To reverse the connotations of a homefelt word like cold, to turn coldness into a bracing quality, neither the death of affect nor the absence of living warmth would seem to be an impossible defiance . . . Yeats accomplishes it." English was what Yeats had to work with, and he pressed it to the bone. It was the only dance available to him, and he danced beautifully.

The Consequences

There were many ways to have a say in turn-of-the-century Ireland. What shows up in the literate tradition was no doubt supported by an even greater diversity of choices available to the millions seeking to articulate their situation in the Hiberno-English of story, song, and chat. Whatever the choices, they were definitely not free. Constraints were everywhere stored in the answers to the questions everyone had to address about who had to be talked to, about what, in what way, and to what end. The same constraints had their effects on literary production. No matter how strong their claim to art for art's sake, the writers of the revival ran into all the social and political pressures of their day. These pressures were the contexts for their breakthroughs. They also set the limits, not just on what could be said, but on how whatever was said could be heard.

The Irish writers' breakthroughs into articulateness were not especially well received by the literate of Dublin. Moore and AE were eccentric enough to be ignored; Lady Gregory received the same fate, mostly for being a lady. Synge, Joyce, and O'Casey had a harder time of it. Synge stands out most surely. The opening of his *Playboy of the Western World* in 1907 was greeted with two weeks of rioting in the name of the women and peasants whom he was accused of defiling and misrepresenting (Kilroy 1971). He did not present everyone's favorite account of the ideal peasants, but something closer to the real peasants, albeit in a farce, surrounded by the real pressures of life in the Irish countryside. Everyone in the middle class seemed to have some complaint about the production; neither women, nor peasants, those he had supposedly harmed, had much to say. His next play, *The Tinker's Wedding,* was considered volatile enough to not make it to the Abbey Theatre for decades.

O'Casey's *The Plough and the Stars,* almost twenty years later, was greeted with an equivalent uproar that revealed many of the same tensions (Lowery 1984). O'Casey presumed to speak for the experience of the tenement people as they lived and died their way through the Easter Uprising of 1916. The rest of the Dublin theater population disagreed with his stand, and they yelled back in the name of the women and patriots of Ireland. Again those spoken for were largely silent and certainly unheeded if they did find a voice.

In the case of both Synge and O'Casey, we are presented with an active suppression of their literary voice. Joyce escaped the nation before reaching the spotlight. He gave up Ireland, and he gave up English for daily discourse. In *Finnegans Wake* (1939:171; cited in Kiberd 1979:13), he explained that "He even ran away from hunself and became a farsoonerite, saying he would far sooner muddle through a hash of lentils in Europe than meddle with Irrland's split little pea." Ireland returned Joyce's sentiment, and while he was condemned and celebrated around the rest of the world, Joyce's name carried little recognition in his home town. Even Clongowes Wood College, the boarding school he made so famous in the opening chapter of the *A Portrait of the Artist as a Young Man,* managed to leave him out of its magazine until decades after his death (Bradley 1982). In the late 1920s, Joyce was joined in exile by O'Casey. The line from Stephen Daedalus (Joyce 1916:203) that Ireland is "the old sow that eats her farrow" seems apt from the perspective of its authors.

Again Yeats is the ambiguous figure. He was better received than his contemporaries, and he continues to this day, almost half a century after his death, to mold the image of Ireland, his "terrible beauty," as it is spoken about around the world. This is not all for the good. Critics have it that it is not until Ireland recovers from Yeats's recovery of Ireland's past, that the culture can again deal with its present and future situation. "Wherever you look," Kiberd (1984:12) complains, "you can see that Yeats is still calling all the shots." That is much more than White-Thunder or Horace ever managed to do. In Yeats, fluency and articulateness seem to merge. But is it articulateness? Did Yeats dent the conditions that made the Irish situation so difficult? Without answering this question, we can appreciate its importance for understanding the nature of articulateness. In one passage anyway,

Yeats (1909:311) himself owned up to how hard it is to articulate what is not already predigested:

> Last night there was a debate in the Arts Club on a political question. I was for a moment tempted to use arguments merely to answer something said, but did not do so, and noticed that every argument I had been tempted to use was used by somebody or other. Logic is a machine, one can leave it to itself; unhelped it will force those present to exhaust the subject, the fool is as likely as the sage to speak the appropriate answer to any statement, and if the answer is forgotten somebody will go home miserable. You throw your money on the table and receive so much change.
>
> Style, personality—deliberately adopted and therefore a mask—is the only escape from the hot-faced bargainers and the money-changers.

By "logic," Yeats could well mean language, or culture and social structure. It talks without us, simply using our mouths to fill the air with words, to keep the chatter up and everything in its place. Style was Yeats's attempt to establish his own voice against the machine, and it rivaled in its day the efforts of James Connolly and Patrick Pearse to lead the downtrodden to a socialist rebellion. But Yeats could no more escape the long-term power of the English language than the others could escape the political and economic powers of the European world system to place Ireland last in distribution of goods. To the extent that Yeats has been enfranchised, that is the extent to which we must worry about his articulateness.

There is a fit between what can be said and what can be purchased (Brown, 1983/84; Rossi-Landi, 1980; Shell 1982; Taussig 1977). You throw your words on the table, and you receive so much change. Like languages, money systems acquire us, and expropriating their currencies for our own use is a difficult task. Coming up with words free of their invidious connections with already existing arrangements—free of the hot-faced bargainers and money-changers—takes more than ingenuity. The fool is as likely as the sage to say what counts. This is no reason to stop trying to change the world, or to stop trying to articulate our situation. It is reason, however, to blur the line between sage and fool, between Horace and Yeats. It is reason to understand that the articulate may not have said it all. Synge and O'Casey sought out those who had been left out of the articulation game of twentieth-century Ireland and found gold in their talk. The fools seemed to say it all too well. The rest of Ireland condemned their efforts. Yeats brought much less of the periphery to his work, and his vision was adopted by the verbal-ideological core as the front cover for the next few generations of Irish imagery. His cold eye and silver tongue continue to move us all, but to where? Do his words bring strength to the weak, or softness to those in pain?[10] Style, articulateness, may not be enough.

BEYOND ARTICULATENESS

This paper has run a treacherous course in holding the mutterances of White-Thunder and Horace up for comparison with those of the Irish masters of the early twentieth century. I have done this while fully aware that when I next crave the pleasure of great reading, I will go to the collected works of one of the Irish writers. If the voices of White-Thunder or Horace are collected anywhere, they are likely in the dusty folders of the Bureau of Indian Affairs or metropolitan social work agencies. They may contain interesting data about some problems, but they will not make good reading.

I have forced this comparison to make a case for a defense of the inarticulate and to raise the question of our own embedded disabilities. On the defensive note, we can start with a sadness that neither White-Thunder nor Horace has a collected corpus. We can appreciate their dilemma further with the realization that their silence has not been totally neutral; some of their words have been whitewashed and written down in official folders somewhere. Their words have been important enough to have been likely altered for official readers; their words were made bureaucratically safe. If we arrange to listen to them stripped of this interference, we could well find them with much to say. Fluency and inarticulateness are not good analytic terms for distinguishing kinds of persons. They are better terms for distinguishing kinds of situations. As we move slowly away from a linguistics of speakers towards a linguistics of participation and from a psychology of intelligence and skill to a psychology of concerted arrangements for information dispersal, it will be good to have one less static trait designation for calling each other names (McDermott & Tylbor 1986). Articulateness and inarticulateness are not the properties of persons or of their utterances; they are the properties of situations that arrange for the differential availability of words and ways of appreciating words across persons in a community.

---

[10] This phrasing comes from Sean O'Casey's *Autobiographies*. As a child, O'Casey had a serious and painful eye ailment that led to near blindness for the rest of his life. "His mother, recommended to it by a neighbor, applied a poultice of sodden tea-leaves, a remedy that had once cured the neighbor's child of a horrid redness of the lids; but no strength crept into the weakness, nor did any softness creep into the pain" (1939:13). This is a crucial theme in O'Casey. His writings were designed to give strength and softness.

As difficult as it is to appreciate the powers of the inarticulate, it is even more troublesome to understand the embedded impotence of those who can fill up conversations and pages with coherent, appropriate, and even creative lines. The masters of the Irish literary renaissance have given us lines that may last forever. They have helped to write this paper, and they keep a small army of researchers busy asking good questions about the nature of the word and the world. We should all aspire to accomplish as much. But there is only so much to be done with articulateness, theirs or ours, for it develops always in the wake of conditions that required it in the first place. The Irish masters had their situation; it gave them problems to work on, a language with which to address their problems, and severe limits on what could be done. They altered the language surely, but the problems and limits seem to remain. In this play between breakthrough and constraint, we have to decide how much to rely on our received competencies and how hard to press for new ways of talking.

The Irish writers of the time were primarily the descendants of what once was, in Synge's words (1982 II:231), "a high-spirited and highly cultivated aristocracy." They were Protestant, land owning, well educated, and in many ways English. Joyce was the exception, the product of an emerging Catholic bourgeoisie. The Anglo-Irish ascendancy was a class on the wane. Articulateness was their most stable treasure. Poised between the English of the Empire and the Hiberno-English of their homeland, they tiptoed their way to poetry. They were perfect for making exactly the breakthrough that they did. They could listen to the voices of peripheral Ireland, not in search of a politics, but in the name of their art. Their lives were not threatened by their choices. Even the selfless Synge, furious with any injustice and mistrustful of any form of hierarchy, lived off a small family fund, sent to him by his brother—the landlord. For their efforts they were yelled at, but not shot. They brought to Dublin what the literate and articulate did not want to hear, but not what they had to murder or destroy. They spoke for the peasantry and for the women of Ireland, and they were condemned. But no one let either the peasants or the women speak out. The peasants and the women were not even afforded the privilege of being condemned; they were only romanticized. They were absorbed into a great silence, muttering perhaps, without breakthrough. The articulateness of the masters was the other side of that silence—a middle-class privilege.

What then is articulateness but the right to speak in ways that others can hear? It beats muttering, but it threatens us with the danger of total conformity, with the danger of reproduction as a way of life. With great breakthroughs, there are new things said. We must treasure them and emulate them. But if we do not use them to organize new ways of putting our lives together, our greatest breakthroughs can be easily erased.

We are all embedded in our situation. Try to say all that is on your mind and notice, as did Joyce, "Here comes everybody." Try to solve a problem and the everybody who had a hand in its construction will show up. All your words can be thwarted, run off, and displaced. Our words are resisted not just by the complexity of the world, but by the history of our words embedded in our relations with each other. Our words are tools we use to shape each other, and they cannot be relied upon at the same time to chart for us a clear path through life. We must understand our situation, no matter how pleasant, as systematically unavailable to us for an easy articulation of how the world works, or of what we should do next.

Any new articulateness must confront our history. It is never easy. It is never complete. We have no choice but to seek it. I will take an articulate life over a lifetime of mutterances, asides, and screams, but it is not enough. On the negative side, it keeps us lording (Joyce, as if making the point of this paper, spells it "louding") our skills over those without access to the right turn of phrase. On the empty side, it keeps us from locating the conditions that foster the "collective illusion" that we settle for as reality.[11] On the bright side, it is the sine qua non for social action. For a starting place, short of killing an Egyptian at random, it is our only choice. Even if dum tacent clamant (silence speaks louder than words), it too ad captandum vulgus (can mystify the masses), diem ex die (over and over). If we are to organize against the conditions that keep us working against ourselves, we had best bring our tongues with us. They will be stepped on, and they cannot do the job alone, but, O Loud, our words will be essential to the organization of any new day.

REFERENCES

Atkinson, J. Maxwell and John Heritage (eds.). 1984. Structures of social action: Studies in conversation analysis. Cambridge: Cambridge University Press.
Bakhtin, Mikhail. [1934/1935] 1981. Discourse in the novel. The dialogic imagination, ed. by Michael Holquist, 259–422. Austin: University of Texas Press.
———. [1940] 1984. Rabelais and his world. Bloomington: Indiana University Press.

---

[11] The description of culture as a "collective illusion" is from Murphy and Murphy (1974). A conversational version of the same idea can focus on interactional co-lusion (McDermott & Tylbor 1986).

Basso, Keith. 1971. "To give up on words": Silence in Western Apache culture. Southwestern Journal of Anthropology 26. 213–230.

———. 1979. Portraits of "the Whiteman." New York: Cambridge University Press.

Bateson, Gregory. 1972. Steps to an ecology of mind. New York: Ballantine.

———. 1977. The thing of it is. Earth's answer, ed. by Michael Katz, William Marsh, and Gail Thompson, 142–154. New York: Harper & Row.

Bauman, Richard. 1983. Let your words be few. New York: Cambridge University Press.

Becker, A.L. 1979. The figure a sentence makes: An interpretation of a classical Malay sentence. In Givon, 243–259.

———. 1982. Beyond translation: Esthetics and language description. In Byrnes, 124–38.

———. 1984. Biography of a sentence: A Burmese proverb. Text, play and story: The construction and reconstruction of self and society, ed. by Edward Bruner, 135–155. Washington: American Ethnological Society.

Birdwhistell, Ray. 1977. Some discussions of ethnography, theory and method. About Bateson, ed. by John Brockman, 103–141. New York: Dutton.

Bliss, Alan. 1972a. A Synge glossary. Sunshine and the moon's delight, ed. by S.B. Bushrui, 297–317. Gerrards Cross: Colin Symthe.

———. 1972b. The language of Synge. J.M. Synge: Centenary papers, ed. by Maurice Harmon, 35–62. Dublin: Dolmen.

———. 1979. Spoken English in Ireland 1600–1740. Dublin: Dolmen.

Bloomfield, Leonard. [1927] 1964. Literate and illiterate speech. Language in culture and society, ed. by Dell Hymes, 391–396. New York: Harper & Row.

Bradley, Bruce. 1982. James Joyce's schooldays. New York: St. Martin's Press.

Brown, Michael. 1983/84. Ideology and the metaphysics of content. Social Text 8.55–83.

Byrnes, Heidi (ed.). 1982. Contemporary perceptions of language: Interdisciplinary dimensions. Georgetown University Round Table on Languages and Linguistics 1982. Washington, D.C.: Georgetown University Press.

Cassirer, Ernst. 1945. Rousseau, Kant and Goethe. New York: Harper.

Cazden, Courtney, Vera John, and Dell Hymes (eds.), 1972. Functions of language in the classroom. New York: Teachers College Press.

Conklin, Harold. 1959. Linguistic play in its cultural context. Language 35.631–636.

Dore, John and R.P. McDermott. 1982. Linguistic indeterminacy and social context in utterance interpretation. Language 58.374–398.

Dumont, Robert. 1972. Learning English and how to be silent. In Cazden, 344–369.

Eliot, T.S. 1943. Four quartets. New York: Harcourt Brace Jovanovich.

Ellmann, Richard. 1982. James Joyce. Second edition. New York: Oxford University Press.

Feuerwerker, Yi-tsi. 1975. Women as writers in the 1920's and 1930's. Women in Chinese society, ed. by Marjorie Wolf and Roxanne Witke, 143–168. Stanford: Stanford University Press.

Fillmore, Charles. 1979. On fluency. Individual differences in language ability and language behavior, ed. by Charles Fillmore, Daniel Kempler, and William Wang, 85–101. New York: Academic Press.

Giddens, Anthony. 1979. Central problems in social theory. Berkeley: University of California Press.

Gilmore, Perry. 1985. "Gimme room": School resistance, attitude, and access to literacy. Journal of Education 167.111–128.

Givon, Talmy (ed.). 1979. Discourse and syntax. New York: Academic Press.

Goldman, Shelley and R.P. McDermott. 1987. The culture of competition in American schools. Education and cultural process, ed. by George Spindler, 282–299. Second edition. Prospect Heights: Waveland Press.

Goodwin, Charles. 1982. Conversational organization. New York: Academic Press.

Hyde, Douglas. 1892. The necessity for de-Anglicizing Ireland. Irish historical documents 1172–1922, ed. by Edmund Curtis and R.B. McDowell, 310–313. New York: Barnes and Noble, 1968.

Hymes, Dell. 1967. Why linguistics needs a sociologist. Social research 34.632–647.

——. 1973. Speech and language: On the origins and foundations of inequality in speaking. Daedalus 102.59–82.

——. 1975. Breakthrough into performance. Folklore performance and communication, ed. by Dan Ben-Amos and Kenneth Goldstein, 11–74. The Hague: Mouton.

James, William. 1907. Pragmatism. New York: Longman's Green and Company.

Jefferson, Gail. 1978. What's in a 'nyem'? Sociology 12.135–9.

——. 1984. On stepwise transition from talk about a trouble to inappropriately next-positioned matters. In Atkinson and Heritage, 191–222.

——. 1985. On the interactional unpackaging of a 'gloss.' Language in Society 14.435–466.

Joyce, James. 1916. A portrait of the artist as a young man. New York: Viking.

——. 1939. Finnegans wake. New York: Random House.

Kenner, Hugh. 1983. In a colder eye: The modern Irish writers. Baltimore: Penguin.

Kiberd, Declan. 1979. Synge and the Irish language. Totowa: Rowman and Littlefield.

——. 1982. George Moore's Gaelic lawn party. The way back: George Moore's The untilled field and the lake, ed. by Robert Welch, 13–27. Dublin: Wolfhound.

——. 1984. Inventing Irelands. The Crane Bag 8.11–23.

Kilroy, James. 1971. The "Playboy" riots. Dublin: Dolmen.

Kroeber, A.L. 1944. Configurations of cultural growth. Berkeley: University of California Press.

Labov, William. 1972. Language in the inner city. Philadelphia: University of Pennsylvania Press.

Lowery, Robert (ed.). 1984. A whirlwind in Dublin: "The Plough and the Star" riots. Westport: Greenwood.

McDermott, John. 1976. The culture of experience: Essays in the American philosophical grain. New York: New York University Press.

———. 1986. Streams of experience: Essays in the history and philosophy of American culture. Amherst: University of Massachusetts Press.

McDermott, R.P., K. Gospodinoff and J. Aron. 1978. Criteria for an ethnographically adequate description of activities and their contexts. Semiotica 24.245–275.

———and Henry Tylbor. 1986. On the necessity of collusion in conversation (revised). Discourse and institutional authority, ed. by Sue Fisher and Alexandra Todd, 123–139. Norwood, NJ: Ablex.

Montague, John. 1979. The rough field. Third edition. Dublin: Dolmen.

Murphy, Robert. 1971. Dialectics of social life. New York: Basic Books.

Murphy, William. 1981. The rhetorical management of dangerous knowledge in Kpelle brokerage. American Ethnologist 8.667–685.

———. 1986. The appearance of consensus in Mende political discourse. Unpublished ms.

Murphy, Yolanda and Robert Murphy. 1974. Women of the forest. New York: Columbia University Press.

O'Casey, Sean. [1939] 1963. Autobiographies. Volume 1. I Knock at the door. New York: Macmillan.

O Cuiv, Brian. [1950] 1980. Irish dialects and Irish-speaking districts. Dublin: Dublin Institute for Advanced Study.

Philips, Susan. 1972. Participant structures and communicative competence. In Cazden, John and Hymes (eds.), 370–394.

Rosaldo, Renato. 1984. Ilongot naming: The play of associations. Naming systems, ed. by Elizabeth Tooker, 11–24. Washington, DC: American Ethnological Society.

Ross, Haj. 1982. Human linguistics. In Byrnes, 1–30.

Rossi-Landi, Ferruccio. 1980. On linguistic money. Philosophy and Social Criticism 3/4. 347–372.

Sankoff, Gillian and Suzanne Laberge. 1973. On the acquisition of native speakers by a language. Kivung 6.32–47.

de Saussure, Ferdinand. 1915. A course in general linguistics. New York: Philosophical Library, 1959.

Schegloff, Emanuel. 1979. The relevance of repair to syntax-for-conversation. In Givon, 261–286.

———. 1980. Preliminaries to preliminaries: 'Can I ask you a question?' Sociological Inquiry 50.104–152.

———. 1982. Discourse as an interactional achievement: Some uses of 'uh huh' and other things that come between sentences. Analyzing discourse: Text and talk. Georgetown University Round Table on Languages and Linguistics 1981, ed. by Deborah Tannen. Washington, DC: Georgetown University Press, 71–93.

Shell, Marc. 1982. Money, language and thought. Berkeley: University of California Press.

Silverstein, Michael. 1981. The limits of awareness. Working Papers in Sociolinguistics, no. 84. Austin: Southwest Educational Development Laboratory.

Spindler, George and Louise Spindler. 1973. Dreamers without power: The Menomeni Indians. New York: Holt, Rinehart and Winston.

Synge, John Millington. 1982. Collected works. 4 volumes. Gerrards Cross: Colin Symthe.

Taussig, Michael. 1977. The genesis of capitalism amongst a South American peasantry: Devil's labor and the baptism of money. Comparative Studies in Society and History 19.130–155.

Thompson, William Irwin. [1967] 1982. The imagination of an insurrection: Dublin, Easter 1916. Stockbridge: Lindisfarne Press.

Wexler, Philip. 1982. Structure, text, and subject: A critical sociology of school knowledge. Cultural and economic reproduction in education: Essays on class, ideology, and the state, ed. by Michael Apple, 275–303. Boston: Routledge & Kegan Paul.

White, Leslie. 1949. The science of culture. New York: Grove Press.

Wilde, Oscar. 1889. The decay of lying. Poems and essays, ed. by Kingsley Amis, 241–261. London: Collins, 1956.

Wolf, Eric. 1982. The mills of inequality: A Marxist approach. Social inequality, ed. by Gerald Berreman, 41–57. New York: Academic Press.

Yeats, William Butler. [1901] 1924. Samhain: 1901. Plays and controversies, 1–16. New York: Macmillan.

———. [1909] 1965. Estrangement. The autobiography of William Butler Yeats, 311–336. New York: Collier.

———. [1928] 1983. Among school children. The Poems of W.B. Yeats, ed. by Richard Finneran, 215–217. New York: Macmillan.

APPENDIX

A FLOWERING ABSENCE
By John Montague

How can one make an absence flower,
lure a desert to sudden bloom?
Taut with terror, I rehearse a time
when I was taken from a sick room:
as before from your flayed womb.

And given away to be fostered
wherever charity could afford.
I came back, lichened with sores,
from the care of still poorer
immigrants, new washed from the hold.

I bless their unrecorded names,
whose need was greater than mine,
wet nurses from tenement darkness
giving suck for a time,
because their milk was plentiful

Or their own children gone.
They were the first to succour
that still terrible thirst of mine,
a thirst for love and knowledge,
to learn something of that time

Of confusion, poverty, absence.
Year by year, I track it down
intent for a hint of evidence,
seeking to manage the pain—
how a mother gave away her son.

I took the subway to the hospital
in darkest Brooklyn, to call
on the old nun who nursed you
through the travail of my birth
to come on another cold trail.

Sister Virgilius, how strange!
She died, just before you came.
She was delirious, rambling of all
her old patients; she could well
have remembered your mother's name.

Around the bulk of St. Catherine's
another wild, raunchier Brooklyn:
as tough a territory as I've known,
strutting young Puerto Rican hoods,
flash of blade, of bicycle chain.

Mother, my birth was the death
of your love life, the last man
to flutter near your tender womb:
a neonlit barsign winks off & on,
motherfucka, thass your name.

There is an absence, real as presence.
In the mornings I hear my daughter
chuckle, with runs of sudden joy.
Hurt, she rushes to her mother,
as I never could, a whining boy.

All roads wind backwards to it.
An unwanted child, a primal hurt.
I caught fever on the big boat
that brought us away from America
—away from my lost parents.

Surely my father loved me,
teaching me to croon, *Ragtime Cow-*
 boy
Joe, swaying in his saddle
as he sings, as he did, drunkenly
dropping in from the speakeasy.

So I found myself shipped back
to his home, in an older country,
transported to a previous century,
where his sisters restored me,
natural love flowering around me.

And the hurt ran briefly underground
to break out in a schoolroom
where I was taunted by a mistress
who hunted me publicly down
to near speechlessness.

So this is our brightest infant?
Where did he get that outlandish ac-
 cent?
What do you expect, with no parents,
sent back from some American slum:
none of you are to speak like him!

Stammer, impediment, stutter:
she had found my lode of shame,
and soon I could no longer utter
those magical words I had begun
to love, to dolphin delight in.

And not for two stumbling decades
would I manage to speak straight again.
Grounded for the second time
my tongue became a rusted hinge
until the sweet oils of poetry

eased it and light flooded in.

Reprinted with permission from John Montague, *The Dead Kingdom.* Winston-Salem,
NC: Wake Forest University Press, 1984, pp. 89–91.

CHAPTER THREE

The Autobiographical Impulse

Harold Rosen

Emeritus, University of London Institute of Education

To begin somewhat autobiographically: in April of this year I was preparing a paper for the National Association for the Teaching of English and was casting about for a short exemplar of my opening point. I think I found it. I want to return to it now because I think my nugget contained more than I realized at the time.

Some time last year I found myself immersed in three very long mimeographed volumes by Dell Hymes.[1] He had pushed them into my hands with typical generosity when he noticed that I was plowing my way through them in his outer office at the University of Pennsylvania. They constituted a vast elaboration of the now very familiar notion of communicative competence, and it could be described as an unremitting polemic against Chomsky's concept of competence. I did not find it an easy read. It was both dense and microscopic, pursuing its argument through every possible theoretical twist and turn; every concept was subjected to critical scrutiny. It was a kind of intellectual war of attrition. However, I persisted over several days for all the reasons you can guess at. For as they used to say in my family— draughts is draughts and chess is chess and there's no point in getting the two confused. I reached a point in the argument where Dell Hymes, having taken us step by step through a demonstration of the inadequacy of Chomsky's model, says with seductive simplicity, ". . . a fair request would be to do better." What happened next? Just this. I cite the text verbatim (Hymes 1973:14–15):

Let me mention here Mrs. Blanche Tohet, who in the summer of 1951

---

[1] The three volumes consisted of Hymes (1973) plus a new foreword and postscript written in 1982; all three have been published in French (Hymes 1984) but not in English.

had David and Kay French and myself wait for a story until she had finished fixing eels. A tub of them had been caught the night before near Oregon City. Each had to be slit, the white cord within removed, and the spread skin cut in each of its four corners, held apart by sticks. The lot were then strung up on a line between poles, like so many shrunken infants' overalls, to dry. Mrs. Tohet stepped back, hands on hips, looking at the line of eels, and said: "Ain't that beautiful!" (The sentence in its setting has been a touchstone for aesthetic theory for me ever since.) All then went in, and she told the story of Skunk, when his musk sac was stolen and carried down river, how he travelled down river in search of his "golden thing," asking each shrub, plant and tree in turn, and being answered civilly or curtly; how down the river he found boys playing shinny-ball with his sac, entered the game, got to the "ball", popped it back in, and headed back up river; how, returning, he rewarded and punished, appointing those that had been nice to a useful role for the people who were soon to come into the land, denying usefulness to those who had been rude. All this in detail, with voices for different actors, gestures for the actions, and always, animation. For that, as people will be glad to tell you, is what makes a good narrator: the ability to make the story come alive, to involve you as in a play. Despite the efforts of white schools and churches, there are people in whom such style lives today. Knowing them, it is impossible to think of them just as tacit grammarians; each is a voice.

For me that passage was much more than a respite or rest in the onward march of academic prose. It brought into the sharpest focus some key questions about narrative in general and autobiographical narrative in particular. What impulse drives a world-renowned scholar at the critical shift in his text, at its pivot or fulcrum, to scan his own past, to demand imperatively from it the recall of a few hours of experience, and cast them into this story about a story? How can he justify chatter about fixing eels amidst the interwoven propositions and abstractions of the rest of the text? It must be a reminder to us that his vast erudition is a superstructure erected on and motivated by meanings which had their beginnings and verifications in a past rich with encounters of this kind. I can do no more than surmise that in the process of the construction of many kinds of texts, spoken and written, the memories of the past are in constant play flashing beneath the still surface like gleaming fish in a still lake. We could enlarge Vygotsky's notion of the subtext of every utterance to include this clandestine presence of memory. This dramatic shift in rhetoric in Dell Hymes declares that the autobiographer locked away in a closet is for an instant coming out to propose another way of meaning and to recruit its persuasive power. Narrative, Chambers (1984) insists, is about desire and seduction. And autobiography permeates the seductive strategies of ordinary people. They are always at it with their damned anecdotes and what an impatient nineteenth-century judge once called their "dangerous confabulations."

Hymes begins with an intriguing phrase to handle his transition, "Let me mention here . . ." It is the storyteller's throwaway guile which advertises as a parenthesis what turns out to be a central and bold effort to enlist your assent. The whole business of fixing eels could be written off as mere embroidery or even cheap bait. I think not. To tell the tale of one's own experiences is to trust what memory offers not in the sense of indiscriminate use of what it transmits but rather in rendering oneself hospitable to surprises both in the *what* and in the *how*. If Hymes is right and each one is a voice, it is a voice coming from a situated person. This kind of autobiography is memory verbalized into art—common, popular, unprivileged—that is to say, without a sanctioned locus in time and space. It marshalls the ruses of discourse. Mrs. Tohet's story, for all I know, may already have figured in a collection of folk-tales, where it would sit bereft of voice, bereft of the story of one particular telling.

We are looking at the story of a story. This is by no means a rare feature of autobiographical speech. It not only provokes responses in the same mode, chains of narrative, but provokes other tales in the teller. If we tell of other people, we recollect too the tales they told.

Memory again. We remember what others tell us they remember. That familiar device of narrative fiction, the story-within-the-story, has like so much else been borrowed from the oral story teller. Take the opening of Eco's *Name of the Rose* (1983). We are to suppose that we are hearing a diligent contemporary scholar pursuing a manuscript across Europe which turns out to be the autobiography of a medieval monk and constitutes the main text of the novel. Thus we begin with the contemporary scholar's tale

> . . . as I was browsing among the bookshelves of a little antiquarian bookseller on Comentes . . . I came upon a little work by Milos Temsvar . . .

And the tale of the monk begins.

> I prepare to leave on parchment my testimony as to the wondrous and terrible events that I happened to observe in my youth.

From a lifetime spent in the study of American Indian languages, Hymes has plucked this single instance. It comes with these components,

1. the eel-fixing

2. Mrs. Tohet's traditional tale; more exactly a stylized summary (a sequence of "how, . . . how . . . etc."), which omits the represented speech of the actors
3. a coda which shifts back to a non-narrative model in which Hymes makes clear his motive for telling the story but with a certain mockery ("It's impossible to think of them as tacit grammarians") which never figures in his main text.

Thus the whole of this three-layered narration is intended to give power to his argument and general theme. And that is just how it is with us when spontaneous autobiography is inserted into the flow of conversation. Mrs. Tohet herself has no such readily construed designs on us. She is handing on from her culture a composition of events in such a manner that it constitutes "an experimentation with life" and moral weight is enfolded in the tale. Here you might say that we have arrived at the opposite of autobiographical narrative. But that would be too easy. Though she is retelling a traditional tale which belongs with countless others, in its composition she imposes on it, literally and metaphorically, her own intonation, which is only another way of saying that her own experience makes its unique contribution to the communal one. A reanimator must not refuse her own learned life. This is not to propose that her tale is autobiographical; but I *do* want to suggest at this point no more than that autobiography is not easily tidied away into its most recognizable forms nor are our autobiographical moments simply microversions or primitive versions of the classic volumes of Gorki, Boswell or Rousseau.[2]

Let me put alongside Hymes an analogue taken from a very animated spontaneous conversation. The occasion, to put it briefly, is a small gathering of five people in an Afro-Caribbean club, four of them black, one a white researcher, David Sutcliffe. They are discussing their feelings

---

[2] Dell Hymes's awareness of these issues is put powerfully and delicately in a joint paper (Hymes and Cazden, 1980:130):

"In sum, our cultural stereotypes predispose us to dichotomize forms and functions of language use . . . And one side of the dichotomy tends to be identified with cognitive superiority. In point of fact, however, none of the usual elements of conventional dichotomies are certain guides to level of cognitive activity. In particular, narrative may be a complementary, or alternative mode of thinking."

Just to leave us in no doubt, he concludes with what he calls *Warm Springs Interlude,* rich with his own autobiographical narrative and observations of narrative in the lives of the Indian people he knows: "It is the grounding of performance and text in a narrative view of life. That is to say, a view of life as a potential source of narrative. Incidents, even apparently slight incidents, have pervasively the potentiality of an interest that is worth retelling . . . A certain potentiality, of shared narrative form, on the one hand, of consequentiality, on the other." (p. 135)

about and attitudes towards white people. One of them, Miriam, a
night-shift worker, at one point dominates the discussion.

> Now I've got five children, all born here, between the ages of 18½ and
> 23. I've got three sons. And I would rather see them come through my
> door with a colored girl. Admittedly, a whole lot of colored girls, born
> in England, they are only colored *outside*. They are everything white like
> you people. They've got white minds. But I would still prefer that color
> coming through my door.

We move through (a) autobiographical data—which establishes her
speaking rights (compare Dell Hymes locating himself with his friends
outside Oregon City), (b) explicit statement of attitude (which Hymes
held back to the end), (c) analysis, (d) restatement of attitude ("coloured
on the outside")—in stronger form.

The discussion then becomes noisy and heated as the group members
try to decide whether they too are prejudiced. At this point Miriam
intervenes again with, "Well, there's a lot you could say about this
sort of thing" which turns out to be a signal that she is about to capture
conversational space. There follows what constitutes by far the longest
turn in the whole lengthy discussion. The discussion itself is the equivalent of Hymes's general text. It surrounds this narrative moment.

> M: Well, there's a lot you could say about this sort of thing. Because,
>   I mean, for instance, this, em, boy who seems to be very unlucky
>   with his chosen white girl, he's been going out with a girl, an
>   English girl, for three years. He's been going to the girl's parents'
>   home and they accept him.
>
>   Oh well it was alright—they were only young. But when they got
>   to eighteen . . . of course I didn't even care to know the parents,
>   did I? (ironic?). When they got to eighteen, one morning there was
>   a knock on my door; (I had) just got into bed. And, mm, by the
>   time I got downstairs, there was this woman turning back from the
>   door. So I called to her and she turned back. And she introduced
>   herself. She was of course my son's girlfriend's mother. And she
>   called to *get to know me,* because she didn't know me after going
>   out with . . . her daughter going out with my son for three years.
>   She just lived round the corner to me anyway. And what she called
>   to say to me: (mimics) "Did Andy tell you anything this morning?"
>   I said: "Anything about what?" Well I was at work the night before,
>   and when I got home Boy had gone to work. So I said no. And
>   *she* was crying tears, and she said: "Well, we had such a row at
>   home last night because my husband and I, we just can't get on
>   with each other any more. Because mm—my husband is annoyed
>   with our daughter going out with your son. Because they are getting

older and they might decide to get married. And if they have children the children are going to be half-castes." I say (hard voice) "And you wait three years to say that? You didn't see what colour my son was when he was coming to your home over *three years?!* And if they have children and they don't want half-caste children— I say, 'Listen love, your daughter is going to have them, and you don't want them—I don't want them either (laughter). I've already warned my son not to come home pregnant.' " (laughter)

I: (over the din): I think it's on both sides. Now we tell them at work: "You are prejudiced, *I* am prejudiced."

The whole of that would bear closer analysis. I must confine myself to a few points:

1. Miriam's conversational move shifts to her own life story which she trusts as a powerful form of argument.
2. It incorporates a fragment of the other woman's life story (I'll call it tip-of-the-iceberg autobiographical speech), "we had such a row at home last night."
3. To sustain the invasion of conversational space Miriam must deploy the ruses of the storyteller or forfeit it—thus her distribution of irony, especially in dialogue. But above all to maintain shape, a shape that has to be generated in the very act of utterance. The triumphal final joke seals the ending.
4. Unlike the momentary (but not insignificant) self-reference like,

> But my kids are English by birth because they were born in King Street Hospital and Paul was born in Whippendale Road—you can't get more bloody English than that.

when Miriam says, "one morning there was a knock at my door," the group will hear that as an announcement of the probability that a complete story is to follow and their listening posture will change accordingly.

To invoke autobiography is to take chances. One problem is how to avoid yet another excursion into liberal individualism. Another is how to avoid using autobiography as mere case history fodder and nothing more. There is the difficulty too that, in a sense, all utterances in day-to-day conversation, however generated, however self-protective, however deceitful, however self-censored, constitute, as Goffman showed, a presentation of the self, but they are also a contribution to that never-finished business, the *construction* of a socially-constituted self. Both of these processes invoke the earlier phases of the operation. Quite young children can be heard saying, "when I was little . . ." To participate in conversation means among other things staying alert to autobiographic clues and traces, however oblique. Even the stereotype is a clumsy, but sometimes necessary, effort to do this. Thus the autobiographical impulse is a way of listening as well as a way of telling: it is essentially dialogic.

THE AUTOBIOGRAPHICAL IMPULSE IN INSTITUTIONAL DISCOURSE

Attentive examination of everyday discourse reveals that narrative surfaces easily and inevitably and without inhibition when the conversation is among intimates and no obvious and fateful judgments turn on the encounter (a job, jail, health, divorce). Oppressive power distorts and muffles it. Certeau (1980:41–2), in a remarkable paper, suggests that memory emerging as narrative is one means available to us for asserting our authority against institutionalized power, more precisely the discourses of power.

> Memory . . . produces at the opportune moment a break which also inaugurates something new. It is the strangeness, the alien dynamic, of memory which gives it the power to transgress the law of the local space in question; from out of the unfathomable and ever-shifting secrets, there comes a sudden "strike" . . . details, intense singularities, which already function in memory as they do when circumstances give them an opportunity to intervene: the same timing in both occasions, the same artful relation between a concrete detail and a conjuncture, the latter figuring alternately as the trace of a past event, or as the production of some new harmony.

He goes on to link "intense singularities" with story-telling. Scientific discourse, he says, exerts a careful maintenance over space which "eliminates time's scandals."

> Nonetheless, they return over and over again, noiselessly and surreptitiously, and not least within the scientific activity itself: not merely in the form of the practices of everyday life which go on even without their own discourse, but also in the sly and gossipy practices of everyday story-telling . . . a practical know-how is at work in these stories, where all the features of the "art of memory" itself can be detected . . . the art of daily life can be witnessed in the tales told about it. (p. 42)

And, I would add, inevitably they are nearly always autobiographical.

To point this out does not necessarily mean that we must hasten to justify it by allocating the interest to some already established terrain and refer it, let us say, to the certain microfeatures of texts like deixis or cohesion (Halliday & Hasan 1976), or in a semiotic vein to explore the deep semantic structure of narrative (Greimas as discussed by Hawkes 1977), or in a narratological vein to look for signs of the implied or pseudonarrator. These are in themselves far from trivial enterprises. However you may know everything about the anatomy and physiology of a horse but that will tell you little or nothing about the horse as a commodity, or as a totem, or its obsolescence as a form of transport and beast of burden. My concern here lies in the periphery of the well-established discourses about narrative. The reason is simple. We need to understand, no matter how speculative and partial our efforts at this stage, the full significance of something which in our culture and in many (all?) others is a resource drawn on so heavily by everyone. Beyond that there is the need to understand why the autobiographical impulse is so constantly thwarted, put down, and often explicitly outlawed in our educational system and in "high" discourse.

Ronald Fraser's (1984) autobiography uniquely combines his own recollections with the testimony, collected in interviews, of all those he knew in his childhood; it is thus a many-voiced work. All the voices speak of the same past. At the very end in a two-sided conversation he attempts to fix the impulse behind this exacting task:

— I've always thought history served one purpose at least. By discovering the major factors of change one can learn from them. The same ought to be true of an individual's history.

— Yes . . . you want to be the subject of your history instead of the object you felt yourself to be . . .

— the subject, yes, but also the object. It's the synthesis of the two, isn't it.

— the author of your childhood then, the historian of your past. (p. 187)

To be the subject and object, both author and historian of one's own past, is asking a lot, but in this case justified by the book which precedes it. Come down the scale, or should I say across to another scale, to all those little anecdotes, recollections, episodes, and reminiscences which we all trade in, and we might say that a modest version of Fraser's aspiration asserts itself. Some can be the autobiographers of whole epochs of their lives and, using the written language, control it judiciously to keep subject and object always harmoniously in harness. But the impulse is the same whether we know it or not. Bakhtin (Volosinov 1976:87) says,

> In becoming aware of myself I attempt to look at myself through the eyes of another person . . . Here we have the objective roots of even the most personal and intimate reactions.

I know of someone who wrote about her childhood, setting out to recount the games and inventive pastimes which seemed to her both inexhaustible and full of meaning. At the end of it she said thoughtfully, "It's about a lonely childhood." Thus in the art of articulating autobiography we do not simply unmask ourselves for others, we too await to know the face under the mask.

GENRE

Once the autobiographical impulse makes enough space for itself, the tactics for which have been learned in many interactions, the archaeological practices of memory come under a minimum control of *genre*— the loose rules of which have been acquired through use, observation and the lessons of success and failure. The impulse is kept on a loose rein but a rein nonetheless. I am using the word genre in Bakhtin's sense. He proposes that speech genres are an essential part of language acquisition and have important consequences for thought.

> . . . to learn to speak means to learn to construct utterances . . . we learn to construct our speech in generic forms and when we hear the speech of others we deduce its genre from the first words; we anticipate in advance a certain volume . . . as well as a certain compositional structure; we foresee the end; that is from the very beginning we have a sense of the speech whole. (Cited in Holquist 1983:314).

As utterance moves towards monologue, it is possible to perceive these genres much more clearly (a plan of action is proposed, a lay sermon delivered, such a one is denounced, a case is argued, etc.), though of course the monologue is always dialogic even when the other is silent. The autobiographical spoken narrative is so distinctive as to be swiftly recognized and identified. Bakhtin attributes to it certain features. For him (Medvedev/Bakhtin 1978:133) all speech genres constitute a way of thinking and learning.

Every significant genre is a complex system of means and methods for the conscious control and finalization of reality.

and

A particular aspect of reality can only be understood in connection with a particular means of representing it. (p. 134)

This is to take all those discussions about the relationship between thought and language on to a different plane and suggest that we think in the genres we have been furnished with through our experience of discourse. What Bakhtin calls "the anecdote" requires the speaker to find and grasp the unity of an anecdotal event in life but it also "presupposes an orientation towards the *means* for the development of narrative."

Every genre has its methods and means of seeing and conceptualising reality which are accessible to it alone. (p. 133)

These methods and means have been analyzed with great finesse by structuralists like Genette (1980), Barthes (1982), and others but I am not aware of their having applied them to an autobiography or more particularly to autobiographical speech when the speaker already shares the past of his/her autobiography with those spoken to. These methods and means make the narrative of personal experience an essentially social activity. Such narratives are an interplay of concern for the material and a concern for the reception of it by others. But this is *not* to juxtapose the private and the public. The episodes of life past were already shaped by their social content and they are articulated in a socially constructed genre (i.e. methods and means socially created) and they are proffered as part of a social interchange.

However, these methods and means may well conceal from us, if we examine the text only, what is in the awareness of the participants and is shaping the narrative. Dunning (1985), working with oral narrative in her own classroom, elicited hospital stories from three of her students, aged fourteen. These stories do not arise from a sociolinguistic experiment. They were told in a regular story-telling session conducted with the whole class. Dunning is able to show how certain features of the story can be accounted for by the fact that all three story-tellers are negotiating their standing in the class.

David's standing at the time of his story-telling is fragile. He is back in school after a minor operation and, as Dunning says, "suffering from the familiar re-entry pangs . . . after an absence." Thus in his story there are methods and means used to enable him to build up a tough, defiant, comic, slightly risqué character for himself and to suppress the anxiety he almost certainly felt at the time. This is an extract from David's story with the response of the listeners.

> D: I didn't go to sleep [the] last night. I was mucking around late. Nurse came in and 'it us 'cause we were mucking around in there.
>
> Pupil: Might've known.
>
> D: Night of the operation, we was reading comics. Beano. . . .We 'ad the lights on and we 'eard the nurse say, 'Get that light out' and we didn't take no notice, just kept on reading. Then she came in next minute and hit us, just about, so I turned it out.
>
> Teacher: Hit us "just about". Did she hit you or just threaten to hit you?
>
> D: She said, 'Get into bed like this' (illustrates with a cuffing gesture) and I were just sitting there looking at 'er.
>
> P: Yeah David.
>
> P: Hard David.

David is receiving, and continues to receive beyond this point, the message from the class that his renegotiation of his standing is going quite well. This kind of narrative event is an interanimation of production and reception. The narrators, no longer invisible authors, have known or partly known motivations and aspirations. Here there is shared history. The personal narratives enter into a disclosure already begun which will continue beyond the ends of stories. In this respect written autobiographical discourse is quite different. It must enter the silent unknown.

Some while ago I began a written autobiographical narrative which would contrast sharply with an improvised narrative of the same events.

- Of course she thought of it. It wouldn't have crossed my mind.
- It would be nice, she said, a nice thing to do.
- Course, said my sister, you shouldn't get too big for your boots.
- You don't remember, said my mother, why should you remember? *I* remember.
- What'll I say to him? Remember me? The corner near the window, your favorite pupil. Turns out I am a genius. My mother thinks you ought to know. How's the little school going? Punishment Book filling up nicely?
- Such a clever-dick don't need a rehearsal, said my sister.
- Have a bit of heart, said my mother. You knock your kishkas out

for twenty years teaching a bunch of snotty nosed momzeirim and in the finish what you got to show for it? Felling-hands, pressers, cutters, machinists, button-hole makers, market boys. Why shouldn't he know, now and then, that one of them won his matric?

- Passed, I said, not won, passed, together with thirty other future Nobel prize winners.
- Two a penny, said my sister. Pish, pish. It's a nothing.
- He'll go, he'll go, said my mother. A thank-you costs nothing.
- Did I say I wouldn't?
- My mother brushed the crumbs off the table into the palm of her hand and stood looking at them. She was so full of pride. She didn't know where to put it all.

Imagine a live telling of that story to the younger members of my family and you will know at once that the means and methods would have to be radically different. Nor, I hasten to add, would it be allowed to become a monologue. (I must leave it to you to work how it might go in different settings and why).

It must be clear that I am in certain respects privileging the auto-biographical genre. If I do so, it is because some genres offer greater possibilities than others for certain purposes, are more dialogic, deploy a wider range of resources, are more open to individual working. The genre of parade ground language offers no play at all (though Yossarian had a try). In spontaneous conversation among intimates, self-imposed controls are at their lightest. In that setting the autobiographical impulse is likely to be strong and following it leaves the greatest room for maneuver; authorship asserts itself in everyone. Holquist (1983:314) puts it well.

> . . . so that we may be understood, so that the work of the social world may continue, we must all, perforce, become authors. To use the shift of signs to represent the world is to use language for social relations . . . Insofar as we wrest particular meanings out of general systems, we are all creators; a speaker is to his utterance what an author is to his text.

In the *now* of our speaking our efforts to find meaning in the world have as their richest resources the *then* of our past, perceived as events saturated with values and feelings. We do not, as we often say, relive the experience; we rework it to fashion it into a sense which we need to discover for its validity now and to share with others. We do not put on a rerun of the past; there is no switch we can throw and let the cameras run. To tell of the past is to negotiate it, sometimes with love, sometimes with hate, but always with respect. The existence of a genre, learned in thousands of tellings, offers us a framework which promises order and control. I have only to begin, as I did very recently, like this:

> My mother, who was always in a state of near paupery, always gave money to beggars in the street.

and I know that that sentence emerges from a long apprenticeship in the genre and that it is no sooner uttered than a set of choices beckons me which are all narrative choices, some of which will be so imperative that they might betray me into a loss of meaning or, as Derrida (1978:4–6) puts it, to stifle the force under the form.

AUTHENTICITY

Labov (1972:396) noted that oral accounts of personal experience command a unique attention from listeners.

> Many of the narratives cited here rise to a very high level of competence; . . . they will command the total attention of an audience in a remarkable way, certainly a deep and attentive silence that is never found in academic and political discussion.

But in spite of his interesting analysis he does not attempt to account for that "deep and attentive silence." I have been suggesting that the particular kind of attention we give arises because

1. the power of narrative in general corresponds to a way of thinking and imagining
2. it speaks with the voice of "commonsense"
3. it invites us to consider not only the results of understanding but to live through the processes of reaching it
4. it never tears asunder ideas and feelings; it *moves* us by permitting us to enter the living space of another: it is perceived as testimony
5. it specifically provides for the complicit engagement of the listener.

To try to put all this in one word I suggest *authenticity*. Let's explore this a little further.

Barthes (1982:251) said that narrative is present at all times and in all places and that all human groups have their stories. So do individuals. But narrative is certainly not present in all places. In fact, there are places which are tacitly declared to be "no-go" areas where, as Foucault

(1970, 1977) suggests, both space and the discourse which belong with it are closely policed. Autobiographical stories often lie completely concealed beneath the genres which come to be defined precisely by their omission of personal stories. We are actually taught in the education system how to cover our narrative tracks and even to be ashamed of them.

Gilbert and Mulkay (1984), two sociologists, in a wicked book, tell us how they discovered that a very sharp controversy was going on in an area of biochemistry called oxidative phosphorylation. They go on to conduct research which would reveal how the dispute was played out, how scientists speak about such things. They interviewed those involved in Britain and the United States and examined the published papers. You can guess what emerged. In the interviews stories came tumbling out, like this one.

> He came running into the seminar, pulled me out with one of his other post-docs and took us to the back of the room and explained this idea that he had . . . He was very excited. He was really high. He said, "What if I told you that it didn't take any energy to make ATP *at* a catalytic site, it took energy to kick it *off* the catalytic site?" It took him about 30 seconds. But I was particularly predisposed to this idea. Everything I had been thinking, 12, 14, 16, different pieces of literature that could not be explained and then all of a sudden the simple explanation became clear . . . And so we sat down and designed some experiments to prove, to test this.

> It took him about 30 seconds to sell it to me. It was really like a bolt. I felt, "Oh my God, this must be right! Look at all the things it explains."

The authors' comment reveals what happens to such stories in the academic culture:

> In the formal paper we are told that the experimental results suggested a model which seemed an improvement on previous assumptions and which was, accordingly, put to the test. In the interview we hear of a dramatic revelation of the central idea which was immediately seen to be right . . . and which led to the design of new experiments.

Bakhtin would perhaps say, "There you have the difference between *internally persuasive discourse* and *authoritative discourse*." Standing behind them are two great forces always at work in language, the *centripetal* and the *centrifugal*. The centripetal is constituted from everything which pulls us towards a center of linguistic norms at every level, the pressures to conform to one language, one dialect, one set of rules, the order of certain discourse etiquettes, and indeed genre conventions. The counter force is centrifugal which is constituted from everything which pulls away from the normative centre, the mixing of dialects, lexical and syntactical innovation, play with language, defiance of the genre conventions, use of a genre considered to be inappropriate, persistence of stigmatized language, phonological mockery. According to Bakhtin (1981:272),

> Every concrete utterance of a speaking subject serves as a point where centrifugal as well as centripetal forces are brought to bear. The processes of centralization and decentralization, of unification and disunification, intersect in the utterance; . . . it is in fact an active participant in such speech diversity.

There is no escaping centripetal forces; the question is what kind of discourse offers the greatest possibility to the play of centrifugal forces. For it must be clear that centripetal forces control or even suppress that crucial attempt which we all make to struggle against the given and already determined in language, a struggle which is an attempt to assert our own meanings against the matrix of ready-codified meanings lying in wait for us.

For Bakhtin the medium with most promise is the novel. I think there is a case for suggesting that autobiographical utterance is the folk novel. It is most impossible to police and springs up unpredictably outside the surveillance of the grammar book and the style manual. De Certeau (1980) argues that it is one of the means of outwitting established order, what he calls "tactics."

> Where dominating powers exploit the order of things, where ideological discourse represses or ignores, tactics fool this order and make it the field of their art. Thereby, the institution one is called to serve finds itself infiltrated by a style of social exchange, a style of technical invention, and a style of moral resistance—that is, by an economy of the "gift" (generosities which are also ways of asking for something in return), by an aesthetic of "moves", "triumphs" or "strikes" . . . . and by an ethic of tenacity . . . This is what "popular culture" really is and not some alien corpus, anatomised for the purposes of exhibit . . .

Bakhtin saw the centrifugal in operation in parody, verbal masquerades, and in the folk buffoonery of local fairs. However the centrifugal can be attempted by anyone, the young included. In, for instance, Michael, aged 14, writing of his infant days:

There was nothing.
And I was two. Rabbit is my very best friend. I sat in a corner and we

were playing with a thing and then there were reds and yellows and browns. My brother is Gonofan and he told Mummy (whose real name is also Mummy) to come and see the pretty colours. Mummy did not like them and hit the pretty colours.

The deers in the park are brown. I like deers and I touched a deer and it ran away and I ran after it into the woods but she did not have a broomstick. She wanted to eat me so I ran back to Mummy. I ran and ran like Johnny Rabbit ran from the farmer's gun . . .

I ran up the stairs with Rabbit. My bottom hurt and I needed the potty. But I cannot run as fast as Rabbit and I had to leave the brown gunge on the stairs and I wet my eyes but I started to read and so was happy.

Mummy made me some red and blue shoes and
he played nic nac on my shoe
And I was three
He played nic nac on my knee

My Daddy (whose real name is also Daddy) is a good wizard. He did magic on the house and made it change. I went for a ride in the car and when I came back it had changed but there was no room for Daddy in our new house. He should have made it bigger

And I was four
He played nic nac on my door

I was with Rabbit on the pavement and we were waiting for Daddy to make us be on holiday and a young man, really the Giant up the beanstalk, made the door sing like Penny Penguin. She says, "Michael row the boat ashore." I was taken to be mended in hospital.

I think of all those who have labored to discover the essence of the "well-formed story" and wonder what they would make of that. The story eludes the centripetal tug by being double-voiced; its surface texture is the voice of the infant from two to four years (a changing voice in that time, you may have noticed) but it is produced by a fourteen-year-old modernist who knows how to manage the juxtaposition of images, abrupt transitions, montage. The opening words defy centripetal narrative, "There was nothing."

Deborah Tannen (1979) noted the widespread use of terms in many disciplines to deal with patterns of expectations (frames, scripts, schemata, scenes and so forth). There are two ways in which this pattern of expectations can enter narrative activity: (a) the recognition of an experience as a scene or several scenes with narrative potential; (b) conforming to a pattern of expectations in the composition of actual narrative which tells the story of the scene. Now suppose we separate (a) and (b) by—a day, a month, twenty years. We now complicate the notion of frame enormously. Instead of a structure of expectation derived from past experience (i.e. a form of memory) and related to the presenting experience, we now have the intervention of memory in a different way. The *form* of presentation (narrative) fits the frame notion comfortably. But what does this telling filtered by memory and intervening experience do to the original experience? I suggest we now have a fascinating complexity—a new and bigger frame is placed around the original one which is at the same time definitely not discarded. It is this which constitutes the double-voice of autobiography. It is both how it was and how it is fused together. It may well account for the legitimate fictions of autobiography (perfectly "remembered" conversations, for example). To sum up, a recognizable narrative is both constructed by and understood by a frame derived from past experience BUT the experience was originally understood by one frame and is now understood by a new one which includes understanding of the original frame.

Bakhtin was concerned to identify the essential differences between discourses which are, so to speak, compulsory and those which satisfy us by their feel of authenticity. He writes (1981:342) of "two categories":

> . . . in one, the authoritative word (religious, political, moral; the word of a father, of adults and of teachers, etc.) that does not know internal persuasiveness, in the other internally persuasive word that is denied all privilege, backed up by no authority at all, and is frequently not even acknowledged in society (not by public opinion, not by scholarly norms, nor by criticism) . . .

Authoritative discourse, he goes on to say, demands our unconditional allegiance—permits no play with its borders, no gradual and flexible transitions, no creative stylizing variants on it. It is indissolubly fused with its authority. It is all inertia and calcification, whereas

> Internally persuasive discourse . . . is . . . tightly interwoven with "one's own word." . . . [It] is half-ours and half-someone else's . . . [Its] semantic structure . . . is *not finite,* it is *open* . . . this discourse is able to reveal ever newer *ways to mean.* (pp. 345-46; italics in original)

Internally persuasive discourse is the arena in which autobiographical speech finds its scope and its diversity of intentions. Narratology has had a good run for its money but is not permitted to speak of such things (no authors, no intentions!). We must increasingly turn our attention to narrative as a form of participation in interaction when the narration is embedded in dialogue. We know that the story-teller can acquire or be offered the right to narrate, the chance to recruit the desires of the others, to achieve a moment's authority without being authoritative. We also have accumulating evidence that speakers can transform a turn in dialogue into a personal narrative which is a contribution to the goals of the dialogue. Erickson (1984) has shown how within a particular culture this is the prevailing mode and very disconcerting for those who do not share it. Halligan (1984) in studying over a long period the small group discussions of 12/13-year-old students in a black working-class inner-city area found a very similar pattern. In one analysis of a discussion (which turned on whether stealing is a result of poverty) he isolated five major personal anecdotes and demonstrated that,

> These anecdotes are the main structural members upon which the fabric of the discussion is erected, both because the discussion which intervenes is in reaction to them, and because they embody the logical structure of the discussion . . . (p. 78)

You will not suppose that I am under the delusion that stories of personal experience will set the world to rights. I do, however, believe that from the top to the bottom of the educational system, authoritative discourse holds sway but that inroads into it can be made by giving students genuine fuller speaking rights in the classroom. An inevitable consequence will be the emergence of a much greater role for personal narrative. For most students this would constitute a liberation. In the end stories about the past are also about the future. On the other hand, we have only to remind ourselves of the way in which folk story was domesticated into coziness, to remember that stories themselves can kow-tow with subservience. Their very universality contains its own surreptitious menace. They can be used to manipulate, control, create a market, and above all to massage us into forgetfulness and passivity. Nor do I wish to forget that alongside the autobiographical impulse there is the autobiographical *compulse* of the courtroom, of the government inspector, of the attitude tests, of the curriculum vitae, of the torture chamber. There are some very sinister people engaged in hermeneutics! We are not left free to limit our pasts to unpoliced crannies and congenial moments. Stand and deliver. There are many ways in which power attempts to wrest from us our past and use it for its own ends. Our autobiographies also figure in dossiers wrung from us as surely as were confessions by the Inquisition. Such invitations do not coax and tempt memory for they surround it with caution, fear, and even terror.

Yet in spite of the inquisitors, indeed, in stark defiance of them, we have no alternative. We must persist with archaeological expeditions into the substrata of our memories so that, returning, we may look the present in the eye and even dare to peer into the future.

REFERENCES

Bakhtin, M.M. 1981. The dialogic imagination, ed. by Michael Holquist, trans. by Caryl Emerson & Michael Holquist. Austin: University of Texas Press.

Barthes, Roland. 1982. Introduction to the structural analysis of narrative. Barthes: Selected writings, ed. by Susan Sontag, 251–95. London: Fontana.

de Certeau, Michel. 1980. On the oppositional practices of everyday life. Social Text 1:3.3–43.

Chambers, Ross. 1984. Story and situation. Minneapolis: University of Minnesota Press.

Derrida, Jacques. 1978. Writing and difference, trans. by A. Bass. London: Routledge & Kegan Paul.

Dunning, Jean. 1985. Reluctant and willing story-tellers in the classroom. English in Education 19:1.1–15.

Eco, Umberto. 1983. The name of the rose. San Diego: Harcourt Brace Jovanovich.

Erickson, Fredrick. 1984. Rhetoric, anecdote, and rhapsody: Coherence strategies in a conversation among Black American adolescents. Coherence in spoken and written discourse, ed. by Deborah Tannen, 81–154. Norwood, NJ: Ablex.

Fraser, Ronald. 1984. In search of a past. London: Verso.

Foucault, Michel. 1970. The order of things: An archaeology of the human sciences. London: Tavistock.

Foucault, Michel. 1977. Discipline and punish: The birth of the prison. New York: Pantheon.

Genette, Gerard. 1980. Narrative discourse, trans. by Jane E. Lewin. London: Basil Blackwell.

Gilbert, G. Nigel and Michael Mulkay. 1984. Opening Pandora's box. Cambridge: University Press.

Halliday, M.A.K., and Ruqaiya Hasan. 1976. Cohesion in English. London: Longman.

Halligan, David. 1984. Social context, discourse, and learning in small group discussion. PhD dissertation, University of London.

Hawkes, Terence. 1977. Structuralism and semiotics. London: Methuen.

Holquist, Michael. 1983. Answering as authoring: Mikhail Bakhtin's translinguistics. Critical Inquiry 10:2.307–19.

Hymes, Dell. 1973. Toward linguistic competence. Texas Working Papers in

Sociolinguistics No. 16. Austin, TX: Southwest Educational Development Laboratory.

Hymes, Dell. 1984. Vers la compétence de communication, trans. by Frances Mugler, with "Note liminaire" by Daniel Coste. Langues et apprentissage des langues; Collection dirigée par H. Besse et E. Papo, Ecole normale superieure de Saint-Cloud. Paris: Hatier-Credif.

Hymes, Dell, and Courtney Cazden. 1980. Narrative thinking and storytelling rights: A folklorist's clue to a critique of education. Language in education: Ethnolinguistic essays, ed. by Dell Hymes, 126–38. Washington, DC: Center for Applied Linguistics.

Labov, William. 1972. Language in the inner city. Philadelphia: University of Pennsylvania Press.

Medvedev, P.N./M.M. Bakhtin. 1978. The formal method in literary scholarship: A critical introduction to sociological poetics. Baltimore: Johns Hopkins University Press.

Tannen, Deborah. 1979. What's in a frame? Surface evidence for underlying expectations. New directions in discourse processing, ed. by Roy O. Freedle, 137–81. Norwood, NJ: Ablex.

Volosinov, V.N. [M.M. Bakhtin] 1976. Freudianism: A Marxist critique, trans. by I.R. Titunik. New York: Academic.

CHAPTER FOUR

Hearing Voices in Conversation, Fiction, and Mixed Genres

Deborah Tannen

Georgetown University

INTRODUCTION

Bleich (to appear) observes that, in light of growing concern with intertextuality, two elements not usually found in purely cognitive approaches to language, *affect* and *dialogue,* become central. These two elements are central to this lecture as well. The lecture draws on an ongoing research project comparing conversational and literary discourse.[1] The thrust of this research is that ordinary conversation and literary discourse have more in common than has been commonly thought.[2] Whereas conversation is generally thought to be messy, pe-

[1] Research on the material presented here was begun with the support of a Rockefeller Humanities Fellowship. Discussion of dialogue in conversation is drawn from Tannen (1986a). An earlier version of this paper appears as "The Orality of Literature and the Literacy of Conversation" in *Language, Literacy, and Culture: Issues of Society and Schooling,* edited by Judith Langer (Norwood, NJ: Ablex). Revision into the current form was carried out during a sabbatical leave from Georgetown University, with the support of a grant from the National Endowment for the Humanities. I am grateful to Lambros Comitas and the Joint Program in Applied Anthropology of Teachers College Columbia University for providing affiliation during this leave.

[2] Christopher Ricks (1981:42), in reviewing Goffman's *Forms of Talk,* reports feeling "what everybody always feels about the main contentions which issue from somebody else's discipline: that it is odd that certain things need to be said." Just so, it will seem odd to some, in particular to creative writers, that I feel it needs to be said that literary language is made of the stuff of ordinary conversation. W.H. Auden, for example, is reputed to have commented that "poetry is memorable speech"; similar observations are reported by Heath (1985:4), who observes that early American writers believed "their work constitutes a linguistic 'reconstitution' of ordinary language." Furthermore, Heath (1986:287) notes, "It is a paradox of postmodernist literature in the United States that what is considered most literary is that which is most like oral language."

destrian, and error-ridden, literary discourse is considered an exalted form of language. I seek to show that both operate on the same linguistic dimensions to create interpersonal involvement.

In the larger research project, I am examining closely a variety of spoken and written discourse types in order to compare the linguistic means by which they create involvement. I have grouped these linguistic means in two categories: first, patterns of language that create involvement by sweeping the audience along in their rhythm, sound, and shape; and second, those that create involvement by requiring audience participation in sense-making, such as indirectness, tropes, imagery, detail, and dialogue, with many of these intertwined in storytelling. (Like all atomistic schemes, the separation of these aspects of language into discrete categories is a falsification for heuristic purposes. All aspects work together; sound is not separate from sense. For more discussion of this theoretical framework, see the last chapter of Tannen 1984 and Tannen in press).

Of these numerous linguistic patterns which I believe contribute to involvement, I have begun investigation of repetition (Tannen 1987b, in press), detail (Tannen 1987a), and dialogue (Tannen 1986a). This paper draws on and expands my analysis of dialogue.

I begin this discussion by considering the centrality of dialogue in storytelling, and the role of storytelling in creating involvement. Then, to support my claim that dialogue in conversational storytelling is constructed rather than reported, I examine the dialogue in a narrative spontaneously told in casual conversation among friends. After this I demonstrate that constructing dialogue is part of a pattern of vivid storytelling by reference to a study of dialogue in Brazilian and American narration. Next, I consider graphic verbs used to introduce dialogue in an American novel. I move then to three spoken and written genres produced by junior high school students: a school writing assignment, a conversational story, and notes exchanged with friends. Finally, I discuss the emotional basis of cognition with reference to an excerpt from an unusual and unusually effective document: a conference proceedings which makes use of techniques of fiction writing.

WHY DIALOGUE?

Many researchers (for example, Labov 1972, Chafe 1982, Ochs 1979, Tannen 1982a, Schiffrin 1981) have observed that narration is more vivid when speech is presented as first-person dialogue (usually called "direct quotation" or "direct speech") rather than third-person exposition ("indirect quotation" or "indirect speech"), and that the former is more commonly found in conversational narrative (sometimes generally referred to as spoken discourse) than in written expository discourse (but not in written literary discourse, precisely, I suggest, because fiction and poetry are akin to conversation in workings and effect). But there is more to it than that. The creation of voices occasions the imagination of alternative, distant, and others' worlds that is the stuff of dreams and art.

According to Friedrich (1986:17), language "is inherently, pervasively, and powerfully poetic," when "poetic language" is defined as "all parts of a language that exemplify a figure" (24). Furthermore, he observes, "it is the relatively poetic nature of language, formed and articulated through figures of speech, that most deeply and massively affects the imagination . . ." (17). In this sense, constructed dialogue is poetic: It is a figure that fires the individual imagination. Moreover, as Friedrich emphasizes, "the imagination of the unique individual" is "a central reality, perhaps *the* central reality, of language and of its actualization in speech" (16), and, perhaps paradoxically, the activation of the individual imagination is what makes it possible to understand another's speech. This understanding—communication—simultaneously establishes the sense of rapport, of involvement with other individuals, that makes communication a social activity. As a culturally familiar figure, constructed dialogue in conversation and in fiction is a means by which experience surpasses story to become drama—a drama staged in the speech of one individual and enacted in the mind of another. The creation of drama from personal experience and hearsay contributes to the emotional involvement that is crucial for understanding and becomes the basis of human interaction.

To begin, I want to place the phenomenon of dialogue in the context of storytelling.

STORYTELLING AS AN ACT OF MIND

Harold Rosen (this volume) both explains and exemplifies the role of stories in even the most seemingly abstract thought, so that a scholar's "vast erudition is a superstructure erected on and motivated by meanings which had their beginnings and verifications in a past rich with [personal] encounters . . ." Furthermore, Rosen articulates the power of storytelling both to make sense of one's own life and to present one's ideas persuasively (I would say, involvingly) to others. Elsewhere, Rosen (1984) argues that storytelling in literature is a refinement of storytelling in everyday life—and that storytelling is at the heart of everyday life. He calls storytelling "an explicit resource in all intellectual activity," "a disposition of the mind," a "meaning-making strategy" which represents the mind's "eternal rummaging in the past and its daring, scandalous rehearsal of scripts of the future."

Inseparable from the function of stories in creating meaning in individual lives is an interactive function: The telling and hearing of experience as stories are made possible by and simultaneously create interpersonal involvement which carries a metamessage (Bateson 1972) of rapport.[3] That is, hearers can understand and appreciate a story because they recognize its particulars and can imagine the scenes in which such particulars could occur, reconstructing them from remembered associations with similar particulars. That the hearers' experience thus matches the storyteller's, creates a sense of a shared universe— of experience and of discourse. When this occurs in interpersonal interaction, rapport is drawn on and established. When it occurs in literature, the sense of rapport is broadened to include a wide audience and a published author—a community of rapport. Storytelling is a means by which humans organize and understand the world, and feel connected to it and to each other. Giving voice to the speech of characters in a story—and we shall see presently that such voice-giving can be quite literal—creates a play peopled by characters who take on life and breath.

Central to this process is particularity, a theme on which Becker (1984; this volume) has elaborated. The casting of thoughts and speech in dialogue creates particular scenes and characters, and it is the particular which moves readers by establishing and building on a sense of identification between speaker or writer and audience.[4] Particularity has a paradoxical power by which, as teachers of creative writing exhort neophyte writers, the accurate representation of the particular communicates universality, whereas direct attempts to represent universality often communicate nothing. Particularity allows the audience to imagine a scene, and this participation in sense-making is emotionally moving. Generality does not trigger this process and therefore leaves audiences unmoved.

---

[3] The overweening importance of language use to create rapport is a repeated theme of R. Lakoff (for example, 1979). Building on her work, I discuss this phenomenon at length (Tannen 1984, 1986b).

[4] Havelock (1963) discusses this sense of identification as the basis of "subjective knowing" which he says accounts for the persuasiveness of orally performed epic poetry. I am eager, however, to avoid his dichotomy between subjective and objective knowing, a dichotomy that parallels the oral/literate one I have been trying to move away from as well (Tannen 1982a, 1985). I am grateful to A.L. Becker for patiently prodding me to avoid this terminology and attendant imaging.

Neurologist and essayist Oliver Sacks (1986) provides evidence, based on observation of certain brain-damaged patients, that memory and thinking occur in scenes.

STORYTELLING AS DRAMA

Eudora Welty (1984) locates her beginnings as a writer in the magic of everyday storytelling. She was first exposed to this magic when her family acquired a car, and a storytelling (that is, gossipy) neighbor was invited along on family outings. The sound of dialogue casts a spell over the child Eudora:

> My mother sat in the back with her friend, and I'm told that as a small child I would ask to sit in the middle, and say as we started off, "Now *talk*."
> There was dialogue throughout this lady's accounts to my mother. "I said" . . . "He said" . . . "And I'm told she very plainly said" . . . "It was midnight before they finally heard, and what do you think it *was?*" What I loved about her stories was that everything happened in *scenes*. I might not catch on to what the root of the trouble was in all that happened, but my ear told me it was dramatic. (pp. 12–13)

Note that in this telling, Welty herself creates a scene (the child nestled between two adults in the back of a car), an inextricable part of which is constructed dialogue:

> "Now *talk*."
> "I said" . . .
> "He said" . . .
> "And I'm told she very plainly said" . . .
> "It was midnight before they finally heard, and what do you think it *was?*"

Welty knows that narratives in ordinary conversation are artistic creations. She recollects (or, more precisely, she artfully creates) Fannie, a woman who came to the Welty house to sew. Like the gossipy friend who was invited on car trips, Fannie delighted the child with stories about other people which the child did not fully understand but loved to hear:

> The gist of her tale would be lost on me, but Fannie didn't bother about the ear she was telling it to: she just liked telling. She was like an author. In fact, for a good deal of what she said, I daresay she *was* the author. (p. 14)

Welty does not, by this observation, criticize Fannie; rather, she places her among the ranks of talented storytellers.

The parallel between gossip and literature is not unprecedented. It is drawn, for example, by Britton (1982). (M.C. Bateson [1984] draws another parallel: between gossip and anthropology, because of its focus on the details of people's lives). Nonetheless, popular opinion reveres literary storytelling but scorns gossip. This negative view of gossip is voiced in Welty's account by her mother. A native of West Virginia, the elder Welty considered the Mississippi custom of social visiting to be "idling." And she was exasperated by the chatter that delighted her daughter. For example, following a long telephone conversation with her gossipy friend, the mother responded wearily to her daughter's eager curiosity:

> "What did she say?" I asked.
> "She wasn't *saying* a thing in this world," sighed my mother. "She was just ready to talk, that's all." (p. 13)

In keeping with her disdain for gossip, the mother tried to prevent Fannie from telling stories in her child's presence:

> "I don't want her exposed to gossip"—as if gossip were measles and I could catch it. (p. 14)

That oral stories are created rather than reported was made clear by another professional storyteller: a medicine show pitchman, Fred "Doc" Bloodgood. In answer to my query about the accuracy of parts of his pitches (Bloodgood 1982), he responded in a letter: "Anyway, as my dad always told me, 'Never let a grain of truth interfere with the story'." I doubt that Bloodgood's father ever said this, and it doesn't matter whether or not he did. What matters is that "as my dad always told me" is an apt way to transform a general maxim into an instance of particular dialogue.

To sum up the argument that animating voices in dialogue makes story into drama and thus involves the speaker and audience in a community of rapport, I quote Dell Hymes's (1973:15) description of and comment on an Indian woman telling the story of Skunk, which Rosen (this volume) cites early in his lecture:

> All this in detail, with voices for the different actors, gestures for the actions, and always, animation. For that, as people will be glad to tell you, is what makes a good narrator: the ability to make the story come alive, to involve you as in a play.

Given this perspective on the creative act of storytelling in any genre, and of the centrality of dialogue in making stories dramatic, I move to the examination of dialogue in narrative.

REPORTED SPEECH IS CONSTRUCTED DIALOGUE

The conversational discourse analyzed in the larger study from which this section is drawn consists of stories told in conversation either in dyads or in small groups, recorded by someone who happened to be there. The literary discourse examined consists of excerpts from novels. The American novel used is *Household Words* by Joan Silber (1976), which won the Hemingway Award for first novels.[5]

I will begin by demonstrating that dialogue presented in oral storytelling is constructed, not reported, by looking closely at the dialogue in a conversational story. (For more detailed argumentation of this point, see Tannen 1986a; for a related demonstration, in different terms, see Haberland 1986). The point is to show that the lines of dialogue in the narrative were not actually spoken by the characters to whom they are attributed. What, then, are they doing in the story? The speaker uses the animation of voices to make his story into drama.

The narrative was told by a young man who came home from his work as a resident in the emergency room of a hospital to find a group of his friends gathered in his home, hosted by his wife.[6] Asked whether anything interesting had happened at the emergency room, he responded by telling this story.

1 We had three guys come in,
2 one guy had a cut right here.
3 On his arm? [Listener: uhuh]
4 Bled all over the place, right? [Listener: Yeah]
5 These three guys were hysterical.
6 They come bustin' through the door.

---

[5] The American stories were recorded, chosen, and initially transcribed either by me or by students in my Discourse Analysis class Fall 1983. Terry Waldspurger helped identify constructed dialogue and count words in the American stories, as did Maria Spanos for the Greek stories and Susan Dodge for the novel.

[6] Kimberly Murphy recorded and initially transcribed this story. I am grateful to her for finding it, and to her and the speaker for giving permission to use it. Transcription of this and subsequent excerpts from spoken discourse is in lines and, in some cases, verses to facilitate reading by representing in print the prosodic chunking of speech. See Tannen (in press) for discussion of this practice and its theoretical implications. Other transcription conventions:

. Period shows sentence-final falling intonation
, Comma shows clause-final intonation ("more to come")
? Question mark shows rising intonation
: Colon shows elongation of preceding vowel sound
/?/ Question mark in slashes shows uncertain transcription
... Three dots show half-second pause
.. Two dots show less than half-second pause

7 Yknow you're not supposed to come in to the emergency room.
8 You're supposed to go to the registration desk, yknow?
9 and fill out all the forms before you get called back.
10 They come bustin' through the door,
11 blood is everywhere.
12 It's on the walls, on the floor, everywhere.
13 [sobbing] "It's okay Billy, we're gonna make it/?/."
14 [normal voice] "What the hell's wrong with you."
15 W-we-we look at him.
16 He's covered with blood, yknow?
17 All they had to do was take a washcloth at home
18 and go like this ...
19 and there'd be no blood.
20 There'd be no blood.
21 [Listener: You put pressure on it]
22 Three drunk guys come bustin' in,
23 all the other patients are like, "Ugh Ugh".
24 They're bleedin' everywhere yknow
25 People are passin' out just lookin' at this guy's blood here.
26 [Listener: Like "We're okay"]
27 "Get the hell outta here!"
28 [Listener: Yknow he's got stories like this to tell every night, don't
     you?]
29 Yeah [Listener: Mhm]
30 "Get the hell outta here!" yknow?
31 These three guys-
32 "What the hell's wrong with you guys.
33 You don't know anything about first aid?
34 Hold onto his arm."
35 ["innocent" voice] "We raised it above his head."
36 "Oh yeah" shh shh
37 [Listener: So it bled up]
38 Yknow they're whimmin' his arm around
39 [voice change] "Come here Billy.
40 No, come here Billy."
41 Two guys yankin' him from both sides.
42 [sobbing] "Am I gonna die? [loud, sobbing ingress]
43 Am I gonna die?"
44 He's passed out on the cot.
45 Anyway so ... [sobbing] "Am I gonna die?"
46 "How old are you."
47 "Nineteen"
48 "Shit. Can't call his parents."
49 [pleading voice] "Don't tell my parents.
50 Please don't tell my parents.
51 You're not gonna tell my parents, are you?"

52 [Listener: /?/ "We're going to wrap you in bandages"]
53 What happened.
54 Then the cops were there too, the cops.
55 ["bored" voice] "Who stabbed dja."
56 "I didn't get stabbed.
57 I fell on a bottle." ...
58 "Come o::n, looks like a stab wound to me."
59 [Listener A: Well this is Alexandria, what do you think?]
60 [Listener: C: Really no shit.]

There are at least five different voices animated in this narrative, each realized in a paralinguistically distinct representation: literally, a different voice.

Billy's two friends are represented by one voice, and the quality of that voice creates the persona that the speaker is developing for them. In line (13) they are presented as trying to reassure Billy, but the quality of the voice animating their dialogue portrays them as emotionally distraught: (Drawn lines are used to give a sense of intonation contours).

13 [sobbing] "It's okay Billy, we're gonna make it /?/."
    * *
39 [voice change] "Come here Billy.
40 No, come here Billy."

When the friends protest, in line (35),

35 ["innocent" voice] "We raised it above his head."

the quality of the voice suggests belabored innocence that is really stupidity.

Another example of more than one person animated in the story as a single voice is the speaker himself, merged with the rest of the hospital staff. The quality of this voice suggests frustration and impatience but also reasonableness and calm. Dialogue uttered by this persona is the closest to unmarked conversational intonation and prosody:

14 [normal voice] "What the hell's wrong with you."
    * *
30 "Get the hell outta here!"
    * *
32 "What the hell's wrong with you guys.
33 You don't know anything about first aid?
34 Hold onto his arm."
    * *

36   "Oh yeah"
   * *
46   "How old are you."
   * *
48   "Shit. Can't call his parents."
   * *
52   [Listener: /?/ "We're going to wrap you in bandages"]

In line (52) the dialogue of the hospital staff is animated by a listener, who self-evidently was not present to hear it uttered by those whose voices it represents.

Billy himself is animated in the most paralinguistically marked voice: sobbing, gasping, desperate, out of control.

42   [sobbing] "Am I gonna die? [loud, sobbing ingress]
43   Am I gonna die?"
   * *
45   "Am I gonna die?"
   * *
49   [pleading voice] "Don't tell my parents.
50   Please don't tell my parents.
51   You're not gonna tell my parents, are you?"

The paralinguistically exaggerated animation of Billy's voice, and the slightly less marked animation of the choral voice of his friends, contrast sharply with the relatively ordinary quality of the speaker/hospital staff voice. These contrasting voices reflect and create the dramatic tension between the unreasonable behavior of "these three drunk guys" who "were hysterical" and the reasonable, legitimately frustrated responses of the speaker/staff.

Marked in a different direction is the stereotypically flat voice of the policeman, represented as one who is just doing his job and has seen it all before:

55   ["bored" voice] "Who stabbed dja."
   * *
58   "Come o::n, looks like a stab wound to me."

Finally, the other emergency room patients are animated in a single voice, and again, in line (26), dialogue is constructed by a listener:

23   all the other patients are like, "Ugh Ugh".
   * *
26   [Listener: Like "We're okay"]

It is clear in all these examples that the lines of dialogue in this story are not reported, but rather constructed by the speaker, like lines in fiction or drama, and to similar effect. Through the quality of the animated voices as much as (or more than) what they say, a drama is constructed. The animation of voices breathes life into the characters and their story—and the conversational interaction for which the story was created (a gift, perhaps, to make up for the speaker's hitherto absence from the gathering).

DIALOGUE AS INVOLVEMENT

Of 25 stories told by American women about being molested which I compared with 25 stories told by Greek women about the same subject, the American women's stories included one instance of constructed dialogue. The Greek women's stories included 119. Dialogue is one of a range of features which made the Greek women's stories vivid and involving.[7] (See Tannen 1983 for illustration and discussion of this range of features.) The use of constructed dialogue is associated not only with Greek but with other culturally identifiable styles as well— those that come across as especially "vivid." Kirshenblatt-Gimblett (1974) and Tannen (1984) show this for East European Jews, Labov (1972) for American blacks.

There is evidence that Brazilian speech falls into this category as well, and that constructed dialogue is a dimension of that effectiveness. In a pilot study comparing how Brazilian and American speakers told the story of Little Red Riding Hood, Ott (1983) found that the Brazilian speakers used far more dialogue. The American man in her study used six such instances, all formulaic for this fairy tale:

"Grandma, what a big nose you have."
"All the better to smell you my dear."
"Grandma, what big ears you have."
"All the better it is to hear you my dear."
"Grandma, what a big mouth and big teeth you have."
"All the better to eat you with my dear."

The American woman in the study used 15 instances of dialogue,

---

[7] This is not to suggest that Americans do not tell effective stories nor that they do not construct dialogue extensively in their storytelling. The narrative analyzed above makes clear that they do. It is simply to say that in the stories I collected by women about being molested, the stories told by Greeks were more vivid and contained more dialogue. I want to stress, too, that there is no way of knowing whether there was in fact more talk in the experiences of the Greek women; I know only that in telling these stories, they presented themselves as having talked more.

including the formulas found in the American man's story, but also including some improvised variations on them ("What long whiskers you have"; "The better to wiggle them at you my dear") and the casting of other parts of the story in dialogue (for example, the mother tells Little Red Riding Hood, "Go to your grandmother's house . . ."). The Brazilian woman who told the same story used 20 instances of dialogue, and the Brazilian man used 43!

The Brazilian man's version of the fairy tale represents almost all action in dialogue, one of a number of ways that his story is rich in particularity. For example, at the beginning (Brazilian excerpts were translated from the Portuguese by Ott):

> One time on a beautiful afternoon, in her city, her mother called her and said:
> "Little Red Riding Hood, come here."
> "What is it, Mother? I am playing with my dolls, can I continue?"

Long segments of this narration are composed only of dialogue, for example when the child is accosted by the wolf:

> "Little Red Riding Hood, Little Red Riding Hood."
> And Little Red Riding Hood stopped and looked: "Who is there?"
> "Ah, who is talking here is the spirit of the forest."
> "Spirit? But I don't know you."
> "No, but I am invisible, you can't see me."
> "But what do you want?" [imitating child's voice]
> "Where are you going, Little Red Riding Hood?"
> "Ah, I'm going to my granny's house."
> "What are you going to do there, Little Red Riding Hood?"
> "Ah, I'm going to take some sweets that my mother prepared for her."
> "Ah, very good . . . the sweets are delicious, they are, they are, they are, they are . . ." [licking his lips]
> "Do you want one?"
> "No, no, no, no. [Accelerated] Spirits don't eat.
> Okay, okay. Then, now, yes, yes, you are going to take it to your granny . . . remember me to her, okay?"
> "Okay, bye."

Through constructed dialogue and other linguistic means such as repetition ("No, no, no, no."), colloquial interjections ("remember me to her, okay?"), specific details ("I am playing with my dolls") and nonverbal gestures (licking his lips), this speaker created a vivid new story out of a traditional fairy tale.

GRAPHIC VOCABULARY IN LITERARY NARRATIVE

The vividness of the foregoing story samples comes in part from the ordinariness of the diction, the familiarity of colloquial linguistic patterns. The effectiveness of some literary writing seems to derive from an opposite phenomenon: the choice of relatively unfamiliar (from the point of view of daily parlance) graphic lexical items.

My earlier study of dialogue in conversational and fictional narrative focused on how the dialogue was introduced (Tannen 1986a). The most frequent introducers in all four types of discourse studied—American and Greek conversation and fiction—were forms of the verb "say" (most frequently, in English, "s/he said" or "s/he says"). When the spoken English dialogue was not introduced by a form of "said," it was usually introduced by no verb at all, accounting for 26% of dialogue; as in the example above, dialogue was identified as such by its voice quality, or by a form of "go" (for example, as will be seen in a subsequent excerpt from a teenager's conversation, "And so I go 'Oh my God . . .'") or a form of "be" + "like" (for example, also from the teenager's conversation, "and I'm like 'Nothing much'."). "Go" and "like" accounted for 19% of the English introducers in the conversational stories studied. The characteristic that set the novel *Household Words* apart most noticeably from the other three discourse types to which it was compared is its use of graphic lexical items to introduce dialogue, accounting for 27% of introducers in the chapter studied.

In this chapter, the author used the following verbs to introduce dialogue: explain, complain, croon, coo, demand, call, call down, call out, wheeze, cry out, mutter, bellow, murmur, go on, titter, grumble, gasp, whisper, hiss, sob, scream, suggest, groan, intone, grimace, yip, warn, sniff, want to know, shout, wail, repeat, supply, yelp, and snap. Of these, only five are repeated, once each (explain, whisper, scream, shout, and suggest).

It might seem, reading these verbs in a list, that the writing of this novel is overwrought. (The author herself, on reading the list, had that impression—regrettable but significant evidence for the distortion entailed in microanalysis: Wrenching phenomena out of context falsifies their nature.) However, this is not the case. When the graphic introducers appear in the text, they are effective, as seen in the following excerpt in which the heroine, Rhoda, serves lunch to her fifth-grade daughter, Suzanne, and Suzanne's classmate Ina Mae. (In this and subsequent examples, verbs introducing dialogue are underlined.)

Suzanne . . . reached out to give Ina Mae a "feeny bird," a rap on the skull with flicked fingers, as Ina ducked away, <u>screaming</u>, "Get away from me!"

"How about," Rhoda <u>suggested</u>, "clearing off the kitchen table so you can have some good old peanut butter and jelly sandwiches?"

"Oh boy," Suzanne <u>groaned</u> sarcastically. "Oh boy, oh boy, oh boy."

"The boy," Rhoda <u>intoned</u>, beating time with a spoon at the kitchen sink, *"stood on the burning deck,/ His feet were full of blisters./ He tore his pants on a red-hot nail/ So now he wears his sister's."* The girls, unfamiliar with the original poem (a staple of recitations in Rhoda's childhood) failed to find this wickedly amusing. "Oh, Mother," Suzanne <u>grimaced</u>. "Ina, for Christ's sake, would you please pass the jelly? I'm starving, you know."

"You poor old thing," Rhoda said. "You're so hungry you could dydee-dydee-dydee-die." Ina giggled. Rhoda poured a glass of milk for the guest. "Say when," she <u>suggested</u>.

"I *hate* milk," Ina <u>yipped</u>.

"Oh, we never serve milk in this house. This is cow juice. Don't be fooled by the carton." Rhoda smiled mysteriously.

"She thinks she's funny," Suzanne <u>said</u>. (p. 104)

Graphic introducers are an evaluative device, to use a term coined by Labov (1972) to describe linguistic elements that contribute to an oral narrative's point. The author uses them to hone her portrayal of the characters and their personalities, states of mind, and relationships to each other—and to make that portrayal more particular.

IN-SCHOOL WRITING

Given the role of dialogue in creating vivid narration, and the evidence that some styles of written literary narrative use graphic introducers,[8] it is not surprising that a junior high school teacher assigned her class the task of writing a story in which dialogue is introduced with words other than "said." The following is the story produced in fulfillment of this assignment by Michelle Lange:[9]

Bob, Susie, and Lisa were walking in the park when suddenly Bob <u>shrieked</u>, "Look!"

---

[8] The same would not be true of other writers, for example, Hemingway and such contemporary "minimalist" writers as Raymond Carver and Ann Beattie.

[9] I am grateful to Deborah Lange for identifying and bringing to my attention this and the following discourse samples produced by her daughter Michelle and her friends. I am grateful to her, to Michelle, and to Michelle's friends, for allowing me to use them. The samples are presented exactly as they were produced, except, of course, for the distortion entailed in transcribing from audiotape and handwriting to print.

"What?" Susie and Lisa inquired.
"I can't believe it!" Bob again shrieked.
"What is it? Tell us," Susie insisted.
"Look, on the sidewalk, sixty dollars!" Bob exclaimed.
"Oh my gosh," Lisa mumbled as she sighed.
"This couldn't possibly be true," Susie theorized.
"Maybe it's counterfeit," Lisa suggested.
"No," Bill confidently stated, "It's real, all right."
They reached their hands out and grabbed the money off the sidewalk.
"Touch it," Bob suggested, "We have real money in our hands."
"What should we do with it?" Susie asked.
"I know one thing for sure," Lisa warned us, "we can't let our parents know we have this money!"
"Why not?" Bob questioned.
"Because if our parents find we have this money, they'll either keep it, or make us turn it in to the police department," Lisa pointed out.
"There's twenty dollars for each of us!" Susie busted out.
The children each took their share of the money.
"What are we going to do with our money?" Bill inquired.
"I have an idea," Susie replied. "Why don't we make a club house!"
Lisa and Bob chorused, "Great Idea!"
"Maybe we can make it in the woods behind my yard," Bob offered.
"O.K.," Susie and Lisa agreed.
"Let's go to Bill's house now to start planning the materials needed for the club house," Lisa ordered.
"O.K.!" Bob and Susie enthusiastically exclaimed.

Michelle fulfilled her assignment admirably. But the assignment frame aside, the accretion of verbs other than "said" introducing dialogue gives the impression that the fiction writer feared when she read a list of verbs she had used in her chapter. However, in the novel the graphic introducers were interspersed with "said," which still accounted for the majority of instances of dialogue. Furthermore, the connotations and associations of the graphic verbs used in the novel contributed effectively to evaluation, that is, constructing a story world which reflects the point the author wishes to make. In Michelle's composition, total avoidance of "said" gives the narrative a forced quality, and the formal register represented by the verbs she chose is often at odds with the nature of the actions in the story. For example, "theorized" suggests more lofty and abstract thought than that represented by the formulaic expression of disbelief it accompanies. ("This couldn't possibly be true"), as evidenced by the audience laughter that always follows this line when I read the passage aloud.

DIALOGUE IN FRIENDLY CONVERSATION

Lest the impression be left that junior high school students are not adept at constructing and introducing dialogue, I will present another story, one told to Michelle by her friend about having accidentally run into their mutual friend Stacy.[10]

1 We saw her huge big truck, yknow?
2 That new scu- that new car?
3 It's such a scandal, that car! [Listener: I think it's so tacky.]
4 I KNOW.
5 And so I SAW it.
6 And then, I didn't see STACY.
7 I'm like c- trying to cruise after the car,
8 because I see her car, yknow run . . like . . driving?
9 And so I go "Oh my God,
10 I have to go run after it
11 and say hi to Stacy,
12 and go "What's up?"
13 'n I look, to the left.
14 Is that scandalous?!
15 Stacy's look- going [screaming] "Michelle, what's up!"
16 I swear she said that.
17 I swear she said that.
18 And then we we had the biggest cow in front of everyone.
19 They were all staring at us
20 cause we're like hugging,
21 and she said "What are you doing here?"
22 And I'm like "Nothing much" yknow
23 I explained the whole . . weird story
24 and she's like "um . . . well that's cool."
25 And so then we had to crank over to Safeway?
26 Because her mom was gonna be there?
27 Cause she was like doing groceries and stuff?

The dialogue is the very point of this story: the irony that just as the speaker was looking for Stacy in order to greet her by saying, "What's up?", she heard Stacy's voice saying to her, "What's up?" This main point is marked and emphasized by repetition of the external evaluation:

16 I swear she said that.
17 I swear she said that.

Note that in the preceding paragraph I repeated the phrase "What's

---

[10] To accommodate her sociolinguist mother, Michelle taped her private conversation with her friend.

up?" when I could have replaced it, the second time, with the phrase "the same words." I chose to repeat the phrase "What's up?" in order to *create* the effect of the repetition for the reader rather than simply *describing* it. This illustrates the function of dialogue in creating involvement—making it possible for listeners to come closer to imagining the recounted action or speech rather than simply hearing about it.

In the conversational story, where are all those excellent graphic words for saying "said" that were found in the written assignment? These words, which were marshalled when required by a school assignment, were not appropriate to the social situation in which the preceding spoken story was created. The lack of such words may make this story—when transcribed—seem impoverished. But the written story seems impoverished, in comparison to the spoken one, in just the way that doesn't show up in writing: voice quality and prosody. Perhaps one of the reasons that graphic vocabulary emerges in some forms of writing is to make up for the loss of expressive potential in the human voice which was exploited in the hospital story as well.

The spoken conversational adolescent narrative, in contrast with the school assignment narrative, is vivid and fluent. One might be tempted therefore to conclude that junior high school students are more comfortable speaking than writing. This, however, would be hasty. The main difference between these two verbal productions is not that one is spoken and the other written, but rather that one was an outgrowth of a naturally arising communicative situation and the other was not. The oddness of the written assignment was not that it was written but that it asked Michelle to do something she does not often do, and to use a register she does not often use, though she has clearly encountered it. Is there, then, a written genre that arises spontaneously out of the communicative needs of Michelle and her friends? The answer is yes— writing notes to each other.

WRITTEN CONVERSATION: PASSING NOTES

For an example of a written register with which Michelle and her friends are comfortable and which is a natural outgrowth of their social life, I will present some brief excerpts of their verbal production in yet another discourse type, one that, to my knowledge, has not yet been studied, a form of written conversation: notes.[11] Even though they talk to each other every day, in person and on the telephone, there

---

[11] In a paper focused on dialogue journals, Shuy (in press) observes that children's note passing is a potentially useful act of written communication.

are contexts in which Michelle and her friends choose to write to each other rather than speak. Michelle reports that sometimes they wrote notes at home and brought them to school ready to deliver. In this written genre, the diction, vocabulary, and fluency are more reminiscent of the story told in conversation than of the one written for class:

> High! What's up? I'm kool! I'm cranking in science with Norm N. & Nate Noster. Party train up the butt!
>
> * *
>
> You would look so good /w the one and only Tom Baxter! So go for it! He loves you yeah yeah yeah!
>
> * *
>
> [about a friend who got into trouble with a teacher] Karen is dead. Shams! DIES! Dead meat all over the street!

Involving, or poetic, aspects of this discourse abound: formulaic phrases which echo songs, including repetition ("He loves you yeah yeah yeah"), conventionalized sayings ("Go for it!," "one and only," the now-familiar "What's up?"), rhyming ("Dead meat all over the street!"), repetition (as above, plus "dead" repeated in the last excerpt), paraphrase with increasing intensity ("shams, dies"), visual punning ("High!", "kool"), and stylized vocabulary ("cranking," "Party train up the butt!"). The point I wish to emphasize here is that it is not the writtenness of the written assignment that accounts for its linguistic form but the context in which it was produced, and the genre associated with that context.

EMOTION AND COGNITION: MINGLING LITERATE AND LITERARY STRATEGIES

In her memoir of her parents Gregory Bateson and Margaret Mead, anthropologist and linguist Mary Catherine Bateson (1984) recalls her efforts to take into account the emotional basis of cognition in confronting the task of communicating ideas that evolved in interaction. Her discussion of this process shows the error of the assumption that academic discourse is emotion-free, emotion being appropriate to fiction. Appointed rapporteur for a conference her father organized on cybernetics at Burg Wartenstein, Bateson (1984:180) "reached the conclusion that my book would be true to the event only if it followed some of the conventions of fiction" because the "conventions of academic reporting . . . would mean editing out emotions that seemed to me essential to the process."

Bateson contrasts her approach with that taken by Arthur Koestler, who organized a conference at Alpbach on a similar topic at the same time. According to Bateson, Koestler tried to separate ideas and emotions and produced two books, a conventional conference proceedings and a novel: "The emotion was edited out of the formal proceedings of the Alpbach Symposium, which came out dry and academic, and resurfaced in the novel as rage." In contrast, Bateson continues:

> There is a sense in which the emotion was edited into [my] book, for I used my own introspective responses of dismay or illumination to bring the reader into the room, and worked with the tape-recorded discussion so that the emotionally pivotal comments would be brought out rather than buried in verbiage.

The successful result of Bateson's effort is a book entitled *Our Own Metaphor* (1972), a document which uses linguistic means commonly found in fiction to "report" the proceedings of the conference. The novelistic devices, I suggest, make the ideas that emerged in the conference available to readers in a way more closely paralleling the way conference participants were able to perceive them.

To see how Bateson achieves this, consider the following excerpt which begins in the middle of an exposition presented as the dialogue of a participant called Tolly:

"I'll begin with an extremely simple picture, by way of introduction, and then elaborate it. This will be like those initial minutes in the movies when you see the introductory pictures which give you an idea of the kind of movie it's going to be while telling you who the main characters are, and so on.

"Let's imagine a pendulum swinging back and forth." Tolly hunted around for chalk and then he drew this picture. "This means that for some interval of time the pendulum swings to the right, shown by the arrow labeled R. Here's an occurrence, shown by a point, and then the pendulum swings to the left for some other interval, shown by the arrow labeled L. The occurrence is the end of the swing. You can think of the same picture as representing a billiard ball rolling back and forth on a frictionless table between two reflecting boundaries. Left, right, left, right, and the occurrences are the bounces."

Horst did a double-take. "You mean the *point* indicates the moment it changes from right to left?"

Tolly nodded gleefully. "Yeah. That's right. Unconventional." Once Horst had called my attention to it, I realized that this was indeed unconventional. The minute I stopped thinking that the arrow indicated the direction of the pendulum (which it did not, because the diagram of a light changing from red to green to red would have looked exactly the same), I realized that Tolly was doing the strange thing of using an *arrow* to represent something stable (an "interval of condition-holding" he called it) and a *point* to represent change, the occurrence that initiates new conditions. This was the exact opposite of the convention Barry had used in his diagram, where arrows had represented the transition from, say, organic to non-organic nitrogen compounds, or Fred, who had used arrows to represent causation. It was not yet clear whether these conventions were simply freakish and arbitrary, or whether this choice of symbols was a first step toward new kinds of meanings. (pp. 166–67)

It would be possible to double the length of this paper by analyzing the many ways this passage is written like fiction (and also the many ways it is not like a transcript of speech). I will refer briefly to a few.

By calling the speakers by first names (Tolly, Horst, Barry, Fred), Bateson brings us closer to them than we would feel if they were referred to by last names only (for example, Holt) or title-last-name (for example, Dr. Mittelstaedt or Professor Commoner). She presents Tolly's ideas as dialogue rather than paraphrasing them—with attendant interjections and colloquial diction ("say," "Yeah"), contractions ("I'll," "it's," "let's"), fragmented syntax ("Unconventional."), and italics for key words that would have been prosodically emphasized in speech *("point," "arrow")*. The possible responses of readers are represented, prefigured, and created by the dramatized responses of the audience-participants ("Horst did a double-take"). Note, too, that Horst's response is described as an image of nonverbal behavior, requiring the audience to supply the meaning of a double-take much as they would on observing it in interaction. Many of the paralinguistic features which frame speech by letting us know how speakers mean what they say—for example, tone of voice, rhythm, intonation, and laughter—are described and aided by adverbs ("Tolly nodded gleefully"). Moreover, the importance of the ideas is highlighted by representing the narrator's own developing cognitive state ("I realized . . ."), as well as by prefiguring future cognition ("It was not yet clear . . ."). This last device simultaneously builds suspense.

Suspense is also created by the scenically graphic but otherwise puzzling description of apparently irrelevant behavior such as "Tolly hunted around for chalk and then drew this picture." How does it contribute to our understanding of the ideas presented to tell us that the speaker hunted for chalk? Contrast this with the conventional academic-writing locution, "See Figure 1." In the latter case we see only the figure. In Bateson's description, we see not only the figure (or, rather, the "picture"), but also the human interaction that gave rise to it. Furthermore, the interruption in exposition gives readers time to prepare to focus attention on the figure/picture, much as the conference participants prepared to focus on the illustration as Tolly prepared to draw it. Finally, Tolly is represented as using a simile in his opening lines, likening the figure he is about to draw to a movie lead-in.

In deciding that she had to use techniques common in fiction in order to make the abstract ideas discussed at the cybernetics conference available to readers, Bateson acknowledged the emotional basis of cognition. To do this, she presented the ideas as dialogue. We have thus come full circle to Bleich's (to appear) observation, cited at the outset, that dialogue and affect are central.

The emotional basis of cognition is also at the heart of a discussion by Shirley Brice Heath of the process of becoming literate. Heath (1985) explains that the literacy needed for success is not merely a matter of decoding skills but rather entails a complex set of behaviors that are acquired only when written materials are integrated in a life that provides situations in which what has been read is subsequently talked about. Similarly, incipient literates must have models of literate adults with whom they feel intimate. It is the human intimacy, or involvement, that gives motivation and meaning to the acquisition of literacy, as to any other culturally significant activity.

CONCLUSION

I have shown that storytelling—conversational or literary, spoken or written—makes use of constructed dialogue which, by its particularity, occasions the imagination of alternative, distant, and other worlds. By this act of imagination, the hearer or reader participates in sense-making and is thus moved to a sense of rapport that is the means to meaning in both conversation and fiction. I demonstrated that the dialogue in a conversational story was constructed, not reported. Drawing on examples of Brazilian and American narration of Little Red Riding Hood, I suggested that the creation of dialogue is associated with "vivid" storytelling style. I illustrated the overlapping of linguistic patterns in spoken and written discourse types by presenting examples of speech and writing produced by junior high school students in three different contexts. The final section demonstrates how one writer used literary linguistic means to enhance an academic writing task, means which enhance, rather than excluding, emotional involvement.

Such mixing of genres reflects the mixing of spoken and written modes in our lives, much as Heath (1985) notes that people must talk about what they read, to be motivated to read. To dramatize this, I end with an excerpt from an essay about Lubavitcher Hasidim, an orthodox Jewish sect living in Brooklyn, New York. In this excerpt, the author, Lis Harris (1985), constructs (I shall not, for now-obvious reasons, say that she "reports") her conversation with a Hasidic man:

> "Thanks," I said. "By the way, are there any books about Hasidism that you think might be helpful?"
> "There are no books."
> "No books! Why, what do you mean? You must know that hundreds of books have been written about Hasidism."
> "Books about Hasidic matters always misrepresent things. They twist and change the truth in casual ways. I trust Lubavitcher books, like the 'Tanya' [a work written by the movement's founder] and the collections of the rebbes' discourses, because our rebbe got the information in them from the rebbe before him, and so on, in an unbroken chain. I trust scholars I can talk to, face to face."

The effectiveness of presenting this interchange of ideas as a dialogue is by now evident. Harris presents herself as naive to the point of rudeness ("You must know . . ."), so that the Hasidic man can be shown to explain his view in detail. His explanation, furthermore, dramatizes the intertwining of speaking and writing in the passing down of a written text—the Tanya—by the great religious leaders (rebbes) who are also great scholars—interpreters as well as receivers of that text. The text, in other words, is meaningless apart from its interpretation, which is found in people, not in print, and from the interaction among people ("scholars I can talk to, face to face").[12]

Heath (1986) quotes at length the poet William Carlos Williams and cites classical and medieval rhetoricians and grammarians to the effect that "literate knowledge depended ultimately on oral reformulations of that knowledge" (282). Similarly, Heath (1985) notes that early American schools emphasized opportunities for talk and for extended debate about interpretation of written materials. It is for this reason that contemporary academics are forever holding meetings, conferences, lectures, and institutes such as the present one—wanting to see scholars face to face rather than encountering them only through their written productions, and wanting to interact with them.

The Hasidic view of books, and Harris's presentation of it, like Bateson's depiction of the Burg Wartenstein conference, and her discussion of how she depicted it, underline the reason for the centrality

---

[12] A similar image of Hasidic disdain for written materials disconnected from people emerges in Myerhoff's (1978:271–72) account of a great Hasidic rabbi who "ordered that all written records of his teachings be destroyed. His words must be passed from mouth to mouth, learned by and in heart."

of dialogue and its relation to other aspects of language which create involvement in speaking and writing. Like such linguistic patterns as repetition, details, imagery, and formulaic expressions, dialogue provides particulars by which listeners and speakers collaborate in imagining and participating in similar worlds. Along with these and other poetic figures, dialogue helps provide the emotional basis of communication, for there is no understanding without caring.

REFERENCES

Bateson, Gregory. 1972. Steps to an ecology of mind. New York: Ballantine.

Bateson, Mary Catherine. 1972. Our own metaphor: A personal account of a conference on conscious purpose and human adaptation. New York: Knopf.

Bateson, Mary Catherine. 1984. With a daughter's eye: A memoir of Margaret Mead and Gregory Bateson. New York: William Morrow.

Becker, A.L. 1984. The linguistics of particularity: Interpreting superordination in a Javanese text. Proceedings of the Tenth Annual Meeting of the Berkeley Linguistics Society. Berkeley, Ca.: Linguistics Department, University of California, Berkeley, 425–36.

Bleich, David. To appear. The double perspective: Language, literacy, and social relations. Oxford: University Press.

Bloodgood, Fred "Doc". 1982. The medicine and sideshow pitches. Analyzing discourse: Text and talk. Georgetown University Round Table on Languages and Linguistics 1981, ed. by Deborah Tannen, 371–82. Washington, DC: Georgetown University Press.

Britton, James. 1982. Spectator role and the beginnings of writing. What writers know: The language, process, and structure of written discourse, ed. by Martin Nystrand, 149–69. New York: Academic Press.

Chafe, Wallace. 1982. Integration and involvement in speaking, writing, and oral literature. In Tannen 1982b, 35–53.

Coulmas, Florian (ed.) 1986. Direct and indirect speech. Berlin: Mouton.

Friedrich, Paul. 1986. The language parallax: Linguistic relativism and poetic indeterminacy. Austin: University of Texas Press.

Haberland, Hartmut. 1986. Reported speech in Danish. In Coulmas, 219–53.

Harris, Lis. 1985. Lubavitcher Hasidim, Part I. The New Yorker, September 16, 1985, 41–101.

Havelock, Eric. 1963. Preface to Plato. Cambridge, Mass.: Harvard University Press.

Heath, Shirley Brice. 1985. Being literate in America: A sociohistorical perspective. Issues in literacy: A research perspective, ed. by Jerome A. Niles & Rosary V. Lalik, 1–18. Rochester, NY: The National Reading Conference.

Heath, Shirley Brice. 1986. Literacy and language change. Languages and linguistics: The interdependence of theory, data, and application. Georgetown University Round Table on Languages and Linguistics 1985, ed. by Deborah Tannen & James E. Alatis, 282–93. Washington, DC: Georgetown University Press.

Hymes, Dell. 1973. Toward linguistic competence. Texas Working Papers in Sociolinguistics #16. Austin: Southwest Educational Development Laboratory.

Kirshenblatt-Gimblett, Barbara. 1974. The concept and varieties of narrative performance in East European Jewish culture. Explorations in the ethnography of speaking, ed. by Richard Bauman & Joel Sherzer, 283–308. Cambridge: University Press.

Labov, William. 1972. The transformation of experience in narrative syntax. Language in the inner city, 354–96. Philadelphia: University of Pennsylvania Press.

Lakoff, Robin Tolmach. 1979. Stylistic strategies within a grammar of style. Language, sex, and gender, ed. by Judith Orasanu, Mariam Slater, and Leonore Loeb Adler. Annals of the New York Academy of Science 327.53–78.

Myerhoff, Barbara. 1978. Number our days. New York: Simon & Schuster.

Ochs, Elinor. 1979. Planned and unplanned discourse. Discourse and syntax, ed. by Talmy Givon, 51–80. New York: Academic.

Ott, Mary Miglio Bensabat. 1983. Orality and literacy in Brazilian and American storytelling: A comparative study. Ms., Georgetown University.

Ricks, Christopher. 1981. Phew! Oops! Oof!: A review of Erving Goffman, Forms of talk. New York Review of Books July 16, 1981, 42–44.

Rosen, Harold. 1984. Stories and meanings. Kettering, Northamptonshire, England: National Association for the Teaching of English.

Sacks, Oliver. 1986. Reminiscence. The man who mistook his wife for a hat, 125–42. New York: Simon & Schuster.

Schiffrin, Deborah. 1981. Tense variation in narrative. Language 57:1.45–62.

Shuy, Roger. In press. The oral language basis for dialogue journals. Dialogue journal communication, by Jana Staton, Roger Shuy, Joy Kreeft-Peyton, & Leslie Reed. Norwood, NJ: Ablex.

Silber, Joan. 1976. Household words. New York: Viking.

Tannen, Deborah. 1982a. Oral and literate strategies in spoken and written narratives. Language 58:1.1–21.

Tannen, Deborah (ed.) 1982b. Spoken and written language: Exploring orality and literacy. Norwood, NJ: Ablex.

Tannen, Deborah. 1983. "I take out the rock—dok!": How Greek women tell about being molested (and create involvement). Anthropological Linguistics, Fall 1983, 359–74.

Tannen, Deborah. 1984. Conversational style: Analyzing talk among friends. Norwood, NJ: Ablex.

Tannen, Deborah. 1985. Relative focus on involvement in oral and written discourse. Literacy, language, and learning: The nature and consequences of reading and writing, ed. by David R. Olson, Nancy Torrance, and Angela Hildyard, 124–47. Cambridge: University Press.

Tannen, Deborah. 1986a. Introducing constructed dialogue in Greek and American conversational and literary narrative. In Coulmas, 311–32.

Tannen, Deborah. 1986b. That's not what I meant!: How conversational style makes or breaks your relations with others. New York: William Morrow. Paperback: Ballantine.

Tannen, Deborah. 1987a. "I had a little ham, I had a little cheese": Getting involved with details in Greek and American narrative. Paper presented at the International Pragmatics Association meeting, Antwerp, Belgium, August 1987.

Tannen, Deborah. 1987b. Repetition in conversation: Toward a poetics of talk. Language 63:3.

Tannen, Deborah. In press. Ordinary conversation and literary discourse: Coherence and the poetics of repetition. The uses of linguistics, ed. by Edward Bendix. Annals of the New York Academy of Science.

Welty, Eudora. 1984. One writer's beginnings. Cambridge, MA: Harvard University Press.

THE NATURE AND USE OF LANGUAGE AND LINGUISTIC THEORY

CHAPTER FIVE

Emergent Grammar and the A Priori Grammar Postulate*

Paul Hopper

SUNY Center at Binghamton

> But all the phenomena that led to these conclusions can be handled rather straightforwardly in a theory that supplements a strictly grammatical competence with non-trivial principles for putting that competence to use in actual speech.
>
> Newmeyer 1984:972.

> . . . a Platonist, fixing in concepts things which change and flow and adding to these concepts a further fixed concept of flowing.
>
> Dilthey 1958, vol. 5:112.

THE "APGP" AND THE EMERGENCE OF GRAMMAR

Linguistics today seems to be leaning toward two basic approaches to grammar, whose polar extremes are dominated by radically different understandings of the nature of human language. I shall refer to these two attitudes of thought as (a) the "A Priori Grammar attitude," and (b) the "Emergence of Grammar attitude." In suggesting these designations, I will not presume to identify particular linguists with one or

* The final draft of this lecture was completed during a year's leave as a Guggenheim Fellow in 1985–86. I am grateful to the John Simon Guggenheim Foundation for support which enabled me to undertake this and other projects as well as to Deborah Tannen and Wallace Chafe, Director and Associate Director of the Linguistic Institute, for having invited me to share these ideas with the participants. Thanks are also due to Sandy Thompson, Larry Roberts, and Steve Straight for their help with various aspects of the paper, though none of them are to be held accountable for any errors of fact or interpretation in it. I respectfully dedicate it to Pete Becker on the occasion of his "retirement": il miglior fabbro.

the other, since what is being described here are extreme positions; many linguists in practice occupy a place somewhere between these two poles, and either explicitly or tacitly draw from a middle ground. The first of these positions makes the initial assumption that a grammar is a discrete set of rules which are logically and mentally presupposed by discourse; that is, that grammar is logically detachable from discourse and precedes discourse. This is the postulate which I shall refer to as the A Priori Grammar Postulate (APGP). The APGP underlies a variety of current approaches to grammar. The second, the Emergence of Grammar (EOG) attitude, has come to view grammar as the name for a vaguely defined set of sedimented (i.e., grammaticized) 'recurrent partials whose status is constantly being renegotiated in speech and which cannot be distinguished *in principle* from strategies for building discourses.

Viewed from the perspective of the APGP attitude, grammar is complete and predetermined and is a prerequisite for generating discourses. From the perspective of the EOG attitude, grammar is provisional and incomplete and emerges in discourse.

The term "A Priori Grammar" as I use it here derives from Husserl and the classical tradition of phenomenology, but conceptually it has a much longer history. Edie (1977) notes, for example, that Husserl's quest for a "pure" grammar resumes a philosophical theme going back to the Middle Ages and even before; he also observes that "[t]he word 'pure' in Husserl's terminology seems to be a synonym for 'formal' " (Edie 1977:138n). Edie cites from Husserl's *Logische Untersuchungen:*

> Language has not only physiological, psychological and cultural-historical, but also a priori foundations. These last concern the essential meaning of forms and the a priori laws of their combinations and modifications, and no language is thinkable which would not be essentially determined by this a priori. (Husserl, cited in Edie 1977:139–140).

It is clear in Husserl's own writings of this period, and in Edie's paper, that it is the grammatical a priori which is the "first level of logical reflection" (Edie 1977:140). This most abstract level of grammar, logically preceding experience of the world and "empirical" grammar, that is, the specific grammar of a particular language, therefore structures and encompasses both individual grammar and perception of the world. In the terminology of classical phenomenology, it constitutes one of the fundamental "a priori structures of consciousness." Edie sees the task of modern linguistics to be that of taking up Husserl's early project of an a priori grammar. Thus, writing in 1972 (reprinted in 1977), Edie (1977:137) observes that although the idea of a universal a priori grammar has its origins in medieval thought, Husserl's project of a "pure logical grammar"—"probably the most recent full-scale proposal in this area from the side of philosophy"—has been taken up by Noam Chomsky in "a program for the study of grammar which, if it were to succeed, might seem to justify the earlier intuitions of rationalist philosophers and to give a new grounding to this ancient quest."[1]

GRAMMAR FROM TWO PERSPECTIVES

It is a constant theme in modern (post-structuralist) thought that the search for a common ground in conflicts of this kind may in the last resort be futile. Indeed, to attempt to resolve them is, paradoxically, to revert to the very structuralism whose validity is at issue, since it is itself an attempt to postulate a further A Priori which will subtend both structuralism and post-structuralism.

Attitudes Toward the Data of Linguistics

Nonetheless, there are common concerns among linguists which might form a basis for an empirical debate. The most central of these common concerns is unquestionably the nature of the data base for linguistics. The a priori grammarian finds the data supplied by "intuition," that is, private data supplemented with private judgments of grammaticality, entirely adequate as evidence concerning specific grammatical rules. For the EOG linguist, such data have only marginal status; they exist only as re-formed scraps of previous discourses, and, stripped of a context, they elicit intersubjectively shared judgments about grammaticality only to the extent that an obvious context can be reconstructed for them, or that they conform to the more sedimented conventions for constructing discourses, or, it must be added, that they violate or agree with explicit social canons concerning "good grammar."[2]

---

[1] Wilks (1972:40–41) likewise sees in Husserl's *Logische Untersuchungen* an important source, together with Russell's theory of types, for the twentieth-century drive to construct "logical systems powerful enough to distinguish the meaningful expressions of everyday language" (40), and eventually from them theories of linguistics. Wilks traces the direct line leading from Husserl to Carnap and Chomsky: "Chomsky was in fact a pupil of Carnap, just as Carnap was of Husserl" (40).

[2] The crypto-prescriptivism of sentence grammar has often been noted. An especially obvious example is found in Green (1974:63n), where the sentence:

(a) John is endeavoring to stop his hiccups, and Bill is acting like he is for the same reason

is said to contrast in acceptability with:

(b) John is endeavoring to stop his hiccups, and Bill is acting like he is for the same

Since a priori grammar is a set of rules and structures held to precede discourse and therefore to be constant across all contexts, the a priori grammarian is apt to view the sort of decontextualization which characterizes intuitional data as a prerequisite to linguistic analysis, rather than an unfortunate limitation of such data. Actual discourse is always contextualized. Linguists who study spoken language, even when it is transcribed, are rarely tempted to reduce it completely to abstract patterns related by transformations or to suggest that it is fully determined by grammatical rules. The EOG linguist is likely to argue that the recurrent partials encountered in real speech are only fragmentarily captured by the standard notion of "grammatical rules."

Attitudes Toward Temporality

Another difference between the two styles of linguistics is one of attitude toward temporality (see Linell 1982:55–7). It follows from the APGP that a grammar is a static entity, an object, which is fully present at all times in the mind of the speaker. It is therefore essentially atemporal, that is, synchronic. It is moreover homogeneous; even if it is conceived of as modular, these modules are internally homogeneous, presumably simultaneously present, and are assumed to be interrelated by clearly statable "non-trivial principles." From the EOG perspective, on the other hand, language is a real-time activity, whose regularities are always provisional and are continually subject to negotiation, renovation, and abandonment. Moreover, these regularities are not homogeneous, but are of many different kinds, no one of which can be singled out and identified vis-à-vis the others as "grammar." We need only look at the question of word order to find an obvious phenomenon whose status with respect to "grammar" is widely acknowledged to be ambiguous. But actual spoken language is replete with recurrent phenomena which are rarely assigned to "grammar." Indeed, some of the most striking regularities are those known as idioms, figures of speech, turns of phrase, proverbs, sayings, clichés, and so on—the very examples of text-building components whose a priori status between "grammar"

---

purpose.

And so for several pairs of examples involving "reason" and "purpose"—an old schoolroom chestnut, of course. In (a), since "reason" must refer to the infinitival complement of "endeavor," which is a purpose clause, the sentence must be marked as ungrammatical, whereas in (b) "purpose" matches with the purpose clause and the sentence is unobjectionable. Naive speakers of English generally react in precisely the opposite way to these two sentences when pressed. Yet a considerable part of Green's argument depends on the validity of her own private judgments concerning these two and an array of similar sentences.

and "lexicon" has so often been debated. (See, for example, Matthews 1976. It is significant that Andrew Pawley devoted a considerable part of his classes and public lecture [Pawley 1986] at LSA/TESOL Institute to the study of such "formulas".)[3]

The data, problematics, and methodology of linguistics cannot but be profoundly influenced by such considerations as these. The APGP is indifferent to prior texts, indeed its doctrine of absolute freedom in the creation of sentences within the rule system of the grammar ensures that the enormously high proportion of repetitive or partly repetitive utterances which characterize all varieties of actual of speech are treated descriptively in the same terms as such bizarre fictional sentences as "The woman died in 70,000 B.C. who invented the wheel" (given as an example in a recent published paper). Its assumption of the prior givenness of linguistic categories like Noun, Pronoun, Proper Name, and so on makes any generalization about the contexts in which discourse participants will be referred to by proper names, lexical nouns, pronouns, and so on appear to be a coincidence.

LINGUISTIC RELATIONSHIPS, CATEGORIES, AND UNITS IN RECENT RESEARCH

The view that grammar is secondary to discourse—the Emergent Grammar postulate—must be distinguished sharply from assumptions about "functionalism," the view that there are predefined grammatical structures which have discourse-functional correlates. This latter view, to which I return later in the paper, presupposes agreement about the nature and form of grammatical structure and asks only about the relationship between structure and function, wherein function is held to be distinct from form. The Emergent Grammar view entails the investigation of the way in which strategies for constructing texts *produce* the fixing of the forms which are understood to constitute grammar. This approach to grammar is implicit in a considerable amount of recent research, of which one or two examples will now be mentioned.

Goodwin (1979) showed that sentences emerged as a product of dialogic negotiation. Cumming (1984), using somewhat different arguments, has made the same point for monologic discourse: that the

---

[3] It is a familiar experience of anyone learning a foreign language that controlling the "grammar" is a deceptive enterprise, which alone—that is, to the extent that it can be isolated—is of little use to the would-be speaker. The task of foreign-language learning is not so much one of "internalizing" a set of inferentially acquired grammatical rules as one of developing an increasingly expanded repertoire of discourse-building strategies; see Becker (1984).

sentence, far from being prior to the construction of discourse, is in fact an accidental by-product of discourse. Given the unquestioned centrality of the Sentence as a basic structural unit in all contemporary versions of linguistic theory which assume the APGP, the significance of these conclusions can hardly be overemphasized.

The case for viewing the prime lexical categories Noun and Verb as derivative of acts of referring and reporting was argued by Hopper and Thompson (1984). The category Lexical Noun was shown to be associated with the introduction of significant new participants in the discourse, and that of Verb with the reporting of significant new events, while any deflection away from these functions was accompanied by a corresponding loss of characteristic morphosyntactic markers of the two categories. In this paper an analysis in terms of the emergence of the categories Noun and Verb (and, by implication, other "parts of speech") was explicitly contrasted with one in which these categories were postulated as a priori abstract units of grammar.

The Transitivity relation between a verb and its object was shown (Hopper and Thompson 1980) to be correlated with discourse fore-grounding, and to involve not solely the presence of a syntactic object, but a set of parameters which are themselves discourse parameters, such as the discourse-referentiality of both agent and patient, the per-fectivity of the reported event, the effectiveness of the action, and so on.

Recently, Givon and a number of collaborators (see, for example, Givon [1983], especially Givon's introductory chapter) have undertaken a massive and significant study of the quantification of topic continuity in a variety of languages, showing that distinctions among referential forms and constructions respond to broad principles of relative saliency and assumed degree of recoverability among discourse topics.

Du Bois's (1985) work on Preferred Argument Structure makes important observations about the calibration between preferred ways of packaging discourse information in clauses and clausal morphosyntax.

It seems appropriate to amplify the present discussion by some specific examples of Emergent Grammar, and since Du Bois's work has for me greatly clarified certain ideas of my own on Malay, I will describe here some of the applications of this direction of research to problems of clause structure in Malay. In particular, Du Bois's expla-nation of the direction of grammaticization in ergative morphology in the Mayan language Sacapultec has a virtually exact counterpart in Malay. In the following section I will present the outline of a textually-based argument concerning some aspects of emergent clause structure in Malay. A somewhat fuller discussion is given in Hopper (1983), from which some of the following is drawn, but the interpretation of the phenomena in terms of Preferred Argument Structure is new. The textual data used are from a nineteenth century document, the Hikayat Abdullah (Abdullah 1932).

TEXTUALITY AND CLAUSAL GRAMMAR IN MALAY

The variety of Malay discussed here exists in a written text, created in the Perso-Arabic script and transliterated and punctuated by European editors. It is a narrative, about 300 pages long, the life story of a Malay writer, Abdullah, who lived in Malacca and Singapore in the first half of the nineteenth century.

Clause Structure and Clausal Semantics

The relationship between text and grammar is mediated by preferred ways of formulating clauses in specific discourse contexts. Clauses both respond structurally to textuality and are central to the ongoing process of constructing textuality. Like other linguistic units, therefore, clauses cannot be described in isolated, autonomous terms "first" (i.e. a priori) and then fitted into a discourse frame; instead the clause must always be seen as having a particular role in the construction of the text, and its form understood, however imperfectly and incompletely, from that perspective alone.

There is thus no pre-existing ideal (invariant) form for "a clause" from which the clauses actually found in discourse can be derived. But there are certain recurrent types of clause whose frequency reflects the frequency of particular strategies for building texts. One of these strategies is that of foregrounding (Hopper 1977, 1979). Foregrounded discourse is that in which successive events of the discourse are reported, usually carried out by a significant participant or otherwise having a significant bearing on the development of the narrative line. In the construction of a discourse, foregrounding contrasts with backgrounding, in which states and situations are described, motives are attributed, and actions incidental to the main line of the discourse are reported. The semantics and structure of the clause in Malay reflect these two strategies, foregrounding and backgrounding, in both word order and in grammaticized morphology.

The Preferred Argument Structure in Malay

A fairly restricted repertoire of short and simple clause types accounts for a considerable proportion of Malay discourse. Consider, for example, the following passage from the Hikayat Abdullah; in it, one of the central characters, Raffles, is suspicious about a letter he has received:

(1) maka sa-bentar sa-bentar di-ambil-nya   surat itu, di-renong-nya,
     and   from time to time   PASS-take-AGT. letter the PASS.-stare:at-AGT.

kemudian di-letakkan-nya,   demikian-lah laku-nya.
then   PASS.-put:down-AGT. such -LAH   behavior-his

Maka sa-hari-hari adat-nya ia berkereta pada petang-petang;
and   daily   habit his he go:driving on   afternoon

maka pada hari itu sampai malam   kereta   menanti di-pintu, tiada ia
and   on   day that until   evening carriage remain at-door   not   he

mau turun   dari rumah-nya . . .
want go:down from house-his

"and this was his behavior: every now and then he took the letter, stared at it, and then put it down again. It was his custom to go for a drive every day in the afternoon; but on that day his carriage remained at the gate, and he would not leave his house."

This fragmentary discourse is seen to be constructed from simple clausal nuclei accompanied by conjunctions and by adverbials of time and place. When these non-nuclear items are stripped away, what remains are transitive clauses:

di-ambil-nya surat itu "he took the letter"
di-renong-nya "he stared at it"
di-letakkan-nya "he put it down"

and intransitive clauses:

demikian-lah laku-nya "thus was his behavior"
ia berkereta "he went for a drive"
kereta menanti "the carriage remained"
tiada ia mau turun "he did not want to leave"

In this passage, the transitive clauses are foregrounded—they constitute the actions of a central participant carried out in sequence and centrally important to this part of the text. The intransitive clauses, on the other hand, tell us backgrounded information—what usually happened (but on this occasion did not), and so on.

Clause Structure in Foregrounding

The transitive clauses illustrate a further phenomenon of Malay, that in foregrounded discourse the subject-object type of clause is ergative. Thus the third-person agent -nya has this form only if an object is present or implied. (The prefix di- on the verb, often referred to as a "passive," is a grammaticized agreement marker for third person transitive agents.) In the background clauses, which are here all subject-only clauses (no object is present or implied), the third person agent has the form ia if a pronoun.

The importance of the simple transitive clause in foregrounded narrative is confirmed when further samples of the text are examined; it occurs repeatedly, especially when human agents who are central participants in the discourse are involved. These are, of course, the very kinds of clauses to which the characterization "foregrounded" can be most often applied. But a further significant fact having a direct bearing on the structure of foregrounded clauses emerges when the role of lexical nouns as opposed to clitics is considered.

Lexical nouns. The first noteworthy thing about lexical nouns is their relative distribution over clauses in the text. In no clause is there a full noun in both the nuclear roles Agent and Patient. To some extent this is a coincidence—a more extensive text would reveal plenty of examples of clauses in which both Agent and Patient were full nouns. But they would be in a distinct minority; about one in ten in ordinary narrative.[4] Far more typical is the situation in which clauses consist overtly of a verb with at the most one lexical argument.

A second peculiarity is the distribution of these lexical nouns over the nuclear roles. Although in the text as a whole we find that lexical nouns and nonlexical referents (clitics and autonomous pronouns) are about equal numerically, when we examine the assignment of nouns to the nuclear roles of Agent and Patient, we find a considerable skewing. The full nouns are most frequently (on an average of seven out of eight occurrences of lexical nouns) patients and transitive verbs or presentative subjects of intransitive verbs. On the other hand, the non-lexical arguments—clitics, pronouns, and zero anaphora—are about equally distributed over the roles of transitive Agent and intransitive Agent, but are less frequently found in the role of transitive Patient. The favored role for lexical nouns, then, is seen to be the "absolutive"— the intransitive agent or the transitive object. While pronouns occur freely in the role of intransitive agent, the role of transitive Agent—

---

[4] And it must be recalled that we are dealing with a text created in the written mode. In oral texts an even smaller number of clauses with both lexical agent and lexical patient could be expected.

the ergative—is almost always filled by a clitic (-nya if third person singular). Malay is thus entirely similar to what Du Bois (1985) has described for Sacapultec Maya: it has a "Preferred Argument Structure" in which lexical nouns, if any, are absolutives, and agents are reduced to clitics on initial verbs. Less favored are (a) lexical nouns as transitive agents, and (b) pronouns as transitive patients.

Overt case marking and preferred argument structure. Looking again at the text as a whole, we notice the development of a further pattern characteristic of these two less-preferred argument structures. Consider the following two examples of clauses containing a pronominal transitive patient:

(2) tiada-lah di-sahut   oleh Tuan Raffles *akan dia* sebab   marah-nya
    not   PASS.-greet AGT. Mr. Raffles   ACC. him because-of anger-his
"Out of anger, Mr. Raffles did not greet him."

(3) Maka di-naikkan oleh   orang-lah   *akan daku* ka-atas pandang itu
    and   PASS.-lift AGT. people-PRTCLE ACC. me   onto   platform the
"and they lifted me up onto the platform."

The pattern is this: in foregrounded discourse definite lexical transitive agents and definite pronominal transitive patients tend to receive a prepositional marker. Less frequently, a definite lexical patient will also be so marked. This preposition is oleh for the agent and akan for the patient. Moreover, the pronouns themselves have special forms after the preposition:

aku: akan daku "I: me"
ia: akan dia "he/she/they: him/her/them"[5]

The prepositions are thus analogous to case markers, oleh as ergative and akan as accusative. The point to be made is that the overt case markers oleh "ergative" and akan "accusative" appear preferentially in those forms—the lexical transitive agent and the pronominal transitive patient—which are least preferred in global discourse terms, and in which therefore the case relationship is most explicit.

It is especially interesting that these forms are not categorical, that

---

[5] Dia, but not daku, occurs more generally as an independent pronoun; in the text daku appears to be restricted to object of the preposition akan and, interestingly, object of verbs with the explicit transitivizing suffix -kan. But see Favre (1875: 833), where an example of daku without a preposition or preceding -kan is given, suggesting that it was partly grammaticized as an accusative form; Favre notes the apparent phonological development of the initial d after a nasal-final morpheme, that is, akan + aku —> akan (d)aku, with daku being analyzed as an object form.

is, grammaticized; object forms without the preposition are also found. But where the preposition appears it is almost always with a pronoun rather than with a lexical noun.

Clause Structure in Backgrounding

In backgrounded discourse—discourse in which generic remarks and comments are made, motives are being attributed, landscapes and other kinds of settings described, and so on—the Preferred Argument Structure is replaced by one in which lexical nouns are more frequent in all roles. Consider, for example, a passage such as the following:

(4) maka orang Malaka semua-nya menutup pintu rumah-nya
    and people Malacca all-of-them shut   door house-their

maka ada-lah   berkeliling lorong itu beberapa matrus itu mabok,
and there-will all-around streets the many   sailors the drunk

yang ada memechahkan pintu-pintu rumah orang,
some   broke-down doors   house people

dan yang ada mengejar perempuan-perempuan berjalan.
and some   chased   women   walking

". . . and the people of Malacca would all shut their doors, and around all the streets there would be sailors getting drunk, and smashing down doors, and chasing women as they walked."

In this kind of discourse, no single topic is carried through the discourse, but a variety of different topics occur. Consequently, lexical nouns are not confined to the role of transitive patient, but occur freely in all positions, for example:

(5) orang Malaka semua-nya pintu rumah-nya "the people of Malacca would all shut their doors"

To these examples may be added the examples already discussed from the passage about Raffles:

(6) maka sa-hari-hari adat-nya ia berkereta pada petang-petang
    and daily   habit-his he drive   on   afternoons
"and every day it was his custom to go for a drive in the afternoon"

maka pada hari itu kereta   menanti di-pintu
and on   day that carriage remain at-door
"but on that day his carriage remained at the door"

tiada ia mau turun   dari rumah-nya
not   he want go-down from house-his
"he did not want to leave the house"

Predication in Discourse

From the last example, backgrounding can be seen to involve not merely lexical subjects, but a *word order in which a full noun or a nonenclitic pronoun precedes the verb*. Indeed, these two aspects of backgrounding are not clearly to be differentiated: a lexical or pronominal subject is likely to precede the verb in backgrounding precisely because almost always in backgrounding a state or attribute is being predicated of an entity, whereas in foregrounding events are being reported in sequence involving the same agent. Hence the word order Subject-Verb (SV) of backgrounding as distinct from the VS of foregrounding is not arbitrary, but emerges directly from the characteristically different roles of participants in backgrounding (predication) as opposed to foregrounding (reporting what happened). This account of predication as a relationship which emerges from a certain discourse strategy can be compared to the account of predication given by traditional and a priori grammar, in which predication is held to exist, at least implicitly, in all sentences.

The verbal prefixes me(ng)- and (for third person or nonspecified agents) di- accompany a preverbal lexical agent or patient respectively. The first of these, the SV clause type in which the S is a transitive or intransitive agent, is referred to as the Active clause type, and the second, in which the S is a patient of a transitive verb, is referred to as the Passive (see Hopper 1983). Thus the following are examples of the Active and Passive respectively:

(7) maka orang Malaka semua-nya menutup pintu rumah nya
     and   people Malacca all-of-them close   door house their
"and the people of Malacca would shut their doors"

(8) maka dua puncha kiri-kanan itu di-matikan.
     and   two ends   right left the PASS.-knot
"and the two ends right and left are knotted"

These clauses with extended lexical noun subjects lend themselves to a slower tempo, a more static and less dynamic kind of discourse, than the "preferred" clause type with its terse cliticized arguments and a lexical noun, if any, following the verb.

This difference manifests itself in a difference of transitivity between the SV type and the Preferred clause type.[6]

Preferred Argument Structure and Transitivity

"Transitivity" as used here is a relative term referring to the degree to which a clause approaches canonical transitivity. The parameters of canonical transitivity assumed there are those set forth in Hopper and Thompson (1980); they include not only the presence of an agent and a patient, but also the perfectivity of the action, the action's dynamicity and effectiveness, the specificity of the patient, and the volitional involvement of the agent.

As already noted, the Ergative clause type contrasts with the two other types (Active and Passive) as verb-initial to noun-initial, where "noun" can stand for either a lexical noun or an autonomous pronoun. There is, in fact, more than a mere word order difference involved here. For example, the "passive," that is, the patient-verb-agent sentence type, often lacks a recoverable agent; it is often used in the description of artifacts, for example, much like the English passive, and in general where a state predication is made of a patient, as in:

(9) ada pun   apit China itu di-perbuat   dari rotan sega
    now PARTCL press Chinese the PASS.-make from rattan best
"Now the Chinese press is made from the finest rattan"

(10) maka dua puncha kiri kanan itu di-matikan
     and two ends   left right the PASS.-knot
"and the two ends right and left are knotted"

(11) karena binatang itu di-laparkan   beberapa hari
     because animal   the PASS.-starve several   day
"because the animals had been starved for several days"

The Ergative, on the other hand, rarely lacks an agent. In an entirely parallel way, the "active," that is, the agent-verb-patient type of clause, may have a non-specific (e.g., indefinite, generic, abstract, non-individuated) patient, while in the ergative non-specific patients are rare:

(12) maka salah-nya sadikit, ia memakai chara Inggeris sahaja, maka
     and pity-its   a-little he wear   style English only   and

jikalau ia memakai chara China   make sa-orang pun tiada mengenal
if   he wear   style Chinese then no-one   at-all not   know

---

[6] An entirely similar correlation of Transitivity with favored clause types is described by Lambrecht in his studies of spoken French (for example Lambrecht [to appear]).

ia orang puteh ada-nya
he man white indeed

"It was a pity, really, that he wore only English clothes, for if he had
dressed like a Chinese, no one would ever have taken him for a European."

The active and the passive are thus complementary in discourse
terms: the passive is a patient-verb construction whose agent is unimportant, and the active is an agent-verb construction with a vague
patient. The ergative on the other hand reports an event in which two
specific participants in the discourse interact. Now it can be shown
that the ergative clause type, most frequently manifested in its Preferred
Argument Structure form, is more transitive than the other two clause
types presented here, the Subject-Verb-Object type ("Active") and the
Patient-Verb-Agent type ("Passive"). This means that the ergative clause
type is more likely in actual texts to rate higher on an average for the
transitivity features than the other two types; actual counts (Hopper
1983:80–81) yielded an average of 8.62 "plus" parameters (out of 10
parameters) for the Ergative against 4.78 and 5.26 for the Passive and
Active type respectively. Transitivity, with its semantic and structural
concomitants, thus emerges from the discourse situation in which an
event involving two specific participants in the discourse is being
reported, one of which, the agent, is an on-going topic and the other,
the patient, may also be topical or may be new or re-introduced; in
either case, the patient is an actual participant of the discourse, and
not merely a generic concept.

It might be asked why in general terms there should be this correlation
between transitivity and foregrounded events, and whether an intransitive action is unable to qualify as a foregrounded event? Of course
many events in a discourse are intransitive; yet they are in a distinct
minority in foregrounding. More natural seems to be the situation in
which a sequenced event has a limiting object, a second participant,
against which a subsequent event can be sequenced. In an inquiry into
this question (Hopper and Thompson 1979), Sandra Thompson and I
pointed out that intransitive actions which are part of an event sequence
require some other kind of limit:

(13)   I smoked a cigarette and (then) left the room
(14)   ? I smoked and (then) left the room.

We want to add something to the verb to play out the first action
before the second is launched. In these sorts of contexts, the verbal
object plays a limiting role. Intransitive events, which of course have

no second participant, are usually limited with a time adverbial; and there are interesting exceptions such as "dine," "pray," "dance," and others, in which the limiting factor is some kind of socially prescribed event boundary. What they have in common is a unified role in the construction of a narrative, that is, the kind of discourse in which events are reported in sequence.

It is from such natural ways of constructing discourse—"text-building," to use Becker's (1979) insightful term—that the phenomena we think of as "grammar," such as the classification of verbs into transitive and intransitive, perfective and imperfective, and so on, develop and become sedimented.

A Debate over "Functionalism"

Two recent critical tacks undertaken by proponents of a priori grammar have claimed to undermine work in the emergence of grammar by suggesting (a) that there is a fundamental mismatch between the data of sentence grammar and the data of "discourse grammar" (e.g. Morgan 1981), and (b) that "functionalism" cannot be a grounding for structural phenomena unless all known linguistic structures can be assigned a functional explanation (e.g. Sadock 1984).

In regard to the first of these, it is obviously the case that since the study of sentence grammar is undertaken from the point of view of the APGP, it is unlikely that it will ever reach a point where it is capable of being applied meaningfully to discourse; consequently in practical terms, and very conveniently for some, the tasks of linguistics must remain confined to the working out of the calculus of the structures of imaginary utterances (shielded, perhaps, by some disclaimer such as "competence"), occasionally supplemented by reference to equally imaginary uses to which such utterances might be put.

Perhaps a misunderstanding here has to do with an oversimplification in the contrast "sentence grammar—discourse grammar," which assumes that the centrality of the Sentence as a unit is axiomatic and universally agreed upon, and that only the relationship between Sentences and discourse is at issue. The Sentence is in fact by no means unproblematic; discourse studies by Goodwin (1979) and Cumming (1984), among others, have pointed to a secondary emergence of the Sentence either as a collaborative enterprise (Goodwin) or as a rhetorical amalgamation of clauses (Cumming). The problems with the Sentence exist at every level—historical, ontogenetic, psychological, and universal-grammatical. Several linguists (e.g. Kalmar 1978, Linell 1979:62–71, Harris 1980:18) have noted the obvious dependency between the Sentence and written language, specifically in the Western grammatical-rhetorical tradition. Before conclusions about "sentence grammar" can be accepted, they must be anchored in studies proving the autonomy of the Sentence. Few linguists will any longer accept its axiomatic status in an abstract theory. These studies must, moreover, be ones which do not themselves proceed from the assumption of the autonomy of the Sentence, but test the value of the unit Sentence vis-à-vis competing postulated units such as clause, paragraph, topic-chain and so on. The challenge to a priori linguistics is profound. The assumed priority and autonomy of the Sentence are at the head of a line of implications which lead to the "modularity" of syntax, semantics, and pragmatics—the separation of structure from meaning, and meaning from use: "The money, and the cow that you can buy with it" (Wittgenstein 1958:#120 [p. 49]).

Similarly with those who believe they have discovered a "functionalist fallacy"—the alleged fallacy that "functionalism" must fail so long as one single grammatical fact cannot be assigned a discourse-functional explanation (e.g. Sadock 1984). Here too there is a strong assumption that grammar is an a priori set of abstract rules and structures whose nature is not in dispute. The supposed dispute over "functionalism" is held to consist in the choice between two positions: either grammar is redundant, being wholly derivative of function, or function is irrelevant, being a separate system only in part isomorphic with structure. In order to disprove the first of these two positions, it is necessary only to show that some phenomenon universally agreed to be "grammatical" cannot be related to any phenomenon agreed to be "functional." But the terms of the debate presuppose agreement about the deterministic view of grammar as a static, prioristic, complete system. Such a view is ideologically at odds with the view of grammar as provisional and emergent, not isolatable in principle from general strategies for constructing discourses. Until such fundamental philosophical differences can be reconciled, the very nature of "function" and the role of "pragmatics" remain moot. Indeed the term "pragmatics" itself must be put on probation as long as it is understood to be opposed to syntax and semantics as discrete modules competing for priority.

CONCLUSION

As I suggested earlier in the lecture, no single analysis or set of linguistic evidence will decisively validate the Emergence of Grammar approach over the A Priori Grammar Postulate approach to language; specific examples and specific counterexamples are meaningless unless the pre-suppositions which underlie statements about language are agreed upon. We have, in other words, what might be called two competing ideologies, corresponding broadly to the two major intellectual trends of our day: structuralism, with its belief in and attention to a priori structures of consciousness and behavior, and hermeneutics, with its equally firm conviction that temporality and context are continually reshaping the elusive present.

REFERENCES

Abdullah bin Abdul Kadir. 1932. Hikayat Abdullah. Singapore: Malaya Publishing House. (Malay Literature Series No. 4.)

Becker, A.L. 1979. Text-building, epistemology, and aesthetics in Javanese shadow theatre. The imagination of reality: Essays in Southeast Asian coherence systems, ed. by A.L. Becker and Aram A. Yengoyan, 211–43. Norwood, NJ: Ablex.

Becker, A.L. 1984. Toward a post-structuralist view of language-learning: A short essay. An Epistemology for the Language Sciences, ed. by A. Guiora, 217–220. Detroit: Wayne State University Press.

Cumming, Susan. 1984. The sentence in Chinese. Studies in Language 8:3. 365–395.

Dilthey, Wilhelm. 1958. Gesammelte Schriften. Stuttgart: Teubner.

Du Bois, John. 1985. Competing motivations. Iconicity in syntax, ed. by John Haiman, 343–366. Amsterdam: Benjamins.

Edie, James M. 1977 [1972]. Husserl's conception of 'The Grammatical' and contemporary linguistics. Reprinted in Readings on Edmund Husserl's Logical Investigations, ed. by J.N. Mohanty, 137–161. The Hague: Nijhoff.

Favre, P., l'Abbé. 1875. Dictionnaire malais-français. 2 vols. Paris: Maisonneuve.

Givon, Talmy, ed. 1983. Topic continuity in discourse: a quantitative cross-language study. Amsterdam: Benjamins.

Goodwin, Charles. 1979. The interactive construction of a sentence in everyday conversation. Everyday Language: Studies in Ethnomethodology. ed. by George Psathas, 97–122. New York: Irvington Publishers.

Green, Georgia. 1974. Semantics and syntactic regularity. Bloomington: Indiana University Press.

Harris, Roy. 1980. The language-makers. London: Duckworth.

Hopper, Paul J. 1977. Observations on the typology of focus and aspect in narrative language. NUSA 4. Jakarta. Reprinted in Studies in Language 3.37–64, 1979.

Hopper, Paul J. 1979. Aspect and foregrounding in discourse. ed. by Talmy Givon, 213–242. Discourse and Syntax, New York: Academic Press.

Hopper, Paul J. 1983. Ergative, passive, and active in Malay narrative. In Discourse perspectives on syntax, ed. by Flora Klein-Andreu, 67–90. NY: Academic Press.

Hopper, Paul J., and Sandra A. Thompson, 1979. A discourse explanation for 'specified' and 'unspecified' objects in universal grammar. Paper presented at the Annual Meeting of the Linguistic Society of America, Los Angeles.

Hopper, Paul J., and Sandra A. Thompson. 1980. Transitivity in grammar and discourse. Language 56:3.251–299.

Hopper, Paul J., and Sandra A. Thompson. 1984. The discourse basis for lexical categories in universal grammar. Language 60:4.703–751.

Kalmar, Ivan. 1978. Literacy and the sentence. Paper presented at the Annual Meeting of the Educational Research Association, Toronto.

Lambrecht, Knud. To appear. On the status of SVO sentences in French discourse. Coherence and grounding in discourse, ed. by Russ Tomlin. Amsterdam: John Benjamins BV.

Linell, Per. 1982. The written language bias in linguistics. Linköping: University of Linköping, Studies in Communication 2.

Matthews, P.H. 1976. Review of Jerrold Sadock, Toward a linguistic theory of speech acts. General Linguistics 16.236–242.

Morgan, Jerry. 1981. Some observations on discourse and sentence grammar. Studies in the Linguistic Sciences 11.137–144.

Newmeyer, F.J. 1984. Review of Lorraine Obler and Lise Menn, eds., Exceptional language and linguistics. Language 60:4.969–975.

Pawley, Andrew. 1986. Lexicalization. Languages and Linguistics: The interdependence of theory, data, and application, ed. by Deborah Tannen and James E. Alatis, 98–120. Georgetown University Round Table on Languages and Linguistics 1985. Washington, D.C.: Georgetown University Press.

Sadock, Jerrold M. 1984. Whither radical pragmatics? Meaning, form, and use in context: Linguistic applications, ed. by Deborah Schiffrin, 139–149. Georgetown University Round Table on Languages and Linguistics 1984. Washington, DC: Georgetown University Press.

Wilks, Yorick A. 1972. Grammar, meaning and the machine analysis of language. London: Routledge and Kegan Paul.

Wittgenstein, Ludwig. 1958. Philosophical investigations. The English Text of the Third Edition, tr. G.E.M. Anscombe. New York: Macmillan.

CHAPTER SIX

Discourse as an Interactional Achievement II: An Exercise In Conversation Analysis*

Emanuel A. Schegloff

University of California, Los Angeles

INTRODUCTION

Let me begin by making my intentions clear. First, I mean to satisfy one concern of an occasion such as this, which is to have some display by the participating visitors of what they know and of what they do in the enterprise in which they are engaged. In my case it seemed useful that I display in some fashion what data analysis looks like in the mode of work in which I participate, which is concerned with the understanding of talk-in-interaction, whose main mode is conversation, which I take to be the primordial site of sociality and social life.

There are several forms which data analysis takes in this enterprise. In one of these, the effort is to elucidate and describe the structure of a coherent, naturally bounded phenomenon or domain of phenomena,

* Much of the analysis presented here was first developed in my courses at UCLA beginning in 1975–76. In its present form, it was initially prepared as a public lecture to be delivered when I was Scholar-in-Residence at the 1985 LSA/TESOL Institute and was subsequently presented in revised form to Sociology and/or Linguistics colloquia at the University of California, Los Angeles, Santa Barbara, and Santa Cruz. Other versions were presented respectively as the McGovern Distinguished Lecture in the College of Communications, University of Texas, Austin in March, 1986, and as a keynote address to the annual meeting of the Sociolinguistic Symposium at the University of Newcastle-Upon-Tyne, U.K. in April, 1986. My thanks to various persons at these various occasions, and to Charles and Marjorie Goodwin, for comments and questions.

A somewhat different version of this paper was published in the *Social Psychology Quarterly*, 50:2, June, 1987. The present publication is by agreement with the American Sociological Association.

and the way in which it works and is organized. For this, one ordinarily works with a collection of fragments of talk-in-interaction which instantiate the phenomenon and its variants, or which exemplify something of the range of phenomena composing the domain: a set of fragments, then, to explicate a single phenomenon or a single domain of phenomena.

That is not the way I intend to proceed here. Rather I intend to engage in a sort of exercise in which I will bring to bear references to a range of already somewhat described phenomena and organizational domains to explicate a single fragment of talk.[1] Some of the past work I draw on will be previously unknown to some of you; to some the very terms of analysis will be strange; still there may be some new wrinkle even for those knowledgeable in the area. My main intention, however, is not the introduction of previously unknown findings. It is, rather, an exercise in using hopefully already gained knowledge to analyze the sort of data which, in this view, we ought to be able to analyze. And what sorts of data are those? A bit of disciplinary context, in this instance largely sociological, is in order.

I take it that we are engaged, among other things, in the study of the organization of social action. For that is what talking in interaction is. However humble the occasion and however apparently trivial the pursuit, the bits of talk we study are lent dignity by being instances of social action in the real worlds of people's lives—instances through which much grander themes can often be more clearly seen. One point which seems clear to me is that, in a great many respects, social action done through talk is organized and orderly on a case by case basis, and not only as a matter of rule or as a statistical regularity. Particular complements of participants on singular occasions of interaction proceed in to-them orderly ways; or, failing this, have ways of coping with the apparent lack of order which can also be invoked and applied on a single case basis. Permit me two anecdotal exemplars of the relevance of the single occasion as the locus of order.

Many years ago (Schegloff, 1968), I formulated a proposed regularity about a type of conversational occurrence, a formulation which adequately described 499 of the 500 cases I was working with—a good batting average by most social scientific standards. But the puzzle was:

---

[1] Examination of single fragments has been used in other ways as well. For example, Sacks (1975, and throughout his lectures) uses analysis of a single fragment as a way of introducing and constraining an account of a practice or set of practices, as does C. Goodwin (1984). Jefferson (1980) brings to bear the analytic tools and possibilities developed in the first part of the paper on a single extended instance, as a sort of test and payoff of the analysis. For another exercise along the lines of the present effort, see Schegloff (1984 [1976]).

how about the participants in that 500th case; they had achieved the outcome in question (getting a telephone conversation underway) also, somehow. How? And was there some account of the "how" that could include both the single case and the other 499?

The present occasion is also an instance of talk-in-interaction, although not of conversation. Such talks, or addresses, have familiar organizational forms and practices. But if I should now begin producing some bizarre behavior, I daresay most of you, perhaps all of you, would find it insufficient to set this aside as just a statistical anomaly. It would not suffice to consider that all the previous lectures/colloquia you have attended followed one or another canonical form; that there was bound to be a case which deviated; and that this is it. Rather, you would find yourselves making some sense or other of what was going on, and finding some way of conducting yourselves that would deal with this situation. On reflection, of course, that is what you have done in each of the ordinary such occasions in which you have participated in the past; you have found on each singular occasion whether and when to laugh, when to knit the brow, whether and when to applaud, when and how to leave early if it was a bore or you were not feeling well or both, and how to indicate which of these was the case.

Accordingly, the analytic machinery which we develop, intended as it is to explicate the orderly procedures of the participants in interaction (conversational or otherwise), should be able to deal in an illuminating manner with single episodes of talk taken from "the real world." There *is* a constitutive order to singular occasions of interaction, and to the organization of action within them. This is the bedrock of social life— what I called earlier the primordial site of sociality. And social science theorizing, both sociological and linguistic, must be answerable to it, and to the details of its actual, natural occurrences. That is an inescapable responsibility of social theory, and perhaps a priority one, for much other social analysis presumes it. Whatever concerns for macro-social issues we entertain, our ways of dealing with them will in the end have to be compatible with a capacity to address the details of single episodes of action through talking in interaction.

So this is what I mean in proposing to undertake the analysis of a singular episode of interaction, to exemplify and to assess our capacity to deal with the sort of data with which we ought to be able to deal. I mean to provide an exercise in a kind of decomposition, in which various empirically-based analytic resources are drawn on to see how an utterance from an ordinary conversation is put together, what it does, how it works. And thereby to provide by illustration a sort of access to one mode of conversation analysis, and a suggestion of one way to provide an analytic capacity to address the details of singular episodes of ordinary interaction.

ACHIEVING THE TURN IN/AND ITS SEQUENCE: LOOKING FORWARD

The utterance which I would like to examine with you occurs at lines 16-18 of Segment 1 below.[2] The excerpt starts at the beginning of a new spate of talk—a new sequence, if you will, and has been modified to omit most of a separate simultaneous conversation, with the exception of a child's summons to the dog at line 15. The main characters in the interaction are Curt, dressed in white and seated nearest to the camera, the host of this backyard picnic; next to him is Gary (the husband of Curt's cousin), who is involved in the separate conversation for most of this episode but joins into our target conversation near the end of the segment we will examine. Across the table from Gary is Mike, a friend of Curt's but not well known to Gary. Next to him, and across from Curt, is Phyllis—Mike's wife. The main axis of this sequence is talk between Curt and Mike. I will reserve further characterization of the talk and of the setting until later. As I say, I want to focus our attention on Curt's utterance at lines 16-18. (For transcription conventions, see Appendix.)

Segment 1

```
 1. Curt:      (W'll) how wz the races las'night.
 2.            (0.8)
 3. Curt:      Who w'n ⌈ th'feature.  ⌉
 4. Mike:      ⌊ Al won,   ⌋
 5.            (0.3)
 6. Curt:      ⌈ (Who) ⌉ =
 7. Mike:      ⌊ Al.   ⌋ =
 8. Curt:      =Al did?
 9.            (0.8)
10. Curt:      Dz he go out there pretty regular?
11.            (1.5)
12. Mike:      Generally evry Saturdee.
13.            (1.2)
14. Phyllis:   He wins js about every Saturday too:.
```

---

[2] The segment is taken from a videotape recorded by Charles and Marjorie Goodwin in central Ohio in the early 1970s, and a transcript produced by them and Gail Jefferson. My thanks to the Goodwins for the use of this material.

```
15. Ryan:    Bo⌈ : Bo!
16. Curt:      ⌊He- He's about the only regular<he's about
17.          the only good regular out there. 'z Keegan still go
18.          out?=
19. Mike:    =Keegan's, (0.2) out there (,) he's, He run,
20.          (0.5)
21. Mike:    E:⌈r he's uh::                    ⌉
22. Gary:      ⌊Wuhyih mean my:,               ⌋
23. Gary:    My⌈ brother in law's out there,  ⌉
24. Mike:      ⌊ doin real good this year'n   ⌋M'Gilton's
25.          doin real good thi⌈ s year,
26. Curt:                       ⌊ M'Gilton still there?=
27. Gary:    =hHawki⌈ ns,
28. Curt:           ⌊ Oxfrey (run?-) I heard Oxfrey gotta new
29.          ca:r.
30. Gary:    Hawkins is ru⌈ nnin,
31. Mike:                  ⌊ Oxfrey's runnin the same car 'e
32.          run last year,=
33. Phyllis: =Mike siz there wz a big fight down there
34.          las' night,
```

I'm just going to begin with some observations—observations that may help render the utterance investigable, and ones which may help advance its analysis.

A first observation is that the utterance that occupies this turn-at-talk is composed of two turn-constructional units—units of the sort a speaker may set out to build a turn with. In this case, they are both sentences: "he's about the only good regular out there" (together with its included repairs) and "does Keegan still go out." Using the model of turn-taking organization developed in the Sack/Schegloff/Jefferson paper on that topic (1974), a multi-unit turn is of potential analytic interest on those grounds alone. On this model, unless a speaker has somehow provided a projection of some extended type of turn (Sacks 1975; Schegloff 1980) other participants may treat the end of a first unit (such as a sentence) as an appropriate place for them to talk, and, if they do so and start to talk there and encounter no resistance, the turn will end up with one turn-constructional unit in it. This possibility builds in a structural constraint in the direction of minimization of turn size, systematically providing an occasion for transition to a next speaker at the end of a first turn-unit. Talk by a speaker which is made up of more than one unit—a "discourse" in one sense of that term—may therefore be treated as an achievement (Schegloff, 1982),[3] something that took doing in the face of some potential resistance.

---

[3] The present paper is in several respects a sequel to the 1982 paper; hence the inclusion of the numeral "II" in the title.

It may be worth noting that this is one respect in which the model of turn-taking with which I am operating differs from that put forward by Duncan and his associates (Duncan 1972; Duncan & Fiske 1977). Aside from the differences in generality of scope (Duncan's model would be hard to apply here for it deals only with the case of two-person interaction and there are four participants here), the speaker in Duncan's model does not encounter such structurally in-built potential resistance as is provided by possible turn-completion in the Sacks/ Schegloff/Jefferson model, and an utterance such as the one under examination would be of no special interest, at least on these grounds, from the point of view of that model. Of course, not every multi-unit turn will turn out to be interesting (on this or any other account). But having noted this feature about this turn, we can ask if anything special seems to have been done to achieve a multi-unit turn here; or, more precisely, if anything special seems to have been done to get a second turn-constructional unit in. And that leads to a second observation.

The second observation is that this second turn-constructional unit *is* an achievement. In particular, it is not the default product of a failure by another participant to talk after Curt has brought his turn to a possible completion; such a failure of uptake by another could yield a gap of silence which the prior speaker, Curt, might then fill with an addition to *his* talk. This is another way multi-unit turns can get produced.

This multi-unit turn was not produced in that manner, however. Rather, Curt methodically organizes the production of his talk—that is, the first component of his turn—to provide for the addition of another component. Using a device we can call a "rush-through" (Schegloff 1982), he speeds up the talk just before possible completion of the first turn-unit ("there" does not have the "drawl" or sound stretch often found in last words or syllables); he omits the slight gap of silence which commonly intervenes between one unit and another, reduces the first word of what follows to its last sound ("z"), and thereby "rushes" into a next turn-constructional unit, interdicting (so to speak) the otherwise possibly relevant starting up of talk by another at that point. Not only is a multi-unit turn *potentially* of interest as a methodical achievement; this instance was *actually* such a methodically achieved outcome.

Although I will defer until later a fuller characterization of the increment thus added to the turn, note for now that it is a question. As my late colleague Harvey Sacks noted some years ago,[4] if a turn

---

[4] For example, in Sacks (forthcoming [1973]).

has several components (that is, turn-constructional units) in it, one of which is a question, the question is almost always the last of them, for on its completion, the question will ordinarily have made it someone else's turn to talk. So the format we have here, unit + unit where the second is a question, is quite a common one, and one which is the systematic product of orderly ways of organizing talk.

For the next observation, we shift our focus momentarily and look to Mike, one of the other participants. He is, however, more than just another participant; he is the one most directly addressed by Curt's talk. As far as we can tell, Curt shows him to be the addressee by making him the target of his gaze. And, in the context of the preceding sequence and its topic, Mike is the participant who is knowledgeable about the races, who has been telling about them, and who has been the directed recipient of Curt's prior inquiries about them. In noting that Mike is visibly doing,[5] we are noting what Curt is seeing while he is talking. What he sees in the course of his talk is a horizontal or lateral head shake.

It is useful to characterize this head gesture initially in this strictly physical manner, for it allows us clearly to focus on the analysis of its interactional import. Almost certainly, the common initial interpretation of this lateral head shake is the same as Darwin's in *The Expression of Emotion in Man and Animal* (1872) about a century ago; namely, it is a gestural expression of the negative. Although several investigators in the years since Darwin wrote have brought to our attention cultural variations on the western practice of the lateral shake as a display of the negative and the vertical shake (or nod) as a display of the positive or affirmative, within the midwestern American context in which this social occasion occurred, the understanding of Mike's shake as a "negative marker" is one plausible candidate. But even within this cultural context, this gesture will not sustain a single, invariant, necessary "reading," as can be seen in the following fragment from a later moment on the same occasion, first discussed by Marjorie Goodwin (1980) in a paper in which many of the points that follow were elaborated.

While discussing another matter (but still on the general topic of "cars"), Mike has referred to someone he knows who owns "a bunch a' old clunkers," but then immediately corrects himself, as he identifies them as high-priced vintage antique cars, to the amazement of Curt:

---

[5] There is no adequate alternative to the audience/reader viewing the tape and thereby having independent access to the data being described. The audience at the 1985 Linguistic Institute was able to view the tape repeatedly. The reader can be given only a discursive description which presumes and buries under the very analysis which is its point.

Segment 2

```
Mike:   Well I can't say they're ol'clunkers eez gotta
        Co:rd?
        (0.1)
Mike:   Two Co:rds,
        (1.0)
Mike:   ⌈ And
Curt:   ⌊ Not original,
        (0.7)
Mike:   Oh yes. Very origi(h)nal              <---- #1
Curt:   Oh::: reall⌈ y?
Mike:          ⌊ Yah. Ve(h)ry               <---- #2
        origi(h)nal.                          <---- #2
Curt:   Awhhh are you shittin me?=
Mike:   =No I'm not.
```

                                                  (simplified)

There are two vigorous head gestures on Mike's part in this little sequence. What is appealing about this data segment is that the two gestures are produced to accompany virtually identical utterances, but the gestures appear to be sharply contrasting—one a horizontal or lateral shake and the other a vertical one. The first comes at the utterance marked with arrow #1 in the transcript. The head gesture here is a horizontal shake. The utterance it accompanies gives clear evidence that this gesture does not invariably mark the negative; the utterance is markedly positive—"Oh yes. Very original." Two turns later Mike produces a virtually identical utterance, at arrow #2, "Yah. Very original." The gesture accompanying this utterance is a vertical shake/nod.

Two observations will have to suffice here to elaborate our sense of what these gestures can be doing. First, gesture #1 (the horizontal shake) is produced to accompany an utterance which is in *disagreement* with the prior utterance of another, whereas gesture #2 (the vertical shake, or nod) is produced as an *agreement* or confirmation. Although many disagreements are negative sentences and vice versa, not all are. Sometimes, agreements are negative and disagreements are affirmative (if, for example, what is being agreed or disagreed with was a negative). Lateral shakes may, then, mark not a feature of the turn itself (its negative aspect) but a feature of its relationship to another utterance in the sequence—disagreement.

Second, note that the lateral shake can serve as a gestural marker of another feature of these utterances, although it is used to do so only in the first of the two in this little sequence. Lateral shakes can be used as the gestural realization of what linguists call "intensifiers." In the fragment above, note that both utterances under examination include the verbal intensifier "very." The lateral gesture in #1 may be understood not only as expressing the disagreement the utterance is doing, but, in addition, as a gestural expression of the intensifier (or, as Goodwin [1980] called it, a marker of the "out of the ordinary").

In sum, a horizontal or lateral head shake can have at least three distinct uses: as a marker or expression of the negative, of disagreement, and/or of intensification. How does all this bear on the utterance we were in the first instance examining?

We might begin by noticing that the initial component of Curt's turn ("He's about the only good regular out there") offers an assessment, both of "Al" and of "the races." As Pomerantz (1978, 1984) has shown, one type of response which assessments can make relevant, and which with considerable regularity follows them in next turn, is agreement or disagreement, and one of these is accordingly sequentially relevant after Curt's assessment. Because the assessment proposed in Curt's utterance is expressed in an affirmative format, a disagreement with it (were one to be forthcoming) might be expected to be expressed in a negative format. Both the negative and the disagreement uses of lateral shakes thus have a prima facie potential relevance here, provided by the sequential locus of Mike's action—"after an assessment."

But one problem needs to be addressed before proceeding along these lines. In the "Two Cords" segment on which a preliminary basis was developed for alternative readings of the head gestures, the gesturer was the speaker. And this is by no means an accidental or arbitrary cooccurrence. A great many, perhaps the great majority, of gestures are resticted to speakers (Kendon, 1979; Schegloff, 1984). Certainly hand gestures are almost all so restricted. Persons who gesticulate when they are not speaking or using the gesticulations as speech substitutes, and especially when another is speaking, are likely to be seen as anomalous at best.

Head gestures are somewhat different. The vertical shake or nod has a major use as a "continuer" or indicator that a recipient of speech understands that an extended unit of talk is in progress and should continue (Schegloff 1982), and although an ongoing speaker may leave a bit of a silence into which such a continuer may be inserted, thus making the nodder into a virtual speaker at that moment, often enough such nods are nonanomalously produced while another is in the process of talking, and are understood as specifically a recipient's gesture. Lateral shakes also can apparently have a recipient usage, as a kind of mark of sympathetic uptake or receipt, a usage which may be related to the usability of the gesture by speakers as an intensifier. But none of these usages seem in point for Mike's shake in the "only good regular" utterance on which we are focusing. His lateral shake does not appear to be a recipient's or hearer's gesture.

Perhaps we can advance the analysis by asking *where* gestures are placed. Because most gestures are produced by speakers, it is not surprising that one useful way of characterizing their placement is by reference to the talk which they accompany. For some important classes of gesture, it appears that they occur *before* the talk components to which they specifically are tied (Kendon 1977, 1979; Schegloff, 1984); often they have been completed by the time that talk has been produced, but they are almost always initiated before that talk. But this way of characterizing the placement of gesture, or of its onset, seems of little use here; there is no Mike talk relative to which we could assess the gesture's onset.

If we cannot, for now, characterize Mike's gesture by its placement relative to his own talk, perhaps we can locate it relative to Curt's talk, during which it begins. Our next observation, then, is that Mike's lateral shake begins just after *"out"* in Curt's utterance (segment 1, line 17). The point is not, however, the word "out," but its manner of delivery, only roughly captured in the transcript by the underlining; "out" is the carrier both of a pitch peak and of raised amplitude.

The relevance of a pitch peak of this sort (but certainly not of all pitch peaks) is that it marks the enhanced likelihood that the next possible completion of the turn-constructional unit will be an actually intended turn-completion.[6] That is, the developing grammatical structure of an utterance in the course of its production is potentially compatible with alternative points of possible completion. Pitch peaks, and their suppression, are one means by which speakers can indicate which syntactically possible completions are built to be completions on this occasion, and which not. A pitch peak thus can project intended turn completion at the next grammatically possible completion point. In doing so, it can also open the "transition relevance space," the stretch of time in which transition from current to next speaker is properly done. It is after such pitch peaks that intending-next-speakers who aim to get an early start begin their next turns. It is such pitch peaks which speakers suppress to show their parsing interlocutors that imminent syntactically possible completions are not designed to be actual completions. It is such pitch peaks after which speakers may increase the pace of their talk in an effort to "rush through" into a next turn component. Such a pitch peak can, then, mark the imminent

---

[6] See Duncan (1972) on the association of distinctive pitch contours with turn completion. For the more specific points being made here, see Schegloff (1982).

completion of a turn, and the appropriate place for a next turn, and its speaker, to start.

What we have then is the marking of a turn currently in production as about to end, and, directly after that display, a bit of gestural behavior by another which regularly occurs in the company of speech, and regularly precedes that speech. We should then appreciate Mike's head gesture not as that of a hearer, but as that of an incipient speaker, who, as it turns out, ends up not speaking at that point.

We previously characterized the sequential environment "after an assessment" as one in which agreement or disagreement is relevant. We can now add another observation, and that is that in the course of the one remaining word of the turn-constructional unit which is in progress—"there" (segment 1, line 17), Mike accomplishes the minimum head movement necessary to display that he is doing a lateral shake rather than a "look over" to his side; actually he accomplishes a bit more—one "round trip" (i.e., a head turn to the left and return to "centered" position) plus the start of a next lateral move. By the end of the projectedly last word of the turn, then, Mike has produced, and Curt has seen, the projection of an incipient disagreement, embodied in this minimal head gesture.

Previous work on the organization of sequences in talk-in-interaction, for example work by Sacks (forthcoming [1973]) and by Pomerantz (1984), has indicated that, with notable and important exceptions, disagreement and other "rejecting" response turn types are *dis*preferred options. Among the sequential expressions of this status is the deferral of actual disagreements. Sometimes this takes the form of delays in the actual onset of the turn, either by silence or by some form of repair initiator (Schegloff, Jefferson and Sacks 1977), such as "huh?" or "what?" Alternatively, the *start* of next turn may not be delayed, but the disagreement may be deferred *within* it, being preceded by various tokens such as "uh," "well," and the like, and even by pro forma agreement tokens, as in the familiar "Yes, but. . . ." These various delay devices can all serve as "pre-disagreements," harbingers of what is to come. But pre-disagreements involve *more* than just a first indication of upcoming disagreement.

One point of a sequential object such as a predisagreement is that it affords the prior speaker—the speaker of the turn about to be disagreed with—an opportunity to recast their talk, and potentially to recast it in a form which will circumvent the disagreement. The "pre-disagreement" may then end up not preceding a disagreement at all, for if the prior speaker takes the opportunity, and recasts the prior turn, or otherwise changes the sequential environment, the disagreement may be avoided, thereby giving full effect to the dispreference for disagreement. This, at least, is what a number of investigators have found for such previously explored pre-disagreements as were mentioned above.

Returning to our target utterance, we may note that the second turn-constructional unit which Curt achieves by his "rush-through" is specifically responsive to this projected disagreement. Indeed, this second unit—line 17: "(Doe)z Keegan still go out there?"—may most properly be said to follow not the first unit in the turn, but the pre-disagreement accomplished through Mike's head gesture, which, because it is not talk, can be produced simultaneously with the prior talk without "overlapping" with it. Although there is no break between the two components of Curt's turn, it is nonetheless clear that that second component is a preemptive response to Mike's projected disagreement with Curt's proposed assessment. This two-unit turn, this "discourse" in that sense, is thus a thoroughly interactional achievement.

(Note, by the way, that a vertical nod by Mike, adumbrating agreement with Curt's assessment, would not engender the same sorts of sequential relevances or consequences; it would most likely not engender a forced extension of Curt's turn. This should be taken as evidence, contra the stance adopted by Duncan and his associates, that however autonomous the organization of turn-taking may appear to be, no full account can be developed without reference to other, simultaneously operating organizations, such as the organization of agreement/disagreement in sequences involved here, for these clearly bear on the size of turns, and potentially on their distribution. It should be clear as well, in this regard, that the suggestion by various interpreters [e.g., Cicourel 1978, 1981; Corsaro 1981] that conversation analysis is committed to, and perhaps even constituted by, a set of *autonomous* turn-taking rules, is quite wide of the mark.)

That Curt's second unit is responsive to Mike's projected disagreement is reflected in various of its features. We noted earlier that this second component was formatted as a question. Now we can add several further observations. One is that this is a yes/no question, and that this is a question format which itself sets up the relevance of agreement or disagreement in the following turn (Sacks forthcoming [1973]). That is, this increment to Curt's turn retains the relevance of agreement or disagreement by Mike in next turn, but changes the terms with which agreement or disagreement are to be done.

Further, the question proffers a candidate exception to the assessment offered in the first part of the turn. It is a guess at what, or rather whom, Mike has in mind in projecting the disagreement displayed by his lateral shake.

Note that this move by Curt involves more than just the attempted circumvention of a dispreferred disagreement. If the projected disagreement by Mike adumbrated a divergence of outlooks or information, a way in which Mike and Curt were "not together," then Curt's move is potentially exquisite in reversing the implication. For, if successful, it will show that from a purely formal and contentless harbinger of disagreement (the lateral shake), he (Curt) can figure out just whom Mike "has in mind"; that is how "close" their minds are. He knows exactly to whom he is talking, just how that one understood his claim, just how that one might disagree, and so on.

The initial success of this move is striking. Instead of the imminent disagreement of which the lateral shake was a harbinger, we find an apparent agreement. Mike agrees with, and confirms, Curt's guess that "Keegan's out there" and (in keeping with the revised version of Curt's turn which concerns not only "regulars" but *"good"* regulars) he adds that he is "doin real good this year." This agreement-formatted talk is accompanied by a vigorous vertical nod (at segment 1, line 19), embodying by gesture the shift from the disagreeing/negative to an agreeing/ affirmative response. This is precisely what a pre-disagreement is designed to do: it has allowed the conversion of a sequence whose component turns were about to be in a relationship of disagreement to be done instead as an agreement. And it allows the parties to end up in a mutual alignment rather than in an opposition.

At least it seems to. Actually, there are various signs of continuing misalignment between Mike and Curt, which deserve at least cursory mention, even though they cannot be fully explicated here. I call attention first to the form of Mike's response, "Keegan's out there." This is a sequential environment in which Mike could have used what I will call a "locally subsequent reference form," in this case the pronoun "he," to refer to the one who "still goes out." He doesn't. He uses instead a "locally initial" reference form, the same one used by Curt, namely "Keegan." Although this usage form is not well understood yet, there is some evidence (Fox 1984) that this usage shows up (among other places) in disagreement environments, and may be one way of marking them as such.

Second, note that Curt's preemptive inquiry mentions a single case as a candidate exception to the assessment he had proposed. Mike, on the other hand, does not accept so limited a basis for his disagreement. And indeed he should not; for if there were but a single exception, he might appear ungenerous, and to be "doing being contrary," to disagree outright on that basis, rather than agreeing and adding an exception as an "afterthought." Keegan is but the first of his "cases"; his response to Curt is produced in a "list" format, in which M'Gilton is a second case and not a final one at that. When that second one is mentioned,

Curt comes up with a third, another possible exception, Oxfrey, but begins to change the focus of the talk to having "a new car" with which Mike immediately disagrees.

So in various respects, disagreement as a relationship between the parties continues in this sequence, even though at the start of Mike's response, disagreement between successive turns in the sequence has been circumvented. In effect, Mike disagrees, but in a turn formatted as an agreement. From this we should learn that the organization of action, here realized in turns at talk in sequences, has a formal basis as a partially autonomous organization. It is not merely the basis for, or a reflection of, the relationship between the participants.

We can catch a glimpse of how the sequence might have developed were it not for the preemptive guess by Curt. Gary is also sitting at the table, and, although he has not talked in this sequence, he has been intermittently attentive to it. He also disagrees with Curt's assessment about "only good regular," but he has had no preliminary exchange of alignment intentions with Curt. The result is an outright challenge response at lines 22 and 23— "Wuhyih mean, my brother in law's out there" and so on, which, although disattended by both Curt and Mike, is just the sort of disagreement response which it appears the "dance" between Curt and Mike successfully avoided.

ACHIEVING THE TURN IN/AND ITS SEQUENCE: LOOKING BACKWARD

The entire analysis has so far been conducted without respect to what the actual assessment was which Curt proposed in the first component of the target turn, and the import of that assessment within the interactional episode in which it occurs. The analysis has also disregarded two apparent hitches in the production of that first component—two points at which the turn-so-far is stopped, and the turn is restarted, and in one of those cases changed on re-production.

In order to address these as yet unexplicated features of the utterance, it will be useful to review and partially to characterize the sequence in which it occurs. As it happens, this is quite a rich sequence; if not distinctively rich, then one whose riches are relatively easily accessible. But only a small bit of its texture can be touched on here—only two or three points, in fact, which are directly germane to our target utterance.

The sequence as a whole can be characterized as a topic-proferring one.[7] From preceding talk we can infer that Mike had gone to the automobile races the previous evening; Curt, not knowing this, had gone by his house to visit and had stayed quite a long while, even though only Mike's wife Phyllis was home. Previous talk about the races has been immediately diverted into teasing talk about the possible infidelities of the previous evening. Now talk about the races is broached again by Curt. The forms of topic-proferring run through here are quite canonical, but the description of those forms is too bulky to develop in detail. I want to note only that ordinarily several tries are made, through distinct subsequences, as here in "how was the races last night" (line 1), "who won the feature" (line 3), and "Does he go out there pretty regular?" (line 10).

To say that these subsequences are "distinct" is not necessarily to say that they are independent. The several tries or proffers may be related in various ways—most obviously by the same referents appearing in them or informing them, as some reference to "the races" appears to inform the second try in this sequence, "Who won the feature." Another way in which separate contributions to a topic-starting undertaking can be related is that a subsequent proffer not only refers to something referred to in an earlier one, but addresses the *product* of an earlier sequence. In the talk which we are examining, the utterance "Does he go out there pretty regular?" *is* related to prior talk in this way, along the following lines.

Note, first, that Mike's "Al won" (line 4) is delivered in a manner—largely through its prosody—which marks it as "routine," as "a foregone conclusion," as "of course," as "as usual."

Note next that Curt's efforts to "retrieve," and then to verify, the person reference (through "who" at line 6 and "Al did?" at line 8), although clearly prompted by its involvement in overlap, at the same time disappoint the claim built into the prosody of "Al won." Expectable talk can regularly get heard through, and despite, all sorts of acoustic interferences; just aspects of the expectable item are needed to confirm that that is indeed what is being said. In twice failing to hear unproblematically who won, Curt fails to align himself with the "routineness" of Al's winning built into Mike's announcement.

Note, third, that Curt's next contribution to the introduction and establishment of this topic (at line 10) is addressed to just this matter; it makes explicit what Mike's earlier turn had done implicitly, that is, through prosody; and it questions it, rather than asserting it, let alone

---

[7] Other modes of topic organization described in the literature include topic elicitation and nomination (Button & Casey 1984 and forthcoming) and "stepwise transition" (Jefferson 1984; see also Schegloff & Sacks 1973).

presupposing it. "Does he go out there pretty regular?" thus builds upon the product of an earlier sequence, rather than re-addressing its object in parallel fashion.

Note further, however, that in pursuing this matter, Curt has slightly, apparently imperceptibly changed the terms. Mike's "as usual"-marking had been applied to Al's *winning;* Curt has asked about Al's *"going out there."* This might not seem to matter; certainly it does not matter just because some logical or semantic analysis might show the content of two such propositions to be different. But note that after Mike confirms (by a head nod at line 11) that Al goes out there "generally every Saturday," his wife Phyllis chimes in (line 14) that "he wins just about every Saturday too." That is, Phyllis appears to have detected the difference between "winning" and "going out there," has treated it as relevant, and has entered as a speaker into a conversational episode to which she had not otherwise contributed in order to address this difference. The manner of her delivery is related to, though it does not recapitulate, the manner of Mike's "Al won," and suggests one possible basis for her treating this as a relevant and actionable matter. It retains the sense of "as usual," but hints (to my ear) of boredom, ennui, world weariness. It hints, in other words, at a persistent issue between husband and wife (he went to the races, she did not): namely, why go to the races when they, and their outcomes, are so repetitive.

These few observations about the sequence preceding our target utterance will have to suffice to supply the sequential context for the remaining analysis. This analysis is directed to two aspects of the first component of the turn. Twice that turn-constructional unit is stopped before coming to completion, and is rebegun, the second of those times being changed on its reproduction. Both of these occurrences involve the use of the mechanism of "repair," the methodical practices provided in the organization of talk-in-interaction for dealing with problems or troubles in speaking, hearing, or understanding the talk. What, then, can be said about these two perturbations in the production of this turn component?

The first—the cut-off of the turn after "he" and its re-use to restart the turn ("He-He's about the only regular")—seems relatively straight-forward. Two sorts of "troubles" in the talk have been established as environments in which this sort of practice is found. Charles Goodwin has shown (1980, 1981) that when a speaker beginning a turn brings their gaze to bear on recipient and does not find recipient already looking at them, a break in the talk regularly works to attract the recipient's eyes. And in earlier work of mine (Schegloff forthcoming [1973]), I described the use of what I termed "recycled turn beginnings" to manage the emergence of one speaker's utterance from overlap with another's. Here we may note that Curt's turn begins in overlap with other talk (line 15 in which Ryan addresses a dog) which, although from a wholly separate conversation, is at high pitch and volume. Although an occurrence like this allows us to see that, and how, persons attend and adjust to environmental events which are not parts of their interaction proper, this theme cannot concern us further here.

The second of these repairs ("he's about the only *good* regular *out* there") will require somewhat more elaborate treatment. To begin with, how shall we characterize what it is doing, where it is done, and what consequences it has for the interaction?

One characterization might treat this occurrence only as an instance of repair, and focus on those of its features relevant to repair. The repair operation involved is "insertion"; the redoing of the utterance allows the insertion of an element, a word, not present on the first saying. This operation—of restarting the turn to allow the insertion— is begun just after the word before which the new item is to be inserted; or, put differently, the repair is initiated just after "next word" after the slot for the missing word. The sort of terms in this characterization are general for the domain of repair (Schegloff, Jefferson & Sacks 1977; Schegloff 1979); "insertion" is a thoroughly formal term, like deletion, expansion, reduction, and so on. The notion "after next word relative to the locus of the trouble" is also quite a formal characterization, given that it is talk we are dealing with.

Another characterization might specify this occurrence *within* the domain of repair, but focus on it as a specific *type* of repair. Here we note that one quite regular type of repair is the addition of an adjective to a noun, of a modifier to a noun phrase, of a descriptor to a reference— to offer three different terminologies for the same occurrence. Then we might note here that the inserted item is a descriptor, that it is inserted before the reference it is a descriptor for, and that the repair is initiated just after the reference to which the descriptor will apply. This characterization is repair-*type* specific, and formulates what is being done, and where it is done, in terms not of the organization of repair in general, but in terms of a particular subset of repairs. Neither characterization addresses what *this* instance of repair, of *this* sub-type of repair, is doing in *this* turn, in *this* sequence, in *this* conversation (which does not mean that they are less good characterizations, only that they serve different analytic interests). To do so we have to build onto what has already been said, with respect both to what the repair accomplishes and with respect to where it is done.

The turn as initially done (or projected)—namely, "He's about the only regular [out there]"—is built as an assessment occupying "third position" in a sequence which begins with Curt's question "Does he go out there pretty regular" (at line 10), and gets as its response from Mike a head nod and "Generally every Saturday" (at lines 11 and 12). The construction of this assessment in third position in terms of "regular" connects it to Curt's question and Mike's answer. It sequentially deletes Phyllis's turn "He wins just about every Saturday too"; that is, it treats it as sequentially nonconsequential. Phyllis's turn, we noted before, picked up a potentially insignificant shift by Curt from the matter-of-factness of Al's *winning* to the routineness of his *competing.* Her turn was built specifically to add to, and contrast with, the sequence developed by Curt and Mike on Al's participation. That addition and contrast is ignored, is treated as a nonevent, in the first version of Curt's assessment, which returns to the theme of Al's being "a regular" and assesses him as the *only* regular. The second version of the turn, marked specifically by the use of repair to insert the descriptor "good," incorporates a reference to Phyllis's contribution. Indeed, by doing it *as a repair,* Curt displays it overtly being taken into account, as he also displays that initially it had not been taken into account (see in this regard Jefferson 1974).

We should, therefore, appreciate that the repair mechanism by which a descriptor is inserted into this utterance in the course of producing a second version of it incorporates a reference to an otherwise disattended utterance by another participant, and thereby also potentially incorporates its speaker as a potentially active participant in the conversation. And, insofar as our earlier observation about the implied boredom with the races, and complaint about Mike's attendance, are in point, the incorporation of Phyllis's remark adds another critical edge to Curt's turn. Perhaps this will enhance our appreciation of the early start of Mike's incipient disagreement with it.

Correlative with this understanding of the interactional import of the second version of this first turn-constructional unit, and the repair which it incorporates, is a recasting of our account of where this repair is done. To our earlier characterization, which related the repair to that which was being repaired, we can add an account of the placement of the repair within the turn. In that regard, we may note that the repair—the insertion of the descriptor "good" with the import already ascribed to it—is initiated just before the possible opening of the transition space—that is, just before transfer of the turn to another may become relevant and "legal." Since the repair appears in the transcript to be buried well toward the middle of the turn, this may seem to be quite a quixotic proposal. Let me try to justify it in the following manner.

Note first that on rebeginning the turn, Curt uses exactly the same words he used in the first version—"he's about the only." Although I cannot display here the relevant array of data, re-using the same words is a way speakers have of showing, or claiming, "what I am saying now is what I was saying before"; in the present case, it may be taken as claiming to be saying the same thing, except for the change accomplished by the repair.

Note next that the next word after "regular" in the second version of the turn is "out"; "out" with the pitch peak which we noted earlier can serve to project imminent possible completion, opening the transition space, making talk by another relevant, and even making legal overlapping talk by possible next speakers who aim for earliest possible start. Then, if the second version of the utterance is built to display "equivalence-except-for-the-change" with the first, then we may be warranted in inferring that the first was projected to continue in the manner in which the second actually does continue. Then, *after the word "regular"* is *just before the word "out"*—the point at which the turn would be displayed to be possibly incipiently complete, and others entitled to talk.

This then is a potentially last assured position in the structure of the turn for the speaker to undertake a recasting of it, and we should note that Curt speeds up his talk just a bit (that is the import of the left-pointing arrow in line 16 at this point) to get the repair started there, before others—whether Mike or Phyllis—get to address themselves to it. It is, in this sense, a last possible moment before the turn projects a possible completion, and this structural characterization is no less in point just because subsequent developments led to the completion not only of the second version of this turn-constructional unit before the turn actually ended, but the inclusion of a whole additional unit as well. In real time, at the moment at which the repair was done, the turn was projectably almost over.

With this I hope to have provided some sense of the interactional basis for the occurrence in this turn at talk of two distinct turn-constructional units, and for the three tries—including two distinct versions—of the first of these units. I hope we have gained some leverage on the multi-unit turn as an achievement, on the basis for Curt's squeezing a second unit in, on the basis for Mike's incipient disagreement in the critical character of Curt's first unit, on the basis for Curt's upgrading that critical character by revising the first unit, and the use of that revision in the taking note of, rather than the ignoring of, Phyllis' interpolation: a lot about two lines of transcript, but these two lines have served us as instantiations for several different domains of phenomena which intersect on this humble utterance. Let me assure you: we have by no means exhausted the interest of this bit of talk. But as William Bull once put it (1968), although we may not have exhausted the topic, it may well have exhausted us—at least for now.

CONCLUSION

One of my intentions was to exemplify one sort of work practitioners of this form of conversation analysis may do. I hoped thereby to display the capacity of this form of analysis to do what its underlying theoretical conception of talk in interaction requires—namely, to analyze singular episodes of talk which, having been produced as orderly, more or less accessible from moment to moment enterprises by their participants, should be so accessible in principle to professional analysts. In so doing, we tentatively explored one version of a, or the, basic problem for the study of social interaction and the use of language in it. There are, as you know, various versions of "the big problem," such as Chomsky's "how an infinity of new sentences are produced with a finite set of rules," or Labov's "Why does anyone say anything?" Perhaps another big problem can be formulated in the following manner: "How is it that with the use of abstract formal resources interactional participants create idiosyncratic, particularized to some here-and-now, interactions?" For we have come to the analysis of our target utterance, particularized as it is to its distinctive local context, with the tools of a formal sequential analysis which incorporates sensitivity to context, in various senses, as an abstract and formal matter.

Various senses of the term "context" and various ways of lending it definite reference have been threaded throughout this exercise—from "Central Ohio" to "before the word which opens the transition space." What will be understood by the term "context" is intimately related to one's theoretical stance, the form of one's materials, and the controls one imposes on one's analysis. And its mode of relevance to analysis will be variable; recall that the first part of the analysis of our text for the day was conducted before characterizing the sequence in which it was embedded. Let me here just anticipate a theme which there is no time to elaborate: in the final analysis, a notion like "context" will have to remain formally contentless, and be instead what we used to call "programmatically relevant"—relevant in principle, but with a sense always to-be-discovered rather than given-to-be-applied.

Two boundaries may have been blurred by this exercise. One is between the sorts of occurrences which ordinarily qualify as linguistic—verbal or vocalic, and those which don't, such as gestures and other deployments of body parts. These may not always be usefully segregated off neatly.

The other, and correlative, boundary which may be somewhat blurred is that between our conventional understanding of linguistics as a discipline and other, neighboring disciplines, such as sociology and anthropology. For pre-disagreements, and their place in the organization of agreement and disagreement in sequences, are part of an elaborate apparatus involved in the social control of conflict, of which disagreement in talk is one rudimentary form. Among the matters we have been examining is included a mechanism by which parties to interaction can try to nip incipient conflict in the bud; this is an *interactional* achievement, which must certainly be a main pillar in the solution to the problem of social order.

Such topics may not initially appear to be a proper concern for linguistics and for linguists. But the fabric of the social world does not seem to be woven with seams at the disciplinary boundaries. The use of language as a vehicle for social action binds the features of language and the features of action and interaction together, at least in part. This requires a theoretical stance toward language different from some others which are current. It implies certain forms of inquiry. It implies a stance toward the organization of inquiry concerning human social life which interweaves linguistics, together with other traditional and not-so-traditional disciplines, as parts in a larger social science, one which is both humanistic *and* scientific. I have meant to sketch one way of pursuing those implications.

APPENDIX

TRANSCRIPTION CONVENTIONS

The notational conventions employed in the transcripts are taken from a set developed by Gail Jefferson. The most recent version of these conventions may be found on pp. ix-xvi of *Structures of Social Action,* edited by J. Maxwell Atkinson and John Heritage (Cambridge: Cambridge University Press, 1984). In general, the orthography tries to capture how the participants actually talked, without rendering the transcript unreadable. In addition, there are specific conventions. I provide glosses below only for the conventions actually employed in this paper.

     (word)   parentheses surrounding a word indicate uncertainty about the transcription.

     (0.8)   parentheses around a number on a line or between lines indicates silence, in tenths of a second.

     [open brackets indicate the onset of

[simultaneous talk between the linked utterances.

] close brackets indicate the ending of

] simultaneous talk between the linked utterances.

= equal signs come in pairs, at the end of one line

= or utterance, and at the start of a subsequent one; the talk linked by equal signs (whether by different speakers or same speaker) is continuous, and is not interrupted by any silence or other break.

?,. punctuation marks indicate intonation contours; they do *not* indicate grammatical status (e.g., question).

out underlining indicates emphasis; the more of a word is underlined, the greater the emphasis.

:: colons mark the prolongation of the preceding sound; the more colons, the greater the prolongation.

< the "less than" sign marks a slightly early start of the bit of talk which follows it.

run- the hyphen indicates the self-interruption of the preceding sound.

(h) the letter "h" in parentheses indicates aspiration in the course of a word, commonly laughter.

REFERENCES

Atkinson, J. Maxwell and John Heritage (eds.). 1984. Structures of social action. Cambridge: Cambridge University Press.

Bauman, Richard and Joel Sherzer (eds.). 1974. Explorations in the ethnography of speaking. Cambridge: Cambridge University Press.

Bull, William. 1968. Time, tense and the verb. Berkeley and Los Angeles: University of California Press.

Button, Graham and Neal Casey. 1984. Generating topic: The use of topic initial elicitors. In Atkinson and Heritage, 167–190.

Button, Graham and Neal Casey. Forthcoming. Topic nomination and topic pursuit. Human Studies.

Button, Graham and John Lee. (eds.). Forthcoming. Talk and social organization. Bristol: Multilingual Matters.

Cicourel, Aaron V., 1978. Language and society: Cognitive, cultural and linguistic aspects of language use. Sozialwissenschaftliche Annalen 2.25–58.

Cicourel, Aaron V., 1981. Notes on the integration of micro- and macro-levels of analysis. Knorr-Cetina and Cicourel, 51–80.

Corsaro, William. 1981. Communicative processes in studies of social organization: sociological approaches to discourse analysis. Text 1.5–63.

Darwin, Charles. 1872. The expression of emotion in man and animal. London: John Murray.

Duncan, Starkey. 1972. Some signals and rules for taking speaking turns in conversation. Journal of Personality and Social Psychology 23.283–92.

Duncan, Starkey and Donald W. Fiske. 1977. Face to face interaction: Research, methods and theory. Hillsdale, NJ: Lawrence Erlbaum Associates.

Fox, Barbara. 1984. Discourse structure and anaphora in written and conversational english, Ph.D. dissertation, Department of Linguistics, University of California, Los Angeles.

Givon, Talmy (ed.). 1979. Syntax and semantics 12: Discourse and syntax. New York: Academic Press.

Goodwin, Charles. 1980. Restarts, pauses and the achievement of a state of mutual gaze at turn beginning. Sociological Inquiry 50.272–302.

Goodwin, Charles. 1981. Conversational organization: Interaction between speakers and hearers. New York: Academic Press.

Goodwin, Charles. 1984. Notes on story structure and the organization of participation. In Atkinson and Heritage, 225–246.

Goodwin, Marjorie. 1980. Some aspects of processes of mutual monitoring implicated in the production of description sequences. Sociological Inquiry, 50.303–317.

Jefferson, Gail. 1974. Error correction as an international resource. Language in Society, 2.181–199.

Jefferson, Gail. 1980. On "trouble-premonitory" response to inquiry. Sociological Inquiry 50.153–185.

Jefferson, Gail. 1984. On stepwise transition from talk about a trouble to inappropriately next-positioned matters. In Atkinson and Heritage, 191–222.

Kendon, Adam. 1977. Studies in the behavior of social interaction. Bloomington: Indiana University Press.

Kendon, Adam. 1979. Gesture and speech: Two aspects of the process of utterance. In Key, 207–227.

Key, Mary Ritchie (ed.). 1979. Nonverbal communication and language. The Hague: Mouton.

Knorr-Cetina, Karin D. and Aaron V. Cicourel (eds.). 1981. Advances in social theory and methodology: Toward an integration of micro- and macro-sociologies. Boston: Routledge and Kegan Paul.

Pomerantz, Anita M. 1978. Compliment responses: Notes on the co-operation of multiple constraints. In Schenkein, 79–112.

Pomerantz, Anita M. 1984. Agreeing and disagreeing with assessments: Some features of preferred/dispreferred turn shapes. In Atkinson and Heritage, 57–101.

Sacks, Harvey. 1964–72. Unpublished transcribed lectures.

Sacks, Harvey. 1975. An analysis of the course of a joke's telling in conversation. In Bauman and Sherzer, 337–353.

Sacks, Harvey. [1973] Forthcoming. On the preferences for agreement and contiguity in sequences in conversation. In Button and Lee. First presented as a public lecture at the Linguistic Institute, University of Michigan, Summer, 1973.

Sacks, Harvey, Emanuel A. Schegloff and Gail Jefferson. 1974. A simplest systematics for the organization of turn-taking for conversation. Language 50.696–735.

Schegloff, Emanuel A. 1968. Sequencing in conversational openings. American Anthropologist 70.1075–95.

Schegloff, Emanuel A., 1979. The relevance of repair to syntax-for-conversation. In Givon, 261–288.

Schegloff, Emanuel A., 1980. Preliminaries to preliminaries: "Can I ask you a question?" Sociological Inquiry 50.104–152.

Schegloff, Emanuel A. 1982. Discourse as an interactional achievement: Some uses of "uh huh" and other things that come between sentences. In Tannen, 71–93.

Schegloff, Emanuel A. 1984. On some gestures' relation to talk. In Atkinson and Heritage, 266–296.

Schegloff, Emanuel A. [1973] Forthcoming. Recycled turn beginnings: A precise repair mechanism in conversation's turn-taking organization. In Button and Lee. First presented as a public lecture at the Linguistic Institute, University of Michigan, Summer, 1973.

Schegloff, Emanuel A., Gail Jefferson and Harvey Sacks. 1977. The preference for self-correction in the organization of repair in conversation. Language 53.361–382.

Schegloff, Emanuel A., and Harvey Sacks. 1973. Opening up closings. Semiotica 7.289–327.

Schenkein, Jim N. (ed.). 1978. Studies in the organization of conversational interaction. New York: Academic Press.

Tannen, Deborah (ed.). 1982. Analyzing discourse: Text and talk. Georgetown University Round Table on Languages and Linguistics. Washington, DC: Georgetown University Press.

CHAPTER SEVEN

The Judicial Testing of Linguistic Theory

William Labov

University of Pennsylvania

In linguistics, as in many other academic disciplines, we tend to think of theories as internal products, most properly used and evaluated by the scholars who produced them. The general public can hardly be expected to judge the rightness or the value of these theories, without knowing the linguistic data they are based on or the methods used to construct them. We tend to think, moreover, that people involved in everyday affairs are strongly biased by their immediate needs and interests, so that they are not likely to weigh the correctness of scientific theories with the objectivity that is called for. On the other hand, those who work in isolation from political and practical concerns are thought to be more objective in their approach to research and knowledge. It is not uncommon for scholars to assert with pride that they are interested in knowledge for its own sake, and not for any practical application it might have.

In harmony with this academic view, professors have warned their students of the bad consequences of efforts to apply their theories to the pressing issues of the larger social world. It is not hard to demonstrate that in the course of popularization, scientific ideas are often weakened and distorted. Students learn that losses in scientific accuracy and objectivity will more than cancel out any gains that might result from their engagement in the social struggle.

In the presentation here, I will not try to estimate the fairness of this portrait of the academic world, nor its freedom from the bias of partisan politics. Most readers have ample experience of their own to judge the matter. I will be looking at the other side of the coin. I will be dealing with situations where linguistic data, theory, and conclusions are presented in a forum far removed from the academic scene, where lawyers and judges work to resolve questions of fact that have important consequences in the world at large. It will appear that objectivity is highly prized in these judicial contexts, perhaps more highly prized than in the laboratory or the classroom.

The course of this discussion will involve us in the familiar problems of the relations between theory and practice, theory and data, theory and facts. Within the academic framework, facts are valued to the extent that they serve a theory, and only to that extent. Academic linguists see themselves engaged in the business of producing theories: theories are the major product and end-result of their activity. It seems to me that there is something backwards in this view, and we should seriously consider whether it might be reversed.

The discussion to follow will consider three cases where linguistic testimony played an important part in a judicial decision. They cover only a small fraction of the range of issues on language and the law that have been brought to linguists' attention in recent years. In these three cases, linguistic data and theory were introduced to support an expert opinion on the facts of the matter under consideration.

It is true enough that almost all linguistic testimony comes in the form of expert opinion, with a system of advocacy where one can expect to find an opposing expert opinion. This can happen in civil suits, automobile accidents, or criminal cases of various kinds. But in the cases I will report here, there is a more serious issue of taking sides on matters of right and wrong. In each of these cases, the facts are part of a larger situation involving justice and injustice, and the linguistic testimony has been used in the search for justice—at least as the linguist sees it.

THE U.S. STEEL CASE

In the 1960s the American steel industry was the focus of a number of federal actions to eliminate practices that discriminated against minorities and women. One of these class action suits was located in Pittsburgh, on behalf of black steel workers in that city. The linguistic issues concerned the fairness of a legal notice that informed the steel workers that they would have to give up their claims in the local suit to accept a partial settlement of a national suit.

The Pittsburgh case was rooted in the history of black steel workers over the previous two decades. Blacks had come from the South to work in the steel industries of Chicago, Gary, Cleveland, and Pittsburgh during the war years and after. Some had been brought as strike breakers, but almost all had come as lower-paid workers, in janitorial and furnace-type jobs that were considered less desirable and paid less than others. A complex system of tracking made it difficult for them to move upward, since if they moved to a better-paying track they would lose the seniority they had gained in the lower-paying one.

In the late 1960s a number of federal suits were brought under Title VII of the Civil Rights Act of 1964, to correct such practices and establish equal pay for blacks and whites, men and women. The Equal Employment Opportunity Commission and the legislation that established it made possible the creation of class action suits, where a single attorney could obtain corrective action for a very large number of clients. One such suit was brought on a national basis against the nine major steel corporations, and settled by a consent decree under federal judge Pointer in Birmingham in 1974. A certain amount of money was to be paid to black and women steel workers as compensation for the lower salaries they had received, and corrective action was to be taken to eliminate many of the practices considered unfair by the courts (though the steel industries never admitted that they had discriminated).[1]

In Pittsburgh, attorney Bernard Marcus had worked over many years to establish a class action suit representing some 600 black steel workers at the local Homestead works against U.S. Steel and the union. He hoped this suit would bring considerably more profit to the steel workers than the national settlement was likely to do.[2] He had experienced many difficulties in getting the class action established, and had carried an appeal as far as the Supreme Court to obtain permission to communicate with his clients. He had joined forces with the NAACP Legal Defense Fund to pursue the case. The linguistic issue arose at a moment where it seemed that new action by all the other parties involved might reduce the class he was representing to almost nil.

An "Audit and Review Committee," representing the steel union, the companies, and the government, was about to send out checks in settlement of the national case. To accept the check, local steel workers would have to give up their claim in the local case. Marcus felt that

---

[1] Consent decrees I and II issued by Judge Sam C. Pointer, Jr. on April 12, 1974, signed by representatives of the Department of Justice, the Department of Labor, the Equal Employment Opportunity Commission, Armco Steel, Bethlehem Steel, Jones & Laughlin, National Steel, Republic Steel, U.S. Steel, Wheeling-Pittsburgh Steel, Youngstown Sheet & Tube, and the United Steelworkers of America. It included provisions for back pay, goals, and timetables for hiring, promoting, transferring, and training minorities and women.

[2] Jimmie L. Rodgers and John A. Turner vs. United States Steel Corp., Local 1397, AFL-CIO and United Steelworkers of America, AFL-CIO, Civil Action 71-793 in the U.S. District Court for the Western District of Pennsylvania.

the letter the committee was sending out explaining the issues, along with the legal notice of waiver, was biased in favor of accepting the check and against continuing the local case.[3]

In the fall of 1975, Marcus called me and asked me if I could, as a linguist, examine the letter for objectivity and comprehensibility. I assembled a group of four who might be able to throw light on the matter. Two would be concerned with the comprehensibility of the document. Mort Botel of the University of Pennsylvania Graduate School of Education was one of the country's leading experts on readability, and the author of one of the widely used indices of readability. Jeff van den Broek (1977) was then engaged in a dissertation on sociolinguistic variation in syntactic complexity in the Flemish of Maaseik, and had done extensive work on measures of syntactic complexity.[4] Two would be concerned with possible bias in the document. Anthony Kroch's dissertation (1979) dealt with the semantics of quantifier scope,[5] and he examined the text for semantic bias of quantifiers and other grammatical features. My own contribution centered on the empirical question as to whether the formulations of the letter actually did produce a semantic bias in those who had to make the decision.

The notice was a 12-page document, under the authorship of the joint committee representing the steel companies, the steelworkers' union, and the government agency. It introduced the consent decree and the local case (the *Rodgers* case), and notified readers that they were members of both classes. It urged the steel workers to read the notice carefully, and to get help if they did not understand it. It explained the relations of the two cases, and the consequences of signing the waiver or not signing it. The last page was the legal notice of waiver itself, which was one long sentence in technical legal language. This sentence was also to be printed in small type on the back of the check to be signed.

Our group testified in Pittsburgh February 17–18, 1976, before Judge Hubert Teitelbaum in a hearing on the comprehensibility and objectivity of this notice of rights. Botel was qualified as an expert on readability, and made a strongly favorable impression on the judge. We presented the data on readability by half-pages of the letter, as shown in Figure 1. At the top of the diagram are some general titles that give some idea of the content of the pages concerned.

The vertical axis on the left shows the Botel readability measure,

---

[3] Notice of rights to back pay under Consent Decree I U.S. et al. v. Allegheny Ludlum Industries, Inc. et al., Basic Steel Industry Audit and Review Committee.

[4] See Van den Broek 1977 for other uses of these measures.

[5] Kroch 1972 deals with the semantics of time adverbials such as *at least,* and Kroch 1979 is concerned with the semantics of quantifiers such as *any.*

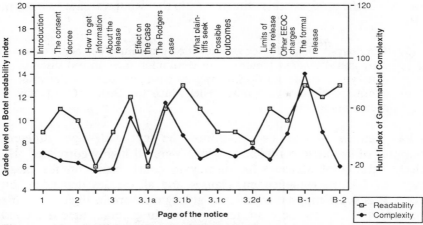

Figure 1   Readability and syntactic complexity of the notice

based on word-frequency as registered in the Lorge-Thorndike list. The measure is in terms of grade-level: it can be seen to vary widely from one section of the document to the other. The index falls to a low level—that is, readability is high—in the section on "How to get information," which begins:

(1)   You should read this letter carefully. If you have any questions which are not answered by this letter, representatives of the Implementation Committee at your plant will be available to answer such questions at the times and place shown on the sheet which you have received along with this letter.

The grade level index is also quite low in the discussion of possible outcomes, where on page 3.1c we read:

(2)   Whichever of the parties in *Rodgers* (either plaintiffs or the defendants) are successful, the unsuccessful parties would be entitled to appeal to a Court of appeals and possibly could appeal to the United States Supreme Court. Such appeals could result in affirmance or reversal of any judgment entered by the District court. Accordingly, it is likely that it will be at least several years even after trial of this case before it is finally known whether plaintiffs or the plaintiff class will receive any back pay or injunctive relief in the *Rodgers* case. Consequently, it is unlikely that there would be any final resolution of the *Rodgers* case, including appeals, before 1979.

On the other hand, the grade level is quite high, and readability low, when the notice deals directly with the Rodgers case, as on p. 3.1b:

> (3) The *Rodgers* plaintiffs seek an injunction prohibiting defendant Company and defendant Unions from continuing such alleged discriminatory policies or practices, as well as back pay, punitive damages, attorneys' fees, and any other relief which the District Court may deem appropriate.

Van den Broek had also examined the text with eight different measures of syntactic complexity, which were all highly correlated. He selected the Hunt Measure for display in court, based on the mean length of T-Units (independent clauses and all clauses dependent on them). It is superimposed on the readability measure in Figure 1, using the vertical index on the right, to show that in general, there is a good agreement between the two measures. The sections that show the lowest grade levels for readability also show the lowest syntactic complexity, and vice versa. Both measures reach a climax with the formal release, which begins with the sentence:

> (4) I, the undersigned, acknowledge receipt of the gross sum shown on the face of this check, in consideration of which I irrevocably and unconditionally release United States Steel Corporation, the United Steelworkers of America, the past and present parents, subsidiaries, divisions, offices, directors, agents, local unions, members, employees, successors and assigns of either of them (severally and collectively "Releasees") jointly and individually, from any and all claims known or unknown which I, my heirs, successors and assigns have or may have against Releasees and any and all liability which Releasees may have to me or them: (1) resulting from any actual or alleged violations occurring on or before April 12, 1974, based upon race, color, sex or national origin, of any federal, state or local equal employment opportunity laws, ordinances, regulations, orders, the duty of fair representation or other applicable constitutional or statutory provisions, orders or regulations; and/or (2) resulting at any time from the continued effects of any such violations by Releasees of any such laws, etc.

The readability and complexity measures diverge at the end of the release, where the language shows complex arrangements of fairly ordinary words as in

> (5) This release is the sole and entire agreement between me and Releasees and there are no other written or oral agreements regarding the subject matter hereof.

Kroch was qualified as an expert in linguistics, and testified on the semantic bias introduced by words like EVEN, AT LEAST, and ANY. He explained to the court that in passages like (2), it was always possible to characterize a length of time by either a least lower bound—WILL BE AT LEAST THREE YEARS —or a most upper bound—WILL BE FINISHED IN LESS THAN FOUR YEARS, and the consistent choice of the former showed a clear bias. He showed that EVEN and ANY introduce further bias toward the writer's point of view that no progress towards the resolution of the case is likely. The multiplication of these presuppositions and negative implications all led to the idea that one should accept the offer and abandon further action.

Judge Teitelbaum carefully followed Kroch's testimony on what the sources of bias were and how they might be eliminated. Here, for example, is an extract from Kroch's discussion of the third sentence in (2) above, as he applies arguments based on Gricean implicatures and his own work on the semantics of time adverbials:

(6) KROCH: Beginning with the words "Accordingly, it is likely that it will be at least several years even after trial of this case before it is finally known whether plaintiffs or the plaintiff class will receive any back pay. . . ." When you indicate only the lower bounds of a time period and not the upper bounds there is a strong suggestion by the reader that it may well drag on indefinitely. Now, I understand that lawyers want to be careful not to make promises that they can't fulfill and that things often go on longer than you might think. However, this document is addressed to laymen who will read it as ordinary English. They won't read these qualifications as being particularly lawyers' qualifications; they will read them as ordinary English and a speaker of ordinary English at least assumes that when a phrase like "at least" is used that the author is using it because he cannot say something more clear and helpful to him. That, on the other hand, it could have said something like, "It is likely that within three or so years this case will be settled." Now, that is slanted the other way . . .

THE COURT: Would it be perfectly unslanted if it said, "You should be advised that it may be three years before this matter is settled." Is that in the middle?

KROCH: Well, frankly, I would take that as in the middle, but whether it is perfectly unbiased is not a question that I can judge immediately.

Throughout the trial, the courtroom was quite full, and several benches were occupied by steel workers from the Homestead plant. We noticed that they paid a great deal of attention to Kroch's testimony, and enjoyed particularly his exchanges with the judge and the defense attorneys.

My own testimony had two parts. One concerned the distribution of elements with semantic bias as against the distribution of readability and complexity. Figure 2 shows the biasing elements that we identified by the half-page, against the background established by Figure 1. It is immediately evident that these biasing elements—ANY, EVEN, AT LEAST, etc.—were not scattered randomly throughout the text. Instead, they are concentrated at just those points where the text is simplest: first, in the section on "How to get information," and then in "Possible outcomes." Our answer to both questions: "is the letter comprehensible? is it objective?" were therefore "Yes." But where the document was comprehensible, it was not objective; and where it was objective, it was not comprehensible. We need not think of such a distribution of bias as the result of deliberate manipulation. Where the authors of the letter tried most earnestly to simplify their language and help the reader decide what to do, they naturally introduced their own way of looking at things—that the Pittsburgh steel workers should take the money and run.

So far, our testimony rested in part on accepted techniques of measurement, in part on linguistic theory, and in part on the specific organization of the document. We emphasized the negative implications of ANY in passages like (2). ANY is a negative polarity element and

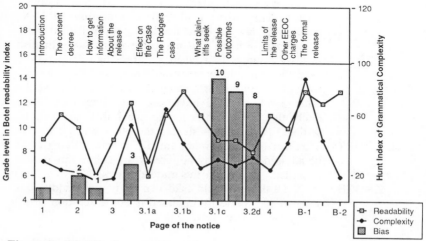

Figure 2 Distribution of biasing elements in the notice

demands negative contexts in sentences like "I (don't) think anything about it." There is a further implication that the occurrence of ANY in neutral contexts strengthens negative interpretations of the existential situation. In (2) the repeated use of this quantifier leads to the implication that even if a judgment is arrived at, there may not be any parties found injured; and even if parties are found to be injured, there may not be any pay awarded. The weakest point in the expert testimony was that our view of semantic bias rested on the linguists' interpretations and any agreement we could elicit from the judge. It was evident that the judge felt that he was as competent as anyone else to interpret the meanings of the words. He was more impressed by the objective measures of readability than by the linguists' analyses of semantic bias. I therefore introduced the results of an experiment designed to determine if the negative implications of ANY were sufficient to influence readers' judgments in a material way.

In this type of field experiment, a situation is constructed where the word or form in question is embedded in an ambiguous sentence, almost evenly balanced by the context. The listener's interpretation is preserved for several more sentences, while he or she discusses the situation. Here, I approached residents of Mantua, a black area of Philadelphia, with a request for help on a case being developed by the NAACP Legal Defense Fund:

(7) This is about a guy in Pittsburgh. He worked for U.S. Steel, for quite a few years. There was a group that was suing the steel companies for back pay, on account of discrimination in hiring policies, so that there were a lot of black people who were earning less money for a long time. So one day he got a letter from the company with a check for $700. If he signed the check within 30 days, he could cash it; but he had to sign a release, giving up any claim or connection with this suit for back pay. He had to figure out what were the chances: if there was a good chance of collecting on the suit, to let the check go; if the chances weren't so good, to cash the check and forget about the back pay. So he went to a lawyer. And the lawyer told him *there was no question about his getting any back pay.* Now how would you deal with that? would you take his advice?

The semantic question revolves around the interpretation of the italicized clause, which was alternatively delivered in two forms to subjects:

(8a) there was no question about his getting any back pay.
(8b) there was no question about his getting the back pay.

Answers to the questions did not always reveal the interpretations made by listeners, but in 16 out of 22 cases, there was a clear indication as to whether people thought the advice was positive—that he would get the back pay, and he should wait for it; or negative—that he would not get the back pay, and should not wait. The effect of *any* was clear:

Table 1.   Negative implications of ANY vs. THE in U.S. Steel Experiment

Interpretation of lawyer's statement on chances of suit	*any* back pay	*the* back pay
positive	2	8
negative	5	1
undetermined	4	4
	11	11

Probability by Fisher's Exact Test, p = .036

This result supports our analysis of the negative implications of ANY in these contexts: the use of ANY can effectively alter listeners' interpretation of a situation and their probable course of action.

The Outcome.

The judge was at first favorably inclined towards our testimony, and in fact asked Mort Botel if he would act as AMICUS CURIAE and rewrite the notice:

> (9) THE COURT: Do you want to do something for history and do it in this case?
> BOTEL: Well, I agree with Mr. Marcus when he said before that this is worth doing.
> THE COURT: Doctor, it is only worth doing as far as I am concerned if it is done by the experts totally independent of counsel and without the interjection of any legal concepts in it, but really stating what is there.

Unfortunately, the judge was not willing to accept the delay that Botel estimated would be necessary to produce a revised notice in truly neutral and readable form. He did ask for a brief on the law concerning the responsibility to communicate to the public, and found none. The judge finally decided to rewrite the notice himself, taking officially into account the existence of these biasing elements. Actually, he changed it very little, and we can consider the case lost.

Judge Teitelbaum ruled against the plaintiffs, arguing that "any benefits which might theoretically be gained by such a revision are far

outweighed by the detriments that would attend a lengthy delay."[6]
Nevertheless, he entered into the opinion the following appreciation of
the new issues raised:

> (10) In support of their position, plaintiffs have offered the testimony
> of various experts in the fields of linguistics and (for want of a
> better term), "readability." I have listened attentively to that tes-
> timony and, candidly, cannot say that I find it to be utterly devoid
> of merit. Indeed, I am inclined to believe that the general question
> of the "readability" level of class and other legal notices is one
> which might well require serious judicial consideration at an ap-
> propriate time.

He added in a footnote that neither the parties nor the Court had been
able to find a case which addresses the "readability" level argument
advanced by plaintiffs.

Though the U.S. Steel case was not won, it introduced into federal
courts the issue of the responsibility of the judicial system to communicate its instructions clearly to the public that must act on them.
Since that time, considerable progress has been made in that respect.
My own participation in this case convinced me that the federal courts
did offer a forum that would attend to and assess objective evidence
on these issues.

THE "THORNFARE" CASE

In 1982, Wendell Harris and I used similar methods to develop testimony in federal court on the "Thornfare" legislation, which involved
a parallel challenge to the objectivity and comprehensibility of a legal
notice. Letters were being sent out to 80,000 welfare recipients notifying
them that they would get assistance for no more than 90 days a year,
since they had been reclassified as "transitionally needy." We were able
to support a legal challenge to this letter by Community Legal Services
of Philadelphia. Research in the community by Harris and myself was
introduced in court to show that the letter was a biased guide to action:
whereas the legislature had provided eight different grounds for appealing such a reclassification, the letter led readers to believe that
there were no such grounds.[7]

On December 24th, Judge Norma Shapiro enjoined the state from

---

[6] Opinion of March 8, 1976, in the case of Rodgers v. United States Steel Corp., No.
71-793.

[7] Labov and Harris 1983 provides a more complete report on this case.

further terminations, and ordered that a new letter be sent out which was more objective and comprehensible. While fewer than one out of 50 people had appealed the first wave of 17,000 letters, one out of seven appealed the second letter. Stronger legal challenges were made to the Thornfare legislation in the months that followed, and this may be considered only a successful delaying action. But as one attorney put it, "we helped quite a few people get through the winter."

THE PRINZIVALLI CASE

In October 1984 I received two tape recordings from attorney Ronald Ziff of Los Angeles. The first tape contained excerpts from a series of telephoned bomb threats made to Pan American Airlines at the Los Angeles Airport. They included such phrases as:

(11)   . . . uh, it's gonna be planted on that plane by [a minority] Communist group and I hope you die on it. It's gonna be a bomb, a nuclear bomb that's gonna be able to kill you and everybody on that plane, and I hope you know it by now.

(12)   . . . there's gonna be a bomb going off on the flight to L.A. It's in their luggage. Yes, and I hope you die with it and I hope you're on that.

(13)   It's like gonna be a big shoot out tonight up in the air when that plane takes off. On 815 there's gonna be a big shoot out tonight up there.

(14)   At eleven when it takes off at 11:15 tonight we're gonna shoot it down. They will shoot it down up in the air after it takes off for tonight.

The second tape had recordings of Paul Prinzivalli speaking the same words. He had been accused of making these telephone calls and was awaiting trial under a series of felony charges. The recording was made by Sandra Disner of the UCLA Phonetics Lab, who with Peter Ladefoged was working for the defense, particularly on voice-print identification data that showed that the two recordings had different voice qualities. They had referred Ziff to me because the defendant was from the New York metropolitan area of Long Island, and apparently people thought that the bomb threat caller was also from New York. I was asked to contribute my knowledge of the New York City dialect to bear on the case.

As soon as I played the tapes I was sure that Prinzivalli was innocent. He obviously was a New Yorker: every detail of his speech fitted the New York City pattern. But it was equally clear that the bomb threat caller was from Eastern New England. In any phrase, one could hear the distinctive features of the Boston area. Every phonetician familiar with the area who heard the tapes came to the same conclusion within a sentence or two, and non-phoneticians who knew the Boston area had the same reaction. In the course of my work for the case, I made recordings of several Bostonians; they all recognized the bomb threat caller as coming from their area without any question.

There was therefore no doubt about the guilt or innocence of Prinzivalli. The problem was how to convey this linguistic knowledge to a judge in the Los Angeles area who, like many other West Coast people involved, heard the two speech patterns as very similar. One could of course testify on the basis of an expert phonetician's opinion that the two dialects were different. But it seemed to me that unless that opinion could be supported by objective evidence that would bring home the reality of the situation to others, there was a serious danger that an innocent person would be convicted of a major crime, with a heavy prison sentence. It is well known that Americans are not sensitive to dialect differences, and from the standpoint of the West Coast, the difference between New York and Boston is hardly noticeable. The differences might appear great to a phonetician attuned to sound patterns, but not necessarily to an untrained listener raised on the West Coast.

Until I arrived in Los Angeles, I knew nothing more about the case than what was on the tapes, and that this was evidence being used to accuse a man of felony charges carrying heavy prison sentences. Here I will present the background facts that were given me after the trial: some have been reported in recent newspaper accounts.

The defendant was a cargo handler for Pan American, the airline involved. He was said to have a grudge against the airlines, because of their handling of shift schedules, among other things, and had been heard to say that he would "get even" with the company. Several executives of Pan American thought the bomb threat calls sounded like Prinzivalli, though others who had worked closely with him thought they did not. He was arrested and released on bail. The bomb threats continued and his bail was increased to $50,000 which he couldn't raise. When he was returned to jail, the bomb threat calls stopped. A month later the district attorney offered to release Prinzivalli on time served if he would plead guilty to three felony counts. He refused, and spent the next eight months in the Los Angeles County jail, awaiting trial.

To prepare for the trial, I first made detailed phonetic transcriptions of the two sets of recordings. I then made instrumental measurements of the formant positions, using the linear predictive coding algorithm

at the Linguistics Laboratory of the University of Pennsylvania, and
the various charting programs which we use for displaying vowel
systems. I did all of this measurement myself, though the other pho-
neticians at the laboratory—Franz Seitz, Sharon Ash and David Graff—
all contributed their critical thinking to the investigation. Since I was
to present the testimony, it was important that I be able to answer for
the continuity of the data and the procedures used throughout by
personal knowledge.

I also made recordings of several Bostonians speaking the same
words, and was able to confirm the similarity of the Boston pattern
to the phonetic features of the tape. Several new and remarkable
characteristics of the Boston dialect appeared in these investigations,
which I did not introduce into the testimony, but do lend further
certainty to our conclusions.

The trial was held in Los Angeles on the week of May 6th, without
a jury, before Judge Gordon Ringer.[8] The defense had been willing to
wait for an opening in Ringer's calendar, since they shared the general
high opinion of his intelligence and ability. The prosecution presented
evidence from ticket-reservation clerks who had given descriptions of
the bomb threat voice at the time, from executives at Pan American
who believed that the voice on the recorded bomb threat calls was
Prinzivalli's, and evidence that he was a disgruntled employee.

The defense began with efforts to introduce evidence from voice-
print identification by Disner and Ladefoged. Although Ladefoged opposed the free use of voice-prints to identify voices as the same, he
has since concluded that voice-print identification is more evidentiary
than we had thought, and can be used to argue that two voices are
different. Disner's analysis showed that the individual voices on the
tapes had different qualities. However, there was considerable legal
argument on the admissibility and reliability of voice-print identification.

I testified on Friday May 10th. I was qualified as an expert on
linguistics on the basis of my phonetic studies of New York City and
other areas, of sound changes in progress and dialect diversity in the
United States. The testimony was divided into four parts: auditory
comparison of the dialect features; differences in phonological structure;
relation to established knowledge of the dialect areas; and instrumental
measurements of the vowel systems. As an expert witness, my role was

---

[8] The account of the trial that I will present below is limited to my own testimony,
the preparation for it, and information I received from the defense attorneys on what
happened immediately after. There was other important testimony that I did not hear,
in particular the statements of Disner and Ladefoged, since I was not allowed to be in
the courtroom while they were testifying.

to present an opinion, along with an account of the various steps that I had taken to reach that opinion, and the evidence that was the basis of it. But my aim was to present that evidence clearly enough so that Prinzivalli's innocence would appear to the judge as a matter of fact, rather than a matter of opinion.

In the first part, I played the tape recordings submitted to show the steps I had gone through to form an opinion. The most effective instrument here was the Nagra DSM loudspeaker, which projected to the four corners of the courtroom a clear and flat reproduction of the voices. Several people who had thought the voices sounded similar were suddenly struck with the differences that they now heard when the sound was projected through the Nagra.

I first called attention to the contrast in the pronunciation of the words BOMB and OFF in the phrase, AND A BOMB GOING OFF, as spoken by the bomb threat caller and the defendant, and displayed the IPA transcriptions of Figure 3.

I also prepared a third tape with copies of the words BOMB and OFF in close juxtaposition, as spoken by the bomb threat caller and the defendant, so that it would be immediately apparent that the vowel quality of BOMB and OFF was the same for the bomb threat caller, but different for the defendant. All of the tokens of short o and long open o words spoken by the bomb threat caller are low back-rounded vowels. But the defendant shows the characteristic New York City distinction between low central /a/ in POSITIVE, lower back /ah/ in BOMB, and the high, over-rounded and ingliding /oh/ in OFF.

The second part of my testimony introduced the theoretical basis of the argument: the concepts of phoneme, phonemic inventory, and phonemic merger. The notion of word class and phonemic identity are difficult enough to establish among linguists, but much more so for the nonlinguist who thinks about language in terms of words and sounds rather than structure. The major emphasis was put on the merger of COT and CAUGHT in the Eastern New England area (as in

There's gonna be a bomb going off on the flight to L.A.

| Bomb Threat | deᵛz gənə bi ə bɔᵒm goɪn ʊf ʊn ðə flaˤɪt tu ɛl eⁱ |

| Defen- dant | deˆz gɔnə bi ə bʊm goɪŋ oᵊf ən ðə flɑɪt tuˤ ɛl eˆⁱ |

Figure 3 IPA transcriptions of the bomb threat caller and the defendant's pronunciations of BOMB and OFF.

Pittsburgh and throughout the Western United States), and on the structural difference between dialects that make such a distinction and those that don't. I also drew attention to some diagnostic phonetic features in the tape recordings, such as the tense front vowel in AIR as spoken by the bomb threat caller, with a following /j/: [ejə].

At this point the judge remarked that the tape of the bomb threat caller did sound to him like Robert Kennedy. But for reasons to appear later, it was important to draw attention away from such direct impressions, and focus instead on abstract structural features of the two recordings. In addition to the merger in the low back vowels, the bomb threat caller showed a consistently fronted nucleus of /ay/ in DIE and FIVE. It was evident that this nucleus was structurally identified with short /a/, while the defendant's New York City pattern showed the expected coincidence of the nucleus of /ay/ with the low central vowel /ah/ of ON.

Most significant was the vowel in THAT in the phrase, "I hope you're on that" in (12) above. In New York City, this is always and absolutely a lax /ae/, and never shows the tensed and fronted phoneme /aeh/. But in Eastern New England, THAT can have the tensed, raised and fronted vowel, at roughly the same position as New York City THERE. In fact, the sentence "I hope you're on that" was mistranscribed in the text originally submitted to the court as "I hope you're on there." Most people still heard it as "there" until I replayed it through the Nagra loudspeaker and pointed out the unreleased /t/ at the end which was clearly audible. Such a pronunciation of THAT is not a real possibility for a New Yorker: of the thousands of short A words measured in our New York City studies, not one ever showed tensed /æh/ or /eh/ before voiceless stops.

The third part of my testimony introduced evidence from American dialectology, to show that the phonological differences between Eastern New England and New York City were established facts in linguistic scholarship. A copy of Kurath and McDavid's *The Pronunciation of English in the Atlantic States* (1961) was introduced into evidence, and the following data was displayed from the table of low back phonemes of each dialect region (p.12):

Table 2. Low Back Vowel Phonemes in ENE and NYC

word class	Eastern New England	New York City
cot, crop, stock, etc	ɒ	ɑ
loss, frost, off, etc	ɒ	ɔ
law, salt, talk, hawk, etc.	ɒ	ɔ

The first column shows for Eastern New England a single phoneme for three word classes: short *o* words ending in voiced stops, which are low central unrounded in New York City, and short *o* words ending in voiceless fricatives, which merge in New York City with the third class of original long open *o* words in the phoneme / ɔ /.

I added to this evidence the figures from my own study, "The three dialects of English" (Labov in press), which include the distribution of the COT-CAUGHT merger for the United States as a whole. These data are drawn from a 1966 study of the speech of long-distance telephone operators, and include information on the perception of speech as well as production.[9] They show the merger located in Eastern New England, an expanding area around Western Pennsylvania, Canada, and most of the western United States. There is no sign of this merger in the New York region or the surrounding mid-Atlantic states.

The last part of the testimony introduced instrumental measurements of the vowel systems of the bomb threat caller and the defendant, providing confirmation of the auditory impressions and the structural analyses.

The vowel system of the bomb threat caller is shown in Figure 4a. This is a two-formant chart, with the first formant on the vertical axis, and the logarithm of the second formant—approximating the perceptual relations—on the horizontal axis. Though we had measured the entire trajectory, and had evidence on differences in trajectories, the patterns appear most clearly in the distribution of vowel nuclei, as shown by the single point for each word selected to represent the nucleus in a systematic way.

Figure 4b showed a comparable analysis for the defendant. To support such displays, it was necessary to present to the court the theoretical concept of formant, and its relation to vowel quality, with some of the limitations involved. It was also necessary to explain the differences between linear predictive coding analysis of the digital signal and spectrographic analysis, which had become involved with the problem of the admissibility of voiceprint evidence. Since we had not used spectrographic techniques in our analysis of the vowel system, our

---

[9] In this study, operators were asked for the telephone number of a Mr. [həri hak], spoken with a low front central vowel. Operators from a one-phoneme area first looked up the spelling H-A-W-K, since it is more common than H-O-C-K. In the course of the discussion that followed, they also gave their own pronunciations of these two words, as well as COT and CAUGHT, reacted to my own two-phoneme pronunciation, and were led to give some information on their own geographical background. Though the mechanization and centralization of telephone information makes it impossible to pursue this approach, it gave a fairly fine-grained view of the status of the merger at that time.

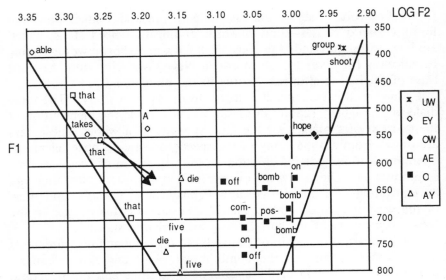

Figure 4a. Vowel system of the bomb threat caller

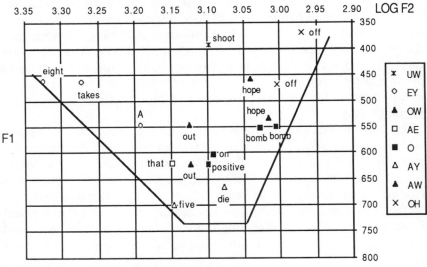

Figure 4b. Vowel system of the defendant

evidence was free of the legal challenges that had been made to voice-print evidence, which uses the electro-mechanical spectrograph.

The significant features of Figures 4a and 4b were presented through a series of simpler displays. Figure 5a showed the single low-back phoneme of the bomb threat caller, with the vowels of BOMB, OFF, ON, POSITIVE and COMMUNIST all in the same low-back range.

Figure 5b showed the corresponding data for the defendant, with the three distinct phonemes characteristic of the New York City system. Most short *o* words like ON, POSITIVE and COMMUNIST have a low central vowel that is represented by the phoneme /a/. A small number of short *o* words are lengthened and backed, and join other long *a*

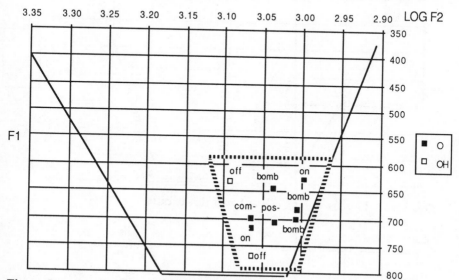

Figure 5a.   /o/ phoneme of the bomb threat caller

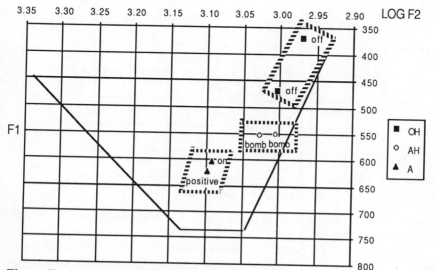

Figure 5b.   /a,ah,oh/ phonemes of the defendant

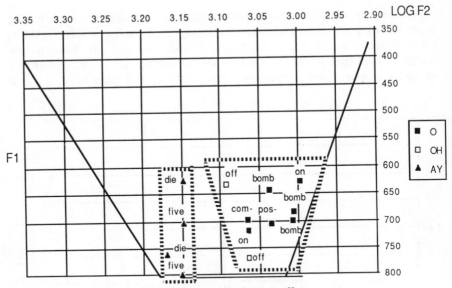

Figure 6a. Low front /ay/ of the bomb threat caller

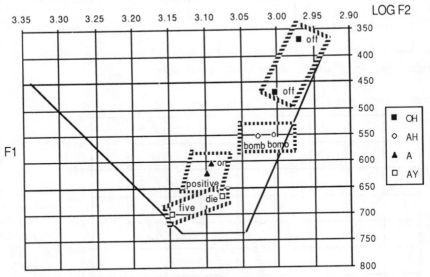

Figure 6b. Low central /ay/ of the defendant

words like FATHER in the phoneme /ah/: BOMB is a member of this class (Cohen 1970).

Figures 6a and 6b dealt with the fronting of /ay/ which marks the Eastern New England dialect; in this system, the nucleus of /ay/ is identified with the nucleus of the /ah/ phoneme that merges traditional long *a* words like FATHER and HALF with words where post-vocalic / r / is vocalized as in CAR and MARKET. In all of these words, the /a/ nucleus is fronted and shows a good margin of security separating it from the low back phoneme that merges /o/ and /oh/. The only representatives of these two fronted phonemes in the bomb threat calls are the /ay/ words. Figure 6a showed the consistent fronting of /ay/ in the bomb threat calls. The comparable Figure 6b showed the situation for the defendant: here /ay/ ranges across the bottom of the vowel system, and the nucleus is not separated from the /a/ phoneme in ON, POSITIVE and COMMUNIST.

At this point it was not necessary to introduce more diagrams or explain the implications of the instrumental data in greater detail. The judge intervened to interpret the diagrams himself, since he saw clearly the relation between the previous testimony and the instrumental display.

I concluded my testimony by stating that all of the linguistic features found in the bomb threat call could be identified with the linguistic features of the Eastern New England dialect, and that the defendant's speech consistently showed the features of the New York City dialect. In answer to the defense attorney's final question, I stated that the two recordings were spoken by different people.

Judge Ringer then asked the defendant to rise and recite the pledge of allegiance to the flag: "I pledge allegiance to the flag of the United States of America and to the Republic for which it stands, one nation, indivisible, with liberty and justice for all." The defendant did so, and the judge asked me if I could point out any relevant dialect characteristics in what he had just said. I was able to indicate a number of defining features of the New York City dialect in including the high back ingliding /oh/ in all, the tensed /æh/ in STAND, and in particular the tensed /æh/ in FLAG. New York City has tense /æh/ before all voiced stops, including /g/. Other Mid-Atlantic dialects have the phonemic split between lax /æ/ and tense /æh/, but none of them have tense /æh/ before /g/. As one passes from New York to Philadelphia, the first sub-class to drop out of the tense category is short *a* the words before /g/: FLAG, BAG, RAG, etc. This confirmed the previous testimony that Prinzivalli's speech showed the specific and consistent features of the New York City dialect.

The prosecution asked only a few questions on cross-examination. Most of the questions concerned the identification of individuals, and whether I could say if a given speech sample belonged to a given person. In response I tried to point out that I had no expertise in the identification of individuals, but that my knowledge concerned speech communities. Though sociolinguistic studies have found from the outset that communities were more consistent objects of description than individuals, there are limits on the range of variation for any individual who belongs to that community.

The question that naturally followed was whether an individual New Yorker could imitate a Boston dialect—whether Prinzivalli could have disguised himself as a Bostonian. My reply was that when people imitate or acquire other dialects, they focus on the socially relevant features: the marked words and sounds, but not on the phonological structures. I was able to cite Payne's work in King of Prussia (1980), which shows that all children acquire the low level sound rules of the Philadelphia area in a few years, but only those with parents raised in Philadelphia reproduce the phonological distribution of Philadelphia lax /æ/ and tense /æh/. If it could be shown that the defendant had had a long familiarity with the Boston dialect, and a great talent for imitation, then one couldn't rule out the possibility that he had done a perfect reproduction of the Boston system. But if so, he would have accomplished a feat that had not yet been reported for anyone else.[10]

On the following Monday morning, Judge Ringer called the attorneys to the bench and asked them if they wanted to continue the case. Since the prosecuting attorney did not consent to dismiss the charges, additional testimony was submitted on voice-print identification. The following morning the prosecuting attorney summarized his case. When the defense attorney rose to present his final argument, Judge Ringer said that there was no need for to him to do so. He acquitted the defendant, finding on the basis of the linguistic testimony evidence of a reasonable doubt that Prinzivalli had committed the crime. In discussion in chambers and to the press, he stressed the clarity and objectivity of the linguistic evidence, a point on which all the attorneys agreed.

Prinzivalli was offered his job back at Pan American, on condition that he did not sue for damages or back pay. He filed suit for damages; the case has not yet been resolved, but he has been reinstated at Pan American and is now working in Long Island. In a letter of thanks to me he said that he had waited 15 months for someone to separate fact

---

[10] A current case in Southern New Jersey involves a parallel problem of identifying the voice of a recorded threat with the voice of a particular person. Here the specific characteristics of the Philadelphia dialect have been useful in arguing that the defendant did not make the call attributed to him. In preparing testimony for this case, Sharon Ash of Penn Linguistics Laboratory carried out experiments to determine whether people trying to disguise their voices altered the phonological features of their dialects. She found that subjects changed many aspects of their speech in attempting to disguise their voices, but the specific phonology of Philadelphia became more prominent.

from fiction, and when he heard it done in the courtroom he was much moved.

CONCLUSION

These three cases are taken from a larger set where linguistic evidence was used to testify in the search for a just interpretation of the facts of the matter. I have chosen them to illustrate the possibilities open to a science of linguistics which draws on observation and experiment to establish its conclusions. All our efforts were not equally successful. But in each case, the objectivity of this approach to linguistics was favorably received by those who are quite removed from the academic issues that determine success or failure within our field.

I have been struck by the intense interest of both attorneys and judges in the objectivity and reliability of evidence. In our legal system it is assumed that there will be advocates and experts on each side. It is assumed that each side will use every rhetorical device to strengthen its case. There is no claim for impartiality in argument. Therefore all the more value is put on the solidity and objectivity of evidence that is inserted into this system of advocacy, which creates belief and justifies decisions in the face of contending parties. It has been pointed out to me that judges in particular are grateful for evidence that allows them to decide a case with confidence, and commit themselves to sleep at night without wondering if they have sentenced an innocent person to jail or let a criminal go free.

The bridge between the facts of a case and the conclusion cannot be made without the help of linguistic theory. No web of inferences and deductions can be made without general principles that rest on a long history of observation and testing. Here I have illustrated the application of the theory of negative polarity, and the association of negative polarity with distinctive meaning. I have also dealt with the theory of the phoneme, intimately connected with the fundamental concept of the arbitrary character of the linguistic sign.

When we contrast linguistic theory with linguistic practice, we usually conjure up a theory that builds models out of introspective judgments, extracting principles that are remote from observation and experiment. This is not the kind of theory I have in mind when I search for a way to establish the facts of a matter I am involved in. It is hard to imagine that a concept like subjacency or the Empty Category Principle would be used in court to decide a question of fact.

We are, of course, interested in theories of the greatest generality. But are these theories the end-product of linguistic activity? Do we gather facts to serve the theory, or do we create theories to resolve questions about the real world? I would challenge the common understanding of our academic linguistics that we are in the business of producing theories: that linguistic theories are our major product. I find such a notion utterly wrong.

A sober look at the world around us shows that matters of importance are matters of fact. There are some very large matters of fact: the origin of the universe, the direction of continental drift, the evolution of the human species. There are also specific matters of fact: the innocence or guilt of a particular individual. These are the questions to answer if we would achieve our fullest potential as thinking beings.

General theory is useful, and the more general the theory the more useful it is, just as any tool is more useful if it can be used for more jobs. But it is still the application of the theory that determines its value. A very general theory can be thought of as a missile that attains considerable altitude, and so it has much greater range than other missiles. But the value of any missile depends on whether it hits the target.

REFERENCES

Cohen, Paul. 1970. The tensing and raising of short [a] in the metropolitan area of New York City. Columbia University Master's Essay.

Kurath, Hans & Raven I. McDavid, Jr. 1961. The pronunciation of English in the Atlantic states. Ann Arbor: University of Michigan Press.

Kroch, Anthony. 1972. Lexical and inferred meanings for some time adverbs. Quarterly progress reports of the Research Laboratory of Electronics of MIT: 104.19–23.

Kroch, Anthony. 1979. The semantics of scope in English. New York: Garland Publishing Co.

Labov, William. In press. The three dialects of English. Quantitative analyses of sound change in progress, ed. by P. Eckert, New York: Academic Press.

Labov, William and Wendell Harris. 1983. Linguistic evidence in the Thornfare Case. Ms.

Payne, Arvilla. 1980. Factors controlling the acquisition of the Philadelphia dialect by out-of-state children. Locating language in time and space, ed. by W. Labov, 143–178. New York: Academic Press.

Van den Broek, Jeff. 1977. Class differences in syntactic complexity in the Flemish town of Maaseik. Language in Society 6.149–182.

POETRY: LINGUISTIC ANALYSIS AND LANGUAGE TEACHING

CHAPTER EIGHT

Poetry and Pedagogy

H.G. Widdowson

University of London Institute of Education

Different domains of inquiry and practice are fenced in by delimiting conventions which determine what counts as a relevant topic and what are the appropriate ways of treating it. Thus disciplines and occupations are defined. These conventions constitute what has been called a paradigm (Kuhn 1970), an epistemological or methodological schema which, so to speak, sets the conceptual coordinates for inquiry. Within the paradigm certain things are done, and others, by fiat, are not: They are, indeed, beyond the pale. In the paradigm of applied linguistics and language teaching, for example, certain topics are immediately recognized as self-evidently relevant: integrative tests, comprehensible input, relative clauses, group work. Other topics are, just as readily, dismissed as irrelevant: astronomy, gastronomy, the imagery of *Macbeth,* the erotic verse of the Earl of Rochester. What I want to discuss in this paper would generally speaking be firmly put in its place in the irrelevant category. I want to talk about literature, more particularly about poetry. Poetry and pedagogy. It might seem that the only relation between them is phonological. I hope to show otherwise.

The conventions of the paradigm not only determine which topics are relevant. They determine too the approved manner of dealing with them: what counts as data, evidence and the inference of fact; what can be allowed as axiomatic, what needs to be substantiated by argument or empirical proof. The paradigm, therefore, is a sort of cultural construct. So it is that the disciplines which concern themselves with language, from their different epistemological perspectives, constitute different cultures, different ways of conceiving of language phenomena and different ways of using language to convey their conceptions. Their positive function is to provide inquiry with the necessary conditions for its operation: for without some conceptual delimitation of domain, there can only be fitful intuition and random thought. But these cultures have their negative side as well. For they also serve the customary social role of establishing group solidarity and closing access to outsiders. So the way language is conceived by another discipline, informed by another set of beliefs and values (the culture of a different tribe of scholars) tends to be seen as irrelevant, inadmissible, or misconceived.

The academic community would provide plenty of scope for case studies in ethnocentric prejudice and cultural intolerance. This means that those who try to promote cross-cultural relations by being inter-disciplinary are likely to be ostracized by both sides and to be stig-matized twice over as amateur or mountebank. The role is even less enviable for those who would seek to mediate not only across disci-plinary boundaries laterally at one level of abstraction but also across different levels of abstraction by referring academic inquiry to the realities of practical applicability. This is what applied linguists claim to do. This is what I want to do in this paper: to try to mediate across these two dimensions. I shall seek to show how poetry is, or might be, treated in the paradigm studies of linguistics and literary criticism on the one hand, and, on the other, how these treatments relate to the practical pedagogy of language teaching. In this way I hope to dem-onstrate that poetry is indeed a legitimate topic for applied linguistic inquiry (alongside integrative tests, comprehensible input and so on) and that the association of poetry with the paradigm is, again, not just a matter of phonological accident.

What meanings are signified in the language of literature? More particularly, how and what does language signify when it is used in lyric poetry? And what do scholars from the linguistic and literary domains of inquiry have to say on the matter? Consider, to begin with, these two pairs of expressions:

A1 Arnold drank some beer.
2 Mary smoked a cigarette.

B1 Swiftly the years, beyond recall.
2 Solemn the stillness of this spring morning.

Linguists and language teachers of a persuasion which gives primacy to sentence structure will immediately recognize the first pair of expres-sions as their sort of data. Familiar grist to the mill. Two sentences, two exponents of the same syntactic structure, two sentence patterns cut to the same basic shape, NP V NP, Subject Verb Object, transitive verbs in the simple past tense, and so on. At one level of analysis, the same surface constituents, sentence patterns from the same substitution table, generated from the same rules: parallel structures exemplifying instances of the same grammatical constituency.

So much, at least for the moment, for the first pair of expressions. Now for the second. A gleam now appears in the eyes of literary scholars. This is *their* kind of data. These are not two separate sentences but the text of a poem:

> Swiftly the years, beyond recall.
> Solemn the stillness of this spring morning.

In spite of what the punctuation might seem to suggest, these are not actually sentences at all in the syntactic sense (as the linguist would be quick to point out) since they lack a crucial constituent: they have no finite verb. Although they are arranged in parallel, they are not to be taken as structurally equivalent sentences but as lines of a poem. Confronted with them we are required to infer some relationship between them, other than that of formal resemblance. This point is made by Empson (1961:24–25), who discusses this little poem (actually a translation from the Chinese) in his book *Seven Types of Ambiguity*. And this is what he says:

> Lacking rhyme, metre, and any overt device such as comparison these lines are what we should normally call poetry only by virtue of their compactness; two statements are made as if they were connected, and the reader is forced to consider their relations for himself. The reason why these facts should have been selected for a poem is left for him to invent; he will invent a variety of reasons and order them in his own mind. This, I think, is the essential fact about the poetical use of language.

But here another voice intervenes, that of a linguist, but from a somewhat different paradigm from the first: one which does not confine attention to sentences but is concerned with discourse also and the pragmatics of meaning as interactively achieved in context. Compactness and the absence of overt connection are not the exclusive features of poetry, he points out. It is a commonplace in pragmatics that the interpretation of any discourse, written or spoken, will require the inference of relations between expressions which have not been explicitly spelled out. Confronted with two adjacent expressions, the language user will invoke the cooperative principle in Gricean fashion, assume the second expression is relevant to the first, engage interpretative procedures or practical reasoning and work out the most plausible connection or implicature. This is an essential fact, not just about poetry, but about *all* uses of language. So it is (our pragmatic linguist continues) that if we also consider the *first* pair of expressions as instances of language use in context and not as sentences to be formally analyzed, then we would seek to infer a relation, bringing to bear as much outside information as might be available to draw out a contextual implication from the utterance (see Sperber &, Wilson 1986). Perhaps Arnold and Mary are husband and wife. Arnold objects to Mary's smoking. He asks her to desist. She for her part objects to his habit of drinking beer for breakfast instead of a more conventional beverage. Quarrel and reconciliation. They make a pact: no beer, no cigarettes. But neither, we must suppose, can long sustain this self-denial. And on one fateful day the pact is broken and

> Arnold drank some beer. (So, or this was because—)
> Mary smoked a cigarette.

A fanciful reconstruction no doubt. But the point is that this kind of expansion or contextual complementation is a natural process in the achievement of meaning and has to be applied by the analyst too in order to explicate how the utterances of two parties in an interaction can be understood as coherent. Garfinkel (1972a:317) describes the task of conversation analysis in the following terms:

> *What the parties said* would be treated as a sketchy, partial, incomplete, masked, elliptical, concealed, ambiguous (note), or misleading version of *what the parties talked about.* The task would consist of filling out the sketchiness of what was said.

Read *poets* instead of *parties* here, and the whole of Empson's literary critical enterprise in his book could without distortion be described in just these terms.

But if poetry cannot be distinguished from ordinary uses of language by this requirement that the reader must realize implicit, concealed, ambiguous relations, how then can it be distinguished? How is this simple two-line poem different from the adjacent utterances about Arnold and Mary and their marital problems, whether occurring in conversation or in a written account?

First, there is the matter of context. Our ability to infer a coherent relationship between the first pair of expressions as utterances, to recognize the second as relevant to the first, would not normally be a matter of invention, but would depend on access to information about their contextual circumstances, and this of course could then be textualized in a fuller, expanded version, thus making clear what was being talked about when these things were said. Labov and Fanshel

(1977) have demonstrated how this might be done. But in the case of the poem, we have no such information to refer to; there is no contextual connection. All we have is the poem. Two expressions which do not even correspond to sentences, presented in isolation. Two parallel lines. Nothing more. We could experiment with expansions. We might, to begin with, try restoring the lines to syntactic respectability by providing finite verbs, and normalizing the word order:

> The years run on swiftly beyond recall (*or* The years are swift beyond recall.) The stillness of the spring morning is solemn.

But what is the connection between swiftness of the years and the solemnity of the spring morning? Perhaps the second is a consequence of the first:

> The years are swift beyond recall. So the stillness of this spring morning is solemn.

But why? We might (as Empson suggests) invent all kinds of reasons. For example:

> The years are swift, they pass by quickly and once they have gone it is not possible to bring them back, or to remember them, or both, and that is to be expected, it is normal, everyday. But this spring morning is still, as if time has stopped, as if life were held in abeyance and yet it cannot be because it is spring and that is a time when life returns after the winter; and this odd paradox is out of the ordinary, and reveals something strange and indeed solemn, like a religious revelation, the stillness like the stillness in a holy place . . .

We could go on, spinning out possible interpretive paraphrases. There is no context to control invention, and no communicative purpose to indicate when we have arrived at a satisfactory approximation to meaning. Possible expansions just proliferate, because, as Garfinkel (1972b) again has pointed out, only purpose can delimit the otherwise inconsequential process of making meaning explicit.

The poem, of course, has long since disappeared, dissipated by prose paraphrase. What then if we sought to make its meaning more explicit by poetic rather than prosaic means, providing an expanded version in verse. We could try:

> The years run swiftly on, their past
> Fades to a distant time, and all
> The present moments are the last,
> As years recede beyond recall.

And yet the stillness of this day
Holds all time, motionless, to bring
A sense of present things that stay
To solemnise this morning spring.

This (I venture to suggest) is not a bad effort. But it does not solve anything. We are still no wiser as to what the two lines of original poem taken together might mean. The prose paraphrase gives only a gloss on the meaning and eliminates the poem in the process. The poetic version just gives us another poem, returning us again to the problem we started with.

We have expended a good deal of effort in our attempts to infer a relationship between these two lines. This would normally indicate a lack of relevance (see again Sperber & Wilson 1986). And yet it is of the nature of poetry to claim relevance, whatever the processing cost may be. We cannot converge on a single satisfactory meaning: instead the meaning is dispersed into divergent interpretations. And yet the poem seems to hold these together in some essential implicational way in the unity of its own composition. The lines have none of the vague indeterminacy of their paraphrase: they sound definite, sure, even assertive. Why should this be so when the meaning is, in conventional terms, so elusive?

Because, I suggest, we have been looking for the wrong kind of meaning. This brings me to the second way in which the poetic lines differ from ordinary utterances.

When, in the company of the formal linguist, we considered the first pair of expressions, we treated them as structures in parallel, related paradigmatically, constituent corresponding to constituent, sentence patterns from the same substitution table. To interpret these expressions as utterances in context, we were required by our pragmatic linguist to relate them differently; not as paradigmatically *equivalent,* but as syntagmatically *combined.* The expressions were related as sentences because they exemplified the same syntactic pattern, related paradigmatically in parallel. But the expressions were related as utterances because, once apprised of a possible context, one followed on from the other, in sequence or in consequence. A happened and *then* B happened: Arnold drank some beer and *then* Mary smoked a cigarette. Or: A happened and *so* B happened: Arnold drank some beer and *so* Mary smoked a cigarette. The meaning of these expressions as utterances is a function of how they combine with context and with each other. Not so with the sentences. They do not combine at all. They just appear in association by virtue of their form.

What, then, of the second pair of expressions? We have been trying to interpret them as if they, too, were related by combination in the matter of ordinary utterances. But are they so related? They are lines in a poem. Lines are of their very nature paradigmatic in character, they appear in parallel, vertically aligned, one above the other. Furthermore, they very commonly assume a metrical regularity, and are themselves constituents of verse form and rhyme scheme. In short, they enter into a relationship of structural equivalence in respect of their prosody in just the same way as the first pair of expressions related in respect of their syntactic structure. In this respect, lines are like sentences.

And yet in other respects, they are not like sentences at all. What is said within the lines, the propositions which are expressed *are* meant to be relevant to each other as utterances in some way, as purposeful sayings, and not just as separate sentential structures. They are connected. But not by combination. They are connected by association, and it is this which brings about the mode of meaning in poetry which I refer to as representation.

Representation might be defined as a mode of meaning which is signified by association over and above that which is signaled by the conventional means of combination. It realizes relevance by correspondence, so to speak, rather than connection. So it expresses a perspective on reality which transcends reference; an alternative order, a realignment of experience, beyond what can be formulated by rational codes and categories; unorthodox, unofficial, a world in parallel, accessible only to art. This is the kind of meaning we must look for in our poem.

Swiftly the years, beyond recall.
Solemn the stillness of this spring morning.

Two expressions, bounded by a capital letter and a period *as if* they were complete sentences. But they are not complete sentences since they lack finite verbs, as we previously noted, and lacking finite verbs there is no marking for tense or aspect. So the propositions expressed are not finite either. They have no referential location in time, past, present, or future. But although they have no location *in* time, they exist *as* time, and this existence is represented differently in each line. The years exist dynamically by their association with adverbial meaning: *swiftly, beyond recall;* the morning exists statically by its association with nominal and adjectival meaning: *stillness, solemn.* The dynamic continuousness of years, and the static punctual moment of the spring morning coexist on the same plane of infinity and in a different dimension from that which we can refer to conventionally by tense and aspect marking on finite verbs.

Now, from the particulars of these lines to a more general observation. For without the general, particulars have no point. In this represented world of literature, normal standards of truth and rationality do not apply. Other conditions for significance hold sway: not better nor more valid but different. We need both. Consider, for a moment, the case of metaphor. The use of metaphor is not the prerogative of poets: it permeates our daily discourse (see Lakoff & Johnson 1980). But it is customary to avoid *mixed* metaphor. When it occurs we generally regard it as a solecism calling for apology and susceptible to ridicule. So even when we depart from the conventions of custom we are constrained by some principle of rational consistency. Mixed metaphor is incongruous, comic, not to be taken seriously. But it is of very common occurrence in poetry, where it excites no such derision. Here, for example, is another poem about time: not two lines now but fourteen, a sonnet by Shakespeare.

> Like as the waves make towards the pebbled shore,
> So do our minutes hasten to their end;
> Each changing place with that which goes before,
> In sequent toil all forwards do contend.
> Nativity, once in the main of light,
> Crawls to maturity, wherewith being crowned,
> Crooked eclipses 'gainst his glory fight,
> And Time, that gave, doth now his gift confound.
> Time doth transfix the flourish set on youth,
> And delves the parallels in beauty's brow;
> Feeds on the rarities of nature's truth,
> And nothing stands but for his scythe to mow.
>   And yet, to times in hope, my verse shall stand.
>   Praising your worth, despite his cruel hand.

Over the eight lines of the octet the metaphor is consistent. Time is associated first with the waves of the sea, then with the rising and setting of the sun. The images are congruent, their effect a sort of seascape. But then, from line nine, with the onset of the sestet this harmony is disrupted by a series of discordant images. Time, first, pierces the blossom of youth, or runs it through as with a sword. What are we to make of that? Why should time transfix *a blossom* rather than a living thing; why should it *transfix* a blossom rather than destroy it, or wither it, or blast it with blight? Then in the next line, another image is invoked, that of a spade digging into the soil[1]; and this is immediately followed by yet another in which time is likened to a beast of prey, and then finally it appears as the traditional figure with the scythe.

Coherence, the recognition of relevance, is elusive here. Instead we have a series of disparate images, an effect of conceptual diffusion. If we were to apply normal rational standards of consistency so as to infer some relevant connection we would find the incongruity intolerable: we cannot take proper bearings on the meaning. But if we consider these images not as combined by connection but as associated by correspondence then we can begin to see that their very incongruity expresses an awareness of reality which cannot be subjected to conventional control, whose instability and elusiveness can only be *represented* in this way by the lack of referential coherence, by a diffusion of images, but held together by the arrangement of meter and rhyme which expresses its own kind of congruence by association. The disordered propositions are given the significance of another and unconventional order by the prosody. This is why the verse shall stand, because it *is* verse. It shifts reality into another dimension.

But it is time now to shift this discussion into a different dimension, from theoretical abstractions to practical application. What bearing does this characterization of poetry have on the business of language teaching pedagogy?

There appears to be at present a tension in linguistics which acts along a continuum between, at one end, the objective specification of general rule, where the study of language is thought of as a science, and at the other end the (relatively) uncommitted delving into data and the assertion of the primacy of particularity, where the study of language is thought of more as an art. The two kinds of linguist I spoke of earlier might find themselves in paradigms positioned at widely separated points of this spectrum. Now there is a comparable tension in language teaching. One pole of attraction draws the teacher towards

---

[1] The relevant entries in the Shorter Oxford English Dictionary read as follows:
Transfix   "To pierce through with, or impale upon, a sharp-pointed instrument"
Delve   "To dig, to turn up (ground) with a spade."
These meanings are dated 1590 and so were attested in Shakespeare's time.
Interestingly (if parenthetically) the new Oxford Shakespeare, published in 1986, includes the following entry in its glossary:
Transfix: "remove"
There is no indication as to what warrant there might be for such a gloss. Certainly there is none in the Oxford Etymological Dictionary. Here, the entry ("to fix by piercing through") is accompanied by a line from *The Fairie Queene,* a poem composed by Shakespeare's contemporary Edmund Spenser:
"Quite through transfixed with a deadly dart."

a pedagogy which asserts the primacy of knowing and which focuses on the formal properties of language; the other attracts the teacher towards a pedagogy which asserts the primacy of doing and allows the learner initiative to discover language through its use in context.

The relevant point about poetry, as I have tried to characterize it, is that it is a use of language which requires meaning to be inferred from context. But the context is created by the patterns of association fashioned within the poem itself. So in the interpretation of poetry there is no disjunction between a focus on meaning and a focus on form. Interpretation can only be achieved by exploring the meanings which are intrinsic to the language itself, in its lexis and syntax, as these are conditioned by the patterns of poetic context. A study of poetry alongside conventional discourses can therefore draw attention to language, not as an abstract system but as a communicative resource. It provides a way (though not the only way) of resolving the needless opposition between form and meaning which has been provoked by recent pronouncements about the acquisition and learning of language (cf. Krashen 1981).

One reason for the inclusion of poetry in language courses, suggested by its very representational character, is that the mode of representation itself can be related to the language learning process. A second reason has to do with the reality which is represented and has to do with the learner's experience of language. And here we confront the very general question of the relevance of literature to life, and return to issues that I touched on at the beginning of this paper.

I spoke earlier of paradigms of inquiry and the way these determine conditions of relevance. Now within the domains of linguistic description, whether this is narrowly focused on the language system or defined more broadly to encompass its use in social context, literature has not conventionally been seen as legitimate data for analysis. The literary establishment has tended to take a complementary view by seeing the matter in reverse: linguistic analysis is not a legitimate operation on literature. Linguistics has, to be sure, dealt with literature from time to time but generally speaking as peripheral to the main business of accounting for normal, nondeviant forms, and the authentic functions of language as directly used in the immediate actuality of social life. There may be an interest in literature but it would not usually be taken seriously as linguistic evidence.

So literature has not generally been seen as a source of data, as *object* language. It is not regarded as reliable either as a source of statments *about* language, or about the social reality which language is used to express. That is to say, it is not legitimate as *meta*-language either. Representation, as I have defined it here, is not regarded as having the same status as referential statements made within the paradigms of established modes of inquiry. A model (be it linguistic, sociological, psychological) is assumed to be ontologically different from a fiction. A novel may make a social comment but not a sociological one. A poem may express a certain psychic state but not a psychological statement. What is said in the name of sociology and psychology needs to be taken seriously: it makes a claim to truth. Novels and poems can be disregarded as being beyond the pale of the paradigm. In no course in the human sciences are they required reading.

One may accept that there is a difference between models and fictions. Models are referential versions of reality, abstract types which claim a correspondence with actual tokens. Fictions are representational versions which cannot be empirically accountable since this referential type/token correspondence is dispensed with in favor of the different sort of representational correspondence already discussed. There is no constraint upon them to tell the truth: all that is required of them is that they should carry conviction. But this does not mean that they are less significant than models, but only that they signify and have significance in a different way. The referential model of reality is more or less empirically valid; the representational model is more or less *experientially* valid.

Let me illustrate the point I am trying to make by invoking the presence of a fictional member of our profession. This is Jim Dixon, the Lucky Jim in Kingsley Amis's novel of that name. Jim Dixon is a lecturer in history in a British provincial university and obliged to convince the authorities there of his academic worth by getting into print if he is to have any hope of tenured employment. Jim Dixon's situation is a familiar one, and will strike a profound chord of recognition in many members of this present audience.

Jim Dixon has written a paper and has submitted it for publication in a learned journal. It has been written in conformity to the approved scholarly conventions. Its title is "The economic influences of the development of shipbuilding techniques, 1450 to 1485." These are Jim's thoughts about it:

> It was a perfect title, in that it crystallised the article's niggling mindlessness, its funereal parade of yawn-enforcing facts, the pseudo-light it threw on non-problems. Dixon had read, or begun to read, dozens like it, but his own seemed worse than most in its air of being convinced of its own usefulness and significance. "In considering this strangely neglected topic", it began. This what neglected topic? This strangely what topic? This strangely neglected what? His thinking all this without having defiled

and set fire to the typescript only made him appear to himself as more of a hypocrite and fool. (pp. 14–15)

This rings true. We have all read, some of us have written, articles of this kind. Although this passage is fiction it conveys through its *representation* of Jim Dixon's particular self-derision aspects of the reality of the academic world that cannot be captured by any other kind of account. Papers from various disciplines of inquiry could expound in their own fashion on the issues that are raised here. The educational question, for example, of what constitutes legitimate research; the sociolinguistic and indeed ideological question of the constraints which are imposed by the schematic structures of conventionalized forms of discourse, the registers or genres of scholarly writing and how they confine individual initiative within a conformity determined by traditional authority. So these disciplines of education, sociology, linguistics can deal with aspects of Jim Dixon's particular experience in their own academic terms—in the very terms, indeed, that Jim himself so dismissively derides as vacuous pretense. This does not mean that the fiction gives us warrant to be dismissive also. Nor that the fictional representation is to be preferred. The point is, rather, that an academic account, in spite of (indeed because of) its conventional criteria of rationality, objectivity and analytic precision, can claim no exclusive patent on enlightenment. Literature, the imagined, fanciful, fictive *representation* of reality is also a force to be reckoned with. It too can give us a valid version of the truth and illuminate our lives.

To return once more to the role of literature in language teaching. Here too the fictive representation of reality has been avoided. Over recent years pedagogic opinion has favored a utilitarian view of learning objectives: the main purpose is seen to be the achievement of practical proficiency. One would not wish to question the importance, indeed the primacy, of this. But too exclusive a concern for this purpose can compromise its achievement by presenting to learners a reduced and meager sampling of the language. The learners come to class with an experience of language which permeates everything they do as social and individual beings. And this experience is compounded of what is directly perceived and what is imagined; of the real and the fictive worlds. Literature plays a crucial formative role in all this. It does not only transpose reality into a different key; it also provides models of an experiential kind for the projection of self in everyday life.

The experience of language that learners bring to the language class is as much representational as referential. It is common to find that in class they are confronted with language which is a very different phenomenon from that which informs their own lives: an impoverished minimal medium for referential transactions, a vehicle of yawn-en-forcement. Of course there must be restrictions on the language intro-duced in class in order to make it accessible, and so it is bound to be restricted in some degree. But it does not follow that it needs to be restricted in *kind*. Representational uses of language have their validity here as well: as a means of engaging the previous experience of learners as mediated through their mother tongue and bringing it to bear on the learning of the new language.

I have tried in this paper to indicate the relevance of literature to life and the learning of language. Literature, I have said, has its own valid revelations of reality through representation. I do not want to suggest by this that we can entirely dispense with rational investigation but only that literary representation too has a role to play in providing insight. Both kinds of discourse are necessary to us. Similarly, it would be absurd to propose that work on literary texts should replace all the customary practices in language teaching classrooms. I suggest only that it has a relevant function, both in developing a knowledge of language as a meaning resource, and also in making learners aware that the language they are learning, like the language they were born to and brought up with, can be creative of realities other than those to which they are socially required to conform. Poetry then can be seen as serving both a pedagogic and an educational purpose in language teaching. It should need no apology.

REFERENCES

Amis, Kingsley. 1961. Lucky Jim. Harmondsworth: Penguin.

Empson, William. 1961. Seven types of ambiguity. Harmondsworth: Penguin.

Garfinkel, Harold. 1972a. Remarks on ethnomethodology. Directions in so-ciolinguistics: The ethnography of communication, ed. by John J. Gum-perz & Dell Hymes, 301–24. New York: Holt, Rinehart, Winston.

Garfinkel, Harold. 1972b. Studies of the routine grounds of everyday activities. Studies in social interaction, ed. by David Sudnow, 1–30. New York: Free Press.

Krashen, Stephen D. 1981. Second language acquisition and second language learning. Oxford: Pergamon.

Kuhn, Thomas S. 1970. The structure of scientific revolutions. Chicago: Uni-versity Press.

Labov, William and David Fanshel. 1977. Therapeutic discourse. New York: Academic Press.

Lakoff, George, and Mark Johnson. 1980. Metaphors we live by. Chicago: University Press.

Sperber, Dan and Deirdre Wilson. 1986. Relevance: Communication and cog-nition. Oxford: Basil Blackwell.

CHAPTER NINE

The Unheralded Revolution in the Sonnet: Toward a Generative Model*

Paul Friedrich

University of Chicago

There is a sort of continuum from a routine conversation to stylized and deeply conventional poetic forms such as the sestina and the sonnet. The sonnet illustrates one extreme case of "poetic language," with acutely constraining rules, patterns, and conventions of all sorts for all levels of sound and meaning. The sonnet, in its gradual changes through history, could serve as an (ideologically conservative) model for a disquisition on "poetry as a cultural system" or as a fascinating instance of a poetic form limited to and deeply ingrained in a linguistically demarcated area (European languages, plus Bengali).[1] It could also be made to serve an argument for extreme limitations on the individual imagination and hence as a qualification to some of the arguments in my book *The Language Parallax*.

But the language of the sonnet—almost as a converse to the language

---

* This lecture appears as Chapter Six in Friedrich (1986). For their critical reading and comments I stand indebted to David Bevington, Dell Hymes, François Meltzer, Donna Jo Napoli, Bonnie Urciuoli, and Robert von Hallberg; for encouragement early on I stand indebted to Lisa Crone (in whose course on *Eugene Onegin* I gave an initial formulation); for both early encouragement and critical comments I stand most deeply indebted to Deborah Friedrich.

[1] Sonnets have been written in Modern Indonesian and, to a much greater degree, in all the major East Indian languages but have remained a minor, ancillary tradition. The notable exception is Bengali, where, starting in the early nineteenth century and continuing recently in the poetry of Jibanananda Das and others, sonnets have constituted a major tradition (some of these sonneteers mastering not only English and French, but Petrarch in the original). The sonnet has been a significant genre in Modern Chinese and, at least in one case, emerged as a primary form for a major Formalist poet, Feng Chih (1905–), who incidentally, in some sense fused the world view of Wang Wei with the form of Rainer Maria Rilke, whom he had studied in Germany.

of dreams—can illustrate the fissures and even the breakdown of order and convention in several ways. Beneath even the apparently rigid paradigms of the Petrarchan sonnet we find a set of formal principles that actually allow for unexpected freedoms of choice and mode— freedoms refreshingly realized by formative sonneteers such as Petrarch himself and Thomas Wyatt. In historical terms again, the premises and potential of the sonnet have recently been loosened up—sometimes exploded—so that today the scope of poetic indeterminacy in the sonnet outweighs the limitations of form; the sonnet actually can open into realms of chaos and indeterminacy while at the same time the individual poems are ordered in diversified and often novel ways. Like dreams, the sonnet form has become a multivisionary means for perceiving and constructing order amid chaos, but also, unlike dreams, of giving intimations of the chaos beneath order and even within order.

THE SONNET IN AMERICA TODAY (1)

To American readers of poetry today as well as to the great majority of our poets the sonnet, like the minuet, is well defined—and passé. Our immediate associations are with Shakespeare, then with Keats and other Romantics (including recent ones such as Millay), and then with the Italian Renaissance. When pressed, the more informed will stipulate fourteen lines in iambic pentameter. And some will recall two structures: the Shakespearean, with three quatrains and a couplet, and the Petrarchan, with an octave followed by a sestet. Sophisticates will remember expanded and contracted sonnets, perhaps unrhymed sonnets, and so forth. And, depending on the universe of discourse, there are semantic notions about stepped progression, logical turns, an argument (thesis, development, resolution), and commitment to "one idea." But the structure of the sonnet, like that of the sonata, is not widely known or discussed.

In our thousands of creative writing classes the sonnet is, like haiku, assigned for a couple of weeks of edifying exercises and basic poetic literacy. But the overwhelming fact of our poetic consciousness is that the sonnet is known, taught, and written as a limited, traditional, conventional, rigid form. A magazine that publishes many sonnets, such as *Plains Poetry Journal,* is unusual. But even in such journals the enormous variation and play that the most traditional rules allow is generally ignored by contributors and editors alike, and the sonnets that appear are almost invariably strictly Shakespearean or Petrarchan. Likewise ignored is the wholesale revolution in the sonnet form that, granted a few pioneers (John Clare, Alexander Pushkin), has largely been achieved by poets such as Frost and Mallarmé writing since the latter part of the last century. Let us turn to two interrelated problems: the obvious freedom of the new practices and the underlying or implicit freedoms in the old rules. We begin with a general, historical background but, after the arrival of the sonnet in England, focus on the English and then the American tradition.

CULTURAL-HISTORICAL SKETCH OF THE FORM

The sonnet ("little sound/song") is one of those rarities in culture history: a complex artifact invented only once by someone whose identity is certain. Giacomo da Lentino (fl.1215–33), one of the Sicilians among the poets surrounding the poet-king Frederick II, invented the sonnet. Fourteen lines of eleven syllables each were structured as two quatrains devoted to exposition and development *(abababab)* and a double refrain of two tercets devoted to the resolution (usually *cdecde*, with *cdcdcd* read as two tercets). The structure itself invited a sharp break or "turn" after the octave. Although the Frederician group was in close touch with Provençal and the German Minnesingers, the sonnet derives from Sicilian (and Arabic) folk song.

This economical and condensed form caught on, became high fashion, and was practiced and refined by other thirteenth-century Sicilians, notably Guido d'Arezzo, who introduced the octave *abbaabba*. Soon afterward poets on the Italian mainland, outstandingly, of course, Dante (1265–1321) and Petrarch (1304–74), gave the form great authority, made the line more flexible, and added several kinds of concluding sestet, particularly the relatively asymmetrical *cdedce*. Many other variants appeared, notably the "tailed" (lengthened) sonnet, the tetrameter sonnet, the retrograde sonnet (with palindrome rhyme), and of course the terza rima sonnet (which violates the strong Italian constraint against a final couplet). The sonnet, with its Classical, Italian, and Catholic symbolism, evolved into a sort of national art form that was used for many themes, addresses, and purposes, including political ones: the morning after a political happening in Florence, dozens of sonnets would appear on the walls. And it was practiced by persons of high and low degree; Michelangelo, for example, is held by some authorities to be an important sonneteer. The Italian sonnet is exemplified by the poem "Tears" by Lizette Woodward Reese (1865–1935) (here and elsewhere I shall try to bring the sonnet into the present by using twentieth-century examples).

Tears

When I consider Life and its few years—
A wisp of fog betwixt us and the sun;
A call to battle, and the battle done
Ere the last echo dies within our ears;
A rose choked in the grass; an hour of fears;
The gusts that past a darkening shore do beat;
The burst of music down an unlistening street—
I wonder at the idleness of tears.
Ye old, old dead, and ye of yesternight,
Chieftains, and bards, and keepers of the sheep,
By every cup of sorrow that you had,
Loose me from tears, and make me see aright
How each hath back what once he stayed to weep;
Homer his sight, David his little lad!

Reese's rhyme scheme illustrates the kind of creative variation to be explored below: rather than having a regular octave, she shifts to *c* (*abbaacca,* which is slant rhymed with the first and fourth lines of the sestet. Her thematic structure, on the other hand, is conventional).

At the center of the medieval Jewish world, Italian Jews such as Immanuel of Rome were writing canonical Italian sonnets in the thirteenth century, albeit in Arabic quantitative meter; but this speech community soon shifted to other directions.

After the sonnet acquired the Italian imprimatur that it still retains, it diffused into other parts of what was to become the sonnet world. It "took" in Provence only somewhat later than on the Italian mainland, and inspired many of the leading troubadors. It arrived on the Iberian Peninsula in the early fifteenth century, was established and produced prolifically by Lope de Vega and others during the "Century of Gold," and has been a basic tradition of Portuguese and Spanish literature ever since (particularly in Mexico). In northern France it had, by the sixteenth century, become a primary form for Ronsard (1524–85) and his circle, and it has attracted many of France's greatest poets, notably Baudelaire, Mallarmé, and Valéry (all using the hexameter). The strength of the sonnet in France and of the French tradition among us is illustrated by Yeats's version of the Ronsard classic: "When you are old and grey and full of sleep, / And nodding by the fire, take down this book, / And slowly read, and dream of the soft look / Your eyes had once, and of their shadows deep. . . ."

Elsewhere we find the sonnet spreading more slowly into the Germanies, not actually reaching them until the seventeenth century, and practiced in a relatively intermittent and uneven way in subsequent years: Rilke is probably the high point in the Germanic community and the greatest influence on sonnet writing in the United States today. The sonnet has been a major form in Greece, forming a sort of companion to the Italian sonnet, and it has been important in Yugoslavia for similar reasons. But in general the sonnet reached the Slavs very late—four to six centuries after Dante—and, for cultural reasons, has played a far lesser role in their literatures. Yet it was used at some point by most of the major Russian poets, such as Mandelstam; and Alexander Pushkin, for his major work, *Eugene Onegin,* "a novel in verse," devised a totally new variant (to which I return below).

Before considering the English-speaking peoples, let me make three general points. The first, which I can barely document, is that thousands of unknown and even unpublished poets have been inspired to write dozens or even hundreds of sonnets; once in a while a great one such as "Tears" is rescued from oblivion. Second, not only are most major sonneteers also major poets, but many of the greatest poets have been drawn to the sonnet. What has attracted them has been significantly independent of cognitive, philosophical, and other considerations at the level of meaning. The content of their sonnets has, in fact, ranged from the courtly eros of Plutarch to Rilke's metaphysics of vision to Baudelaire's often concrete visions of evil to Pushkin's energized narratives and utterly colloquial conversations; perhaps the most basic dimensions amid this variation have been (1) the courtly-elegant versus the colloquial style and (2) profane versus sacred subject matter. But what has fascinated these and other poets and often inspired their poems have been problems of the form of the sonnet.

THE SONNET IN ENGLISH

The sonnet was introduced to England by Thomas Wyatt (1503–42), who, while writing mainly in the variants that he had learned as a diplomat in Italy, also innovated in the *way* he broke the sestet into a quatrain plus a couplet: *cdcdee.* This is the frame for what in my judgment perdures as the most brilliant and forceful sonnet in the English language:[2]

> Whoso list to hunt, I know where is an hind,
>> But for me, *hélas!* I may no more.

---

[2] Wyatt's poem, since dubbed "The Hind," actually was numbered VII in the Edgerton Manuscript and is an imitation of Petrarch's *Rime* 151; diamonds are a Petrarchan symbol of chastity. Otherwise, *noli me tangere,* "Don't touch me," was said by Christ to Mary Magdalene. The sonnet is believed to be devoted to Ann Boleyn, once Wyatt's lover, and the "Caesar" here is Boleyn's eventual husband, Henry VIII.

The vain travail hath wearied me so sore,
I am of them that furthest come behind.
Yet may I, by no means, my wearied mind
    Draw from the deer; but as she fleeth afore
    Fainting I follow. I leave off therefore,
Since in a net I seek to hold the wind.
Who list her hunt, I put him out of doubt,
    As well as I may spend his time in vain;
    And graven with diamonds in letters plain
There is written, her fair neck round about,
    "Noli me tangere, for Caesar's I am,
    And wild for to hold, though I seem tame."

Wyatt's innovations were completed by his near contemporary, Henry Howard, Earl of Surrey, to yield a sonnet with three distinct quatrains *(ababcdcdefef)* and a concluding couplet *(gg),* hence a maximization of rhyme, a relatively stepped progression, and a strong sense of closure. After Surrey, Spenser (1552–99) invented a melodic, concatenated variant *(ababbcdccdcdee)* that, despite its great potential, has been used but rarely since. Then Surrey's scheme was given "deathless" prestige by Shakespeare's 154 sonnets.

It is the Italian forms, however, that have been somewhat favored—for example, by Donne (1573–1631) and Milton (1608–74), the latter of these revolutionizing the sonnet by dropping the sharp break midway and giving the whole poem a single, continuous vision; both took the sonnet away from song and toward a more conceptual focus. Granted some partial exceptions such as Cowper, it can be said that the sonnet was eclipsed by the Neoclassical forms of the late seventeenth and the eighteenth centuries—as it was in Europe generally. But it reemerged as one of the essential vehicles for the Romantic movement, favored and developed by Keats, Shelley, Wordsworth (who wrote over five hundred sonnets), E. B. Browning, Longfellow, and later by the Rossettis and many others. In general, the Italian and the Shakespearean variants were adhered to rather rigidly.

SUMMARY: SURFACE STRUCTURE

Except in the hands of isolated geniuses, the sonnet, until Hopkins and the French Modernists, was governed overwhelmingly by certain rules, most of which, in the conventional view that prevails, are still observed today (some of these are not, of course, peculiar to the sonnet).

The Line. A metrically regular (usually iambic pentameter) line, either with a strong caesura or with a marked increase or thrust of energy in the center. The line, in either case, is strongly felt as a unit, and enjambment is highly marked.

Rhyme. The rule is regular, full rhymes, including many in the same part of speech and even the same inflectional form. The indispensable end rhyme is balanced by internal texture in various ways (alliteration in English, internal rhyme). Overall schemes are of the Italian or English varieties already discussed.

Vision and/or Logical Structure. The sonnet usually argues a single idea, with a break near the middle (accompanied by a full stop between the octave and sestet) or with an argument in three parts—or both (in the sense that there are two interacting structures). As a continuing feature, the sonnet is, at the same time, both markedly stichic and markedly strophic.

Variation. These surface rules lead to many natural variations. Starting with an *abab* sequence, the second quatraine can be reversed, as in Sidney, to *baba;* or an initial octave in *abab* or *abba* can be followed by *cdcd.* On the other hand, an overall chiasmic structure (e.g., *abbaabbaabba*) creates a quite different phonic potential. A different, recursive potential can be achieved by looping back to *ab* in the sestet or the couplet (as in Josephine Miles's "Tally"). Many other variations were devised in the Renaissance or since or have been infused with new life, as in Frost's "Acquainted with the Night," which includes twelve lines in terza rima, then a concluding couplet.

THE MODERN PERIOD

The Modernist—or, perhaps better, the modern period between the late nineteenth and mid-twentieth centuries—witnessed a curious bifurcation. On the one hand, four "giants" of those years eschewed the sonnet because, for example, it was associated too much with traditional forms such as the iambic pentameter, or tended to entail the completion of a rhyme scheme with padded lines, or was too dependent on a Renaissance-style "argument." Eliot, Moore, Stevens, and Williams wrote practically no sonnets (Williams opposed them explicitly), and this despite the fact that all four participated significantly in the American version of the Romantic tradition and were close students of the Renaissance lyric and of modern literature in the Romance languages (or at least of French in the case of Moore and Stevens). To some extent, they wanted to perpetuate not the form but some of the spirit or world view traditionally associated with and expressed through the sonnet. Yeats, Pound, and Auden seem intermediate: they crafted some superb sonnets but contributed little to its evolution. Some other poets added great sonnets to the tradition: Crane, Jeffers, Millay, Robinson, and Owen. Four other "giants" of Modernism, on the other hand, practiced and even favored the sonnet and innovated radically: Hopkins in line length, sprung rhythm, and overall phonic texture; Frost in line rhythms and rhyme schemes; Lawrence in diction and dialect; Cummings in intonation and stanzaic structure. And all four of these poets moved the sonnet closer to conversation.

The troubled, liminal period between the poets just mentioned and the self-conscious pluralism of today went in two directions. Half or so of the leading poets, including Bishop, Jarrell, Roethke, and Olson, ignored the sonnet because of its cultural associations or because its formal powers lead in directions quite different from the ones they were seeking. But many southern poets such as Tate and Ransom did write many sonnets, as did Lowell, Berryman, and their sympathizers, partly in reaction to the Modernists, partly to explore new possibilities such as the unrhymed sonnet; in *History*, Lowell eventually generated 568 "pseudo-sonnets," which, whatever one may think about their quality, opened up a loose and accessible variant of the form to many younger poets.

MORE SURFACE VARIATION

Given the considerable surface constraints just noted as well as others, we find a number of innovations that we can group in terms of initial units of various kinds, two-part divisions, cutting and extending the sonnet, and deviating from the isometric (usually pentameter) line.

Against one powerful rule, which precludes an initial couplet, we find Frost's "The Oven Bird" ("There is a singer everyone has heard / Loud, a mid-summer and a mid-wood bird"). And against an equally powerful constraint, which precludes starting with a sestet, we find his "Mowing" (see below; there is at least one precedent for this, Shelley's "England in 1819").

There are other variations. Herrick's "I sing of brooks," Clare's "Evening Primrose," and Frost's "Once by the Pacific" are all in seven couplets. We occasionally find a sonnet consisting of two seven-line stanzas—for instance, in Robinson's "The Companion." These symmetrical sonnets break the strong rule of dynamic asymmetry in overall form (which is reminiscent of the rule against a sixth-foot caesura in the dactylic hexameter line).

The extended or "tailed" sonnet of the Renaissance reappears, and Hopkins invents the curtailed sonnet, notably exemplified in "Pied Beauty." Semisonnets (four united quatrains) had been devised by

George Meredith (1828–1909), as in his "Modern Love," and other semisonnets have followed since then. To this I would add the "intended sonnet," where what by various criteria was meant to be a sonnet and still feels like one has veered away from the norms of line length, number of lines, and so forth, conventional rules being sacrificed to what the poem is trying to be: for example, Owen's magnificent war poem "Futility." On the dimension of line length, short-liners of many kinds have appeared or reappeared, a typical case being Wylie's Italian "little sonnet" in iambic tetrameter. Much less orthodox have been the experiments of Kinnell and Ashbery; the latter's "Dido" begins, "The body's products become / Fatal to it. Our spit / Would kill us, but we / Die of our heat." Long-line sonnets were pioneered by Hopkins; "The Windhover," for instance, runs to seventeen-syllable lines that break the limits of the printer's page, to wit: ". . . king- / dom of daylight's dauphin, dapple-dawn-drawn Falcon, in his riding." No one has tried to combine a Whitman-style long line with the sonnet format, but this has potential and would technically syncretize two traditions that have long been basic in American poetry. Other, actually realized variations involve the interaction of a real or implied rhyme scheme with forms on the printed page that are unconventional; for example, Cummings's unrhymed sonnet "you shall in all things be glad and young" has the lines grouped in the following blocks on the page: 2–4–2–4–2. These questions of visual layout and other so-called concrete effects of the printed page are maximally removed from the sonnet-as-song values of the Renaissance, or, later, the concern with the potential music of language among sonneteers such as the Rossettis.

GENERATIVE RULES

As has been known for centuries, the octave invented by Guido d'Arezzo can be read at least three ways: as three couplets bracketed by a rhyme, as two quatrains, and as two quatrains overlapping with a quatrain (or even two tercets bracketing a couplet). This can be diagrammed as follows:

a (bb aa bb) a
abba   abba
ab(ba   ab)ba
abb   (aa)   bba

The sestet, too, can be read variously, which means that the sonnet as a whole is always phonically ambiguous to a high degree, or, in other words, that several levels of rhyme have to work together more or less simultaneously. By the same logic, the sonnet should not be conceptualized in terms of overt rhyme schemes but in terms of combinatory possibilities that can be generated by a set of underlying givens.

Three things normally are assumed for the octave: symmetry, the minimum of two rhymes, and no initial couplet. This leaves the following possibilities:

I	II	
abba	*abba*	= 6 octaves
abab	*abab*	
	aabb	

of which the two with *aabb* in position II would be marginal.

If we then assume up to three rhyme words in the tercet *(c, d, e)*, we get the following sestets: *cdecde, cedced,* and so forth. Of the mathematically possible sestets, Petrarch favored at least four: couplets *(cdcdcd)*, repeated, symmetrical tercets (particularly *cdecde* and *cdccdc*), and asymmetrical tercets (particularly *cdedce*). Even within these limits there are four times four or sixteen totally conventional Italian sonnet forms. But at least one anthologized English-language sonnet in the Italian style has been found that ends in one out of fifteen of the total number of possible sestets. If we multiply this total of fifteen sestets times the total of four (non-marginal) octaves, we get a total of sixty possible rhyme schemes with a good precedent in our language. The sestets that I have found, with the names of the poets and the poems, are tabulated in Figure 1.

SUGGESTIVE CONSTRAINTS

The enormous formal potential of even the conventional sonnet is constrained in the most diverse ways.

Sonnets—even a sestet—in triplets are precluded; in English, at least, this is simply an intensification of the limitations and difficulties inherent in the triplet. Given the incantatory power of triplets, a triplet sonnet remains a possibility.

A number of other sestets are not used in English, or at least are very rare: *effgge* (in Auden's "Who's Who") and *cddcdd* and *cdedce* (which are common in Italian—Petrarch also has *cdcece* [in XXVI] and even, with a triplet, *cdddcc* [in XIII]).

The sonnet with a retracted, that is, nonfinal couplet, is rare, although

Italian #1	*c*	*d*	*e*	*c*	*d*	*e*	Berryman, "Sonnet 25"
Italian #2	*c*	*d*	*c*	*d*	*c*	*d*	Hopkins, "Carrion Comfort"
Italian #3	*c*	*d*	*e*	*d*	*c*	*e*	Cummings, "Next to of course God—America I"
cd-	*c*	*d*	*e*	*e*	*d*	*c*	Auden, "Who's Who"
	c	*d*	*c*	*e*	*d*	*e*	Auden, "Our Bias"
	c	*d*	*e*	*c*	*e*	*d*	Wordsworth, "On the beach at Calais"
	c	*d*	*d*	*e*	*c*	*e*	Thomas, "February Afternoon"
	c	*d*	*c*	*e*	*e*	*d*	Robinson, "Souvenir"
	c	*d*	*d*	*c*	*e*	*e*	Pushkin, *Eugene Onegin* (Nabokov)
	c	*d*	*c*	*d*	*e*	*e*	Frost, "Putting in the Seed"
cc-	*c*	*c*	*d*	*e*	*e*	*d*	Frost, "Range-Finding"
	c	*c*	*d*	*d*	*e*	*e*	Berryman, "The Poet's Final Instructions"
	c	*c*	*d*	*e*	*d*	*e*	Robinson, "How Annandale Went Out"
II c-d	*c*	*d*	*c*	*c*	*d*	*c*	Frost, "Design"
	c	*d*	*d*	*c*	*d*	*c*	Santayana, "O World"
	c	*d*	*d*	*c*	*c*	*d*	?
	c	*c*	*d*	*c*	*c*	*d*	Hopkins, "I Wake and Feel the Fell of Dark"
III	*c*	*c*	*c*	*c*	*c*	*c*	?

Figure 1. The Sestets (following an octave in *a* and *b* only)

the *ccdeed* variant was used by Dante Gabriel Rosetti, who was, of course, exceptionally close to the Italian tradition. The *ccdede* variant occurs once in my sample ("How Annandale Went Out"), but the fact that even in French it had to be championed by F. de Malherbe (1555–1629) in a swirl of poetics controversy suggests that powerful constraints are at work. Incidentally, Pushkin used this sestet in one of his rare sonnets, "Madonna."

It was Pushkin, too, who invented a form of the sonnet that occurs in the work of no other poet in no other language except in the work of Nabokov and more recently, Seth. Yet this scheme would be singularly appropriate for English because it maximizes not only the number of (perfect) rhymes but the possible overall variation (assuming multiples of two) as follows: *abab ccdd effe gg*. Consider the following superb translation by Arndt of *Eugene Onegin* 5.2:

> Winter . . . the peasant, feeling restive,
> Breaks a new trail with sledge and horse;
> Sensing the snow, his nag is restive
> And manages a trot of sorts;
> Here passes, powdery furrows tracing,
> A spirited kibítka, racing,
> The coachman on his box a flash
> Of sheepskin coat and crimson sash.
> There runs a yard-boy, having chosen
> To seat his "Rover" on the sled,
> Himself hitched up in horse's stead;
> The rascal rubs one finger, frozen
> Already, with a wince and grin,
> While Mother shakes her fist within.

The constraints enumerated above suggest that the sonnet is often controlled by formal and cultural factors that are relatively subtle and remain to be explored. For one thing, the greater formal variation among the Italians (and persons imbued with Italian such as Pushkin and D. G. Rossetti) suggests that the "native" imagines *il sonneto* more in the generative terms that I have outlined, whereas, except for master experimentalists such as Frost and Robinson, the English-speaking poet thinks of the Italian sonnet in terms of a memorized surface rhyme scheme.[3]

BREAKING THE RULES

In the twentieth century so many variations on the sonnet have emerged that we are in a new sonnet world. These innovations have involved the (unmetered) line, rhyme (e.g., unrhymed versus full rhyme), the role of enjambment, overall gestalt, the continuity of meaning, the types of subject matter, and the attitudes and stance of the poet. Consonant with my general contention that the gist and appeal of the sonnet is primarily formal, let us look at some of the variation in the limited area emphasized in this article: the overall rhyme scheme seen, not as random or incidental variation, but as poets' strategies that arguably contribute to the power of the sonnet.

In one kind of innovation the poet adheres to a conventional format except for one obvious break. Thus, John Crowe Ransom (1888–1974) ends his Shakespearean "Winter Remembered" with "And there I went, the hugest winter blast / Would have this body bowed, these eyeballs streaming"—where "blast" does not rhyme with earlier lines in the poem, and "streaming" only slant rhymes with "-ealing" in lines ten and twelve.

In a second kind, intensification is achieved through cumulative slant rhyme, as in Laura Riding's "The Map of Places," which starts out $abb_1b_2b_3b_3b_4$ ("passes . . . tears . . . are . . . were . . . her . . . there"), and then concludes with four couplets. Hart Crane's sonnet to Emily Dickinson, in a diametrically opposite order, starts with four couplets—which also can be read as two quatrains—and then shifts to ddd_1d_1 before the final couplet ee. Clearly, the repetitiveness of several perfectly rhymed couplets is being played against the freshness of rhymes that are not only slanted but cumulatively so.

By a third general strategy, an overall symmetry of rhyme is preserved even while departing from the traditional formats. Merrill Moore (1903–57), in more than one thousand published sonnets, provides some of the most interesting and numerous innovations in this direction—for example, a rhyme scheme that can be bracketed as follows: *abc deed ff bac ff*. Moore's sonnets hit upon a significant fraction of the mathematically possible full-rhyme schemes.

Fourth, an expectation of rhyme may be created by the initial lines but then be frustrated in various ways. A poem can start with *abba* in iambic pentameter tone and then veer off in the direction of open form. Hopkins, on the other hand, begins "The Windhover" with an octave in final "-ing" before shifting to a regular sestet. In his phonically extraordinary "When I read Shakespeare—" Lawrence shifts asymmetrically between several full and slant rhymes: "wonder . . . thunder . . . *language* . . . daughters . . . rougher . . . chuffer . . . *with* . . . snoring . . . whoring . . . choring . . . goring . . . daggers . . . are . . . gas-tar." Mandelstam uses only *a* and *b* in his poem "Pedestrian": *abab baba bab aba*. Mallarmé's equally brilliant "The Virgin, The Vivid, and the Splendid New Day" revels in final assonance: "aujourd'hui . . . ivre . . . givre . . . fui . . . lui . . . livre . . vivre . . ennui . . . agonie . . . nie . . . pris . . . assigne . . . mépris . . . Cygne" (where octave and sestet are clearly indicated, however).

Some of the most interesting sonnets display unordered or at least highly asymmetrical variation. Kinnell in his "In Fields of Summer" shifts from *a* to *h* but then cuts back to gg_1ii_1h ("look . . . flakes . . . deepening . . . up . . . dew"). Other modern sonnets verge on being prose spread over fourteen isometric lines, which may or may not be isometric. But let us close with Frost's "Mowing" because it illustrates the freshness and power of the move toward asymmetry. Using capital letters for the second member of a slant rhymed pair, we get:

ab c ab de c dE eD eD

which reflects several underlying groupings. On phonic grounds as well as in virtue of its many interacting meanings, Frost was justified in regarding "Mowing" as one of his best ("I come so near what I long to get that I almost despair of coming nearer"; Frost 1964:83).

> There was never a sound beside the wood but one,
> And that was my long scythe whispering to the ground.
> What was it it whispered? I knew not well myself;
> Perhaps it was something about the heat of the sun,
> Something, perhaps, about the lack of sound—
> And that was why it whispered and did not speak.
> It was no dream of the gift of idle hours,
> Or easy gold at the hand of fay or elf:
> Anything more than the truth would have seemed too weak
> To the earnest love that laid the swale in rows,
> Not without feeble-pointed spikes of flowers
> (Pale orchises), and scared a bright green snake.
> The fact is the sweetest dream that labor knows.
> My long scythe whispered and left the hay to make.

Curiously, the sonnets that maximize overall variation of rhyme to the point of lacking it and those that, on the contrary, minimize it to the point of having only *one* end word, *both* eliminate the formal (i.e., rhyme) counterpart to the bipartite semantic structure or argument that has usually been so integral to the sonnet tradition.

POETIC PRACTICE: THE SONNET WITHIN

> All poetry is experimental poetry.
>
> WALLACE STEVENS, *Opus Posthumous*

In symbolic studies today a major theoretical enterprise or exploration is to be explicit about subjective factors and to explicitly relate one's authorial subjectivity to what used to be called the object of analysis. These explorations, depending on the author, may derive from a Neo-Marxist epistemology or an Orientalist, existentialist, or phenomenological philosophy, or (as in my case) as an analogy from the principle of indeterminacy in physics ("the observer is an integral part of the universe of observation"). Whatever the sources—and they must be multiple in all cases—I subscribe to these explorations and have already experimented many times, notably in *The Meaning of Aphrodite;* within the main focus of the present chapter—"toward a generative model"— an essential constituent is my own experience and use of that model.

In the fall of 1982, having read thousands, memorized hundreds, and written dozens over the years and having more time for writing because of a Guggenheim, I decided to explore the inner form of the sonnet while simultaneously writing a set myself. To use either of the standard variants for my own work struck me as atavistic but other options did not.

After some experimentation I resolved to more or less follow certain guidelines.

There would be one central idea, but not necessarily an "argument."

I would use any of the rhyme schemes that could be generated by my model, but I would not sacrifice meaning or a good line simply to satisfy such a scheme. I would use slant rhyme partly à la Dickinson, but often in a sense of "sounding alike" or being sufficiently similar in terms of the number of features shared by two forms in a close phonetic transcription (e.g., the "advent" and "gnats" rhyme in my poem below). Full rhyme was almost entirely for emphasis or other special effects. In other words, a complex system of potential rhyme would generate a poem, but the final surface form did not have to conform to one of the standard sonnet types in the "great tradition."

The lines would be isometric, with their length to be determined by the first line—my usual point of inspiration and departure when writing. These point-of-departure or jumping-off lines could range from nine to twelve syllables, or four to six stress or energy groups (my idea of "energy group" cannot be spelled out here). Despite isometricity, the length and semantic quality of the line should not, once again, be sacrificed by adding or deleting a canonical stress or syllable, more or less. At a more intuitive level, I would avoid a strong iambic pentameter or similar traditional sound or pattern. Thus line length was also part of a generative system rather than a procrustean surface.

Finally, there would be fourteen lines, with strong closure on the last two.

What was new about these guidelines was partly the combination: my particular use of slant rhyme in a sonnet and my definition of slant rhyme itself; the degree of variation not only allowable but allowable in terms of relatively explicit generative rules; and the idea of variable but generally isometric lines, whose length would be determined by the first line that had sprung into being. Other semantic criteria regarding metaphor and "keying," while also operative, will not be discussed here.

For over five months, for an hour or two each morning, early, I wrote sonnets, eventually completing about forty as well as redoing about twenty open or free-verse poems into sonnet form; a half dozen of my earlier poems *already were* sonnets by the new criteria. Typically, I would produce a complete draft in an hour or less on one day and then revise it over two or three days (often during long walks in downtown Chicago). My main experiences were: that these poems tended to fall into two parts simply as a consequence of mental energy— they tended to be composed in two bursts; that few readers noticed that I was using slant rhyme or, at readings, that they *were* sonnets; that stress groups and energy peaks yielded better lines, as a rule, than syllable counts; that some of my free-verse poems were improved by being put into sonnet form, whereas others were improved by being cast into sonnet and then *back* into various free or open forms.

As a sort of control and also to slow myself down I eventually began doing rough draft translations of all my sonnets into Russian. Attempts to have these translations finished by master translators (and native speakers) have indicated that on all counts, notably lexicon, the poems were highly untranslatable (which seems to imply, in the first instance, a relative embeddedness in the semantic nuances of American English).

Of the fifty-odd sonnets only sixteen, seven of them new (as opposed to those reworked from older poems), satisfied my criteria for quality. Of these, nine have been placed in professional poetry journals or in anthologies; one of the better of these (cited below) will appear in the *Kansas Quarterly* (1985). Although some of my sonnets were rewritten dozens of times over the months (scores or hundreds of times if we count "mental rewriting"), "Generation" remains a third draft.

Generation

The Hermit Thrush, crushed by tires in our alley
lies far from Guatemala, from the Yellow-Jacket
who hovers over the thrush's blood, expectantly.
Some message in the bird's code, genetic bits—
runes cut in a runestick—made it wing
south out of the White Pine stands of Ottawa
over the wheatfields like a man seeking home
or, perhaps more, a woman pressing inward
along the sidewalks of her mind that are cracked cement
with dead birds, but where witchgrass and plaintains
sprout in the fissures, pioneering the advent
of a weedy field, then bushes, and then again
high climax stands of conifers swarming with gnats
where thrushes will feed during the northern summer.

Having—to use trade lingo—included the participant-cum-observer in the universe of description, let us now return to that larger universe.

THE SONNET IN AMERICA TODAY (2)

Given the formal potential of even the conventional sonnet that was shown earlier, what is the status of the sonnet today? None of the fifty to one hundred established, recognized poets who have won or at least been nominated for major national prizes (so-called Mandarins) or, for that matter, who have been on the cover of *The American Poetry Review,* currently write sonnets. Ashbery, Bly, Merrill, Merwin, Rich, and Snodgrass wrote sonnets long ago and some (notably Ashbery and Merrill) even published excellent sonnets, but they are not writing sonnets now or encouraging others to do so. The contemporary lack of enthusiasm for the sonnet increases among "pace-setting" younger poets such as Bidart, Dubie, Forché, Gallagher, Graham, Harrison, Strand, and Wakoski (granted, the last of these got started writing poetry with Shakespearean sonnets and has published a superb sestina). Among the poems by "poets under forty" (as of 1975), conscientiously selected for *The American Poetry Anthology,* not one sonnet appears. In fact, it is bizarre, even absurd, to think of the two groups of poets just named as advocating the sonnet. Apparently, recognized poets avoid the stigma of seeming to regress to the sonnet in an obvious way. Undeterred by these biases, however, let us look at some of the new possibilities as actually exemplified by recent poetry.

First we must ask: what is the sonnet today? Where, in American poetry, does one draw the line between the "canonical" sonnet and all other sonnetlike things? In my opinion only two sets of criteria survive. The first are specific and formal. Most poets and critics still hold to the skeleton of fourteen lines, even after everything else has been discredited. Somewhat less diagnostic is that the lines be of equal length, usually about the same visual length, and be reminiscent of iambic pentameter. Finally, there is the less obvious criterion that the rhymes and visual breaks between sections be in multiples of two, that is, that they involve division into equal sets; the only exceptions to this powerful criterion have been the innovations in the direction of randomness noted above. The second set of criteria is really a "fuzzy" set: some necessary and sufficient combination of diction, argument, world view, and perhaps a dozen other things (including, of course, line and rhyme). The basic answer to my initial question, however, is that *no* line exists nor should one be drawn between the many canonical sonnets and other sonnetlike and sonnetoid forms, including the grey marginal area of poems whose authors themselves would not want to call sonnets even though some of their meaning derives from vibrations and resonances within the sonnet world.

It is difficult to relate the conventional sonnet to today's poetic consciousness, notably its decentered pluralism. That the sonnet can still engage criticism is shown by Cunningham, Kelly, A. Stevens, and a few other sonneteers. That sonnets can succeed with the general public is shown by the perennial sales of Millay in practically all major bookstores. Some well-known contemporaries, including Ashbery and Hollander, have written sets of sonnetlike lyrics predicated on a purely formal criterion or variation (e.g., thirteen lines, fifteen lines) very recently, in 1986, the lacuna represented by the absence of the "Eugene Onegin stanza" from four hundred years of English sonnets was filled— as if fulfilling a prediction—by Vikram Seth's *The Golden Gate.* At the grass-roots level sonnets are produced in enormous quantities; for example, both the Poetry Club of Chicago and the Illinois State Poetry Society sponsor "international" competitions in both the Shakespearean and/or Petrarchan sonnet, and I am sure the same happens in some other states. A stronger argument for contemporary relevance is provided by the work of Claude McKay, as bitter, haunting, and "relevant" today as it was four decades ago during the "Harlem Renaissance."

The Harlem Dancer

Applauding youths laughed with young prostitutes
And watched her perfect, half-clothed body sway;
Her voice was like the sound of blended flutes
Blown by black players upon a picnic day.
She sang and danced on gracefully and calm,
The light gauze hanging loose about her form;
To me she seemed a proudly-swaying palm
Grown lovelier for passing through a storm.
Upon her swarthy neck black shiny curls
Luxuriant fell; and tossing coins in praise,
The wine-flushed, bold-eyed boys, and even the girls,
Devoured her shape with·eager, passionate gaze;
But looking at her falsely-smiling face,
I knew her self was not in that strange place.

CONCLUSIONS AND SPECULATIONS

Even the limited area of rhyme dealt with in this article has demonstrated or suggested the potential of, for example, the phonic ambiguities of the octave, the many possible "multiples of two," the options of slant rhyme, and so forth. Once we leave the limits of rhyme and connect the sonnet with other formal dimensions such as the distribution of energy within the line, the total possibilities increase even more. The sonnet explodes when we enter various dimensions of semantics and emotions. Sonnets and sonnetlike poems can achieve a special poignancy or other psychological depth when they entail the realism and pessimism of Frost, the urbanity and idealism of Cummings, the urban neuroticism of Berryman, or the Black defiance and desperation of Claude McKay. The anguish, power, complexity, and occasional ugliness of these world views acquire a certain existential courage when they are ensconced in the implicitly measured, melodic, and generally Romantic forms of "the little song" invented seven centuries ago in Sicily by Giacomo da Lentino.

But this leaves unanswered the question with which I began: what is it about the *sound form* of the sonnet and sonnetlike poem that gives them such vitality and fascination? One answer lies in the arguments advanced by Miller in his famous article "The Magical Number Seven, Plus or Minus Two" (1957), where he showed that, both cognitively and perceptually, the mind tends to favor sets of about seven and tends to lose certain kinds of control as it goes above or below this number. The sonnet, with its phonic and semantic break about midway through fourteen lines, its lines of about five emphatic syllables and ten syllables in all, and other features of this sort, would seem to illustrate Miller's contention as much as the perceptual test data and lexical semantic data that he adduces. At all linguistic levels—phonetic, lexical, syntactic—the sonnet plays around the magical number.

In the second place, a fundamental fact about our linguistic consciousness is the rough dichotomy between the active and the passive command of a language—here sonnet language. While few poets today have an active command in this sense—shades of Florence in 1400!—practically all American poets and readers of poetry have read hundreds of sonnets and often include sonnets among the poems that they cherish and/or know by heart. That is why a poem that resonates within the sonnet world over time acquires a richness of meaning that few other forms can give. The gross historical fact is that the sonnet has been used, or better, achieved in many languages by a large fraction of the most enduring poets—Petrarch, Dante, Camões, Lope de Vega, Shakespeare, Milton, Keats, Baudelaire, Ronsard, Mallarmé, Pushkin, Mandelstam, Rilke, Goethe, Frost, Cummings, Vallejo. This alone would argue for its continued cumulative growth as a lyric form. As long as poets in the European languages study their craft seriously they will be studying a lot of sonnets, and poets such as McKay and Berryman will continue to arise. But the excellence of the poets and the persuasiveness of their poems do not account for the enduring appeal of the sonnet over seven centuries, any more than does "the magical number seven" and similar psychological, scientific arguments. Perhaps no other lyric form enables one to reach a sustained, energetic argument and/or vision *and* a strong sense of closure, of completion—in such short compass. But, after much consideration, the appeal of the sonnet remains, at least for me, something mysterious and largely unexplained.

REFERENCES

Carruth, Hayden. 1971. The voice that is great within us. American poetry of the twentieth century. New York: Bantam Library.

Chomsky, Noam. 1957. Syntactic structures. The Hague: Mouton.

Ellmann, Richard and Ronert O'Clair. 1973. The Norton anthology of modern poetry. New York: W.W. Norton.

Frankenburg, Lloyd. 1956. Invitation to poetry. New York: Doubleday.

Friedrich, Paul. 1978. The meaning of Aphrodite. Chicago: University of Chicago Press.

Friedrich, Paul. 1986. The language parallax. Austin: The University of Texas Press.

Frost, Robert. 1913. "Letter to Thomas Mosher." Selected letters of Robert Frost, ed. by Lawrence Thompson, p. 83. New York: Holt, Rinehart and Winston.

Gross, Harvey (ed.). 1966. The structure of verse. New York: Ecco.

Halpern, Daniel. 1975. The American poetry anthology. New York: Avon.

Harrison, Jim. 1982. Selected and new poems, 1961–81. New York: Dell.

Langley, E.F. 1915. The poetry of Giacomo da Lentino. Cambridge: Harvard University Press.

Lin, Julia C. 1972. Modern Chinese poetry: An introduction. Seattle: University of Washington Press.

Lowell, Robert. 1973. History. Farrar, Straus and Giroux.

Miller, George A. 1957. The magical number seven, plus or minus two: Some limits on our capacity for processing information. Psychological Review 63.81–97.

Mönch, Walter. 1955. Das Sonett, gestalt und geschichte. Heidelberg: F.H. Kerle.

Nabokov, Vladimir. 1981. "The 'Eugene Oneigin' stanza." Eugene Onegin. Volume 1.9–14. Princeton: Princeton University Press.

Nagler, Michael. 1974. Spontaneity and tradition: A study in the oral art of Homer. Berkeley: University of California Press.

Nye, Robert. 1976. The Faber book of sonnets. London: Faber and Faber.

Preminger, Alex, Franke J. Warnke and O.B. Hardison. 1974. Princeton encyclopedia of poetry and poetics. Princeton: University Press.

Pushkin, Alexander. 1981. *Eugene Onegin.* Trans. by Walter Arndt. New York: Dutton (Paperback Original).

Seth, Vikram. 1986. The golden gate. New York: Random House.

Stevens, Wallace. 1977. Opus posthumous, p. 161. New York: Alfred A. Knopf.

Untermeyer, Louis. 1942. A treasury of great poems. New York: Simon and Schuster.

Wyatt, Thomas. 1975. Sir Thomas Wyatt. Collected poems. Edited and introduced by Joost Daalder. Oxford: University Press.

CHAPTER TEN

Bridging Language Learning, Language Analysis, and Poetry, via Experimental Syntax

Kenneth L. Pike

University of Texas at Arlington

INTRODUCTION

Within human experience, intuition, and belief, there are numerous items which seem sometimes to differ sharply—to be distinct, or even contradictory—but which need to be seen in a uniting framework of thought if we are to have an integrated existence. The following pairs may be relevant to such a discussion: the application of science versus the theory of science; applied linguistics versus linguistic theory; science as such versus metaphysical philosophy; metaphysical philosophy versus aesthetics; form versus meaning. I would like to live with them all at once. I try to express this in a poem of mine (1985:45–46):

MATTER AND MIND

Matter alone will not do.
Heart will sue
If neglected.

Heart, alone, is sad.
Mind, neglected,
Is mad.

"Nothing but" is death,
Or hyperbole
Out of breath.

Matter and mind—
Tie them up tight,
Package them right.

My interests, for years, have included crossover relations between such fields. I have wanted higher-level theory to tie them together. I have ached for the development of theory and philosophy that would allow one to do the job at hand without self-reproach for being inconsistent, or unscientific, or anti-intuitive. I wanted a theory that would allow one to live outside the office with the same philosophy one uses inside it. This required the development of a view which allowed one to integrate research with belief, thing with person, fact with aesthetics, knowledge with application of knowledge.

My talk here is an attempt to show my present stage in that quest. This is in spite of the intimidating presence in this audience of persons who know far more than I ever can about various aspects of the search. Then why here? Because I have felt the pressure of three audiences, some members of which may be in the midst of these same struggles and to whom I might suggest a direction to glance—and duck: (a) those who consider themselves heirs to a variety of linguistic tradition which finds little stimulus from its application to language teaching; (b) those teachers who despair of mastering the intricacies of competing claims to truth in theory development; and (c) those from departments with literature overlaps, who may still be struggling with the teaching of poetry, because of its impact on personal insight, in spite of its departures from language-rule norms.

Experimental syntax holds the promise of helping the teaching of modern languages.

By EXPERIMENTAL SYNTAX, in relation to language learning or teaching (or language analysis), I mean the deliberate, systematic, patterned changing of a text in order to force the student to use different grammatical forms to paraphrase the same referential material. When the same story is told forwards, backwards, or "inside out," grammatical usages of conjunctions, verb forms, or phrase and sentence arrangement must change in order to preserve the original referential content in the face of such grammatical sequence changes.

This approach elicits a variety of grammatical elements and orders while allowing the use of a small vocabulary in a constant referential context. This, in turn, suggests that the teacher can have an amplified choice, relative to other alternatives: attention can be focused, for that period, on optional or required grammar changes without simultaneous focus on massive lexical variety.

But how to make this simple enough for beginning teachers to use, even though they have not been trained in linguistics? I was in Khartoum, in the Northern Sudan, about three years ago, and was asked to lecture to the Khartoum International Institute of Arabic, which teaches Arabic to people from many areas. What could I suggest that might be helpful—even though I did not know any Arabic myself? I told them a story, with a simple plot (Pike 1983a):

THE STORY; in sentence sequence a, b, c:
(a) John came home.
(b) He ate supper.
(c) He went to the movies.

Referentially, this means that, first, chronologically, John came home; second, he ate supper; and, third, he went to the movies. One could have started sentences (b) and (c), however, with the word "then." (Or the story can be told in the same order, with further variations, such as "John came home before he ate supper, and then he went to the movies.")

But the same story can be told, in English, with the sequence (b a c):

(b) John ate supper
(a) after he came home.
(c) Then he went to the movies.

Referentially, it is still the same story. And there are still numerous options such as "Before John ate supper, he came home." But to preserve the meaning it is obligatory, not optional, for a signal to show that the TELLING (GRAMMATICAL) order has been changed by some such device as the one here: "after [he came home]."

The other possible orders of the three sentences give further optional or obligatory changes to preserve the meaning:

Sequence (c a b): (c) "John went to the movies," (a) "after he came home," (b) "and had eaten his supper."

Sequence (a c b): (a) "John went home." (c) "Then he went to the movies," (b) "after he had eaten his supper."

Sequence (b c a): (b) "John ate supper." (c) "Then he went to the movies." (a) "He did both after he had come home."

Sequence (c b a): (c) "John went to the movies." (b) "But before that he had eaten his supper," (a) "after coming home."

A person who speaks the language well should be able to make these changes—or related ones—easily. But if a student cannot modify the form of the individual phrase to meet the requirements of changed order, he needs further instruction. And all this would seem to be possible without the need for an extensive technical vocabulary. I would hope, therefore, that after such items have been used in experimental classrooms for a while, that beginning teachers would be able to use it without extreme discomfort to them or to their students, while nevertheless eliciting or teaching a massive grammar change without massive lexical demand at the same time.

Experimental syntax can contribute to the further development of linguistic theory and/or technology in this next decade.

Underlying a simple experiment like this one lies an extensive set of theoretical assumptions. Among them is the belief that it is normal for any and every language to have words for "before" or "after." It was Henry A. Gleason (see the footnote in Pike & Pike 1972:47) who first pointed out to me that that assumption is empirically false. Some of the languages of Papua New Guinea and of Irian Jaya, as I have had occasion to check since, do not have the words "before" and "after"!

It turns out that they do not need them. They have an overriding general pattern in their grammars, such that when stories are told, the sequence of the REFERENTIAL order—the SPATIAL, CHRONOLOGICAL, or LOGICAL order—is left unchanged, except for special circumstances which are met, for example, by embedded quotations (or stories). The telling order (the grammatical order) in general conforms to the referential one. Thus misunderstanding or conflict between "John came home; he ate supper" with "John came home [after] he ate supper" does not normally arise.

This is but one simple manifestation of a vastly important point in the theory of linguistics: the grammatical and referential structure of discourse are not the same, even though they may be isomorphic in simple "straightforward" instances. Perhaps it would help to add: Paraphrase types are not necessarily all universals. And grammatical constraints on discourse structure are not fully explicable by structure within sentences by themselves. Both grammar and reference have essential controls beyond the sentence, and language theory must allow for that, and for contrast grammatically and referentially in such structures.

But once this is affirmed (and probably accepted by many scholars now), we ask: What further experimental-syntax devices can help us uncover some other related structural constraints? We may recall that in the heyday of morphological analysis, declension and conjugation could be used as supplementary search models (although Bloomfield [personal communication], for one, did not wish to ask "How do you say 'X'?" but rather would ask "What would you say under circumstances 'X'?"). Paradigmatic eliciting approaches to find morphological patterns were much more efficient, for rapid discovery, than looking solely at morphemes in long texts. What could be a RESEARCH ANALOGUE for studying the structure of the texts themselves? If one or more such approaches could be developed, it should be helpful. And, in my view, the experimental syntax seen above, in changing sentence orders in texts, might well prove to be one of these.

Another experiment which Evelyn Pike and I have used is also quite simple in principle, and related to the one shown above. It numbers the sentences in a text; it then reverses the order of every pair of sentences, so that sentences 1-2-3-4-5-6 are rewritten in the order 2-1-4-3-6-5; and whatever changes in grammar are necessary for normal structure and for preservation of the original referential content are then made. (Pike & Pike 1972:46-48; Pike & Pike [1977] 1982:8-10.)

This technique led to some unexpected results, when applied to non-Indo-European languages. In Sherpa, of Nepal, when a primary sentence pair reversal (as just described) was applied to the underlying discourse form, the educated Sherpa speaker-writer working with Schoettelndreyer was able to perform the reversals and revisions with no difficulty. When, however, he was asked for a secondary reversal (a reversal of, say, a primary reversal of 1-2, 3-4, and 5-6 to 2-1, 4-3, and 6-5, followed by a secondary reversal to (2)-(4-1)-(6-3)-(5) the Sherpa sometimes rejected the possibility. It seems that there was an underlying grammatical paragraph structure—and the secondary reversal appeared to damage that enough to be resisted. Apparently the primary reversals had added elements which specified certain logical relations which were then harder to rearrange than the initial more simple chronological ones. (Pike & Schoettelndreyer 1972:76-79.)

In the illustration above, I showed grammatical changes with referential structure invariant. In a further experiment, however, the opposite can be done: The high-level grammatical form of the text can be invariant, but with the referential content changed. Using the final grammatical sequence (c b a) as given above, that order, and the connecting words, can be retained, but with change of the referential content: (c) "The little old lady came to the big black house," (b) "but before that she had bought things in the store," (a) "after complaining that there was not enough to eat." (For a more complex story seen as containing a grammatical form with a very different referential content, however, see Pike & Pike [1977] 1982:10-11, 15.)

More complex referential structures can also be studied in a related way. Note the following story (ignoring, for the moment, the parenthesized markings before the printed lines):

(C4c) Clara made up a flimsy excuse.
(B2-A2) It seems that Bill and Abe had met,
(C1-2-3) and Clara, who had gone downtown shopping for a while,

(C4a,B4A,A4A) ran into them—a regrettable coincidence since she detested Bill.
(A3-B3) These two men were having lunch together
(A1) (since Abe was downtown for work)
(A4b,B4b,C4b) and Abe invited Clara to join them.
(B1) Bill, who had left his office on an errand,
(B2–3) and had met Abe, and joined him for lunch,
(A4c,B4c,C4c) was someone Clara didn't want to eat with. So she refused to join them
(C4a) when she passed by the sidewalk restaurant
(A3-B3) where they were.

This story seems only moderately awkward in its telling. But its grammatical complexity is far greater than it seems. Compare this next version of the same general referential content:

(A1) Abe, (B1) Bill, and (C1) Clara had all gone downtown.
(A2,B2,C2) Bill and Abe met while Clara was shopping.
(C3,A3,B3) But while Abe and Bill were eating, Clara wandered past.
(A4,B4,C4) Although invited to join them, she refused (since she detested Bill), saying that she felt ill.

My technique (Pike 1981:47–64) to compare the source of the differences between the two tellings is to begin with an underlying referential matrix of rows and columns in which the successive columns represent successive points in time and action, and each of the different rows represents the actions of a different individual at those comparable times. (See Figure 1.)

The second telling above (and see Pike 1981:50–51) takes one column at a time, indicating what each of the three persons was doing at that time. A still different alternative is rather to take one row at a time, following the action of one individual through the time sequence, and

	1	2	3	4
A:	A1	A2	A3	A4
B:	B1	B2	B3	B4
C:	C1	C2	C3	C4

Figure 1. (Taken from Pike 1981:48) The numbers represent points in a sequence of events in time. The capital letters represent Abe, Bill, and Clara acting at those times.

then to start over again for the next individual. That requires that one say, for example, "Abe did this, but MEANWHILE Bill did that."

But the choice of order for the first telling above was not systematic like these last two. Rather I had deliberately made a RANDOM PATHWAY through the matrix, to see what would happen when, afterwards, I tried to tell the story in that order. (See Fig. 2). This technique I had used in classes, having students make such paths without their knowing in advance the reason for them, and then letting them see the result when they told the story following the path of their choice. In my case, above, as we look back on it, there are many signals to allow the referential material to be retained, in spite of the telling-order changes and in spite of the complexity caused by simultaneous but interlocking events. Note, for example: "It seems that . . . had . . ." (for getting further back in time, before the preceding verb); "for a while" (for crossing two or more columns of time); "were having" (for simultaneity). Yet there are fewer word signals here of nonsequential telling than the numbers of telling changes themselves. The reader must fill in from referential reconstructed background, the remaining parts of the event.

Various other kinds of experimental changes of text reworking (like these above) can be seen. A whole story, for example, can be told backwards, with the last sentence first (Pike & Pike 1972:48); this is a grammatical change. Or the narrator can be replaced, with resultant emotional overtones (49–51); this is a referential change. Or the story

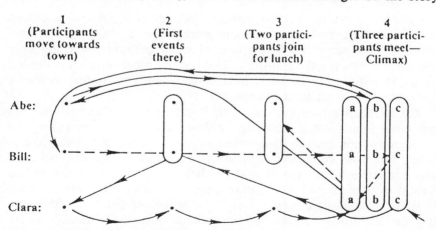

Figure 2. (Taken from Pike 1981:53) The numbers 1–4 are as in Figure 1, for event sequence. The letters a, b, c subdivide the event 4. The arrow at the lower right implies that the narration starts there, then the solid arrows lead to the next activities mentioned. Events indicated by the broken arrows are mentioned after the others just referred to.

can be retold in verse (51); if this brings in rhyme or controlled syllable dynamics, it is a phonological change.

On the other hand there can be various kinds of text creation, built to a particular patterned sequence of clause types. In one of these I took the transitivity sequence of Pike and Pike [1977] 1982:42–44, of bitransitive (with direct and indirect object), transitive (with direct object only), bi-intransitive (with scope, such as required location), intransitive, bi-equative (requiring an evaluator), and equative. (For an earlier more complex suggestion for a listing of clause types, but with paraphrase from each of them to each of the others, see Pike 1975a.) The text (from Pike 1975b:24–25) was made up of one clause from each of these types, in that specified order. In addition, one word (here, book) was chosen, such that that same word had to appear in each of the clauses. The repeated use of that word (or its pronominal substitute) plus an implicit plot, were referential components of the experiment:

BT   I took Bloomfield's book off the shelf and handed it to the young scholar who had just stepped into my office.
T   This classical book bothered him.
BI   It fell to the floor with a thud, from his hand.
I   The book screamed with indignation and pain (and I did, too).
BEq That book seemed important to me.
Eq   It had been, in fact, colossal in its own way—and is still extant.

(It startled me to see how natural such an artificial text appeared to be. But it startled me even more when I saw [same reference] how unnatural the same incident appeared when paraphrased using only one kind of clause—the transitive. Here, again, more research is needed to try to specify for various kinds of texts the constraints on clause sequences that such texts may impose.)

But an even more startling result is seen when referential changes are made which are underlying, implicit assumptions concerning the rules controlling conversation under particular kinds of circumstances. If one forces on children (or "inferiors") the rule "Do not speak until you are spoken to," the formal mathematical representation of the formal rules of social nonnarrative discourse are sharply different from those of a committee meeting with "equality" of all, and with inter-ruptions permitted. Any formalization of discourse, or of speaker-hearer interchange, which does not take account of such differences still has research to do, to cover the normal human situation.

I have struggled with some of these axioms and their results as seen via group theory (Pike 1973), where some 50 different theoretical possibilities are considered. Of these, some are socially normal, and some are hopeless—as seen at the moment—for finding their axioms to map against any normal human situation. But this emphasizes the fact that PURE FORMALISM as such, without attention to referential social axioms, is powerless to capture the relevance of many discourse grammatical functions. Experimental syntax, of a mathematical type, geared to referential axioms, may help further along these lines—or others not imagined as yet.

In my view, some of the material implicit in this approach may be labeled as "premature discovery" just waiting for students of this decade to use it to go beyond us all in using experimental text forms for teaching and analyzing foreign languages.

We have a further step to go in this paper, concerning poetry. But first I emphasize a general claim, as exemplified above: the more isomorphic the grammar and the referential structures, the fewer the grammatical signals needed to retain the meanings without serious loss or distortion. It follows, then, that in a text where the telling sequence closely parallels the happening sequence, fewer grammatical signals are needed, but where there is inversion of sentences or of whole texts, more signals are present.

The poetic kaleidoscope stimulates aesthetic invention and could demand language learning competence.

A kaleidoscope has a substantial number of small pieces of colored glass in a small transparent flat container fastened across one end of a tube. At the other end is a place to look through the tube. But between the two ends, inside the tube, extend three pieces of glass in the form of a triangle. When one looks through the tube, the glass bits which happen to fall to the bottom of their chamber are reflected in the glass and make beautiful symmetrical patterns. Each turn of the tube gives a new pattern but does not add any glass bits to the total available inventory in the kaleidoscope. At one moment, however, the bits in view will not be the same selection as at another moment.

Suppose, now, we start with a given poem, written by a particular living, available author. His poem will have been written against a background of thought and experience or imagination which includes all of the items in his poem. In addition, there will be in his memory or imagination, accessible to him, a large number of items which identify or characterize or relate to the material of the poem. Some, but not all, of this material will have been made explicit in the poem—directly or indirectly. Other parts of that background, essential to the understanding of the poet's meaning and intention, will for the moment be left unstated, or implicit.

Suppose, next, that we ask the author to write a second poem which in some sense is a paraphrase of the first—saying the same thing but in different words and different text structure. The two poems would be GRAMMATICALLY DIFFERENT but—in my terminology—REFERENTIALLY THE SAME.

In order to illustrate this, I take one of my poems written about 20 years ago (Pike [1967] 1976:63) before I had worked on these current materials. The choice of this particular poem was made because it is the favorite of one of my daughters—not because it fits this exercise readily. (The letter (A) identifies the poem, and numbers are added to label the lines; they are not part of the published poem.) The remaining poems, except for Poem (B), were prepared for an unpublished paper on the poetic kaleidoscope presented at the centennial celebration at the University of North Dakota, June 28, 1983.) Poem (A):

(A) (1) TENSION

    (2) String—taut stretched—
    (3) Snap not! Nor grieve
    (4) When frightful bow draws
    (5) Forth the haunting fear.

    (6) Please, Lord, play on.

And the paraphrase, in Poem (B):

(B) (1) THE CRY IS *THERE*

    (2) With bow on string.
    (3) String sings,
    (4) But cries
    (5) With fear
    (6) Of failure.

    (7) Keep me singing,
    (8) Lord. Play on!

I see two interlocking sets of referential relations which are holding the two poems together. On the one hand there is in both the physical relation of string to bow; on the other hand there is the relation of human person to divine person. There is also the set of metaphors, with string representing the human person and bow (or user of the bow) representing the divine person. The pair of pairs can be shown in a matrix, as follows:

	PHYSICAL	PERSONAL
HUMAN	string	me
DIVINE	bow	God

But, as you would suspect, I was not building to that abstract structure when I wrote the kaleidoscopic twist of that poem. What I was in fact trying to do in (B) was to focus on the "where" component of poem (A), to give it a twist in that "place direction." And an earlier version (given in North Dakota) came out as (C):

(C) (1)   WHERE?

    (2) String on bridge,
    (3) String in air,
    (4) Bow on string,
    (5) String sings.

Yet this poem was not satisfying to me. Why not? It had met my requirement of focusing strongly on place. And it had met the requirement of staying within the bits of the world view kaleidoscope and the intent of the original poem. But it felt weak. It was only when I saw that I had lost a part of the matrix of metaphor, using only the physical column of it, that I could hope to do better, consciously, by adding data relevant to the second column.

Let us call the immediately visible material in the kaleidoscope its current HORIZON; the horizon changes with each turn of the kaleidoscope, just as the visible horizon changes if one turns one's head around in a pasture jaunt—or as if one walks a hundred miles in the same direction.

With this in mind we can specify a second problem. For this paper I wanted at least one of the twists to hold rigidly to the first starting poem in two ways: I wanted it to use only material clearly on the momentarily visible horizon of the kaleidoscopic content of poem (A), and I wanted to omit nothing of the major content of that temporarily visible horizon. Yet in (C) not only had I omitted the second column of the matrix, but I had added detail in terms of the nouns "bridge" and "air"—words which were legitimate in relation to the available material in my cultural kaleidoscopic world view, but which could be confusing as an illustration at this point in the present paper if they "seemed" to be adding to the available data. So, in version (B), the personal reference is added to the horizon of the earlier form (C), whereas bridge and air are deleted from it.

Yet, as I have tried to indicate, in the kaleidoscopic approach it is legitimate to add material when it is validly present in the background environment and when it adds to the impact of the new focus. In (D), for example, focus is changed to time (D.1); and time is split into the past (relaxed, before the string was on the violin, D.2–5), and the now (tense, tuned up, on the implicit violin, D.6–8). Added, for the new horizon, are the implicit violin itself, contrasting with the two time states, involving lack of stress (D.3) versus presence of stress (D.8), and futile life (D.11) versus vibrant useful life (D.10). In addition, there is the state of the wrapped-up string (before being used, D.4), and emphasis on pain (D.8), rather than merely stress (stretching the figure to person, implicitly, since pain does not apply to inanimate string). Lacking is explicit emphasis on the bow and the player, although both are implicit.

(D) (1) *NOW,* IT HURTS

    (2) Before, I relaxed,
    (3) Quiet; no stress;
    (4) Wrapped in coil
    (5) In isolated state.
    (6) Now, I'm held;
    (7) Bound, not free!
    (8) Wobbling in pain.

    (9) Wrong perspective!
  (10) Stress gives vibrant life,
  (11) Not futile slack.

The next poem, (E), changes focus from the string to the containing larger constituent—a violin (E.1). Poem (A) does not specify what kind of instrument it was. (An artist, drawing an illustration for the poem in Pike 1967:63, used a nonviolin for a model.) It is clear, therefore, that there was reader ambiguity in the reader's interpretation kaleidoscope—although not in the kaleidoscope of the writer.

(E) (1) VIOLIN UNDER STRETCHED STRING

    (2) Now, there's music.
    (3) Without *you,*
    (4) Who hears my tears?
    (5) Autonomous *string*
    (6) Can't sing.

    (7) Play on!
    (8) Let pain remain.
    (9) Continue the refrain.
  (10) *Play on!*

But another change is seen. A further referential PERFORMATIVE INTERACTION set is added: The violin (not the bow) becomes the explicit "you" in (E.3) in relation to the implicit personal "I" (or "my") in

(E.5–6). Then in (E.7–10) the grammatical implicit "I" seems to be (ambiguously) the person (me) or else the physical string, whereas the implicit "you" seems to be either the performative impersonal bow or personal God, or both. (Note that we treat the "I-thou" axis as pertaining to the grammar, regardless of what particular person is talking, but that we treat the specific speaker or/and hearer as referential in the performative interaction set.)

In the next poem (F), I attempted to put the focus on the PURPOSE implicit—not explicit—in Poem (A). Here, clearly, the author is needed to provide the information—if he remembers or knows. But life without purpose is empty, and poetry written without intent does not satisfy me (although explicit purpose is not necessary—even as it is not given in (A).) Note the title of (F), which tries to mention here—as in the other poems—the focus. (But a poem does not need to do so. The purpose under some circumstances could be better achieved by letting the focus come out later in the poem, as a surprise, for example.) That focus takes some of the attention away from the one hurting, to place it on the ones who are to hear (F.1)—and to benefit (F.6) by that hearing of the singing. So the focus has changed, relative to the persons in the performative interaction:

(F) (1)　　FOR OTHERS—SING

　　(2) Must life be tense?
　　(3) With opposite pulls?
　　(4) No rest, relaxed? At all?

　　(5) Your vibrant life
　　(6) Is joy for others.
　　(7) No chord *can* sing
　　(8) Until taught tautness.
　　(9) Sing, don't sag.

Next I wanted to change the focus to the background of the situation being talked about. Specifically, I wanted to emphasize the necessity for context to be involved in anything relevant. But instead of treating this with positive elements of the kaleidoscopic background I chose, in (G), to approach it NEGATIVELY—referring to autonomy as absence of adequate context. And lack of that context, for the string, would be its absence from the bow and violin and player. This would mean "no music"—or death (G.10–11), in terms of pushing the metaphor of uselessness further, or of failure to reach a desired goal of making music. But in retrospect (I did not see it at the time), I still had difficulty in getting the added metaphor of death to carry an adequate load, through a mere mention of it. I needed, apparently, something more like the two columns of the matrix, above, with physical versus personal. So I added the metaphor of seed dying to get fruit (G.4–5) as analogous, by implication, to a person being able to help others through the experience of tension. A POETIC UNDERLYING MATRIX, that is, may have rows or columns added for further development and impact.

(G) (1)   AUTONOMY IS DEATH

(2) Service to God
(3) Is death to man.
(4) Seeds must die
(5) For fruit to grow.
(6) Death to self
(7) From tension springs
(8) Like string which sings
(9) From inner stress.

(10) Autonomy is death,
(11) Real death.
(12) Die for the good—
(13) Or die for good.

A further comment must be made on one general component of the structure of this set of poems as a whole. Each of them is in two parts, as indicated by the line inside them (e.g. between (G.9–10). This was not my conscious intent, but a parallelism growing out of trying to paraphrase the first poem (A) which "happened" to have two parts, with a shift in the I-thou-here-now axis. There, it was from the PER-FORMATIVE AXIS in (A.1–5), with its implicit talking of God to person (or, ambiguously, of self admonishing self), followed (in A.6) with person talking to the Lord. In (B.1–6), it is also ambiguously string crying to self, or crying to God.

Flexibility in the use of one's mother tongue is part of one's mastery of one's mother tongue. So that one can affirm, in this sense, that a child has not mastered the use of the mother tongue. Mastery includes control for eloquence and flexible control for aesthetics and its fore-grounding (focusing). Aristotle (in his Poetics; translation by Telford 1961) long ago contributed to the development of rhetoric. (For a summary of the view of Socrates see Young, Becker, and Pike 1970.2–5; there, Plato is interpreted as regarding "rhetoric as the art of rational discourse rather than the art of eloquent expression," and Aristotle is quoted as insisting that "it is not sufficient to know what one ought to say, but one must also know how to say it.")

Language learning, in the sense of knowing how to use language for ends of persuasion or aesthetics, requires much more than a mere knowing of forms and rules. It requires knowing ways of using rules to break rules—ways of allowing intuition of the relevance of similarities to break forth into poetic or prose metaphors with startling clarity. And some of these techniques are taught in college courses in composition or literary production; they cannot be assumed as known by the child—although my grandson at 12 years of age was writing poetry which I, at least, enjoyed.

FLEXIBILITY as an aid to an intuitive grasp of pattern must be CULTIVATED, just as logical thinking must be cultivated—and such language and thought development cannot be separated into autonomous categories, or events or time periods in life. New thoughts in science result in invention of new terms or concepts or definitions of terms. New thoughts in aesthetics result in new poetry or new essays or books. And training for such development continues to the grave—unless one makes a grave mistake and stops too soon. (Someone has said that having many birthdays is good for you—the more you have the longer you live.) And various kinds of experimental composition are related to such aims. One, seen in Young, Becker, and Pike (1970:123–30) shows how to stimulate insight by compositions varied according to focus placed on the same material in relation to structures emphasizing contrast versus variation versus distribution; and these in turn intersect with emphasis on particle (static), wave (dynamic), and field (relational) perspectives.

All of this implies, once more, that language and culture and growth are not autonomous. Nor can the observer be separated in his growth and being from the culture, things, and environment in relation to which that observer happens to be growing and learning as an adult in thinking, remembering, and being. Much work has been done recently under the label of Cognitive Science in specifying some steps which must be taken to learn more about development of such networks (or frames—and compare my terms distribution, universe of discourse, field, and cohesion). See, for example, de Beaugrande and Colby (1979) on narrative models and interaction; Johnson-Laird (1980) on mental models; Waltz and Pollack (1985) on interactive interpretation; D'Andrade (1981) on implicit cultural sources rather than formal ones, for cognition and guided discovery; Sabbah (1985) on a connectionist approach to visual recognition; and Charniak (1981) on the analogy between a linguistic case approach and the frame approach in artificial intelligence. See also stratificationalism (Lamb 1966) for a different network approach.

In my view, a child is born with the INNATE POTENTIAL to learn to handle deliberate focus shifts such as are seen in the kaleidoscopic poetry shifts, but both the young and old need to learn such matters from available oral or written culture or from teachers—or must have initiative and imagination to develop some such devices on their own.

There are further implications for linguistics, literary criticism, and philosophy growing out of the kaleidoscope approach.

Various linguists and many literary critics have written about poetry.

Jakobson (1960:350) suggested that poetics is an integral part of linguistics. More recently, with Jones (Jakobson and Jones 1970), he discusses rhymes, strophes, and lines as constituents, and "variables which form a salient network of binary oppositions" (16–18), odd versus even (18–22), outer against inner (23–24), central against marginal (29), and others. Ross (1981), for example, more recently discusses the number of lines holding a poem together (267), punctuation (269), thematic content (269), and balancing, by repetition (270–72) and conjunctions (275–77).

Wellek and Warren (1942:144) assumed that "Every reading aloud or reciting of a poem is merely a performance of a poem and not the poem itself"; and "each performance contains elements which are extraneous to the poem and individual idiosyncrasies of pronunciation, pitch, tempo, and distribution of stress."

Some authors have used a kind of kaleidoscopic shift by changing the person being quoted. Browning is one who has impressed me most in this direction. In *The Ring and the Book* the same murder event is discussed, in some 500 pages, by several different persons from their respective viewpoints. (In Pike and Pike [1977] 1982:7–11 and E.G. Pike 1983:43–48, these differences would be treated as "vectors" of the event.) Sullivan (1969) has an extensive analysis of this work of Browning's. Gunter ([1972] 1975:40) has students take a poem and "put it in bread-and-butter syntax," or he rearranges normal syntax into a poem (40). He notes, "Such exercises as these tell us a world about norms and departures therefrom . . . and motives and strategies." Yip (1976) has students make experimental versions of translations of Chinese poems, showing (8–9) how Chinese images often "form an atmosphere" which "evokes" but does not state the "aura of feeling."

I have not seen attempts at the marking of contrastive intonation with its impact on poetry—either of one's own poems (except Pike, for example, 1981:45); or in the contrastive writing of the pitch of several persons who have read aloud, and have had recorded, their reading of someone else's poem (Pike 1982:93–95, on a poem by Dickinson, which I first presented in a meeting in Michigan in 1953).

There have been various poets who have discussed different versions of their own poem or poems of other writers. Holmes (1960:36–50), for example, discusses the "biography" of five of his. And I have discussed a bit of my own (plus additional references) in Pike (1984). But the variants in such approaches are different from the planned, kaleidoscopic, systematic scheme controlling focus—which is different from the other kinds of experimental syntax which I have done (as, for instance, those mentioned in earlier sections of this paper).

The focus changes treated in the kaleidoscopic twists here were chosen to treat, successively, change of grammatical focus from referential class (Poem A), to referential slot (B-place, C-place, D-time, E-place), to referential role (F), and to referential cohesion (G).

The source of the stimulus to try this was the TAGMEME, with its four cells on all levels of the hierarchies of phonology, grammar, and reference. (For a mathematical understanding of this structure, see Pike 1983c.) For all of the poems, the referential material includes the entity "string" as a physical, observable object—as a member of a referential CLASS of objects relevant to the poems. (By metaphor, it is simultaneously a person). The referential ROLE for each of the poems is its relevance as a possible source of music. (By metaphor, it is simultaneously a possible source of service to other people.) Its referential SLOT (or position) is on the bridge of the violin, under the bow, once it has been taken out of its pre-used coiled state. (And, by metaphor, it is related in some local social setting to other people around it.) Also, in its referential COHESION, it is in the larger framework of the world where all people have problems, seeds must die for plants to grow, and God is assumed to be integrating or promoting goodness through people.

In grammatical structure, the general pattern of each of the poems has the double form (shown by the line) with the grammatical (generalized, rather than referentially specific) role of problem followed by solution (A, B, D, E, F). But (G) shifts across a POETIC RIFT, I shall call it, from specific contrast to general contrast in death types. And the off-norm (C) loses its impact not only from the lack of the matrix, discussed above, but for lack of this basic grammatical structure. (I shall not attempt, here, to analyze the grammatical differences in clause or sentence or phrase types contained in the different poems.)

Much of the recent treatment of tagmemics by Pike and Pike ([1977] 1982) has utilized the concepts of the four-celled tagmeme (see index under these cell labels). The concepts are applicable both in theory and in practice to any of the levels of the hierarchies of grammar, phonology, and reference. The most extensive treatment of a text for grammar and reference, from this viewpoint, is by E. G. Pike (1983). The only extensive application to the phonological hierarchy is given by K. Pike (1983b) in relation to a poem by Langston Hughes. The mathematically-described relationships between the characteristics of the four cells of the tagmeme are given by K. Pike (1983c).

For the purposes of this paper, however, I emphasize that a tagmeme of any hierarchy is a unit in CONTEXT—that is, that NO unit exists in AUTONOMY from other parts of its system. The concept of the presence of an obligatory referential slot component of any unit specifies that there must be an IMMEDIATE context within which the unit functions as a constituent of some larger element as part of a whole, or as a member of a taxonomic set, or as a part of some other relation. Similarly, the referential cohesion component puts such a unit into the still larger context of a BACKGROUND SYSTEM which may control some features of it—or which it may in its turn control; autonomy, again, is rejected. (For theoretical discussion of the need to reject autonomy see Pike 1985.) A further feature of referential context is its PURPOSE or RELEVANCE in the eye of the observer—its role, which once again eliminates autonomy, because of the relation of an item to observer (rather than treating a unit as a thing-in-itself). And the referential class cell in its normal non-abstract form contains an entity or event or relation or context (including imaginary or mental ones)—e.g. especially the visible or audible ones.

In general, furthermore, the concreteness of many of the referential class items, treated (at least for the moment) as having boundaries, makes them viewable as PARTICLES (or as static). Their place in a referential slot, whether nuclear or marginal, or on a cline, makes them able to be viewed dynamically (or as WAVE). And the n-dimensionality of a background system lends itself to treatment as holding all things in cohesion (in a FIELD structure), in a matrix of reality. And to these more formal components is added the personal observer component (of relevance to other observers—or to an understanding of the relation of things to things); observer is not autonomous from thing, nor thing from observer. And here philosophy interlocks with language, in a metaphysical approach to the referential worlds in which we respectively seem to find ourselves as we see ourselves.

Material on grammatical class elements is seen in older works where they enter into immediate constituent hierarchies, or into rule-governed relations between units and each other, or between units and their containing structures. Cohesion networks of the grammatical hierarchy may be found in the work of the stratificationalists. Grammatical role data occurs in work of the case grammarians. For poetry, on the other hand, note that Ramanujan ([1967] 1975) has a kind of cohesion factor in which special things—e.g. honey—have standard meanings in many Tamil poems. And Leech (1969:236) discusses referential cohesion in poetry in that, for example,

The work of some poets, such as Dryden, cannot be understood fully without a detailed social and political history of the times. . . . A knowledge of intellectual and moral systems must be assumed in many cases. . . . Often, interpretation depends on familiarity with literary traditions, conventional symbolism, mythology, and so forth.

But each of the four cells is relevant to each level of each hierarchy. In this chapter, the background material which is held constant is that of the underlying referential structure. The kaleidoscopic twists do not change that—although they may, as we have seen, bring in formerly implicit material, or delete some of it. And that implies that the changes which we have made, in terms of actual inner structure, have been that of the grammatical structure of the texts rather than that of the underlying referential structure. And we have not taken the space or time here to point out the details of the grammatical changes at these levels.

Nor have we shown the kind of analytical techniques which would be required to give the detail of the background referential structures referred to. For that, we would have had to chart the chronology of each event, and of each character in each event. (The string was at first coiled, then put on the violin, then stretched; the player prepared his violin, then played a tune.) (For these techniques, and others, see Pike & Pike [1977] 1982 and E. G. Pike 1983.)

The shift of referential material from one grammatical cell to another does not leave the first cell empty; a kaleidoscopic twist leaves every grammatical cell filled again.

This appears extraordinary when first seen. Why does not the "emptying" of a cell leave it empty? It is because no unit of grammar can take place in a mental-physical vacuum. To be human is to be in contexts—contexts of various kinds; contexts of interlocking kinds; contexts of hierarchial kinds; contexts of levels; contexts mental and physical; contexts of n-dimensionality, of simultaneity, of mutual relevance.

Several things can be going on at once in any language event but especially in a poem.

Every utterance has the three hierarchies involved, coming together in particular utterances (or writings). Each text is called, in tagmemics, a member of the GREATER LEXICON. That is, not only individual words, but a total text, carries the intersection of phonology, grammar, and reference (see E. G. Pike 1983:70–72).

But in addition to such interlocking there is also the double meaning of a pun or of a metaphor. In the poems here, the matrix (as given above) represents the double layerings of the meanings of these poems.

Compare Friedrich (1979:41): "Poetry aspires . . . to represent . . . the many-tracked complexities of a symphony . . . [The Iliad has] such orchestration of many levels of form, imagery, and idea." Or, as I have said earlier (Pike [1967] 1976:108), "this kind of poetic writing may be called anti-redundant, because of its n-dimensionality." And rhyme, or other devices, have importance by calling the reader's attention to some dimension of relationship which might not otherwise be seen quickly or easily, if at all; or, in Holmes's (1960:vii) terms, "Some passages [including prose] concentrate whole essays, and the poems say more than books." And Kennedy ([1966] 1979:487) says that poetry may give pleasure by "the sudden recognition of likenesses." This may contrast with a logic which wishes to have just one meaning per word in some of its technical phases. But life is multifaceted—and language best reflects that fact in poetry. The kaleidoscope of life itself also has backgrounds of various kinds. For example, Vern Poythress, independently (personal communication 1983), has begun work using the kaleidoscope for representing multiple perspectives in theology.

The observer enters the data, via emics or etics, as insider or outsider.

Some 30 years ago (Pike [1954, 1955, 1960] 1967) I coined the term emic (from the term phonemic) to extend the concept of inner-system relevance in phonology to all fields of human behavior. This contrasts with an etic approach (from the term phonetic) which has at least two overlapping uses: an approach to someone else's insider-emic system by an adult outsider from the viewpoint of his or her own foreign but (there) emic system; the other is the use of an etic system developed scientifically with categories which are intended to be universally-assignable (or partly assignable) to any language or culture in the early stages of analysis of that language or culture. The initial etic assignments may miss some emic features of the language being studied, or may imply or posit the presence of some which are not emically relevant to it.

Reeder (1984:53), a phenomenologist, uses the term "horizon" somewhat differently from mine here but in a way which suggests the need for a careful study of their relationships. He says that "there must be room for metaphorical (and sometimes just plain muddled) accounts of phenomena which lie at the horizons of our explicit knowledge." And he tells us (95) that Husserl (in Hua VI:86) used the term "for different types of horizon, including spatial, temporal and worldly horizons." Ricoeur (1981:178) speaks of "the horizon of a world towards which a work directs itself," and "The emergence of the sense and the reference of a text in language is the coming to language of a world and not the recognition of another person."

Gunter ([1972] 1975) says that "our experience . . . is filtered through the culture of our tribe"; and "Culture is an unseen envelope of custom and experience . . . [It is] a lens through which our experience must pass." León-Portilla (1963:37) says of the old Aztecs that "in their poetry is an authentic theory of metaphysical knowledge."

Richards (1963:165), however, would reject the close tie of observer to poem, by asserting of poems that "They are living, feeling, knowing *beings* in their own right . . . A poem is an activity, seeking to become itself."

In the treatment of a scientific system, and the emics of that system as itself an emic unit of the scientist at work, universals and particulars are relative to the view from within such a system. As Cassirer ([1960] 1966:90) says, "Every scientific concept is in fact both universal and particular: its task is to set forth the synthesis of both of these factors." And in our material, a particular poem, of a particular pattern, is an element of the greater lexicon expressing something referential within that grammatico-phonological pattern.

But in poetry, as in other literature, there are two emic views, related to the poles of my "I-thou-here-now" axis: the intent of the writer, and the interpretation by the hearer. They only partly match. In my view, authors have the right to say what they wish—including meaning which comes by the use of intonation or voice quality, and with as much of it written as they are capable of writing. On the other hand, readers, when they desire to gain an understanding of writers as those writers understand themselves, must deduce or guess at various elements which are at best implicit, and known to the author, or else not in that author's temporary horizon, or not known to the author but relevant to the material at the time of reading. Leech (1969:225) feels that "the individual reader projects special significance wherever his critical judgment lets him do so."

In my view one should try to understand what the author of a poem intends (which is what I want readers to try to do with my material, before doing something quite different). But readers have a dilemma in that in fact they cannot always do so even if they wish; and at times they are not deeply interested in that, but rather in widening their own experienced world under the impact of the poem.

How, then, can we express the dilemma? Perhaps Fruchtman (1984) has captured a bit of it in the title to a paper: ' "How do I know that I mean what you mean when you say: You mean what I mean": A linguistic model of modern Hebrew poetry.'

SUMMARY

I have wanted, in this chapter, to suggest ways in which the teaching of foreign languages could, over the next decade, exploit ways to make additional, useful exercises for teaching the use of conjunctions or special phrase forms, without major linguistic theory being needed by the students. This I would hope to see accomplished by the use of more extensive experimental changing of small texts. In addition, the use of complicated texts could lead to further teaching, by forcing extensive reworking when simultaneous events are shown in experimental rearranging of their grammatical form of presentation.

The use of the poetic kaleidoscopic experimental change of focus, on the other hand, could serve as a stimulus for the more advanced training of people who need stimulus to change their observer stance for the writing of interesting compositions, or aesthetic expression. This could occur without demanding of them a change of belief or data, but rather by a shift of attention, with corresponding focus on who they are and on their views of their perspectives on life's small or large problems.

These same exercises, when studied through any or every linguistic theory—not just the one I happen to enjoy—should force more attention to text structure, in relation to the analysis of alternative types of grammar when referential structure or background is invariant. Or it could lead to more attention to referential structure, while the grammatical structure is kept more or less invariant (i.e. while the content is changed).

In addition, the exercises might lead to fun, to enjoyment, to aesthetic reactions in studying formal or technical matters, when otherwise interest would lag. After all, we want fun in linguistics and composition, as well as in volleyball.

I end with another poem to highlight the aesthetic I-thou-(here-now) relation:

POEMS ARE WINDOWS

Through which one looks
Via eyes
Of feeling soul
On other's toil.

REFERENCES

d'Andrade, Roy G. 1981. The cultural part of cognition. Cognitive Science 5.179–95.

de Beaugrande, Robert, and Benjamin N. Colby. 1979. Narrative models of action and interaction. Cognitive Science 3.43–66.

Browning, Robert. [1897] 1927. The ring and the book. Walter Hampden edition. New York: Crowell.

Cassirer, Ernst. [1960] 1966. The logic of the humanities. Translated by C. S. Howe. New Haven: Yale University Press.

Charniak, Eugene. 1981. The case-slot identity theory. Cognitive Science 5.285–92.

Friedrich, Paul. 1979. Language, context, and the imagination: Essays by Paul Friedrich, selected and introduced by Anwar S. Dil. Stanford: Stanford University Press.

Fruchtman, Maya. 1984. "How do I know that I mean what you mean when you say: You mean what I mean"—A linguistic model of Hebrew poetry. A paper presented to the Seventh World Congress of Applied Linguistics, Brussels.

Gunter, Richard. [1972] 1975. Reading poems. Columbia, South Carolina: Hornbeam Press.

Holmes, John. 1960. Writing poetry. Boston: The Writer, Inc.

Jakobson, Roman. 1960. Closing statement: Linguistics and poetics. Style in language, ed. by Thomas A. Sebeok, 350–77. Cambridge: MIT Press.

Jakobson, Roman, and Lawrence G. Jones. 1970. Shakespeare's verbal art in *Th'expence of spirit*. The Hague: Mouton.

Johnson-Laird, P. N. 1980. Mental models in cognitive science. Cognitive Science 4.71–115.

Kennedy, X. J. [1966] 1979. Literature: An introduction to fiction, poetry, and drama. 2nd edn. Boston: Little, Brown and Company.

Lamb, Sydney. 1966. Outline of stratificational grammar. Rev. ed. Washington, D.C.: Georgetown University Press.

Leech, Geoffrey N. 1969. A linguistic guide to English poetry. London: Longmans.

León-Portilla. 1963. Aztec thought and culture: A study of ancient Nahuatl mind, trans. by Jack Emory Davis, Norman: University of Oklahoma Press.

Pike, Evelyn G. 1983. Grammatical and referential hierarchies in a prose text: Toward its systematic exegesis. In Pike & Pike 1983, 4–73.

Pike, Kenneth L. [1954, 1955, 1960] 1967. Language in relation to a unified theory of the structure of human behavior. The Hague: Mouton.

———. 1971. Implications of the patterning of an oral reading of a set of poems. Poetics 1.38–45.

———. 1973. Sociolinguistic evaluation of alternative mathematical models: English pronouns. Language 49.121–60.

———. 1975a. Focus in English clause structure seen via systematic experimental syntax. Kivung 8.3–14.

———. 1975b. On describing languages. Lisse: Peter de Ridder Press.

———. [1967] 1976. Stir, change, create. Huntington Beach, CA: Wycliffe Bible Translators.

———. 1981. Tagmemics, discourse, and verbal art. Ann Arbor: Michigan Studies in the Humanities.

————. 1982. Linguistic concepts: An introduction to tagmemics. Lincoln: University of Nebraska Press.

————. 1983a. Experimental syntax: A basis for some new language-learning exercises. Arab, journal of language studies 1:2.245–54.

————. 1983b. Phonological hierarchy in a four-cell tagmemic representation: From poem to phoneme class. In Pike & Pike 1983, 74–103.

————. 1983c. The tetrahedron as model for the four-cell tagmeme in its multiple relations. In Pike & Pike 1983, 104–24.

————. 1984. Towards the linguistic analysis of one's own poems. The Tenth LACUS Forum 1983, 117–28. Columbia, South Carolina: Hornbeam.

————. 1985. The need for rejection of autonomy in linguistics. The Eleventh LACUS Forum 1984, 35–53.

————, and Evelyn G. Pike. 1972. Seven substitution exercises for studying the structure of discourse. Linguistics 94.43–52.

————, and Evelyn G. Pike. [1977] 1982. Grammatical analysis. Dallas and Arlington: Summer Institute of Linguistics and University of Texas at Arlington.

————, and Evelyn G. Pike. 1983. Text and tagmeme. Norwood, N.J.: Ablex.

————, and Burkhard Schoettelndreyer. 1972. Paired-sentence reversals in the discovery of underlying and surface structures in Sherpa discourse. Indian linguistics. 33:1.72–83.

Ramanujan, A. K. [1967] 1975. The interior landscape: Love poems from a classical Tamil anthology. Poems translated by Ramanujan. Bloomington: Indiana University Press.

Reeder, Harry P. 1984. Language and experience: Descriptions of living language in Husserl and Wittgenstein. Washington DC: Center for Advanced Research in Phenomenology and University Press of America.

Richards, I. A. 1963. "How does a poem know when it is finished?" Parts and wholes, ed. by Daniel Lerner, 163–74. New York: Free Press of Glencoe.

Ricoeur, Paul. 1981. Hermeneutics and the human sciences: Essays on language, action, and interpretation. Translated by John B. Thompson. Cambridge University Press.

Ross, Haj. 1981. Robert Frost's "Out, Out—": Crossing the boundaries in linguistics, ed. by W. Klein and W. Levelt, 265–82. Boston: Reidel.

Sabbah, Daniel. 1985. Computing with connections in visual recognition of Origami objects. Cognitive Science 9.25–50.

Sullivan, Mary Rose. 1969. Browning's voices in The ring and the book: A study of method and meaning. Toronto: University of Toronto Press.

Telford, Kenneth A. 1961. Aristotle's poetics: Translation and analysis. South Bend, Indiana: Gateway Editions.

Waltz, David L., and Jordan B. Pollack. 1985. Massively parallel parsing: A strongly interactive model of natural language interpretation. Cognitive Science 9.51–74.

Wellek, Rene, and Austin Warren. 1942. Theory of literature. New York: Harcourt, Brace.

Yip, Wai-lim (ed. and translator). 1976. Chinese poetry: Major modes and genres. Berkeley: University of California Press.

Young, Richard E., Alton L. Becker, and Kenneth L. Pike. 1970. Rhetoric: Discovery and change. New York: Harcourt, Brace and World.

LANGUAGE LEARNING AND TEACHING

CHAPTER ELEVEN

From Context to Communication: Paths to Second Language Acquisition*

Muriel Saville-Troike

University of Illinois, Urbana-Champaign

A major topic of discussion recently among researchers in the field of second language acquisition has been the appropriate relationship—and directionality—of theory and data. There have also been recent claims from at least one international leader in TESOL that neither theory nor research data are relevant to second language instruction. As one who is vitally concerned with both research and its application, I was therefore particularly pleased to be asked to address the theme of this year's LSA/TESOL Institute—Linguistics and Language in Context: The Interdependence of Theory, Data, and Application.

I am firmly in the camp of those who believe that theory should be "grounded" in data. I believe that collecting data only to confirm or disprove a priori hypotheses is likely to exclude crucial evidence for phenomena which occur in the process of language acquisition which are merely not salient to the investigator. For my research I have adapted the "grounded theory method" developed within the field of sociology by Glaser and Strauss (1967), and I would like to briefly outline this method and the procedures I have used for data collection and analysis before I discuss and illustrate the results so far.

The present discussion will be based on research I have been con-

* This research has been supported in part by the Bureau of Educational Research and the Research Board of the University of Illinois. I am particularly grateful for the collaboration and assistance of Mary Fritz, Jo Anne Kleifgen, Erica McClure, Charlotte Blomeyer, Jie Cao, Rey-Mei Chen, Ya-Mei Chen, Lawrence Colker, Atteya El Noory, Soonai Ham, Keiko Koda, O Ook Whan, and James Stanlaw, and for the extensive cooperation of children, parents, and teachers.

ducting for the last four years on children in Illinois who are acquiring English as a second language. I will concentrate primarily on the data which relate to the earliest stages of emergence of their English. I have focused on 40 individual children during this time, for periods ranging from four months to four years each. They have ranged in age from 2 to 12 years, and have spoken eight different native languages. The data base includes over 200 hours of videotape, as well as a variety of language and academic achievement measures.

1. Theory building using this method begins with collection of data on naturally occurring behaviors and experiences within comparison groups. In this study, comparison is among age levels and among native language backgrounds. The constant factors are place of residence (all of the children live in the same University housing complex), and the fathers' educational level and current occupation (all are graduate students or visiting scholars at the University of Illinois).

2. A second important characteristic of this method is collection of data which will place the observed behaviors and experiences in a holistic context. For my research this has included collecting background information on families, prior schooling, and peer contacts, as well as the videotapes and the language and academic achievement measures. Since part of the analysis involves trying to obtain a phenomenological perspective on the viewpoint of the subjects who are being studied, my data collection procedure also includes interviews with the children, their parents, and their teachers, some based on playback of the videotaped observations.

3. Analysis may focus on any number of topics, but grounded theory building must include organization of the observed data into conceptual categories which reflect their regularities and interrelationships. It is critical to such an approach that this level of abstraction be descriptive of the actual data: inductive rather than deductive in nature.

4. The descriptive model which results from such analysis is then used to generate theoretical propositions that account for the data, or as a base against which to evaluate the adequacy of other theories. The theory then provides hypotheses to be tested against additional data collection and analysis in a continuing interactive process, but it is in the first instance empirically "grounded."

RESEARCH SITES

I have collected data for this study in three different sites. The first is the housing complex where my subjects and their families live. It is a

University-owned community for married students and their families, composed of quadroplex units which closely resemble all low-rise public housing, plus a Community Center for group meetings and social activities, and several play areas for the children. Most of the families in the complex are from foreign countries, with the largest numbers from Korea, Japan, and Arabic-speaking nations. The community is self-contained in many respects, but nearby supermarkets stock extensive selections of Asian food, and nearby churches have separate services in Korean and Chinese and house Saturday School classes for children which supplement the bilingual instruction that is provided by the public schools.

The typical father of children in my sample has a master's degree and is pursuing advanced study at the University of Illinois in commerce, engineering, or one of the physical sciences. He speaks enough English to pass TOEFL enrollment requirements, and is quite consumed by his work at the University for the duration of his residence, which averages two years. The typical mother has a bachelor's degree, but speaks little or no English. With few exceptions, English is never used in the home by adults, although children often begin to use English even with their siblings after the first year in this country. There are exceptions, but women in this population with young children generally stay at home and have few contacts other than with other women who are from the same country. My access to this community has been through two channels. First, through foreign students and research assistants who live there, who both provide first-hand information about school-age subjects' out-of-school activities and contacts, and interview children and parents in their native languages. My second channel of access is as a participant in a weekly English conversation session in the Community Center for mothers with accompanying toddlers under the age of three. The sessions are informal, and there is no explicit instruction in English.

The second setting for my research is the Child Development Laboratory, which is a University-operated nursery school. Most of the children who attend are English speakers, as are all four of the adults who teach there. During the past year, however, the group has included two monolingual speakers of Chinese, one of Japanese, and one of Korean. None of the teachers have had any training in teaching English as a second language, and there is no explicit language instruction in the program.

Nursery classes for three and four year olds run for three hours a day on all days that the University is in session. My procedure there has been to focus a videocamera on one non-English speaking child at a time, who is outfitted with a wireless microphone, and to record all of the naturally-occurring activities for that three-hour period over the duration of several months. Additionally, I have obtained audiotape and videotape of the same children interacting at home with parents and siblings, or playing with friends inside and outside their homes.

The third setting for my research is the Martin Luther King Elementary School in Urbana. Because it includes the University housing complex in its attendance area, over one third of the King School student body are native speakers of languages other than English. All children in the school are assigned to a regular English-medium classroom, and limited English speakers are pulled out of these classes for 30 minutes of ESL instruction a day. Emphasis in these ESL sessions is placed on teaching vocabulary that the children will need in their regular classrooms, and on teaching the forms of the Latin alphabet and beginning reading and writing skills. There is no attention to formal grammar, and production errors in English are seldom corrected. Additional scheduling modifications include the assignment of speakers of a number of different native languages to pull out classes conducted in their native languages for another period each day. My research at King School has primarily involved periodic videotaping of focal subjects in naturally-occurring instructional and social contexts, but data collection has also included playback and interview procedures, and has been augmented by more formal elicitation in both first and second languages.

STAGES OF DEVELOPMENT

The toddlers who accompanied their mothers to the weekly conversation session were at Stage 0 in the descriptive model in Figure 1, i.e., they were unaware of other languages around them. They evidenced no need for a lingua franca, playing happily and noisily at their mothers' feet while speaking their respective native languages to one another. This group included the two-year-old daughter of another American participant who spoke English in response to Japanese, Chinese, and all other languages alike. Although the children did not share a common language and were engaged to a great extent in parallel monologues, they did communicate to some extent, and successfully called others' attention to actions and objects they wanted to display, made claims and offers, and shared expressions of amusement or displeasure.

Each of these English sessions also included some organized group activity for the children, where an English speaking adult led the toddlers in finger plays or rhythmic activities, and the mothers joined in. The children followed directions in English beautifully, including stamping their feet or hitting rhythm sticks to such verbal directions as "fast"

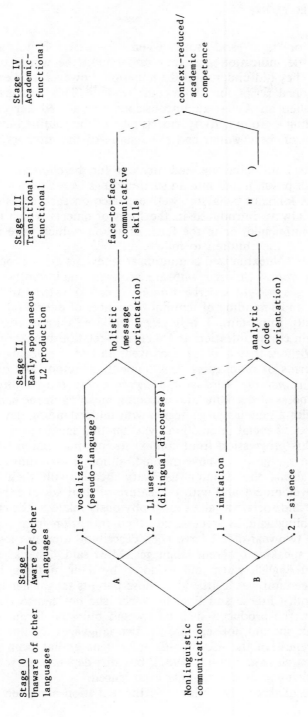

Figure 1. Stages of Development in Second Language Acquisition

and "slow," or "loud" and "soft," when they were told to do so, but there was little indication that they understood the words that were being used. They did understand the situation, however, and evidenced a well-developed script for "follow the leader." This was graphically illustrated when an American unconsciously scratched her ear while she was leading a group activity, not as part of the routine but because it itched. All of the children and even some of the mothers followed suit.

The events I am describing had meaning for the children in several respects. Both physical and human surroundings were familiar to them, and the same kinds of behaviors were expected on each occasion. New content was always introduced in the form of objects which could be seen and manipulated, or in the form of actions which were modeled nonverbally for the children to follow.

Such highly contextualized communicative events are, of course, also common for young children who are acquiring their mother tongue. Early meaning is thought to derive from children's knowledge of "scripts," or a general understanding of familiar sequences of events (e.g. Nelson 1981). Equally important, I believe, is children's knowledge of the participants in communication and their role-relationships, of the emotional tone or key that is being conveyed, and of the norms of interaction. In terms of ontological development, therefore, *the basic unit of meaning is not the word or the sentence, but the communicative event;* the process of decoding and encoding meaning in the early stages of contact with a new language begins with understanding the meaning of the context of social interaction, whether that language is a second or a first. This progression from context to communication holds true for all of the age groups I have studied, although the communicative tactics and forms the children use vary greatly with their level of cognitive development and with the nature of their social experiences.

Cognitive and social variables most obviously relate to the children's level of metalinguistic awareness, and their transition from Stage 0 to Stage I. The two-year-olds I have been describing were not aware that people were speaking different languages. Most said "Thank you" and "Bye-bye" in English when told to do so by their mothers, but little else. One exception was a little girl whose parents taught her labels for objects in both Chinese and English. When she pointed to things and named them, she produced such compound bilingual forms as "feiji-airplane," but she did not separate the two languages for this purpose. Earlier awareness of the use of different languages has been reported in other research (e.g. Vihman 1982), but this depends on social conditions which none of my subjects experienced.

At the age of three, the children in this situation are often enrolled by their parents in one of the nearby private or University nursery schools. Both because of their more extensive contact with speakers of English and their more advanced cognitive development, children of this age generally become aware that other people talk differently than they do within three or four weeks in the new setting. Under Stage I (see Figure 1), I have indicated the categories of communicative phenomena which occur immediately after children's awareness of people speaking different languages begins to emerge.

TYPE A AND TYPE B LEARNERS

First, there appears to be a fairly clear-cut division among children at this point between what I will call Type A and Type B learners, which basically reflects a difference in their social orientation. Type A learners might also be labelled "other-directed" and Type B "inner-directed," to adapt David Riesman's (1950) terms.

One communicative tactic for Type A learners at this point of metalinguistic awareness was to continue to vocalize, but to produce what I call "pseudo-language," which is similar to the jargoning produced by some native speakers of English during the transition period from about nine months into early in their second year (cf. Halliday 1975, Ziajka 1981, Painter 1984). According to Ziajka, in a first language it "sounds like meaningfully inflected sentences, but without using actual words . . . unlike babbling, which lacks stress, pitch and juncture" (1981:113).

The non-English speaking children who use this tactic produced what they claimed (in their native languages) was English, but which in fact was a string of nonsense syllables which may or may not have included an actual English word or phrase. They were aware that people around them were making different sounds, and while they did not yet recognize the conventional nature of the new language, they evidently did think it had meaning, in at least a general sense.

Pseudo-English has been reported to me by several mothers of three-year-olds. One Bengali-speaking mother provided me with an audio recording of her daughter using it while talking on a toy telephone to an imaginary English-speaking friend, and I videotaped a Japanese boy using this medium with English-speaking adults and children at the nursery school. On one occasion he pounded out letters on a typewriter and then brought this paper over to a Japanese adult who was in the room. He told her in Japanese that it was English, read it aloud in nonsense syllables, and then translated the passage into Japanese. Several times during the same class session he used pseudo-English with other children and with adults. When we played these segments of the videotape back to him later, he translated the pseudo-English used in events he could remember into Japanese.

Vihman (1982) reported the appearance of jargon in a two-year-old's second language, and attributed it to mimicry or "parroting" utterances "recalled from memory after a delay of unknown length" (p. 277). I do not believe that is the case in the instances I have observed. This appears to be genuinely creative vocalization, although there is no way to be sure if the children who were able to translate these utterances actually attributed specific meaning to them at the time or were being creative in their reporting to us as well. We can be quite sure that these children perceived the new language first in terms of its sound. Meaning was still perceived in the context, and some was associated with that sound.

Whereas older Type A children came to King Elementary School with an already-developed awareness that people speak different languages and so did not go through that initial stage of metalinguistic discovery, they too often made extensive use of nonverbal vocalizations for communicative purposes during the earliest stage of second language acquisition. By the age of 8 to 12 this often took the form of elaborate collaborative speech play, including plays on one another's names and long alliterative exchanges. An analysis of the form and function of their communicative acts when engaged in peer play during the first month of school showed that, for instance, a third (33.3%) of their communicative acts in the category of acknowledgments to others were performed with nonspeech sounds, as were almost an equal percentage (29.2%) of organizational devices such as greetings and bids for attention. The next most common form of social interaction for children in this age range was entirely nonverbal: e.g. gestures and facial expression. It is important to note, however, that not all of the children engaged in social interaction with peers during this period; some who did not were merely much less assertive than others, or appeared to hold themselves aloof (reported in Saville-Troike, McClure, and Fritz 1984).

Another Stage I communicative tactic of Type A learners was the continued use of their native language to speakers of other languages, even after they realized that different languages were being used. Such simultaneous use of two languages by different participants in a communicative event is what I have termed "dilingual discourse" (Saville-Troike 1987).

I first observed this phenomenon at the beginning of the school year among five-year-olds entering kindergarten who had only recently arrived in the United States and had not had much prior contact with speakers of other languages. The tactic worked well enough for the most part when the children were involved in play, especially when there were objects to be manipulated, but failed in other situations. A number of the five-year-olds soon tried to respond with something that sounded the same as the language being spoken to them—a Korean speaker would mimic an English greeting in response, for instance, and an English speaker would mimic Japanese. None in this age group continued exclusive use of their native languages to others beyond a period of two or three weeks, and most stopped after a few days.

The children who engaged in this phenomenon for the longest period of time were two brothers from Taiwan who attended the nursery school, a three-year-old and a four-year-old whom I have called Didi and Gege (which in Chinese mean "younger-brother" and "older-brother," respectively). Except for the lack of a common verbal code, their exchanges with other children and teachers in the class looked and even sounded normal to a casual observer in most respects. This interactive dilingual discourse in which they engaged, in addition to fulfilling a phatic function, surprisingly often yielded a meaningful exchange of information. Analysis of this phenomenon has been of particular interest to me in my efforts to discover principles governing the negotiation of meaning at this stage which are entirely independent of the content or form of the linguistic code.

The most obvious clues to meaning in the dilingual discourse involving the three- and four-year-olds were derived from the extralinguistic context of the interaction—especially objects upon which mutual attention could be focused, or the presence of some unusual and obviously noteworthy condition—much as in the case with the younger toddlers. Gege, the four-year-old, soon differed from his younger brother Didi in shifting the pragmatic intent of almost half of his initiating utterances to adults to requests for English labels, even though he was still doing so in Chinese, usually asking, *Zheige shi shenma* ("What is this?"). It is interesting to note that although Gege's English-speaking teachers almost always correctly interpreted his *intent* and responded appropriately, not a single one learned even this simple question form in Chinese. This illustrates how even meaningful input need not necessarily lead to second language acquisition where expectations of learning and other social factors (such as differential power relationships) are not conducive to the process.

Another way in which the dilingual discourse of both Didi and Gege with adults and other children differed from the parallel monologues of the toddlers was in the *structure* of communicative exchanges, which participants adhered to even without sufficient extralinguistic context for content to be mutually comprehensible. For example, when a narrative was expressed in one language, the speaker of the other maintained an attentive expression and nodded periodically to provide feedback and encourage continuation. In a social conversation, as when playing house, the participants cooperated by following shared rules for turn-taking, and by using the social routines which were appropriate for that context, even though in different languages. And in the didactic exchanges which occurred during more formal periods of small group instruction, the tripartite Initiation-Response-Feedback structure of "teacher talk" was maintained by all parties, whether speaking English or Chinese.

Dilingual discourse thus provides evidence for the deepening meaning of a communicative event as a context for language acquisition. This meaning develops from the emergent understanding toddlers have of setting, sequence, roles, and norms to include also aspects of the discourse structures. In this case the understanding of these components was part of the communicative competence that the Chinese children had already acquired through social experiences in their native language, but which was not language-specific.

In contrast to the pseudo-language and the continued first language phenomena I have just described, when Type B "inner-directed" learners recognized that people around them spoke a different language, one response was a period of silence which sometimes lasted for several weeks. Other "inner-directed" children began to imitate English words spoken by adults or other children to themselves at this time, although they were not asked to do so. In fact, although imitation by some of the children was audible to all who were present, some used such a low vocal level that their imitation was only detectable with the wireless microphones that were clipped close to their mouths. The microphones also allowed us to discover that in a few cases where children apparently spoke spontaneous English words or phrases aloud during this period, they were actually repeating forms that were fed to them in a whisper by another child.

One challenge in this study has been to map the second language development of children who did not produce any English at all during this stage. The audible evidence we have that some Type B learners vocalized to themselves in imitation of others suggests that others who were overtly silent may, in fact, have been subvocalizing in a similar manner. These undoubtedly include the two "silent" children in this sample who began to speak English in whole sentences without going through a one-word production stage at all.

It is important to emphasize, however, that children who are silent at this stage do not necessarily become successful language learners. One kindergarten child, for instance, suddenly stopped speaking at all at the point of metalinguistic awareness, which for her occurred after about three weeks of chattering indiscriminately to everyone in Japanese. She remained silent in all English contexts for the remainder of the school year, and spoke only to other Japanese children and to Japanese-speaking adults. When asked why she had stopped talking, she said she realized that she could not understand the language others were using, and that it was too hard. Unlike most other Type B children, she did not make any discernible attempt to learn English, and in spite of months of informal exposure, she showed no signs of even beginning to acquire it.

The transitions between the early stages of acquisition undoubtedly require some insight on the part of the child, but this appears to be gradual for most children rather than a sudden "ah-hah" experience. Three-year-old Didi, for instance, explicitly said in Chinese, "This is English" and "This is Chinese," but only in reference to written English letters and Chinese characters. Four-year-old Gege, on the other hand, clearly recognized spoken English words as being different, since he repeated them to himself with Chinese translations, even as he continued to produce only Chinese to others. A born pedagogue, he also unsuccessfully tried to teach the nursery school teachers how to say things in Chinese.

Data on the quantity of private speech provide further evidence for the gradual increase in metalinguistic awareness at the four-year-old level. Gege's use of Chinese to himself in the presence of English speakers decreased over a four-month period that was analyzed (Chen 1985), while younger Didi's did not. Even so, it was many weeks before Gege abandoned dilingual discourse and began to produce English to others. When asked why he had done so, he explicitly said that he realized they were not going to speak Chinese, and now that he was learning English he would use that language.

Even at the age of six, a child may not have fully developed the concept of a different language. Near the beginning of the first grade one boy brought a letter from his mother to the teacher which was written in Japanese. His mother had probably told him that his teacher would not be able to read Japanese and that he should read it to her. He did so, slowly and carefully enunciating every word—but without any translation. He obviously did not realize that she would not understand Japanese (Mary Fritz, personal communication). Another Japanese speaker, age eight, spoke Japanese initially to every new child or adult he encountered at the beginning of school. While he clearly realized that many would not understand him, he used this tactic to sort out those who could from those who could not. He made no evident connection yet between language identity and physical traits or ethnicity.

HOLISTIC VS. ANALYTIC STRATEGIES

In Stage II, when English first appears in children's spontaneous production, two basic developmental strategies can be inferred from the data. The first strategy I have labeled "holistic" or "message-oriented"; the second I am calling "analytic" or "code-oriented." (I have elsewhere [Saville-Troike et. al. 1984] called these "chunking" and "stringing.") The difference between the specific language forms and skills which children in these two categories exhibit is not entirely unlike those described by Nelson (1973) in her differentiation of "referential" and "expressive" groups of children acquiring their mother tongue. In her words, "one is learning an object language, one a social interaction language" (p. 22).

In analyzing the English vocabulary which children in these two groups produce spontaneously in the first month of contact with English, the following results are typical. Kazu, a five-year-old analytic learner who was a Type B (inner-directed) imitator in Stage I, named objects in his environment, counted them, and labeled attributes such as color and shape. Soo-mi, a holistic learner in the same kindergarten class who had been a Type A (other-directed) vocalizer in Stage I, produced no labels at all for objects during the ten hours that she was videotaped during a month except in direct response to the question from an adult "What is that?", although she talked a great deal. Her earliest spontaneous utterances included "No," "Me too," "I color too," "My first," "I am thirsty," "Not here," "I want to there," "I want a this," "I want that way," and "That are bad."

The analytic Kazu also practiced more complex forms in Stage II, and even created patterned drills for himself, although he had encountered none at school. Sequences of his recorded private speech include "Finished. I finished. I have finished. I am finished. I'm finished" and "I want. I paper. I want paper." Another early imitator, nine-year-old Akiko, continued to whisper English words to herself (using Japanese phonology), following each with a Japanese particle *deshyo,* which might be freely translated as "check," as she appeared to consciously store them in memory.

The type of strategy a child evidences during the early emergence of English in Stage II is usually related to the social orientation he or she evidenced earlier, but there are exceptions. Most Type A (other-directed) learners produced whole messages from the beginning, even when they required a combination of English routines, native language, gestures, nonspeech sounds, and pictures. This combination of tactics was particularly effective in sustaining social interaction with other children. The first spontaneous English of Type B (inner-directed) learners, on the other hand, was frequently a single lexical term (usually the name of the topic the child wanted to convey information about). Completion of the proposition for them required a cooperative addressee, who typically asked one or more questions that allowed the child to respond with a simple "yes" or "no." This tactic was more effective with adults than with other children.

This difference can be illustrated with exchanges between two seven-year-old boys and their teachers at about the same point in their English language development. Both were quite successful.

The first, who was message-oriented, used the following tactic to communicate to the teacher that another child, Taki, had thrown a pencil at him while passing out supplies:

> Child: *TEACHER. TEACHER.*
> The teacher goes over to him.
> Child: *TAKI.*
> *PENCIL.*
> *Makes throwing motion.*
> *TAKI.*
> *UN . . . HE.*
> *Makes throwing motion again.*
> Teacher: *TAKI, PLEASE DON'T THROW PENCILS.*

The second child, who was code oriented, made use of the following sequence to respond to the teacher's question about why another child had not come to class:

> Child: *PICTURE.*
> Teacher: *SHE'S MAKING A PICTURE?*
> Child: *YES.*
> Teacher: *WILL SHE COME WHEN SHE'S FINISHED?*
> Child: *YES.*

Three-year-old Didi used another holistic tactic, just replacing a Chinese word in an utterance with its English equivalent. For instance, when the teacher offered him a cherry, he said, *Women ye you yingtao* ("We also have cherries"). The teacher said, "Cherry," and Didi repeated, *Women ye you cherry.* His early English vocabulary (all of which occurred in Chinese utterances) consisted of names for things that interested him in the environment, such as "balloon," "airplane," "skyscraper," and "squirrel," even though he also knew the terms for them in Chinese.

In spite of his early Type A social orientation, four-year-old Gege used analytic strategies. He appeared to consciously disapprove of mixing English words with Chinese, and corrected his younger brother Didi when he did so. The only English words that Gege incorporated into Chinese utterances were terms unique to the English context which he could not express in Chinese, such as letter names, place names, and some food items. His very limited early productive vocabulary in English included "McDonalds," "Valu Check," "Green Street," "butter pecan," "jelly beans," and "fried chicken." At the same time, Gege continued to practice other English words and phrases to himself apparently until he felt ready to use them.

Context remained vital to the decoding and encoding of meaning at this stage of development, whichever strategies were in use, although linguistic as well as nonverbal context began to be part of the event knowledge that was taken into account. Children made extensive use of prior utterances to build on, repeating parts with a minimal substitution and then gradual expansion or elaboration. They also relied on consistent frames or formats to provide a known context within which to interpret and learn new information. This is consistent with Fillmore's (1985) finding that limited English speakers learn best in highly structured lessons with consistent scripts. In familiar contexts, even the recognition of only a single word (in speech or in written text) often allowed correct interpretation of meaning and an appropriate response. In one third-grade class I observed, for instance, the teacher complimented a new student from Venezuela at some length on the pyramid he had just constructed by gluing toothpicks together. She ended with the question, "What geometrical shape is that?" Jorge had only a few days' experience with English, but he apparently already understood that when an adult asks a question which includes the word "shape," a student is supposed to respond with "circle," "square," or "triangle," which were among the initial vocabulary terms taught in his ESL class. Since the nonverbal context made it clear that the teacher was talking about his toothpick pyramid during this otherwise unintelligible stream of speech, he was able to make sense of the situation and answer correctly, "triangle."

Holistic vs. analytic developmental strategies in the acquisition of a second language may well relate to more general top-down vs. bottom-up strategies, or to relatively more field dependent vs. field independent styles of learning, and that question deserves further consideration. It is quite apparent that the predominance of early holistic vs. analytic strategies relates to children's level of metalinguistic awareness, and to their intentionality in learning. Although I hope I have made clear in the data presented here that there is no absolute division by age, younger children tend to favor the former and older children the latter.

LATER DEVELOPMENTAL PHENOMENA

I will offer only a very brief summary of the later developmental phenomena at this time. By Stage III (which I have labeled "transitional-functional"), an "other-directed" social orientation and holistic strategies quite uniformly led to competence in face-to-face social interaction with peers, judging from the quantity of interaction these children chose to engage in, and their apparent success in achieving their communicative goals. "Inner-direction" and analytic strategies sometimes led to social interaction skills, but sometimes did not, judging from lack of sustained interaction with English-speaking peers and unsuccessful attempts to initiate play or gain entry into ongoing activities. (This is why indication of those skills is in parentheses in the model.)

However, the Type B (inner-directed) learners were more successful in reaching Stage IV (labelled "academic-functional"), which is characterized by competence in context-reduced language skills, as measured by reading and writing tasks and performance on tests of knowledge in academic content areas that were administered in English. For some, achieving social competence came only *after* a relatively high level of academic competence was reached. Some of the Type A (other-directed) learners who were very successful interpersonal communicators plateaued at fairly early levels of development, their very success seeming to have reduced their motivation to learn more complex linguistic forms. (This is why there is a dotted line between Stages III and IV for that group of children in Figure 1.)

I would attribute these differential outcomes to the greater disposition on the part of the more analytic children to make efforts at conscious and intentional learning. While such a disposition may not necessarily enhance the acquisition of social interaction skills, it clearly contributes to success in school.

Another difference in the groups of children which began to appear by Stage III was the more rapid attrition of native language skills in Type A learners who were "other-directed" and message-oriented. This difference appeared even though the parents of all of these subjects continued to speak only their native languages at home, and even though all school-aged children received the same amount of native language instruction. Since metalinguistic awareness is often tied to the development of literacy skills, this finding is probably related to the greater vulnerability of first language skills among children who begin to learn a second language prior to reading their first, as was the case for younger Finnish children in Sweden reported by Skutnabb-Kangas and Toukomaa (1976; see John-Steiner [1985] for a discussion of this point).

Language dominance tests are administered to all of the foreign children at King School twice each year, and the pattern of scores for hundreds of them in that setting over the past 10 years clearly shows that those who first encounter English in kindergarten shift in dominance quite rapidly, and the decline in their native language ability continues as long as they stay in the country. Children who first encounter English in the first or second grade shift at a slower rate, and children who do not encounter English until the third grade or beyond shift more slowly at first and then appear to level off after the second year. Evidently only they seem to be successful in maintaining a balance between their two languages. This process, and its effect on cognitive development for the children both in the United States and after they return to schools in their home countries, is a major focus on the next phase of my research.

IMPLICATIONS FOR SECOND LANGUAGE ACQUISITION

Now I want to turn to the generalization or theoretical propositions that can be inferred from these data about the nature and processes of second language acquisition.

The most obvious is that from beginning to end, the process of decoding and encoding meaning in both first and second language development can be seen on a continuum from nonlinguistic to linguistic communication. Even for young children, the meaningful contexts within which communication may take place are not merely what can be immediately perceived by the senses, but rather events which also include schemata for act sequences, participant roles, emotional tone, and norms of interpretation (i.e. knowledge and ability to identify/ abstract and interpret *salient* aspects of the setting). With time, through further social interaction experience and cognitive development, "meaningful context" additionally comes to include discourse structures and more complex grammars of expectation. Once acquired through the medium of a native language, these scripts are available for interpretation of meaning even when the language forms used by other participants in the event cannot be understood.

This process applies across all ages, including older children's development of scripts for school, which enables them to make sense of what is going on in their classrooms before learning the language of instruction. It also applies to the English-speaking nursery school teachers, whose development of scripts for relating to young children enables them to make sense of two little boys who are speaking Chinese.

Development within this process is both syntagmatic and paradigmatic in nature, with children learning meaningful sequences within recurring events, and developing a repertoire of forms for their expression and rules for their selection. Given the socially and contextually embedded nature of language, one of my major conclusions is that I do believe that an ultimate explanatory theory for language acquisition ought not to differ significantly from theories which explain development in other sociocognitive domains (e.g. see Serafica 1982, Turiel 1983).

The well-known generalizability of decontextualization in child development lends further weight to this point, with what Werner and Kaplan (1963) call the "autonomization of symbols" considered a basic process of overall cognitive development. Phylogenetic parallels can be hypothesized as well, as in Kay's (1977) proposal that language evolves in the direction of autonomous, context-free systems of symbols. We might here also invoke the principle of uniformitarianism, which has been accepted in the natural sciences since the nineteenth century.

Although this conclusion supports a theory of innate origins in some respects, a second obvious finding to be drawn from these data is that the process of natural language acquisition is not unitary, and may take different paths. This contradicts the claim made by Krashen and Terrell (1983) that there is a single "natural approach to second language acquisition." Different types of learners follow very different approaches, though some individuals in one group may at different times employ some learning or communication strategies favored by the other group. Not even the often presumed "natural" progression from concrete interpersonal interaction to abstract context-reduced language skills holds true for all learners, and for many the sequence may be exactly reversed. As a pedagogical implication, therefore, it would follow that different approaches to teaching will be better suited to children who are on different learning paths, and that different approaches may be effective at different times for particular individuals. Thus there can be no single "best" or "natural" method or sequence for instruction.

At the same time, not all paths are equally effective for reaching the same goals. Just because an approach to second language acquisition can be shown to be a "natural" one, it does not necessarily follow that a child should not be shown a different road. When goals include academic competence and the maintenance of bilingual skills, for example, children who have a higher level of metalinguistic awareness have a clear advantage. Such an orientation can be taught, or at least considerably enhanced, by appropriate instructional procedures.

Another implication for language teaching has already been widely recognized—that meaningful context is critical for language learning. There has not been adequate recognition, however, that this context includes understanding of culturally defined aspects of a communicative event, such as role-relationships and norms of interpretation, of holistic scripts for the negotiation of meaning, as well as observable aspects of the setting. This is initially a top-down process rather than bottom-up: students begin with meaning.

On the other hand, overemphasis on providing contextual meaning for students may actually inhibit their development of context-reduced/ academic competence. This is underscored by evidence that face-to-face communicative skills do not necessarily precede or even lead to decontextualized ones, and that quite different strategies may favor the achievement of one or the other.

The attainment of "communicative competence" is a viable goal, as that construct has been defined by Hymes (1966), Savignon (1972), and Canale and Swain (1980) to include context-reduced as well as interpersonal communication. In practice, however, instructional methods and materials which go under this rubric often focus exclusively on social skills, and are likely to shortchange students for whom academic competence is an important goal. Because of this endemic confusion in the field, I would like to urge that "academic language competence" replace "communicative competence" as the primary goal for English instruction for the vast majority of children who need this more advanced competence for success in school.

A final issue that my findings relate to is one that requires serious consideration, but for which I can offer no simple answer. The acquisition of English as a second language by young children is quite likely to be at the expense of their native language development, even within the relatively supportive first language environment that I have described. If balanced bilingualism and L1 maintenance are conditions to be cultivated, as many of us believe, we have an ethical responsibility to recognize the vulnerability of young learners, and to find ways of keeping language options open to them at least until they reach an age of informed consent.

REFERENCES

Canale, Michael and Merrill Swain. 1980. Theoretical bases of communicative approaches to second language teaching and testing. Applied Linguistics 1.1–47.

Chen, Rey-Mei. 1985. A naturalistic study of private speech. Masters thesis, University of Illinois at Urbana-Champaign.

Fillmore, Lily Wong. 1985. When does teacher talk work as input? Input in second language acquisition, ed. by Susan M. Gass and Carolyn G. Madden, 17–50. Rowley, MA: Newbury House.

Glaser, Barney G. and Anselm L. Strauss. 1967. The discovery of grounded theory: Strategies for qualitative research. Chicago: Aldine.

Halliday, M. A. K. 1975. Learning how to mean: Explorations in the development of language. London: Arnold.

Hymes, Dell. 1966. On communicative competence. Paper presented at the Research Planning Conference on Language Development among Disadvantaged Children. New York, NY: Yeshiva University.

John-Steiner, Vera. 1985. The road to competence in an alien land: A Vygotskian perspective on bilingualism. Culture, communication, and cognition: Vygotskian Perspectives, ed. by James V. Wertsch, 348–371. Cambridge: Cambridge University Press.

Kay, Paul. 1977. Language evolution and speech style. Sociocultural dimensions of language change, ed. by Ben Blout and Mary Sanchez, 21–33. New York: Academic Press.

Krashen, Stephen D. and Tracy D. Terrell. 1983. The natural approach: Language acquisition in the classroom. Oxford: Pergamon Press.

Nelson, Katherine. 1973. Structure and strategy in learning to talk. Monographs of the Society for Research in Child Development 38(1–2), Serial Number 149.

Nelson, Katherine. 1981. Social cognition in a script framework. Social cognitive development: Frontiers and possible futures, ed. by John H. Flavell and Lee Ross, 97–118. Cambridge: Cambridge University Press.

Painter, Clare. 1984. Into the mother tongue: A case study in early language development. London: Frances Pinter.

Riesman, David. 1950. The lonely crowd. New Haven, CT: Yale University Press.

Savignon, Sandra. 1972. Communicative competence: An experiment in foreign language teaching. Philadelphia, PA: Center for Curriculum Development.

Saville-Troike, Muriel. 1987. Dilingual discourse: Communication without a common language. Linguistics 25(1):81–106.

Saville-Troike, Muriel, Erica McClure, and Mary Fritz. 1984. Communicative tactics in children's second language acquisition. Universals of second language acquisition, ed. by Fred R. Eckman, Lawrence H. Bell, and Diana Nelson, 60–71. Rowley, MA: Newbury House.

Serafica, Delicisima C., ed. 1982. Social-cognitive development in context. New York: The Guilford Press.

Skutnabb-Kangas, Tove, and Pertti Toukomaa. 1976. Teaching migrant children, mother tongue, and learning the language of the host country in the context of the socio-cultural situation of the migrant family. Tutkimuksia Research Reports. Tampere, Finland: University of Tampere.

Turiel, Elliot. 1983. Interaction and development in social cognition. Social cognition and social development: A sociocultural perspective, ed. by E. Tory Higgins, Diane N. Ruble, and Willard W. Hartup. Cambridge: Cambridge University Press.

Vihman, Marilyn May. 1982. Formulas in first and second language acquisition.

Exceptional language and linguistics, ed. by Loraine K. Obler and Lise Menn, 261–284. New York: Academic Press.

Werner, Heinz and Bernard Kaplan, eds. 1963. Symbol formation. New York: Wiley.

Ziajka, Alan. 1981. Prelinguistic communication in infancy. New York: Praeger.

CHAPTER TWELVE

Do We Learn to Read by Reading? The Relationship between Free Reading and Reading Ability

Stephen D. Krashen

University of Southern California

Do those who read more read better? On the basis of experimental research, Smith (1982) and Goodman (1982) have argued that "we learn to read by reading," that is, we learn to read by attempting to make sense of what we see on the page. We thus learn to read the same way we acquire language: by obtaining "comprehensible input" (Krashen 1982). If this is true, we would expect the relationship between the amount people read and how well they read to be positive (but not perfect; see discussion at the end of this paper).

In this paper, I review studies that attempt to determine whether there is a relationship between the amount of pleasure reading done and reading ability, as measured by tests of reading comprehension. Three kinds of studies are presented:

1. Free reading programs done in school (e.g. Sustained Silent Reading, Self-Selected Reading).
2. Students' reports of free reading outside of school.
3. Reading resources, or the availability of books and other forms of print.

I will argue that free reading consistently relates to success in reading comprehension, and that the apparent counterexamples to this generalization are easily dealt with.

Table 1.   Studies of Sustained Silent Reading

I. SSR as part of a regular program:

study	grades	duration	measure	results
Oliver 1973	4–6	1 month	RC	equivalent to comparisons
Oliver 1976	4–6	3 months	RC	equivalent to comparisons
Evans & Towner 1975	4	10 wks	RC	equivalent to comparisons
Collins 1980	2–6	15 wks	RC vocab	equivalent to comparisons
Lawson 1968	6	3 months	vocab RC	SSR superior regular program superior
Wolf & Mikulecky 1978	7	9 wks	RC vocab	equivalent to comparisons
Elley et al. 1979	high school	2 years	RC writing	equivalent to comparisons
Schon et al. 1984 (Tempe)	high school	4 months	RC	equivalent to comparisons
Schon et al. 1984 (Chandler)	high school	7 months	RC vocab	equivalent to comparisons
Schon et al. 1985	7–8	8.5 months	RC vocab	SSR tend to be superior in L1; controls in L2
Aranha 1985	4 L2	9 months	RC	SSR superior

II. SSR as supplement to regular program

study	grades	duration	measure	results
Sperzel 1948	5	6 weeks	RC vocab	equivalent to comparisons
Maynes 1981	2–6	one year(a)	RC	no additional gains
Minton 1980	9	one semester	RC vocab	SSR superior SSR superior
Schon et al. 1982	2–4	one year	RC	SSR superior
Manning & Manning 1984a	4	one year	RC	equivalent to comparisons; SSR superior with "peer interaction" (e.g. book sharing)

III. SSR as the exclusive language arts program

study	grades	duration	measure	results
Farrell 1982	8	one year	RC	significant gains(b)
Elley & Mangubhai 1983	4–6 L2	2 years	RC grammar listening	SSR superior SSR superior SSR superior

IV. Other SSR (full information lacking)

Arlin & Roth 1978	3	10 weeks	RC	significant gains(b)
Cline & Kretke 1980	junior high school	3 years	RC	equivalent to comparisons

a: one year = one academic year, fall to spring
b: no comparison group used
L2: students read in a second language
In Aranha (1985), SSR readers as a group were significantly better than controls; further analysis revealed significant differences for girls but no significant difference for boys.

IN-SCHOOL FREE READING PROGRAMS

Sustained Silent Reading (SSR)

Table 1, a slightly expanded version of a table that originally appeared in Krashen (1985a), presents research on "Sustained Silent Reading" (SSR). In SSR, about five to 15 minutes of the usual language arts class is devoted to free reading: children read what they want to read (and teachers read what they want to read; devotees of SSR claim that it is important that students see teachers enjoying reading; e.g. Petre 1971; Mork 1972).

Examination of the first few studies in Table 1 shows that the worst outcome of SSR programs is "no difference": Children do just as well on tests of reading comprehension (and vocabulary) when a few minutes of their language class time is devoted to free reading. Since SSR is much easier on students and teachers than "skill-building" exercises, a result of no difference means SSR is preferable. The studies that show no difference between SSR and traditional instruction are, however, short-term programs. Anyone who has observed SSR knows that for many children, little reading takes place during the first few weeks; the children haven't found a book yet! As we shall see, when reading programs run for a longer term, they are consistently successful (see Sadowski 1980 and Wiesenberger & Birlem 1983 for similar suggestions).

A more detailed discussion of SSR studies can be found in Krashen (1985a). Some of the studies in Table 1 are worth discussing in a bit more detail here, however. In the Schon et al. studies, students read in Spanish, their primary language. In Schon, Hopkins and Davis (1982), not only did the students gain in Spanish reading comprehension (and vocabulary), but they also showed gains in English reading vocabulary equivalent to comparison students, showing that literacy in the first language can improve without cost to the second language.

Schon, Hopkins, and Vojir (1984) carried out two similar studies with bilingual high school students. No difference was found for growth in Spanish or English reading. In one case (their Tempe study), the duration may have been too short. In addition, teachers of the experimental groups in this study reported that U.S.-born Spanish speakers "were not interested in reading in Spanish and rarely if ever used the specially provided reading materials in Spanish . . ." (p. 36). Spanish speakers born in Mexico, on the other hand, were eager to read in Spanish. In Schon, Hopkins and Vojir (1985), a junior high school study, most comparisons were not statistically significant, but there was a trend for those who read in Spanish to improve more in Spanish reading and vocabulary, while comparison students tended to improve more in English. Closer analysis revealed, however, that only five of the 11 experimental group teachers actually carried out Spanish SSR conscientiously. The classes taught by these five achieved significantly better gains in both English and Spanish.

Two SSR studies involving comic books can be interpreted as cases supporting the efficacy of SSR. In Sperzel (1948), three groups of 15 students served as subjects, with two groups reading only comic books! Sperzel reported no difference among the three groups in gains in reading comprehension or vocabulary:

gains in:	reading comprehension	vocabulary
comic book readers	3.8	1.3
comic book readers*	2.2	3.1
comparison group	2.3	2.3

(Scores in terms of months gained on the Gates Reading Test)
* = this group was asked to keep a word list "to make sure the group read the words and not the pictures" (p. 110).

It should be noted that all three groups made excellent gains in reading comprehension, considering the short (six-week) duration; "normal" progress would be about 1.5 months. In addition, Sperzel noted that the comic reading was very popular:

> The period was eagerly looked forward to and was one of the first items taken care of in the planning of the day's work. Invariably one of the first questions was, "What time will we have our comics?" The respectful attitude of the children was especially noticeable during the period. No one bothered anyone else. They tiptoed quietly about the room as they exchanged their books. As far as the rest of the world was concerned it simply did not exist for these boys and girls (p. 110).

Arlin and Roth (1978) compared comic book readers with "regular" book readers, and classified subjects into good reader and poor reader groups. All groups made impressive gains:

Gains in Reading Comprehension
(10 weeks of SSR, 20 minutes daily)

	comic book group	book group
good readers	5.8	6.4
poor readers	2.6	9.9

(Grade equivalent scores in months; Gates-MacGinitie Reading Test)

Arlin and Roth's worst-performing group (poor readers who read comics) matched expected growth, gaining 2.6 months in 10 weeks. The other groups did much better. It should also be pointed out that the book readers read books "selected by the school librarian and the two classroom teachers to represent books of high interest and appropriate reading level" while the comic book readers read comic books "which might be considered educational," such as Classics Comics (pp. 206-207). Thus, the comics might have been less interesting than the books.

Perhaps the most impressive of all the free reading studies is Elley and Mangubhai (1983), which is one of the few studies I found in the professional literature which examined the effects of reading exposure in a second language (see also Aranha 1985, included in Table 1, and Williams 1981, Table 6). Fourth and fifth graders studying English in the Fiji Islands were divided into three groups for their 40-minute EFL period: One group had audiolingual instruction, a second received SSR, and a third had the "Shared Book Experience" method, a reading exposure approach developed by Holdaway which involves reading out loud to children (sometimes from enlarged or "giant" books), discussion of the story, and activities based on the story, rather than on a preordained grammatical syllabus (see Holdaway 1979 for more details). The following table shows that the two reading exposure groups (termed "Book Flood") were clearly superior to the audiolingual group in reading comprehension for the first year of the study:

Gains in Reading Comprehension

	audio-lingual method	SSR	shared book experience
grade 4	6.5	15	15
grade 5	2.5	9	15

(Months of growth; STAF Reading Comprehension Test)

Similar gains were reported for the second year of the study, with the Book Flood groups performing equivalently, and both outperforming the audio-lingual group on reading, listening comprehension, and grammar tests.[1,2]

Self-Selected Reading

Self-Selected Reading programs differ only in small ways from Sustained Silent Reading programs. Typically, more time is devoted to reading, students may keep a record of books read, and discuss what they read with the teacher during short conferences. As is the case with SSR, students read what they want to read. Tables 2 and 3, from Krashen (1985a), confirm that when such programs are given a chance to run for about an academic year or longer, they consistently succeed. Table 4, a revised version of a similar table in Krashen (1985a), analyzes the effect of duration of treatment, combining SSR and Self-Selected Reading Programs. (Combining "7 months to one year" and "greater than one year" categories, and "no difference" and "negative" studies to allow statistical analysis, the difference between short-term and long-term programs is statistically significant (chi square = 5.56, p<.025, df = 1).

Yap's (1977) in-school free reading study does not fit neatly into Tables 1, 2 and 3. Yap reported on the Hawaiian English Project, an "individualized language arts program" used statewide in Hawaii. This

---

[1] Book Flood students also did better in other subjects, such as English and Mathematics. There was even a tendency (p<.10) for Book Flood students to outperform comparison students in tests of Fiji language, another demonstration that the development of literacy in one language helps the development of literacy in general (see Cummins 1984 for a discussion of this "common underlying proficiency").

Elley and Mangubhai also report some variation in progress in the Book Flood classes. As was the case with Schon, Hopkins and Vojir (1985), this variable was related to whether the treatment was carried out faithfully: "Most experimental groups made substantial improvements; those which did not had teachers who restricted the use of books, and did not follow the guidelines provided (p. 65). On the other hand, "only one control class made better than average progress (in the first year)." In this class, "the teacher had exposed her pupils to daily story book reading, from her private collection of books" (p. 65).

[2] A case of a decline in reading attitudes and in amount of outside pleasure reading after an SSR program was reported by Minton (1980). The positive results listed for this study in Table 1 do not give the true picture—SSR clearly "flopped" in this school. While SSR students did gain more during the SSR semester than they did over the previous semester, gains were small (four months in reading comprehension compared to no gain at all during the previous semester), and the program was very unpopular. Minton outlines the reasons for this: The program was implemented with very little staff consultation, inservicing was inadequate (the staff received only a memo describing SSR, and were invited to a few voluntary meetings), and the entire school did SSR at exactly the same time, which made it very inconvenient for students in industrial arts and physical education classes!

Table 2. Self-Selected Reading Compared to Regular (BASAL) Programs

study	grades	duration	measure	results
Jenkins 1957	2	one year	RC	self-sel superior
			vocab	self-sel superior
Bohnhorst & Sellars 1959	1–3	2 years	RC	self-sel superior
Sartain 1960	2	3 months	RC	no difference(a)
Sartain 1960	2	3 months	RC	regular superior(b)
Gordon & Clark 1961	2	4 months	RC	self-sel superior
Greenman & Kapilian 1959	3–4	one year	RC	self-sel superior
Aronow 1961	4–5	2 yrs, 4 mths	RC	self-sel superior
Healy 1963	5	one year	RC	self-sel superior
Lawson 1968	6	3 months	RC	regular superior
			vocab	regular superior

a: "good readers"
b: "slow readers"

Table 3. Studies of Self-Selected Reading Without Control Group

study	grades	duration	measure	results
Boney & Agnew 1937	1–3	3 years	RC	positive
Sharpe 1958	2	3 months	RC	positive
Cyrog 1959	1–2	2 years	RC	positive
Cyrog 1959	2–4	3 years	RC	positive
Carson 1957	2	one year	RC	positive
			vocab	positive
Largent 1959	3	7 months	RC	positive
			vocab	positive
Crossley & Kniley 1959	3	one year	RC	positive
Jenkins 1955	3	5 months	RC	positive
Jenkins 1955	5–6	one year	RC	positive
Dickinson 1959	4	one year	RC	positive
			vocab	positive
Johnson 1951	5	3 months	RC	positive
Smith & Becker 1960	5	2 years	RC	positive(a)
Burrows 1950	5	6 weeks	RC	positive
Kingsley 1958	6	one year	RC	positive
			vocab	negative
Safford 1960	3–6	one year	RC	negative
Anderson, Hughes, & Dixon 1957	1–6	six years	RC	positive

positive = students exceeded published norms
(a) students exceeded city average

Table 4. Sustained Silent Reading and Self-Selected Reading Programs: Analysis of Results According to Duration of Treatment

	Results (tests of reading comprehension)		
duration	positive	no difference	negative
less than 7 months	6	8(a)	3
7 months–1 year	11	4	1
greater than one year	7	2	0

positive: SSR or self-selecting students outperform comparison students or published norms (see tables one, two, and three)
a: In seven of these studies, SSR or self-selected reading was part or all of the language arts program; "no difference" can thus be interpreted as evidence in favor of reading exposure (see text).

study involved 202 second graders studied over two years. Yap found strong correlations between "reading level," based on the number of books a child reads, and scores on the California Reading Test (r = .77 for comprehension and .84 for vocabulary). The amount of reading done was a much stronger predictor of test performance than measured IQ was. (Students were required to correctly answer comprehension questions to receive credit for having read a book.)

On the other hand, Harris, Serwer and Gold (1967) found "low positive correlations" between the "number of books read completely" (p. 702) and reading attainment for minority second graders. It is not clear from their report, however, whether the books were self-selected, and the exact correlation and level of significance is not given.

Another potential counterexample is Stallings (1986), who reported a negative correlation between amount of class time devoted to silent reading and reading CTBS scores (California Test of Basic Skills) for 43 high school reading classrooms "focussed on basic reading skills" (p. 92) (n = 903 students). In addition, those students making the greatest gains over a year spent the least amount of time in silent reading in class (9%, compared to 21% of the time spent by those students who made no gains over the year; note that 9% of a 50-minute class is 4.5 minutes, while 21% of a class is 10.5 minutes, only a six-minute difference). This study is a genuine counterexample only if "student silent reading" was genuine SSR, with self-selected books read for pleasure. (Stallings also reported a negative correlation between use of leisure books in class and class attendance, r = −.34. She suggests that such classes may have lacked "rule clarity" and structure, a factor that related to better attendance [r = +.34]. It may be the case that high school students do not appreciate the value of SSR and do not take it, and classes that contain it, seriously. In fact, an inspection of Tables 2, 3, and 4 shows that only one high school study out of five shows positive results; this one study is Minton [1980], a problematic SSR program that resulted in small gains. For discussion, see footnote 2.)[3]

---

[3] The results of some other studies also seem to be counter to the generalization that in-school free reading programs are effective. Closer analysis reveals, however, good reasons for these results.

In Cline and Kretke (1980) no differences were found between SSR and non-SSR students in a three year program. All SSR students in the study, however, came from a population of good readers who scored, on the average, two years above grade level. It is thus no surprise that SSR did not produce superior gains in this study; SSR is for less mature readers, its aim being to interest them in outside reading. It probably has little effect on the already mature reader.

Ingham (1981) describes the impact of large quantities of additional books being supplied to middle school (ages 9 to 12) students in two schools in England. Publishers donated over 7000 volumes (5600 at the beginning of the project), which were made available to students mostly through classroom libraries. Quantity of reading and gains in language were reported for the two experimental (book flood) schools (one "inner city" school and one "outer city" school) and for two comparison schools. The project lasted three years (the book flood books were introduced in the middle of the first year).

Analysis of "reading record forms" filled out by students for each book they read revealed that the experimental students did more reading in five comparisons out of six (the exception was the age 12+ group in the outer city experimental school):

"Outer city schools"

age	10+		11+		12+	
	E	C	E	C	E	C
different titles read	554	290	471	322	249	307
total number of books read	1095	447	773	666	456	782
number of students	77	83	74	80	70	79

"Inner city schools"

age	10+		11+		12+	
	E	C	E	C	E	C
different titles read	415	404	479	299	886	412
total number of books read	776	590	688	582	1240	1250
number of students	94	94	89	86	86	83

"total number of books read" = number of "reading records" filled out by students and returned
E: experimental (book flood) students
C: comparison students

Book Flood students, however, showed only "slight or negligible" advantages on standardized tests of reading comprehension when compared to control students. Ingham suggests several possible causes for the failure of the book flood to make a substantial difference. An important observation was that the headmasters of all schools in the study, experimental and control, "had made every effort to obtain a good supply of books for the children. Although these may not have been in classrooms, there were several thousand

FREE READING OUTSIDE OF SCHOOL

Reported Pleasure Reading

The studies presented in Table 5 probe the relationship between the amount of voluntary reading students say they do outside of school

books in each school, reaching a total of about 9000 in one school. An additional 5000 books need not then make a very substantial difference" (p. 204).

A reanalysis of the quantity of books read confirms this suggestion. Although book flood students did read more, they didn't read that much more than control students. Based on data from the preceding table, I calculated the average number of books read per student:

age	10+		11+		12+	
	E	C	E	C	E	C
outer city schools	14.2	5.4	10.4	8.3	6.5	9.9
inner city schools	8.3	6.3	7.7	6.8	14.4	15.1

The difference between book flood and control students is marked only for 10-year-olds in the outer city schools—during the first year of the project. For the rest of the comparisons, differences are small, from about one to three books a year! We would not expect this small a difference to have much of an impact. As Ingham points out in several places, the book flood did not bring with it any change in school procedures; there were, for example, no SSR times added to experimental schools (see e.g. pp. 31–32). As Ingham notes (p. 213), it is crucial to determine how books are used.

It is interesting to note that the amount of reading reported in Ingham's study is not overwhelming. Cleary (1935) asked junior high school students to keep a record of their free reading for one semester. Seventh graders averaged 15 books over the semester, eighth graders averaged 14, and ninth graders, eight. To compare these figures with Ingham's readers, we need to double Cleary's figures, since her study lasted only one semester—the average number Cleary's students read is considerably greater than those in Ingham's study.

Lamme (1976) studied the free reading habits of 65 students in the United States of about the same age as Ingham's students (grades 4 to 6; ages 9 to 11):

grade	books read per year	standard deviation
4	23.5	16.7
5	27.5	8.2
6	31.4	9.6

Even if we subtract summer reading (about five to six books, according to Heyns's [1978] data on sixth graders; Brink [1939] reported that high school students read an average of three books over the summer, with a range of from zero to 22. His data is probably an underestimate of summer reading, since students were asked to recall specific titles), these figures are clearly larger than experimental and control students in the book flood study. These comparisons lead to the interesting question of whether American children read more than British children.

McCreath (1975) is another apparent counterexample. In her study of 89 junior college students enrolled in a reading improvement course, McCreath reported that the correlation between the amount of free reading done and gains on the Nelson-Denny test over one semester was not significant. In Krashen (1985a), I suggested that this result may have and scores on reading comprehension tests. Data on the amount of free reading done was obtained either by questionnaire (Sheldon & Cutts 1953; Evans and Gleadow 1983; Wahlberg & Tsai 1983, 1985; Roberts, Bachen, Hornby & Hernandez-Ramos 1984; Telfer & Kann 1984; Hafner, Palmer & Tullos 1986; Neuman 1986a), or by asking subjects to keep a diary or log (Greaney, 1980; Fielding, Wilson & Anderson in press; Long & Henderson 1973; Lamme 1976).

In most of the studies in Table 5, modest but positive correlations are reported between reading achievement and amount of reading done outside of school. One exception is Wahlberg and Tsai's low correlations between "frequency of spare time reading" and reading achievement. Wahlberg and Tsai's results may be due to the fact that the measure of reading achievement in both studies was a questionnaire, not a reading test, that measured four "cognitive processes in reading: knowledge, comprehension, study skills, and application" (p. 61), clearly quite different from the reading comprehension measures used in other studies. The sample item presented in their 1983 paper was:

What is the best place to find the meaning of a word you do not know?

---

been due to the short duration of the study and the lack of variation in reading ability and reading exposure of these students (p. 101). Of additional interest is the fact that these subjects were apparently those with reading problems, and they were not, as a group, heavily involved in free reading. McCreath does provide some data on her subjects' free reading, but did not study a comparison group.

Other researchers who have asked college students the extent of their free reading have reported higher figures:

Percentages of College Students Reporting "Frequent" or "Daily or Almost Daily" Free Reading

study:	McCreath	Jones 1950 undergraduates n = 497	Reinhardt 1930 freshmen n = 66 males, 174 females	Kingston 1960 undergraduates n = 155
reading			m f	m f
newspapers:	73	98	78, 61	
magazines:	62	80		87, 73
books:	38	50		
(other than texts)				

With the exception of the females in Reinhardt's sample, McCreath's students appear to read less than unselected college students, a finding consistent with the hypothesis that there is a relationship between free reading and reading comprehension. (It is interesting to note that in Jones's study, book reading was more frequent among freshmen, 62%, than it was among seniors, 46%. In McCreath's sample, older students, those over 23, did more reading than younger students. The older students still lag behind comparison students from other studies in magazine and book reading, however.)

Table 5.   Reported Pleasure Reading and Reading Achievement

study	subjects	results
Schoonover 1937	high school	r = .079 between number of books read over six years and scores on reading test; all students involved in free reading program
Sheldon & Cutts 1953	grades 1–12 n = 521	parents report that "almost half of the above-average and superior readers have reading as an out-of-school interest . . . about one-fourth of the average and only one-tenth of the below-average readers seem to be interested in reading at home." (p. 519)
Hansen 1969	grade 4 n = 48	no relationship between reading achievement and number of books read (size of correlation not reported)
Long & Henderson 1973	grade 5 n = 150	r = .18 to .22 between time spent reading and subtests of Gates-MacGinitie Reading Test
Thorndike 1973	14 years old n = 39,307 (15 countries)	correlations between hours of reading for pleasure and reading comprehension: all 15 countries: r = .16 12 developed countries: r = .29
Lamme 1976	grades 4–6 n = 65	r = .30 between number of books read and test of reading comprehension
Lambert & Saunders 1976	high school	skilled readers non-skilled readers 42 25 non-readers 26 51 "skilled" = top 50% of STEP test "reader" = reads five hours or more per day for pleasure "non-reader" = reports no free reading chi square = 12.023, p<.001 phi coefficient = .29 (a)
Greaney 1980	grade 5 n = 920	correlations between time devoted to reading and performance on the Drumconda English Test (comprehension and vocabulary: books = .31 comics, popular magazines = .13
Newman & Prowda 1982	4,8,11th graders n = 7,787	partial correlations between hours per week of reading for pleasure and tests of reading (sex, amount of educational material in the home partialled out): grade 4 r = .22 grade 8 r = .25 grade 11 r = .27
Evans & Gleadow 1983	grade 11 n = 78; adults n = 66 middle class	no relationship between reported leisure reading and reading proficiency (British Columbia Reading Assessment)

Wahlberg & Tsai 1983	age 17 n = 2,300	correlations with reading achievements frequency of spare time reading = .23 amount of leisure reading = .09
Telfer & Kann 1984	4,8,11th grade n = 234	r = .21 between time spent reading for enjoyment and reading scores on Gates-MacGinitie test for 11th graders. "statistically nonsignificant trend among 4th and 8th graders" (p. 538)
Roberts, Bachen, Hornby & Hernandez-Ramos 1984	grades 2,3,5	correlation between reading achievement (CTBS, SAT, SRA) and number of books read in last two weeks: grade 2 r = .01 n=127 grade 3 r = .22 n=134 grade 5 r = .21 n=203
Wahlberg & Tsai 1985	age 9 n = 1,459	correlation between reading achievement & frequency of spare time reading = -.03
Neuman 1986a	grade 5 n = 59	"heavy readers" (about 6 books per month) score higher on *Reading Progress Scale* than "light readers" (about one book/month) heavy readers = 2.8 light readers = 2.3 (maximum = 4 points)
Hafner, Palmer, & Tullos 1986	grade 9 n = 80	no difference between good readers and poor readers in "number of books or magazines read"; good reader = upper half of scores on Davis Reading test poor reader = lower half of scores on Davis Reading test.
Fielding, Wilson, & Anderson in press	grade 5	minutes per day reading best predictor among leisure time activities of reading achievement, vocabulary, gains in reading

a: calculations done by S.K. from Lambert and Saunders' raw data.

(In a world atlas, in an encyclopedia, in a dictionary, in a newspaper, don't know)

Samples from their 1985 paper were:

"Does a poem have to rhyme? (a) yes (b) no (c) I don't know.

"Where should you look to find the best route from Columbus, Ohio to Toledo, Ohio? (a) on a road map (b) in a geography book (c) on a globe (d) in a history book (e) I don't know."

Another possible reason for Wahlberg and Tsai's low correlations may be the questions used to determine the amount of reading done.

In their 1983 study (see Table 5), "amount of leisure reading" did not correlate with reading achievement (r = −.09). This measure, however, reflected only time spent doing pleasure reading on one day ("How much time did you spend reading just for your own enjoyment yesterday?"). In their 1985 study, "frequency of spare time reading" was a composite of this question and a question probing general reading, and also failed to relate to reading achievement (r = −.03). When general reading was probed alone ("frequency of spare time reading," 1983 study: "How often do you read for your own enjoyment during your spare time?"), a positive correlation was found (r = .23).

The correlations reported in several other studies in Table 5 are, most likely, attenuated. In Long and Henderson (1973), only students who could read at grade level or above were included in the study: "thirty-three (fifth grade students) were eliminated because they were not reading at grade level" (p. 194).

Thorndike's (1973) reported correlations between "hours reading for pleasure" and reading comprehension in 15 countries could also be attenuated in some cases, since in some countries education is limited to a privileged few. This could explain the lower correlation reported in Table 5 for the full set of 15 countries; less developed countries may be those with less universal education and a lower range of reading ability among its school children.[4]

In Schoonover (1937; see also 1938) all subjects were involved in a voluntary free reading program and averaged about 55 books read per year outside of school, a great deal of reading—the low correlation reported between free reading and reading achievement (r = .079) is thus also attenuated. (Gallo [1968] reported that the eleventh graders he studied averaged about 11 books per year; for data on the amount of free reading done by younger students, see footnote 3). Similarly, in Evans and Gleadow (1983) the subjects, as a group, read quite a bit: 90% of the adult subjects and 70% of the (grade 11) students were pleasure readers, averaging between one and three books a month, equalling or exceeding Gallo's eleventh graders (see above), and a great deal of newspaper and magazine reading was also reported. Evans and

---

[4] To test this hypothesis, I computed correlation coefficients between (a) correlations from Thorndike's (1973) data between reading comprehension and amount of pleasure reading done (pp. 118–119) and (b) standard deviations of reading comprehension tests (pp. 124–125). As predicted, a relationship was found: The more variability (the higher the standard deviation), the more pleasure reading and reading achievement correlate. For the 10-year-olds, r = .533; for the 14-year-olds, r = .553. Both correlations are (just barely) significant at the .05 level. Rank order correlations were also calculated: For the 10-year-olds, rho = .66 (p<.05); for the 14-year-olds, rho = .59 (p = .05) (two tailed tests used in all cases).

Gleadow explain their failure to find a significant correlation between amount of reading and reading proficiency by hypothesizing that "literacy skills are well established by secondary school and unguided practice does little to refine them" (p. 14). Another possibility is that their sample did not vary enough in amount of reading or in reading proficiency (mean scores of the reading used were high, 82.7/96 for the adults and 78.7/96 for the eleventh graders; standard deviations were not reported, nor was the size of the nonsignificant correlation between amount of reading and reading proficiency).

Additional Studies of Reported Pleasure Reading

Guthrie (1981) reported a relationship between reading comprehension and reading achievement using a different methodology. Estimates of "reading volume," the amount of reading done by adults (based on readership surveys and other sources) was compared to performance on tests of reading comprehension (from Thorndike 1973) for three countries. Guthrie concluded that "for the three nations of New Zealand, the United States, and Iran, reading comprehension achievement and volume of reading were highly associated" (p. 20)[5]:

Scores on Reading Comprehension Tests:				
14 year olds		18 year olds		Reading Volume
New Zealand	29.3	New Zealand	35.4	1. New Zealand
U.S.A.	27.3	U.S.A.	21.8	2. U.S.A.
Iran	7.8	Iran	4.4	3. Iran

Finally, Kasdon (1958) interviewed 50 "superior readers," college freshmen who scored in the top 2½% on a reading comprehension test (Cooperative English Test). Twenty (40%) of the sample attributed their reading competence to the fact that they read a great deal, and 12

---

[5] Smit (1983) suggests additional reasons for the New Zealand students' high performance on reading tests. First, according to Smit's observations, "a psycholinguistic view of reading prevails in New Zealand and seems always to have prevailed. Reading has been taught as a meaning-getting process. New Zealand's reading program has been strongly influenced by Marie Clay, Kenneth Goodman, and Frank Smith . . ." (p. 124). In addition, there is "little use of commercially prepared workbooks," and "children are encouraged to discuss books they have read or have had read to them" (p. 124). In his response to Smit, Guthrie (1983) adds, from his own observations of schools in New Zealand: "What continually struck me was the large number of attractive books within classrooms. These books gathered no dust but were read, reread, exchanged, and adored . . ." (p. 124). These comments agree with the results of studies presented in the text and support the idea that successful programs are those that help children get meaning from texts, encourage reading, and provide lots of books.

more of the group gave interest in reading as the explanation for their high reading proficiency. Only five subjects credited a school experience.

READING RESOURCES

In some studies, indirect measures of free reading are used, such as number of books owned or the amount of "reading resources" available. Table 6 presents these studies, which consistently show a relationship between "reading resources" and reading achievement, ranging from strong (e.g. Milner 1951; Williams 1981) to modest (e.g. Thorndike 1973).[6]

---

[6] A few studies attempt to correlate the amount of free reading done with school success in general. Cleary (1935) reported that seventh, eighth, and ninth grade boys in "rapid progress" English classes reported doing more outside free reading over a semester than students in "slow progress" English classes. (According to my calculations, however, the difference is not significant; chi square = .702.) No difference was found for girls:

	books read by:	
	rapid progress students	slow progress students
boys	16	10
girls	13	13

Swanton (1984) found that "gifted" sixth graders said they had larger personal collections of books than "regular" sixth-grade students:

Number of books owned:

	"gifted" students	"regular" students
over 100	43 (35%)	22 (19%)
between 10 and 100	74 (61%)	78 (67%)
under 10 books	2 (2%)	15 (13%)
other	3 (2%)	2 (1%)

I performed a chi square analysis on the first three rows; the difference between "gifted" and "regular" students was significant (chi square = 16.76, p<.001). To determine the strength of the relationship, the "between 10 and 100" and "under 10 books" categories were combined and a phi coefficient computed. The result, phi = .19, gives a relationship quite similar in strength to other studies relating free reading and reading achievement discussed in the text.

Several other researchers confirm that "gifted" children read more and read more widely (e.g. Termin & Oden 1947, cited in Barbe 1965).

Schoonover (1937) reported only a .134 correlation between number of books read and IQ test scores for 56 high school seniors and a correlation of .272 between number of books read and scholastic attainment. All of these students had participated in an extensive free reading program for the past six years; thus, the correlation may be attenuated (see discussion in text).

SUMMARY

In-school programs (Tables 3,4) show outstanding results in promoting the development of reading comprehension. Sustained silent reading and self-selected reading programs are in general at least as effective as traditional direct teaching programs in developing reading ability, and when they are carried out over a long term (at least seven months), they are consistently more effective.

Out-of-school free reading studies (Table 5) typically show positive correlations with reading achievement, but the correlations are modest, ranging from .2 to .3. While some of these correlations may be attenuated, they are clearly less than the effects of in-school reading (note e.g. Yap's [1977] .77 correlation between number of books read by a child in school and scores on a reading comprehension test).

The reasons for the apparent greater effectiveness of in-school programs are not clear. Students doing free reading in school may select more challenging books; also, out-of-school studies rely on self-report, which may not be completely reliable. What is clear is that free reading consistently relates to reading achievement; apparent counterexamples are probably the result of too-short duration of studies, and the use of restricted samples.

"Reading resources" studies (Table 6) consistently show that reading achievement is related to the amount of reading that is available.

Table 6. Reading Resources and Reading Achievement

study	subjects	results
Milner 1951	grade 1 n = 21 pairs	own "several" or "great many" storybooks; high scorers on reading test = 15/21 low scorers on reading test = 0/21 (chi square = 23.33, df = 1, p<.001; phi coefficient = .74)
Sheldon & Carillo 1952	grades 1–12 n = 521	parents of good readers (read one grade above grade level) report more books in home. more than 100 books: good readers = 72% average/poor readers = 32%
Hansen 1969	grade 4 n = 48	reading achievement relates to "home literacy environment" (literacy materials in the home; amount of reading done with child; reading guidance and encouragement; parents as model reading examples)

Thorndike 1973	age 10 n = 34,344 age 14 n = 39,307 age 18(a) n = 29,474	correlations between reading comp. and "reading resources"(b): age 10: r = .26 age 14: r = .32 age 18: r = .16
Briggs & Elkind 1977	age 5 n = 33 pairs	children who learn to read early taken to library more often by parents
Williams 1981	age 8–18 n = 368	correlation between comprehension test scores (cloze test) and "reading resources" (c) = .51 (English as a second language in Nigeria)
Shields, Gordon, & Dupree 1983	ages 8–13 n = 35	correlation between reading achievement and parents' buying "extracurricular books for child" (r = .37)
Roberts, Bachen, Hornby, & Hernandez- Ramos 1984	grades 2,3, 5	correlation between reading achievement (CTBS, SAT, SRA) and availability of print (newspapers, magazines, books received as presents): grade 2 r = -.08 n = 127 grade 3 r = .33 n = 134 grade 5 r = .19 n = 203
Manning & Manning 1984b	kindergarten n = 10 pairs	more parents of early readers check out library books for their children (8/10 compared to 1/10 from comparison group)
Wahlberg & Tsai 1985	age 9 n = 1,459	correlation between reading achievement and reading material in home = .30
Stevenson 1985	adults (reading age 12 or less)	books in home (childhood): many books: 9.7% a few books: 52% no books: 38.3%

a: or age at final year of secondary school. Students from 15 countries were tested.
b: "reading resources" composite of:
   1. About how many books are there in your home?
   2. How often is a dictionary used by anyone in your home?
   3. Does your family receive or do you regularly read a daily newspaper?
   4. About how many different magazines does your family receive each month?
(Thorndike 1973, p. 65)
c: "Responses grouped under the heading of *reading resources* showed the extent to which English books and reading materials other than textbooks were available in the home and school, or from any library. Responses under this heading also gave information concerning the availability of an English dictionary." (p. 38)

DISCUSSION

The idea that genuine reading is helpful is scarcely controversial; nearly everyone agrees that free reading is desirable. Some scholars, however, assume that skills must first be taught directly and are made "automatic" by reading (e.g. Mork 1972: 441; Sadoski 1980:153–4). Those who adopt this view approve of free reading, but recommend a "balanced" reading program, claiming that reading programs are "every bit as valuable as having the child complete pages in workbooks or fill up pages of skill exercises" (Mork 1972:440 in reference to SSR). The alternative hypothesis is that genuine reading for meaning is far more valuable than workbook exercises—in fact, it is the source of "skills": we learn to read by reading (Smith 1976; 1982; Goodman 1982).[7]

The correlations reported between free reading and reading achievement could be interpreted as showing that those who have mastered the reading "skills" through drill and exercise are able to go on and enjoy more free reading. Experimental studies showing free reading programs in school to be as good as or better than traditional programs cannot be interpreted in this way, however, and support only the hypothesis that it is free reading itself that is responsible for the progress shown by these students.

The results of the research on free reading thus confirm the Smith-Goodman view that we learn to read by reading, as well as the hypothesis that the essential ingredient in language acquisition in general is comprehensible input, messages the acquirer understands (Krashen 1982, 1985b). While comprehensible input may not be sufficient for language acquisition, it is necessary (see discussion at the end of this paper).

There is, in addition, good evidence that free reading is the source of competence in other areas of literacy, such as vocabulary (Smith 1982; Nagy, Herman, & Anderson 1985), writing style (Smith 1983; Krashen 1984), and grammar (Chomsky 1972; Elley and Mangubhai 1984). The practical implications are clear: students need to get "hooked on books" (Fader 1976). While this may seem obvious, encouraging voluntary reading is often the last resort in literacy programs, which all too often emphasize drills and exercises at the expense of real reading.

ENCOURAGING READING

If free reading is important, the question that needs to be asked is how to encourage it. First, of course, we need to be sure books and other reading matter are available. It has been shown that more reading takes place when readers have more access to reading material, whether

---

[7] A similar controversy exists in second language acquisition. Some writers claim that conscious knowledge of rules ("learning") can be converted into subconscious automatic knowledge ("acquisition"). Indeed, most second language teaching materials assume this is the only way second language competence is attained. The alternative hypothesis is that subconscious acquired competence results only from comprehensible input (for supporting arguments, see Krashen, 1985b).

at home (Morrow 1983; Neuman 1986b) or in school (Powell 1966; Morrow 1982). In addition, children who live closer to libraries read more than those who live farther away (Heyns 1978).

Research also suggests that children read more when their parents read more (Morrow 1983; Neuman 1986a; 1986b) and there is good evidence that the use of "literature activities" at home or at school, such as reading to children and discussing stories, leads to more voluntary reading (Lomax 1976; Morrow 1982, 1983; Morrow and Weinstein 1982, 1986; Neuman 1986a; 1986b). One recent study shows that reading aloud also stimulates more voluntary reading by college freshmen (Pitts 1986).

Light Reading

Another avenue to establishing a reading habit that may be overlooked in school programs is encouraging lighter reading. There is suggestive evidence that light reading can build reading ability and can also lead to more "serious" reading.

Consider the case of comic books. Readability studies (R.L. Thorndike 1941; Wright 1979) show that readability of popular comics ranges from second to sixth grade, which means that some are quite challenging for elementary school students, while others may be ideal for less mature readers who need high interest/low vocabulary material. (An example of the latter is *Archie,* a comic series that is of interest to junior high school and high school students but is written at about the second grade level [Wright 1979]). Research studies consistently show that comic book readers do as well in school as noncomic book readers, and show no deficits on tests of language ability. There is suggestive evidence that comic book reading can directly help the development of reading ability (see discussion of Sperzel 1948, and Arlin and Roth 1978, above). Contrary to popular opinion, comic book readers do as much book reading as, or more than, noncomic book readers. (This research is reviewed in Krashen forthcoming).

Of interest to us here is the possible role comics can play in encouraging additional reading. A spectacular case of comic books being used in this way was reported by Dorrell and Carroll (1981) in an article entitled "Spider-Man at the Library." Dorrell and Carroll studied the effects of including comic books in a junior high school library, comparing circulation during the 74 days after comics were introduced and the 57 days before they were available. As indicated in the table below, the presence of comics resulted in an 82% increase in library use (traffic) and a 30% increase in circulation of noncomic books (comics were not circulated):

Effects of Including Comic Books in a Junior High School Library

	precomic period	comic period
number of students who used library (a) (daily average)	272.61	496.38
circulation (daily average)	77.49	100.99

a: Does not include students brought to library by teachers for class assignments.
precomic period = 54 days; comic period = 74 days
(from Dorrell and Carroll 1981)

Dorrell and Carroll also reported that the presence of comics in the library did not result in any negative comments from parents, and that teachers, school administrators, and library staff supported and encouraged the idea of having comic books in the library. (For an extremely interesting case history of comics promoting reading in young children, see Haugaard 1973).[8]

Another example of light reading that can encourage additional reading is "Teen Romances." The small amount of research done on this genre produces results very similar to those reported for comics: According to Pollack (1981), *Sweet Dream Romances,* written for girls aged 10 to 15, are written at the fifth grade level; by way of comparison, note that the mean readability level of best-sellers in 1974 was calculated to be 7.4 by Schulze (1976, quoted in Monteith 1980). Parrish and Atwood (1985) surveyed 250 junior and senior high school girls and reported that most of the girls read Teen Romances: During the school year, 50% of the eighth graders had read from one to five, and 100% of the ninth graders had read at least five Teen Romances. Also, "an astonishing 12% of the twelfth graders had read in excess of thirty novels this school year" (p. 24). Reading Teen Romances does not seem to prevent other kinds of reading. Parrish and Atwood found

---

[8] There has been some concern about the possible negative effects comics may have on behavior. There is, in fact, some research relating comic-book reading and problem behavior, but other studies show that comic book readers are just as well-adjusted as noncomic book readers. (For a review, see Krashen, forthcoming). Clearly, there is nothing intrinsic to the comic book format that is harmful. While some comics may be objectionable, current comics contain some engaging and thought-provoking stories, a development that several writers credit to Marvel Comics' Stan Lee and his introduction, in the early 1960s, of the "super-hero with problems" (see e.g. Schoof 1978, Brocka 1979, Inge 1985).

that "students who read the romance novels read many other kinds of literature also" (p. 25).

Teen Romances seem to bring students into the library. According to Parrish and Atwood, "Eighth and ninth graders . . . get their romance novels equally from friends, bookstores and school libraries. Tenth graders favor drug/grocery stores and the school library. Twelfth graders showed the most diversity: Over half got their books from friends and the public library, 37% from bookstores and the school library, with little use of home and drug/grocery stores" (p. 24). Thus, despite the easy availability of Teen Romances, the school library still plays a significant role as a source of reading for this genre. (For thoughtful discussion of the value of Teen Romances as literature, see Sutton 1985a, 1985b).

The fear has been expressed that if children are allowed to do light reading, they will only do light reading and may not progress further. Schoonover (1937, 1938) studied 56 high school seniors whose school program had emphasized voluntary free reading over the last six years; these students averaged about 55 books of outside reading per year. Schoonover found that 73% of the books these students reported reading were included on three "approved" reading lists, and that students' reading tastes "gradually progress toward a point at which they voluntarily select the better books" (1938:116). The research on comics and Teen Romances also suggests that at least some light reading may have value and may help in getting students "hooked on books."

CONCLUSIONS

The issue of free reading and reading comprehension is important for theoretical and practical reasons. On the theoretical side, demonstrating a relationship between free reading and reading ability gives additional support to the related hypotheses that we "learn to read by reading" (Smith 1976, 1985; Goodman, 1982) and that we acquire language by obtaining comprehensible input (Krashen 1982). On the practical side, it underscores the value of free reading programs for children, and the importance of providing easy access to books.

As noted at the beginning of this paper, we expect the quantity of free reading to correlate with reading ability, but we did not predict the correlation to be perfect, since other factors will also play roles:

1. It is reasonable to assume that reading ability will be affected by what is read, that despite the benefits of light reading, a diet of only

light reading will probably not lead to advanced levels of competence. The research provides modest support for this hypothesis; there is some evidence that school-age children who are better readers tend to show a greater preference for certain kinds of books, such as historical fiction and science fiction (Thorndike 1973; Hafner, Palmer, & Tullos 1986).

2. Affective and social factors also play an important role (Athey 1985, Stevenson 1985). Smith (1982) refers to the condition of sensitivity: For children to learn to read, they must assume they will be successful. Smith (1984, 1985) suggests that successful readers need to "join the literacy club," that is, consider themselves to be the kind of people who read and write. In Dulay and Burt's terms, the "affective filter" must be low (Dulay and Burt 1977, Dulay, Burt, and Krashen 1982).

3. Other factors affect performance on reading comprehension tests, such as test-wiseness and background knowledge (Smith's "non-visual information").

Finally, we would not expect free reading programs to have much of an effect on students who are not ready to do free reading: very young children and other less mature readers will get their comprehensible input elsewhere.[9]

Despite the presence of these other factors, the amount of free reading done consistently correlates with performance on reading comprehension tests, a result that confirms the hypothesis that we learn to read by reading, and that also confirms the importance of E.B. White, Judy Blume, Archie, and Spider-Man for young readers.

---

[9] There are several sources of comprehensible input for beginning readers: (a) There is good evidence that environmental print (signs, advertisements) is an important source of reading for them (Smith 1976, Y. Goodman and Altwerger 1981). (b) Reading out loud to beginning readers provides them with familiarity with the style and vocabulary of written language (Smith 1982), and helps get them interested in reading (for a review of this research, see Krashen 1985b; see also Wells 1985 for a report of the positive effects of story-telling and reading out loud to children). (c) In methods such as language experience, texts are produced that are based on the reader's own oral utterances. This helps ensure a text that is interesting and comprehensible. Research on language experience has shown this approach to be generally successful, but not always better than alternatives. The reason for this, in my view, is that in these studies language experience is combined with extensive drills and exercises (see e.g. Kendrick & Bennett 1966, Hahn 1967, Stauffer 1970). In Guthrie (1977) a program labeled "language experience" faired poorly. Guthrie notes, however, that the program labels may not have revealed what was crucial: "Programs that engaged students in actual reading/language activities for large amounts of time may have been the successful ones, and programs that captured attention for these activities only briefly may have been less effective" (p. 244).

REFERENCES

Andersen, Esther. 1948. The Elementary School Journal 48.258–267.

Anderson, Irving, Byron Hughes, and W. Robert Dixon. 1957. The rate of reading development and its relation to age of learning to read, sex, and intelligence. Journal of Educational Research 50.481–494.

Anderson, Richard, Elfrieda Hiebert, Judith Scott, and Ian Wilkinson. 1985. Becoming a nation of readers: The report of the commission on reading. Urbana, IL: University of Illinois Center for the Study of Reading.

Aranha, Mabel. 1985. Sustained silent reading goes east. The Reading Teacher 39.214–217.

Arlin, Marshall, and Garry Roth. 1978. Pupils' use of time while reading comics and books. American Educational Research Journal 5.201–216.

Aronow, Miriam. 1961. A study of the effect of individualized reading on children's reading test scores. The Reading Teacher. November, 1961, pp. 86–91.

Athey, Irene. 1985. Reading research in the affective domain. Theoretical models and processes of reading (3rd ed.), ed. by Harry Singer and Robert Ruddell, 527–557. Newark, DE: International Reading Association.

Barbe, Walter. 1965. Characteristics of gifted children. Psychology and education of the gifted: Selected readings, ed. by Walter Barbe, 248–257. New York: Appleton-Century-Crofts.

Bohnhorst, Ben and Sophia Sellars. 1959. Individual reading instruction versus basal textbook instruction: Some tentative explorations. Elementary English 36.185–190, 202.

Boney, C. De Witt and Kate Agnew. 1937. Periods of awakening or reading readiness. Elementary English Review 14.183–187.

Briggs, Chari and David Elkin. 1977. Characteristics of early readers. Perceptual and Motor Skills 44.1231–1237.

Brink, William. 1939. Reading interests of high-school pupils. School Review 47.613–621.

Brocka, Bruce. 1979. Comic books: In case you haven't noticed they've changed. Media and Methods 15.30–32.

Burrows, Alvina. 1950. Caste system or democracy in teaching reading? Elementary English 27.145–157.

Carson, Louise. 1957. Moving toward individualization—a second grade program. Elementary English 34.362–366.

Chomsky, Carol. 1972. Stages in language development and reading exposure. Harvard Educational Review 42.1–33.

Cleary, Florence. 1935. Recreational reading in junior high school. The Nation's Schools 16.31–33.

Cline, Ruth and George Kretke. 1980. An evaluation of long-term SSR in the junior high school. Journal of Reading, March, 1980.503–506.

Collins, Cathy. 1980. Sustained silent reading periods: Effect of teachers' behaviors and students' achievement. The Elementary School Journal 81.109–114.

Connor, Ulla. 1983. Predictors of second-language reading performance. Journal of Multilingual and Multicultural Development 4.271–88.

Crossley, Ruth and Mildred Kniley. 1959. An individualized reading program. Elementary English 36.16–20.

Cummins, Jim. 1984. Bilingualism and special education: Issues in assessment and pedagogy. Clevedon, Avon, England: Multilingual Matters.

Cyrog, Frances. 1959. The principal and his staff move forward in developing new ways of thinking about reading. California Journal of Elementary Education 27.178–187.

Dickinson, Marie. 1959. Through self-selection to individualizing reading procedures. California Journal of Elementary Education 27.150–177.

Dorrell, Larry and Ed Carroll. 1981. Spider-man at the library. School Library Journal 27.17–19.

Dulay, Heidi and Marina Burt. 1977. Remarks on creativity in language acquisition. Viewpoints on English as a second language, ed. by M. Burt, H. Dulay, and Mary Finocchiaro, 95–126. New York: Regents.

Dulay, Heidi, Marina Burt, and Stephen Krashen. 1982. Language two. New York: Oxford University Press.

Elley, Warwick, Ian Barham, Hillary Lamb, and Malcolm Wyllie. 1979. The role of grammar in a secondary school curriculum. Wellington, New Zealand: New Zealand Council for Educational Research.

Elley, Warwick and Francis Mangubhai. 1983. The impact of reading on second language learning. Reading Research Quarterly 19.53–67.

Evans, Howard and John Towner. Sustained silent reading: Does it increase skills? The Reading Teacher 29.155–156.

Evans, Peter and Norman Gleadow. 1983. Literacy: A study of literacy performance and leisure activities in Victoria, B.C. Reading Canada lecture 2.3–16.

Fader, Daniel. 1976. Hooked on books. New York: Berkeley Books.

Farrell, Ellen. 1982. SSR as the core of a junior high school reading program. Journal of Reading, October, 1982, 48–51.

Fielding, L.G., P.T. Wilson, and Richard Anderson. A new focus on free reading: The role of trade books in reading instruction. Contexts of literacy, ed. by T.E. Raphael and R. Reynolds, New York: Longman. (Cited in Anderson, Richard et al., 1985. Becoming a nation of readers, National Academy of Education.)

Gallo, Donald. 1968. Free reading and book reports—An informal survey of grade eleven. Journal of Reading 11.532–538.

Goodman, Kenneth. 1982. Language and literacy vols. 1 and 2. Boston: Routledge and Kegan Paul.

Goodman, Yetta and Bess Altwerger. 1981. Print awareness in pre-school children. Occasional Papers No. 4. Program in Language and Literacy, Arizona Center for Research and Development, College of Education, University of Arizona.

Gordon, Ira and Christine Clark. 1961. An experiment in individualized reading. Childhood Education 38.112–113.

Greaney, Vincent. 1980. Factors related to amount and type of leisure time reading. Reading Research Quarterly 15.337–357.

Greenman, Ruth and Sharon Kapilian. 1959. Individual reading in third and fourth grades. Elementary English 31.234–237.

Guthrie, John. 1977. Follow through: A compensatory education experiment. The Reading Teacher 31.239–244.

Guthrie, John. 1981. Reading in New Zealand: Achievement and volume. Reading Research Quarterly 17.6–27.

Guthrie, John. 1983. Response to Smit. Reading Research Quarterly 19.124.

Hafner, Lawrence, Barbara Palmer, and Stan Tullos. 1986. The differential reading interests of good and poor readers in the ninth grade. Reading Improvement 23.39–42.

Hahn, Harry. 1967. Three approaches to beginning reading instruction—ITA, language experience, and basic readers—extended to second grade. The Reading Teacher 20.711–715.

Hansen, Harlon. 1969 The impact of the home literary environment on reading attitude. Elementary English 46.17–24.

Harris, Albert, Blanche Serwer, and Lawrence Gold. 1967. Comparing reading approaches in first grade teaching with disadvantaged children—extended into second grade. The Reading Teacher 20.698–703.

Haugaard, Kay. 1973. Comic books: Conduits to culture? The Reading Teacher 27.54–55.

Healy, Ann. 1963. Changing children's attitudes toward reading. Elementary English 40.255–257, 279.

Heyns, Barbara. 1978. Summer Learning and the Effects of Schooling. New York: Academic Press.

Holdaway, Don. 1979. The foundations of literacy. Exeter, New Hampshire: Heinemann Educational Books.

Inge, M. Thomas. 1985. The American comic book. Columbus, OH: Ohio State University Library.

Ingham, Jennie. 1981. Books and reading development: The Bradford book flood experiment. London: Heinemann Educational Books Ltd.

Jenkins, Marian. 1955. Here's to success in reading—Self-selection works. Childhood Education 32.124–131.

Jenkins, Marian. 1957. Self-selection in reading. The Reading Teacher 10.84–90.

Jones, Harold. 1950. The extracurricular reading interests of students in a state college. School and Society 72.40–43.

Johnson, Mabel. 1951. Individualizing reading experience. New York State Education 38.654–673.

Kasdon, Lawrence. 1958. Early reading background of some superior readers among college freshmen. Journal of Educational Research 52.151–153.

Kendrick, William and Clayton Bennett. 1966. A comparative study of two first-grade language arts programs. Reading Research Quarterly 2.83–118.

Kingsley, Marjorie. 1958. An experiment in individualized reading. Elementary English 35.113–118.

Kingston, Albert. 1960. College study and reading maturity. Journal of Developmental Reading 3.199–202.

Krashen, Stephen. 1982. Principles and practice in second language acquisition. Hayward, CA: Alemany Press and Oxford: Pergamon Press.

Krashen, Stephen. 1984. Writing: Research, theory and applications. Oxford: Pergamon Press.

Krashen, Stephen. 1985a. Inquiries and insights: Essays on language teaching, bilingual education, and literacy. Hayward, CA: The Alemany Press.

Krashen, Stephen. 1985b. The input hypothesis: Issues and implications. New York: Longman.

Krashen, Stephen. (forthcoming). Comic book reading and language development.

Lambert, Kathleen and Edna Saunders. 1976. Readers and non-readers: What's the difference? English Journal 65.34–38.

Lamme, Linda. 1976. Are reading habits and abilities related? The Reading Teacher 30.21–27.

Largent, Mary. 1959. My third-graders are eager readers. NEA Journal 48.64–65.

Lawson, Hoyle. 1968. Effects of free reading on the reading achievement of sixth grade pupils. Forging ahead in reading, ed. by J. Allen Figurel, 501–504. Newark, DE: International Reading Association.

Lomax, Carol. 1976. Interest in books and stories at nursery school. Educational Research 19.100–112.

Long, Barbara and Edmund Henderson. 1973. Children's use of time: Some personal and social correlates. The Elementary School Journal 73.193–199.

Manning, Gary and Maryann Manning. 1984a. What models of recreational reading make a difference? Reading World, May, 1984: 375–380.

Manning, Maryann and Gary Manning. 1984b. Early readers and nonreaders from low socioeconomic environments: What their parents report. The Reading Teacher 38.32–34.

Maynes, Florence. 1981. Uninterrupted sustained silent reading. Reading Research Quarterly 17.159–160.

McCreath, Ethel. 1975. An investigation of the reading habits, reading interests, and their relationship to reading improvement of students in an urban opendoor junior college. 24th Yearbook of the National Reading Conference, Clemson, SC, pp. 100–105.

Milner, Esther. 1951. A study of the relationship between reading readiness in grade one school children and patterns of parent-child interaction. Child Development 22.95–112.

Minton, Marilyn. 1980. The effect of sustained silent reading upon comprehension and attitudes among ninth graders. The Reading Teacher 23.498–502.

Monteith, Mary. 1980. How well does the average American read? Some facts, figures, and opinions. Journal of Reading 23.460–464.

Mork, Theodore. 1972. Sustained silent reading in the classroom. The Reading Teacher 25.438–441.

Morrow, Leslie. 1982. Relationships between literature programs, library corner designs, and children's use of literature. Journal of Educational Research 75.339–344.

Morrow, Leslie. 1983. Home and school correlates of early interest in literature. Journal of Educational Research 76.221–230.

Morrow, Leslie, and Carol Weinstein. 1982. Increasing children's use of literature through program and physical changes. The Elementary School Journal 83.131–137.

Morrow, Leslie and Carol Weinstein. 1986. Encouraging voluntary reading: The impact of a literature program on children's use of library centers. Reading Research Quarterly 21.330–346.

Nagy, William, Patricia Herman, and Richard Anderson. 1985. Learning words from context. Reading Research Quarterly 20.233–253.

Neuman, Susan. 1986a. Television, reading, and the home environment. Reading Research and Instruction 25.173–183.

Neuman, Susan. 1986b. The home environment and fifth-grade students' leisure reading. The Elementary School Journal 86.335–343.

Neuman, Susan and Peter Prowda. 1982. Television viewing and reading achievement. The Reading Teacher 25.666–670.

Oliver, Marvin. 1973. The effect of high intensity practice on reading comprehension. Reading Improvement 10.16–18.

Oliver, Marvin. 1976. The effect of high intensity practice on reading achievement. Reading Improvement 13.226–228.

Parrish, Berta and Karen Atwood. 1985. Enticing readers: The teen romance craze. California Reader 18.22–27.

Petre, Richard. 1971. Reading breaks make it in Maryland. The Reading Teacher 15.191–194.

Pitts, Sandra Kelton. 1986. Read aloud to adult learners? Of course! Reading Psychology: An International Quarterly 7.35–42.

Pollack, Pamela. 1981. The business of popularity. School Library Journal 28.25–28.

Powell, William. 1966. Classroom libraries: Their frequency of use. Elementary English 43.395–397.

Reinhardt, Emma. 1930. Reading interests of freshmen in a teachers college. Teachers College Journal 2.57–60, 63–64.

Roberts, Donald, Christine Bachen, Melinda Hornby and Pedro Hernandez-Ramos. 1984. Reading and television: Predictors of reading achievement at different age levels. Communication Research 11.9–49.

Sadoski, Mark. 1980. Ten years of uninterrupted sustained silent reading. Reading Improvement 17.153–156.

Safford, Alton. 1960. Evaluation of an individualized reading program. The Reading Teacher 13.266–270.

Sartain, Harry. 1960. The Roseville experiment with individualized reading. The Reading Teacher 13.277–281.

Schon, Isabel, Kenneth Hopkins, and W. Alan Davis. 1982. The effects of books in Spanish and free reading time on Hispanic students' reading abilities and attitudes. NABE Journal 7.13–20.

Schon, Isabel, Kenneth Hopkins and Carol Vojir. 1984. The effects of Spanish reading emphasis on the English and Spanish reading abilities of Hispanic high school students. Bilingual Review 11.33–39.

Schon, Isabel, Kenneth Hopkins, and Carol Vojir. 1985. The effects of special reading time in Spanish on the reading abilities and attitudes of Hispanic junior high school students. Journal of Psycholinguistic Research 14.57–65.

Schoof, Robert. 1978. Four-color words: Comic books in the classroom. Language Arts 55.821–827.

Schoonover, Ruth. 1937. The Negaunee reading experiment. English Journal 26.527–535.

Schoonover, Ruth. 1938. The case for voluminous reading. English Journal 27.114–118.

Schulze, Lydia. 1976. Best sellers evaluated for readability and portrayal of female characters. Master's thesis, Rutgers University. New Brunswick, New Jersey.

Sharpe, Maida. 1958. An individualized reading program. Elementary English 35.507–512.

Sheldon, William and Lawrence Carrillo. 1952. Relation of parents, home, and certain development characteristics to children's reading ability. The Elementary School Journal 52.262–269.

Sheldon, William and Warren Cutts. 1953. Relation of parents, home, and certain developmental characteristics to children's reading ability. II. The Elementary School Journal 53.517–521.

Shields, Portia, Jessica Gordon, and David Dupree. 1983. Influence of parent practices upon the reading achievement of good and poor readers. Journal of Negro Education 52.436–445.

Smit, Edna. 1983. Response to Guthrie. Reading Research Quarterly 19.124.

Smith, Frank. 1976. Learning to read by reading. Language Arts 53.297–299, 322. Reprinted in Smith, F. Essays into Literacy. Exeter: Heinemann Educational Books, 1983, pp. 35–39.

Smith, Frank. 1982. Understanding reading. New York: Holt Rinehart Winston.

Smith, Frank. 1983. Reading like a writer. Language Arts 60.558–567. Also available from Abel Press, Victoria, British Columbia.

Smith, Frank. 1984. Joining the literacy club. Victoria, British Columbia: Abel Press.

Smith, Frank. 1985. Reading without nonsense (2nd ed.). New York: Teachers College Press.

Smith, Lois and Jane Becker. 1960. Self-selection with intermediate children. The Reading Teacher 14.83–88.

Sperzel, Edith. 1948. The effect of comic books on vocabulary growth and reading comprehension. Elementary English 25.109–113.

Stallings, Jane. 1986. Effective use of time in secondary reading programs. Effective teaching of reading: Research and practice, ed. by James Hoffman, 85–106. Newark, DE: International Reading Association.

Stauffer, Russell. 1970. The language experience approach to the teaching of reading. New York: Harper & Row.

Stevenson, Colin. 1985. Challenging adult illiteracy: Reading and writing disabilities in the British Army. New York: Teachers College Press.

Sutton, Roger. 1985a. Girls just want to have fun. School Library Journal 31.52.

Sutton, Roger. 1985b. Librarians and the paperback romance: Trying to do the right thing. School Library Journal 32.25–29.

Swanton, Susan. 1984. Minds alive: What and why gifted students read for pleasure. School Library Journal 30.99–102.

Telfer, Richard and Robert Kann. 1984. Reading achievement, free reading, watching TV, and listening to music. Journal of Reading, March, 1984, 536–539.

Termin, Lewis and Melita Oden. 1947. The gifted child grows up. Stanford, CA: Stanford University Press.

Thorndike, Robert. 1941. Words and the comics. Journal of Experimental Education 10.110–113.

Thorndike, Robert. 1973. Reading comprehension education in fifteen countries. New York: Halsted Press.

Wahlberg, Herbert and Shiow-ling Tsai. 1983. Reading achievement and attitude productivity among 17-year-olds. Journal of Reading Behavior 15.41–53.

Wahlberg, Herbert and Shiow-ling Tsai. 1985. Correlates of reading achievement and attitude: A national assessment study. Journal of Educational Research 78.159–167.

Wells, Gordon. 1985. Preschool literacy-related activities and success in school, ed. by David Olson, Nancy Torrance, and Angela Hildyard. Literacy, language, and learning. Cambridge: Cambridge University Press.

Wiesenberger, Katherine and Ellen Birlem. 1983. The effectiveness of SSR: An overview of the research. Reading Horizons 24.197–201.

Williams, David. 1981. Factors relating to performance in reading English as a second language. Language Learning 31.31–50.

Willet, G. 1919. The reading interests of high-school pupils. English Journal 8.474–487.

Witty, Paul and Robert Sizemore. 1955. Reading the comics: A summary of studies and an evaluation III. Elementary English 32.109–114.

Wolf, Anne and Larry Mikulecky. 1978. Effects of uninterrupted sustained silent reading and of reading skills instruction on changes in secondary students' reading attitudes and achievement. 27th Yearbook of the National Reading Conference, Clemson, South Carolina, pp. 226–228.

Wright, Gary. 1979. The comic book—a forgotten medium in the classroom. The Reading Teacher 33.158–161.

Yap, Kim Onn. 1977. Relationships between amount of reading activity and reading achievement. Reading World 17.23–29.

CHAPTER THIRTEEN

Language Learning and Language Teaching: Towards an Integrated Model

The Bell Educational Trust

INTRODUCTION

The subject of this paper is the relation between language learning and language teaching. Its starting point is a number of propositions which I take to be facts:

1. Highly effective and rapid language learning exists, and can be systematically produced through the exercise of informed teaching.
2. The teaching of English as a foreign or second language (EFL/ESL) includes, in its highest manifestations, evidence on a large and expanding scale of effective learning led by informed teaching.
3. This informed teaching can call on a massive array of published materials, of teaching techniques, and of professional support for the teacher and the learner, and is the product of a highly-developed body of teacher education and training.
4. A large corpus of intellectual knowledge, of research effort, and of theoretical understanding is engaged in the further development of informed teaching and the better understanding of effective learning; this intellectual base is supplied principally through applied linguistics and its associated research.

Of course not all language teaching is "informed" in this sense, not even all EFL teaching. There is still a great deal—perhaps a majority—of inadequate teaching and ineffectual learning. But informed language teaching does exist: It can be defined; it is there to be emulated; it is

299

growing very fast. The existence of informed language teaching cannot be ignored in considering the relations between learning and teaching. Some of us, who spend much of our working life observing and encouraging such teaching, are rather tired of theoretical attitudes which assume that all language teaching is, by definition, ineffective and tedious. We *know* otherwise.

The tasks facing language teaching henceforth are threefold: (a) to understand the nature of the language learning/teaching process; (b) to bring all language learning/teaching up to the level of the best; (c) to improve yet further the standard of the best.

This paper is divided into two parts: first, an outline of the nature of the four paradigms currently in use, and the important differences between them; second, a discussion of the "learning/teaching-dominated paradigm," seeking to show that this is a paradigm which embodies a mutual and reciprocal relationship between language learning and language teaching—in short, that in the best circumstances we teach as we do because we have observed that thereby learners learn better.

THE FOUR PARADIGMS OF LANGUAGE LEARNING AND TEACHING

Four quite distinct paradigms embrace all deliberate, thoughtful consideration of language learning/language teaching throughout the world. They might be labeled theory-dominated, learning/teaching-dominated, mystique-dominated, and literature-dominated.

The Theory-Dominated Paradigm

In this paradigm a single theory is taken as given—currently Krashen's (1981) Monitor Theory, derived from transformational grammar linguistic theory by way of an extension to first language acquisition studies and a further extension into second language acquisition research. Teachers are enjoined to undertake in class only those activities which have been validated by research within this paradigm. Attention is concentrated on aspects of learning, with teaching seen as having a restricted function and as probably being ineffective. The few positive references to teaching are offered as consequences of the theory and are not related to the existing body of language teaching practices. Other models and paradigms are not tolerated, on the grounds that deviations from a single theory would constitute undesirable "eclecticism." The paradigm is fundamentally a branch of theoretical linguistics and is seen as scientific in nature.

The Learning/Teaching-Dominated Paradigm

Here the assumption is that effective language learning is most likely to occur as a consequence of deliberately planned teaching. The planning centers on the design of courses, on techniques of instruction (methodology), and on professionalism in the teacher. The learner's positive contribution to the process is seen as crucial; current trends towards more "learner-centered" instruction reinforce this. Research and theory are regarded as important: Research can illuminate points of difficulty and can contribute to theory. Theory provides the teacher with an understanding and explanation of how learning and teaching take place, but it does not dominate teaching. Professionalism lies in a mixture of the widest possible command of techniques for helping learners to learn, with a growing understanding of how and why the process can be improved. EFL has its intellectual base in the multidisciplinary field of applied linguistics. This paradigm is pragmatic, willing to try out new ideas from other fields and from the other paradigms. It is "eclectic" in seeking aspects of the truth in many places and in being wary of theoretical snake-oil salesmen. (It is worth commenting that although the term "eclectic" is often seen as pejorative in America, it is used with approval in Britain and Europe.) The paradigm is fundamentally a branch of education: It is seen as an art and a skill, informed by wide-ranging principles and aspects of theory, but not dominated by them.

The Mystique-Dominated Paradigm

This paradigm is concerned chiefly with respect for the individual as a "whole person" (its techniques are often called "holistic" or "humanistic" methods), with raising the learner's readiness to learn, with passing much of the responsibility for learning from the teacher to the learner, and with developing interpersonal and group relationships of mutual respect and trust. It embraces many approaches, including The Silent Way, Suggestopedia, Counseling Learning, Neurolinguistic Programming, Total Physical Response, and others. All have origins in fields outside language learning/teaching. All are restricted in their application and do not seek to address the full range of activities involved in the planning of language teaching. Nor do they make use of the large corpus of techniques and methods developed in the mainstream of language teaching. Success, in this paradigm, is held to reside in the meeting of minds, in openness to the contact of personalities, in factors often more mystical than scientific. The paradigm is not basically a branch of any discipline: It is not scientific in the sense in which linguistics is scientific, but it is consonant with some schools of thought in psychotherapy.

The Literature-Dominated Paradigm

One of the most widespread outlooks, philosophies, or attitudes in language teaching is "the grammar-translation method"; that label obscures the fact that a whole paradigm is involved, in which the ultimate purpose was and is to promote the study of literature and literary criticism. Study of the language is seen as a stepping stone, of lower value, to permit the learner to have access to the higher plane of literary texts. In many institutions, no systematic teaching of the language as such is provided: Many literary texts are studied; a number of conventional academic tasks such as translation, prose composition and dictation are practiced; learners are tacitly expected either to have picked up the language from similar exercises while at school, or to spend time in a country where the language is spoken, in order to achieve command of the language. This paradigm is a branch of literary studies and is not concerned with the systematic teaching and learning of language.

Among these four paradigms, none of them is "better" or "worse" than the others, on any kind of moral scale. Each operates within its own universe of discourse; each serves different ends. So, for example, the theory-dominated paradigm serves the ends and purposes of developing and extending second language acquisition theory; the mystique-dominated paradigm serves the ends of establishing personal and group relations of mutual respect and of removing psychological anxiety from the task of learning; the literature-dominated paradigm serves the ends of preserving and strengthening the profession of literature. As for the learning/teaching paradigm, it serves the ends of improving the whole gamut of planning and of implementing programs of language teaching and learning.

One more characteristic needs to be stressed: Three of these paradigms are exclusive and self-contained, in the sense that they discourage borrowing from—and often ignore or deny the existence of—the other paradigms. Only the learning/teaching paradigm encourages teachers to take from elsewhere any and all ideas, concepts, techniques that can be usefully applied to the task of helping learners to learn.

THE "LEARNING/TEACHING-DOMINATED" PARADIGM

Language Teaching

Language teaching is a vast subject, most of it not strictly relevant to this argument. It includes the main operational categories by which language teaching is nowadays organized, that is, the categories of approach, syllabus (or curriculum), methodology, materials, evaluation (or assessment), and teacher training. These are the tools by which informed language teaching is organized so as to bring together learners and teachers in circumstances best suited to enhance learning. At this organizational level there is general agreement that effective learning is most likely to take place if there is good syllabus design, suitable methodology, varied and interesting teaching materials, competent teachers—and willing learners.

This paper concentrates, rather, on the relations between teaching and learning, and asks rhetorically, what are the fundamental actions of teaching that bear on the learning process of the learner? They are, I suggest, the following:

1. Shaping the input to the learner
2. Encouraging the learner's intention to learn
3. Managing the processes of learning
4. Promoting practice and use of the language

Each of the operational categories mentioned earlier, the whole vast array of teaching techniques and materials, the entire system of teacher training—all these are reduced, in the classroom and from the viewpoint of the individual learner, to these four basic teaching activities.

1. Shaping the input. It is a fundamental characteristic of language teaching—and indeed of all education—that the teacher selects and controls the experience from which the learner learns. This selection is partly a matter of preplanning long in advance, for example, in devising a syllabus and choosing suitable course materials, and partly a matter of decision making from moment to moment in the class. Even in passing the responsibility for most of the language activity to the class (as in communicative methodology), the teacher is nevertheless making a decision about the nature of what the learners will experience: The teacher is shaping the input.

2. Encouraging the intention to learn. There are a great many reasons why learners may not learn. Perhaps the single most effective stopper on learning is an absence of an intention to learn. There is a

direct relation between the well-known factor of motivation and the learner's intention to learn. Motivation consists of external conditions and circumstances whose consequences are internal to the learner in the form of an intention to learn. The intention to learn may or may not be conscious; it is part of the teacher's job to monitor this critical factor and to ensure that a flagging intention is massaged and cajoled and wheedled and generally brought back to life.

3. Managing the processes of learning. One description of informed teaching is "the management of learning." But there is a more precise aspect to the task: Every teacher becomes aware that there are a great many different learning processes; that these change from moment to moment and from one level of attainment to another; that they vary between one learner and another; and that each can be best helped to keep the learning in flow by the choice of one or another technique of teaching. It is part of the great richness of methodology in informed EFL that teachers can help learners quite decisively by managing their processes of learning.

4. Promoting practice and use. A visitor to any class where informed teaching is going on may be surprised at the sheer quantity of language— talk, reading, writing, interaction—that takes place. It is a central tenet of language teaching that learners must be provided with a language-rich environment. It is another tenet that learners of a language learn not only by experiencing—by hearing, seeing, reading—but by *doing*. And informed language teaching promotes practice—not "pattern practice" in the old audiolingual sense (though in the hands of some teachers that did lead to some good learning)—but practice in all the aspects of language.

These four basic teaching activities are at the core of informed language teaching. It is part of the argument in this lecture that this development of teaching is not an accident. The changes that have taken place in language teaching—the staggering expansion of methods and materials, the massive effort in teacher training—cannot be dissociated from random events. Nor are they independent of the very great improvements in language learning that can be observed throughout the world, wherever informed language teaching is available. And since it is chiefly within EFL that the majority of informed language teaching has taken place, it can be argued that the explosive spread of English, to reach its present estimated figure of some 1.5 billion users of the language, has been at least partly due to more effective learning as a result of more informed teaching. What is more, it is probable that language teaching has developed as it has in reflection of a growing awareness of the nature of language learning. In order to develop this argument we now turn from language teaching to language learning.

Language Learning

A Fundamental Function of Language Learning. To understand more fully the relation between language teaching and language learning, it is helpful to consider one of the fundamental functions of language. This will take us into areas of speculation that have been unfashionable, at least in the theory-dominated paradigm, for many years, that is, to the analysis of mental processes, of cognition, of thinking. It seems to be universally agreed that all normal adult human beings are aware of "inner speech" or of an interior monologue. We all have "pictures in our heads," "silent speech," and similar metaphors. In fact, human beings typically report that their thoughts are of two types: verbalized and nonverbalized. Verbalized thought includes images, unseen and unheard, of both spoken and written language, when the person is literate.

A major function of verbalization is to act as a "control language" for organizing thought and action. Of course, very many of our actions have no conscious verbalization beneath them: we shift in our seat in order to get more comfortable without necessarily engaging in an interior monologue about it—yet equally one may "say" to oneself "What's that digging into my leg?" or "Where's that draft coming from?"

Further, the interior monologue becomes the controlling basis of speech and of writing, once the necessary additional psychomotor effort begins. (Psychomotor, because it entails commands from mind and brain to the organs of speech, the muscles of the eye, the muscles of the writing hand, and so on.)

These two observations, about the "control" function of the interior monologue, and about its externalization into speaking and reading and writing, apply also to the learning of a foreign language. When we learn a foreign language we are creating an additional alternative control language for our thinking. During the progress of our learning we may become aware that we can first employ the new control language only fitfully, occasionally, for brief periods. Then gradually the ability to do so becomes more frequent, covers longer stretches of time, suffers fewer interruptions through incomprehension or lack of knowledge. And to the extent that we have created an additional control language for our interior monologue, we can then externalize it into speech and writing in the foreign language—though with special problems about accuracy of performance, which we shall return to later.

Components of the Language Learning Process. What must be the minimum essential components of language learning? They are: (a) experience, i.e. input of the necessary language and other information;

(b) a learner, whose qualities and abilities make an inescapable contribution to learning; (c) a stage of comprehension and learning.

Each of these components merits a few words of discussion.

1. Experience. The experience from which learners extract meaning and construct their knowledge of language is not only language experience; it is also experience of life, of the society and culture which uses the language. In short, the experience has to be both systemic (i.e. of language) and schematic (in the sense of constructing mental schemata from our experience). Teaching only the language deprives learners of part of their essential nutrients for learning.

2. The Learner's Qualities. The learner is not a tabula rasa on which the teacher—or the flow of experience—writes a message. Each learner is a dynamic, active, positive (or even negative) contributor to learning. Each learner is different from all others in the same way that he or she has an individual face and fingerprints; but equally an individual shares many characteristics with all other learners. And these characteristics and qualities produce a range of variables, tending either to favor better learning, or to hinder it. The principal qualities brought by the learner to the process are these: (a) Qualities reflecting the learner's identity and individuality: gender, age, previous language experience, special abilities (a "good ear," preference of eye over ear, ability to mimic, self-view as a learner, and so on); (b) Qualities reflecting the learner's volition: e.g., his or her intention to learn, normal attention span, availability of concentration, and so on; (c) Qualities of the learner's mental processes.

Let us recall where the argument has got to. We are outlining a model of language learning that has a close relation to informed language teaching. Here is an example of how that relation emerges in practice. Every teacher quickly discovers that the learning progress of each learner is strongly affected by these sets of factors. Some of them cannot be directly influenced or improved by the teacher—for instance learners with rather slow thought processes cannot have them improved, but nevertheless an informed teacher will know how to give such learners special treatment that will help them to learn better than would otherwise be the case. Other factors *can* be adjusted by the teacher, particularly aspects of their volition, and some negative attitudes toward learning or being taught. The point is that the nature of learning is directly reflected in, and by, the nature of informed teaching.

There is a great deal that needs to be said about mental processes. Here one can only give a flavor of what is involved. First, the label refers to ways of thinking, to learning strategies, to thought processes.

Every informed teacher is aware that all learners dispose of a great range of modes of thought, which they employ—often many of them simultaneously—as they are exposed to language input. One might categorize five main kinds of such processes, beginning with a set of *pervasive mental processes,* continually available: recall (i.e. from memory), imagination, and creativity. Of a different kind are some *control processes,* like watch-keeping ("Is there any language present?"), tracking the flow of meaning, calling up concentration, even switching on and off. There are *identifying processes,* including the *recognition* of meaning already known, and shunting problems to be dealt with by other processes. There are *problem-solving processes,* including internal repetition and recall, guessing, inference, analogy, even translation, and a pattern-matching and hypothesis-forming process which I call a jig-saw process. And there are *internalizing processes* such as generalization, reflection, consign to memory—and even a process which one might call fermentation, by which is meant the low, long-term build-up of learning outside the normal learning/teaching situation. And there are many others: Currently I distinguish about 28 distinct mental processes.

A word about the status of these labels may be necessary: The assertion made here is that experiential evidence among teachers can be in part explained by postulating the existence of a number of cognitive processes operating in at least approximately these ways.

The components mentioned thus far—experience of the language, and qualities of the learner—come together to produce comprehension and learning. And comprehension necessarily precedes learning. By comprehension is meant "understanding the language" (or a small bit of it), "extracting meaning," "following the sense of the language." (This does not refer to the classroom exercise labeled "listening comprehension" or "reading comprehension," but to the individual's growing ability to understand, to comprehend.)

Comprehension, Learning and Memory. It is difficult, if not impossible, to describe and explain how comprehension arises and learning takes place without recourse to the concept of memory. Memory is, in broad terms, the individual's stored experience—in this case, his or her stored experience of language. But not all our past experience is equally accessible. There is much that we "know," in the sense that we have previously experienced it and even extracted some meaning from it, but which we cannot consciously bring back from our memory— though we may be able to do so on a future occasion under different conditions. Within our total memory, then, there is a smaller core of stored experience which we can recall, which is available for use, which forms our accessible previous experience. (See Figure 1 for a visual representation.)

It is our general experience throughout life that what is stored within our memory can slip in and out of recall. "I know it, but I just can't

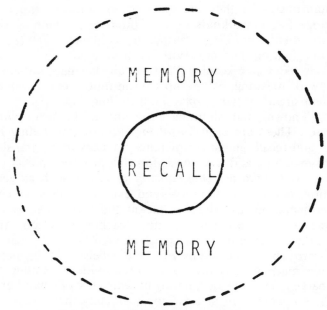

Figure 1. Recall as part of memory

recall it—it will come back to me in a minute": These are common occurrences. Within the field of language, though, learning means being able to recall as it were in a continuous, on-line manner. If we cannot recall, we have not learned—or it may be that we had learned, once in the past, but have lost that particular item from recall: It has slipped into memory outside recall. This process is known as attrition. Attrition affects everyone, with the passage of time. Its effects and consequences are particularly serious for beginners, who have so much less to lose anyway, so that every loss is serious. It is well known to teachers that what a learner has learned, but has lost through attrition, can be quickly restored through further presentation. EFL teaching commonly uses two devices to stave off attrition: first, what are called "spiral syllabuses" (in which new material is presented within a body of re-presented language); and second, plenty of practice and use of what has already been comprehended.

Comprehension takes place as we track the flow of meaning. Any previous comprehension that we make use of, because it is within our recall, constitutes learning. The spoken or implied question "Do you understand?"—if the answer is Yes—relies on previous comprehension recalled. Comprehension precedes learning, whether by a millisecond or ten years. So, learning can be characterized as "comprehension in recall."

But there are two kinds of learning, receptive learning and productive learning. Language teachers are well accustomed to their learners being able to actually produce some of the language they have learned while only comprehending, receptively, other parts of the language; they are accustomed even to actually labeling some teaching/learning items as being more suitable for productive learning or for receptive-only learning. This is another example of language teaching reflecting an awareness of the process of language learning. And it is receptive learning which takes place when we become able to recall that which we have comprehended and can still recall.

How do learners make the transition from receptive to productive learning? By the introduction of additional, psychomotor effort: that is, by making attempts at reproducing in speech or writing that which they have heard or read and understood and can recall. In short, receptive learning plus psychomotor effort gives productive learning. The results of this effort are almost always at first inadequate and inaccurate (as they are also in mother tongue acquisition). But it is a feature of most kinds of human learning that repeated attempts—that is, practice—can improve the accuracy of learners' efforts. The further attempts by language learners to exercise their productive learning are affected by the additional experience of seeing and hearing the language, by self-correction, by peer-correction, by teacher-correction, and by the experience and memory of actually doing it: Speaking and writing provide internal memory of "how one did it" as well as "how good it was," and these internal memories contribute to adjusting the psychomotor effort on future occasions. Improvability is a characteristic of early efforts at language production. Whether improvement actually takes place is another question. But informed teaching recognizes this stage of learning and provides guidance for helping the learner's efforts to improve, if the conditions are suitable.

We have now looked briefly at each of the components of the model of language learning, from experience through the qualities of the learner to comprehension and learning. If this were being presented as a "free-standing" model, so to speak, of language learning without reference to teaching, one might be tempted to leave it at that. But every language teacher quickly discovers that in the context of language learning and teaching other elements, other variables, need to be considered. It turns out that learning is also affected by: (a) the manner in which the experience reaches the learner, that is, the manner of presentation of information; and (b) certain aspects of the learning process, particularly that learning is multiple and gradual.

At this point a metaphor may be helpful. Consider a brand-new color TV set, delivered to your home. It possesses all the necessary components to provide a good picture with good sound. But it is not enough just to possess all the components and to embody a potentiality for giving a good picture. Several further parameters need to be adjusted into a state suitable for proper operation. The set has to be plugged into the electricity supply, which in turn has to be switched on. Then operate the on/off switch on the set and presto!—nothing! Just flashes and mush on the screen. We need an aerial (antenna), and that may need quite a lot of adjustment before it supplies the set with a signal. Why still no picture? Tune it for your local stations. Correct the vertical and horizontal controls. Perhaps, at last, a picture. Turn up the sound, and off we go with "Dallas" or the Muppets.

The first part of the description in this paper of a model of language learning was concerned with the equivalent of the circuits and components of the TV set. The last part will touch briefly on the equivalent of tuning, settings, and performance controls. If the metaphor has any value, it is in reminding us that while any learner can learn a language quite effectively, few learners actually do; that while human beings have the potentiality for learning a language, they also have the potentiality of being prevented from doing so—or even preventing themselves from doing so—partly or completely. It is central to this thesis of an integrated model that informed language teaching is able not only to help learners to learn, but to help them avoid the causes for not learning.

1. Presentation of Information. Teachers are not alone in being aware that both comprehension and learning are vitally affected by the manner in which the information is presented. Madison Avenue is founded in part on the techniques for the best presentation of information; the Medical Research Council in Britain has in its Applied Psychology Unit a strong team of specialists in the presentation of information; and informed language teaching equally relies on it. In our case, we recognize four basic principles or variables, each of which can have either a positive or a negative effect—like shifting the contrast control on a TV set, or the brightness, or color. These variables are organization, variety, interest and impact.

Present-day EFL materials produced within this paradigm are inherently interesting, varied and well-organized—or they can be—and they really do facilitate effective learning.

2. Multiple-gradual Learning. Our habits of literacy accustom us to language in the guise of written text, seen as a string of discrete words separated by white spaces. We are prone to assume therefore that language is learned as a sequence of items, each one presented and

learned or not-learned, then succeeded by another item to be learned or not-learned. Much research presumes just such a "railroad train" nature for language. But language is emphatically not learned like that. Only in the very first seconds of a beginner's first lesson in the foreign language does he/she learn a single item. Thereafter he/she is simultaneously learning very many items, devices, patterns and connections, simultaneously. And "learning the items" entails gradually increasing one's grasp of them: moving from "I *think* I know what that means" to "I'm *sure* I know that"; recognizing the item more quickly, in different voices and accents and typefaces; extending one's range of the meanings and the connections and the restrictions of every item. Language learning is multiple and gradual. Hence it is constantly open to assistance and encouragement from informed teaching.

So much for the model of language learning which is integrally related to informed language teaching. Now, finally, to review the basic teaching activities in the light of language learning.

THE RECIPROCAL RELATION BETWEEN LANGUAGE TEACHING AND LEARNING

Now let us reconsider each of the basic teaching actions in the light of the model postulated above.

1. Shaping the input. Informed teaching not only engages in long-term planning (for example, through the design of syllabuses, course books, teaching materials, and so on) of what is to form the learner's input; in addition, the informed teacher constantly guides and steers the language input, manipulating the interest and variety so that the learner's attention continues to focus on what is to be learned.

2. Encouraging the intention to learn. Again, informed language teaching entails continuously observing the learners' progress and selecting techniques for keeping their learning-readiness at the highest level. Interest and variety help here, too.

3. Managing the learning processes. Sensitive experience on the part of the teacher enables him/her to select from a vast array of techniques (that is, methodology and materials) those best suited to the learner's current learning progress.

4. Promoting practice and use. Teachers are well aware, in the paradigm of informed teaching/learning, of the multiple uses and purposes of practice and use: staving off attrition, facilitating the leap from receptive to productive learning, feeding the multiple and gradual nature of learning, improving productive learning by actually doing.

The thesis of this paper, then, has been: first, that language learning has a number of components; second, that informed language teaching has developed as it has in response to growing awareness of language learning; and third—though the case has not been argued here, only sketched in its platonic, shadowy outline—that, of the four different paradigms of language learning and teaching which currently coexist, only one of them, the teaching/learning paradigm, is seriously conducive to language learning. But that paradigm really is conducive. Within this paradigm, above all in the best of EFL, there now exists a marvelous array of teaching methods and techniques and materials, a highly professional force of informed teachers, a growing research effort geared to improving teaching and learning, a sophisticated intellectual base in applied linguistics—and a great deal of effective learning.

REFERENCE

Krashen, Stephen. 1981. Second language acquisition and second language learning. Oxford: Pergamon.

Author Index

313

Subject Index